AF321637

Decolonizing Diasporas

Decolonizing Diasporas

Radical Mappings of Afro-Atlantic Literature

✦

Yomaira C. Figueroa-Vásquez

NORTHWESTERN UNIVERSITY PRESS
EVANSTON, ILLINOIS

Northwestern University Press
www.nupress.northwestern.edu

Copyright © 2020 by Northwestern University Press.
Published 2020. All rights reserved.

10 9 8 7 6 5 4 3 2 1

Library of Congress Cataloging-in-Publication Data

Names: Figueroa-Vásquez, Yomaira C, author.
Title: Decolonial diasporas : radical mappings of Afro Atlantic literatures / Yomaira C. Figueroa-Vásquez.
Description: Evanston, Illinois : Northwestern University Press, 2021. | Includes bibliographical references and index.
Identifiers: LCCN 2020018934 | ISBN 9780810142428 (paperback) | ISBN 9780810142435 (cloth) | ISBN 9780810142442 (ebook)
Subjects: LCSH: Caribbean literature (Spanish)—History and criticism. | Equatorial Guinean literature (Spanish)—History and criticism. | African diaspora in literature. | Postcolonialism in literature.
Classification: LCC PQ7361 .F54 2021 | DDC 860.99729—dc23
LC record available at https://lccn.loc.gov/2020018934

Except where otherwise noted, this book is licensed under a Creative Commons Attribution-NonCommercial-NoDerivatives 4.0 International License. To view a copy of this license, visit http://creativecommons.org/licenses/by-nc-nd/4.0/.

In all cases attribution should include the following information:
Figueroa-Vásquez, Yomaira C. *Decolonizing Diasporas: Radical Mappings of Afro-Atlantic Literature*. Evanston, Ill.: Northwestern University Press, 2020.

The following material is excluded from the license:
Images, previously published material

For permissions beyond the scope of this license, visit http://www.nupress.northwestern.edu/

An electronic version of this book is freely available, thanks to the support of libraries working with Knowledge Unlatched. KU is a collaborative initiative designed to make high-quality books open access for the public good. More information about the initiative and links to the open-access version can be found at www.knowledgeunlatched.org.

Para los Santos

Santos Vásquez-Rivera

Marcelino Santos-Figueroa

Santa Figueroa-Vásquez

The proposal I am making is that such a discipline can only emerge with an overall rewriting of knowledge, as the re-enacting of the original heresy of a Studia, reinvented as a science of human systems, from the liminal perspective of the "base" (Dewey, 1950) new Studies, whose revelatory heresy lies in their definition of themselves away from the Chaos roles in which they had been defined—Black from Negro, Chicano from Mexican American, Feminists from Women, etc. For these have revealed the connection between the way we identify ourselves and the way we act upon/know the world.

—Sylvia Wynter, "The Ceremony Must
Be Found after Humanism"

CONTENTS

ILLUSTRATIONS

ACKNOWLEDGMENTS

There are many tangled threads that have led me to this book. While I could attempt to trace or unravel those critical moments, what has guided me to and through this project can only be put into words insofar as this book is in your hands.

There is, however, an impetus. I am guided by an ethics forged in diaspora and brandished on the island, the empire, and innumerable points in between. My family, colonial subjects thrust out of our island, made home in impossible places. We call it Nuyorican, diasporican, Boricua, Afro-Latinx, Caribbean. In no world is this book an objective endeavor. It is anchored in the histories I grew up hearing and is haunted by voices often unheard. The years of living in destierro have made me a faithful witness to the experiences of overlapping forms of domination, racialization, and exploitation. This text bears witness to the distinct and ever-present forms of resistance, imagination, and poetics that emerge from the ruptures of colonialism and coloniality.

I was transformed when I read my first novel written by a Latina Caribbean writer. One hot summer, locked inside my abuela Santos's house in Caguas's barriada Morales, a whole new worldview was opened for me and so many possibilities unfolded. I felt as if I had been written into existence. Latinas were writing us into being, in and against a system that erased us by trapping us within predetermined scripts and pathologies. I carried that book, Julia Alvarez's *How the García Girls Lost Their Accents*, from the lush mountains of Tomás de Castro to Vega Baja's resilient Alto de Cuba, reading and rereading diasporic experiences on my island. Uncanny the feeling. At twelve years old I knew that whatever I was going to become, these books had to be a part of it.

Over the last twenty-plus years, that one book became hundreds. During that time, I have attempted to articulate what they conjured in me then and how they summon me now. I find in this literature a reflection of strangers I know, elders I've loved, children I've helped to raise, and ancestors I never knew. When I read these poetics, hear their sounds, see their art and images, complex and beautiful prisms emerge. I see what I've always known and could never know.

We are tied to one another: Cuba, the Dominican Republic, Puerto Rico, Equatorial Guinea. History and language and struggle connect us. Blackness and hope and survival connect us. Tropical islands and hard cities connect us.

Our imaginations connect us. There is a place where we know one another, and perhaps that place is the page.

The risks these artists take in conjuring these poetics are chasms, they are sinkholes. They expose the contradictions of diaspora and the specters of migration. They reveal the machinations of power observed from up close and afar. They resist and collide against facile notions of oppositional consciousness; they are entangled and write back from within shape-shifting power structures. They summon worlds/otherwise that act as talismans and bear azabaches against colonizing notions of home, relations, love, time, space.

I wrote this book because encountering Latinx literature as a twelve-year-old changed my life. I am indebted to these writers and thinkers. So I think alongside them, I trace imaginaries, I dedicate years of my life to studying and sharing these knowledges.

In Equatorial Guinea I went in search of a linguistic connection, and I found long histories of Crossings, an affinity of experiences under colonialism and dictatorship, and liberation struggles fueled by love and fury. Equatoguinean diasporic literature is a product of violent processes that are very different yet reminiscent of the Latinx Caribbean diaspora. I found that the horizons of their archipelagos are dotted with similar preoccupations with intimacy, witnessing, dispossession, reparations, and futures. I also found that when this African literary corpus, peripheralized in almost every sense, is placed alongside the peripheralized literary corpus of Afro-descendants in the Caribbean, it explodes what we know and what we can know about decolonization, liberation, and the ontological experiences of the contemporary Afro-Atlantic Hispanophone world.

This book would not be possible without the generosity of many people. These words of gratitude are insufficient, but please accept them with the fullness of my spirit. Nelson Maldonado-Torres has supported and mentored me for the better part of fourteen years. Thank you for helping me understand and envision the heretical possibilities of ethnic studies and decolonial thought. You have helped me in more ways than I can ever know, and I will be fortunate to mentor others in the same ways that you fostered my growth as a person and scholar. My deepest thanks to you and Celines. Yolanda Martínez-San Miguel took me under her wing and I am so lucky to be cared for by her. Thank you for the years of advice, strategies, and encouragement. Keith Feldman has been a pillar of support for this project since he arrived at Berkeley and has been generous and helpful at every turn. My thanks to Trinh T. Minh-ha for challenging my thinking, encouraging my ideas, and urging me to study and read beyond my own limits. Ramón Grosfoguel helped me in critical times throughout my years at Berkeley. Laura E. Pérez helped me to conceive of the Latinx literary canon in new ways. The brilliant Natasha

Himmelman introduced me to the literature of Equatorial Guinea and for that I will always be thankful! Mayra Santos-Febres, eres mi hermana, mi comadre y me siento tan bendecida por tenerte en mi vida. Vamos a seguir trabajando, bregando e inventando para crear el mundo que sabemos que es posible.

At Berkeley I was able to receive incredible training and mentorship for which I am most grateful. Thank you to the faculty in Ethnic Studies, African Diaspora Studies, History, Rhetoric, and Gender & Women's Studies. I am forever thankful for my peers from graduate school who I am blessed to call friends: George Ciccariello-Maher, Daphne Taylor García, Jason Kim, Jason Chang, Tala Khanmalek, Monica Huerta, Mattie Harper, Craig Santos-Perez, Wanda Alarcon, Norene Ybarra, Kim Tran, Dory Nason, Danika Medak-Saltzman, Leece Lee, Anthony Kim, José Fusté and Jade Power-Sotomayor, Marcelle Maese-Cohen, and Ronald Williams. ¡Carmen Mitchell: presente! My Berkeley Boricua contingent: Mercy Romero, Angelina Villafañe, and Zelideth M. Rivas, mil gracias—the ancestors are with us. The Berkeley Afro-Latin@ Working Group was a dynamic influence. Thanks to: Tianna Paschel, Petra Rivera-Rideau, Juan Herrera, Jennifer Jones, and Rebecca Bodenheimer. Janey M. Lew has been my ES day one. We've seen each other through this process at every step with so much love and patience, which is no small thing (Alex and Ernest, I love you).

When we moved to Michigan I had no idea that I would not only have colleagues and friends, but family. I am grateful to count you as kin and community in East Lansing: Terah and Glenn Chambers (and Langston), Estrella Torrez and Dylan Miner (and Reina and Mexica), Terry Flennaugh and Joy Hannibal (and Elijah), Breannah Alexander and Clay Oppenhuizen (and Alba and Simon), Dali Martínez and Bernadette Castillo, and Maribel Santiago. Delia Fernández I am so glad that we met here and that we get to be friends and family all at once. My love and thanks to little Jonny and Jonathan. Tamara Butler: I love you and I am so very glad to have shared this assistant professor journey with you. Thank you for being a monster friend, a night owl, and a collaborator on so many projects, initiatives, and ideas. Vanessa Holden, Mariama Lockington, and Sir Henry: we love every visit, every text, and every moment we get to catch up. At Michigan State University I had the pleasure to be surrounded by a supportive and loving group of people: Cara Cilano, Justus Neiland, Zarena Aslami, Aleida Martínez and Juan Flores (and Aleina and Julian), Divya Victor and Josh Lam (and Zameen), and Salah Hassan and Sheila Contreras (and Noor and Paz), thank you for every talk, every shared meal, for every single thing. Terrion Williamson, thank you for putting up with my silliness and for being so candid and brilliant. I am thankful to have shared space during these years with David Bering-Porter, Lynn Goeringer, Lucia Cárdenas, Beronda Montgomery, Deborah Johnson, Eric Juenke, Laurie Medina, Stephanie Nawyn, Emery Petchaur, Jeff Wray, Tama Hamilton-Wray, Sarah Fingal and Dustin

Barr, Danny Méndez, Johanna Schuster-Craig, Pero Dagbovie, LaShawn Harris, April-Baker-Bell, Pete Johnston, Lamar Johnson, Bill Vincent, Bill Johnsen, Ken and Liz Harrow, Chezare Warren, Rac and Django Paris, Ellen McCallum and Barb, and Kinitra Brooks. Kristie Dotson—you changed the framework for this book with just a few questions. Thank you and Kyle Powhys Whyte for believing in the project. Kristin Mahoney sat with me through the editing of my manuscript and dealt with my pouting with the utmost generosity and grace. I am so glad you are here and that we get to be friends and colleagues. Kaveh, my gardening buddy, thank you for reminding me to sit back and watch things grow. Thank you to Kathy Dorshimer, Barbara Miller, Marilyn Duke, Marina Patrick, Sara Allison, and Katlyn Wright for all that you do to support our research and work. Many thanks to the MSU Womxn of Color Initiative team and everyone who makes our work at MSU and in the Lansing/East Lansing community possible. My thanks to the MSU librarians, especially to Diana Rivera. Dean Christopher Long listened to me with care at many meetings, supported my research and initiatives, and affirmed my experiences and knowledge. Thank you for being approachable and understanding and for supporting the work of women of color and underrepresented faculty. Benita Sampedro Vizcaya, thank you for supporting me and this project since 2013. You have taken the time and energy to talk me through the nuances of Equatoguinean literary studies, to point me in the right direction, and to redirect me when I was wrong. You've done so with kindness, integrity, and patience. Thank you for reading this manuscript in its draft form and for your necessary input. Xhercis Méndez, thank you for your friendship and intellectual comradery—from our time in the Decolonial Feminist Working Group at Binghamton/Berkeley to Cartagena and Boca Chica and beyond. Niko Karkov, you are perhaps the most generous scholar that I have ever come to know. Thank you for your encouragement, for the collective intelligence, and for the wonderful times we all shared together. Jessica Marie Johnson, thank you for the advice, the laughs, for reading me for filth, for letting me be loud and stubborn, for loving me, and for being a real one. Also, thank you for Crescent, who I love to the stars. You too TC.

I have had the pleasure of working with excellent undergraduate and graduate students at UC Berkeley, Rutgers University, and Michigan State University. I am especially thankful to Keishla Rivera López, who helped me with getting the permissions for this book. Keishla, you've come so far and I am continually inspired by your gusto and tenacity. Briona Jones, you are a light in this world and I am so proud to know you and to be part of your journey. You've helped shape this book in many ways, and I cannot wait to read your books in the near future. Eliana Castro and Liany Martínez, thank you for your brilliance and for the community we have built together. Rebecca Fussell, Erin Alvarez, and Blair Zaid were fantastic graduate assistants who helped with this project in many ways. Stephany Bravo's assistance helped me to complete the final edits of this manuscript and Stephany and

Jada Similton's work as electricians for Electric Marronage were essential to the final stages of production. Many thanks to our English department students and MUSE scholars. Thanks to: Breanna Escamilla, Krsna Santos, Bria Harper, Cameron Clark, Christian Ramírez, Danielle Schwartz, Rashad Timmons, Néstor Espinoza, Amanda Flores, Dianey Leal, Nerli Paredes Ruvalcaba, Stephanie Aguilar-Smith, Benjamin Espinoza, Suban Nur Cooley, Marlisha Marcellin, Kaelyn Muiru, Jennifer Mojica Santana, Cristóbal Martínez, Ronny Ford, and Liz Deegan, for your insights, warmth, and brilliance. My students in my "Decoloniality, Diaspora and the Human," "Poetics of Liberation and Relation," "From the Entrails of the Monster," and "Race, Gender and the Human" graduate seminars asked brilliant questions, offered the opportunities to revisit foundational texts, and made me a better teacher and scholar. Max Monroy-Miller, all of us who were blessed to share space with you in the fall 2015 seminar love and miss you dearly.

Carlos U. Decena: thank you for taking a chance on me as an undergrad and for cheering me on ever since. Sandra Rocio Castro, your mentorship during my undergraduate years made this career possible, I will forever be thankful for all of those nights you let me work in your office at the CLAC, offering me the quiet space to write and research. Frances Tapia Mateo and Engelbert Santana, son mis amigos del alma. My love to Jane Batista-Ortiz, Jennifer Pichardo-Berniz, Tannia Muñoz Ospina, Andrea Ortega, Angela Matos, Jennifer Arnau, Veronica Olivares, Jahaira Infante, Jaqueline Gonzalez, Jennifer Arbelo, Maria Barzola, Yoraydil Brito, and to all of Epsilon. Zaire Dinzey-Flores, thank you for your kindness. Yarimar Bonilla, I am so glad for our times together in Puerto Rico and for your transformative work. Marisa Parham and John Drabinski have offered invaluable advice and support. Lorgia García Peña has brought so much kindness, wisdom, and fierceness to my world: thank you for sharing yourself with me. Omaris Z. Zamora: sis, you are a shining star and I am proud to know you and to traverse this path alongside you. Vanessa Valdés is a beacon of light—thank you for your work and for all that you do to support early career scholars. Nadia Celis Salgado, gracias por todo. Christen Smith, I am thankful for each interaction we have and for getting to know your fierce work in this world. Nicole Fleetwood and Kai, you are like a family to me.

I am grateful to have been chosen for the inaugural cohort of the Duke University Mellon Mays Summer Institute for Tenure and Professional Advancement (SITPA), where I received invaluable mentorship that has extended beyond the tenure of the award. Margot Crawford offered essential support and advice at crucial moments, as did Jacqueline Lazu, Herman Beavers, Candice Jenkins, Mark Anthony Neal, and Kerry Haynie. My deepest thanks to Jarvis McInnis, La Marr Jurelle Bruce, and Jeffrey Coleman for being wonderful interlocutors and friends. The Ford Foundation Postdoctoral Fellowship allowed me the precious time and resources to complete this manuscript under the brilliant mentorship of Tsitsi Jaji. My thanks to the

English Department at Duke University and to the Duke Libraries, especially the staff at the Rubenstein Rare Book & Manuscript Library. The Woodrow Wilson Foundation offered me a Career Enhancement Fellowship and bolstered my belief in my project. I am so grateful to Natalie Léger, Armando García, Pablo López Oro, Cindy Cruz, Carolyn Ureña, Emmanuel Martinez, Judy Rodriguez, Martin Repinecz, Brenda Quiñones-Ayala, Dixa Ramírez, María Chavez, Susana Morris, Therí Alyce Pickens, William García, Randi Gill-Sadler, Mary Pat Brady, and Xavier Totti. The Tepoztlán Institute for the Transnational History of the Americas offered me the invaluable opportunity to workshop two chapters of this book. The Caribbean Philosophical Association has been an intellectual home for me since 2009. My thanks to Lewis and Jane Gordon, Michael and Camille Monahan, Paget Henry and Robin Campbell, Rosario Torres Guevara and Douglas Ficek, Hanétha Vété-Congolo, Carolyn Cusick, and Neil Roberts. I was able to workshop, discuss, and present many parts of this book at Pennsylvania State University, the University of North Carolina at Chapel Hill, Duke University, the University of Kansas, Rutgers University at New Brunswick and Newark, Williams College, Cornell University, the University of San Diego, California State University at Long Beach and Fullerton, Amherst College, Northwestern University, La Universidad del Norte in Barranquilla, the University of Houston, the Univeristy of Texas at Austin, Bowdoin College, and the Massachusetts Institute of Technology. My thanks to all of the departments and colleagues that extended invitations for me to share my work.

Belinda Thurston, owner of Just B Yoga, has been a pillar in our Lansing community and has made healing spaces available to so many women of color. I love the Ypsilanti-based Peters family dearly and I want to especially thank Shani. Bee Queener, I bear witness to your skills and I am spreading the good news. Mil gracias al equipo Yagrumo: José Arturo Ballester, Mayra Santos Febres, y Betty Santiago por todo lo que han hecho para hacer nuestro proyecto de intercambio entre MSU y Puerto Rico una realidad. Team #PPPR you are fierce and fearless: Estrella Torrez, Tamara Butler, Delia Fernández, Xhercis Méndez, Keishla Rivera, Angélica de Jesús, and Jessica Marie Johnson. Angélica has been my co-conspirator in many projects and designed the maps for this manuscript, thank you for your vision. Dr. Stephanie Flemming saved my life and held me up in difficult times. Jochi Melero me ayudo a ver, sentir y vivir de nuevo, Ashé.

I am indebted to the authors, artists, and writers who have made this study possible (some of whom have been included in this work and others who appear in other ways): Remei Sipi Mayo has sido como otra mamá para mi. Juan Tomás Ávila Laurel, Edjanga Jones Ndjoli mi pana, Donato Ndongo, Melibea Obono, Joaquín Mbomío Bacheng, Recardo Silebo Boturu, María Nsué Angüe, M. Jacqui Alexander, Audre Lorde, Aracelis Girmay, Loida Maritza Pérez, Nelly Rosario, Christina Olivares, Ibeyi, Ernesto Quiñonez, Michelle Cliff, and so many others, thank you for your works. Junot Díaz offered me guidance and encouragement when I first started grad school—thank you. María Magdalena Campos-Pons gave me permission to use her stunning image both within the book and on the cover; I am most grateful for the gift of your work. The editors and team at Northwestern University Press have been truly wonderful. Thank you to Gianna Mosser who first believed in this project and who supported me wholeheartedly. Trevor Perri, thank you for your advice and patience and for helping me through each step of the production process. My thanks to the entire editorial, marketing, and design team.

In Hoboken and points beyond, I would like to thank: Tamiah N. Brevard, I am lucky to call you my best friend—thank you for loving and supporting me through all of these years. Alyza and Aubee . . . I love you deeply. I would like to thank my dearest friends who are truly family: Angela Russo, Juan Valdez, Namibia Donadio, Maxx, Melissa Castillo and Miah, Justin Lane, and Anne Bonner, Arthur, and Beatrice. Mucho cariño para Courtney Salerno, Rachel Clowe, Bobbea Bermudez, Tamara Moss Soru, Kate Lee, and Mayra Vásquez Radzinksi. Alix Genter, editor extraordinaire, helped me when I was in a pinch and did so with unending kindness and professionalism.

Peggy Díaz is my big sister and confidant who helps me navigate this world—I would be lost without you and I will never defriend you. Isaiah Díaz Mays, you inspire me with your dreams and willingness to create and write worlds; Amanda Rodríguez Mammas, my very first love, I am so proud to see who you've become. You are both talented and amazing human beings and I am proud to be your aunt. Troy, our spoiled little forever-puppy who reminds me to take walks, to be mischievous, to play, and to cuddle—the unconditional love you give is more than I can ever deserve. Shoeboots lived ferally and fearlessly—no turtle can replace you. My brothers Peter Díaz and Juan Rodríguez and nephew Everett Díaz are deeply loved. Cheka, Brandon, Yaslene, Jasmine, Cassandra, and Mateo, you are so special to me and I am thankful for our bond. A mis tías, tíos, y primos que tantos hay—de la familia Vásquez-Rivera de Caguas y la familia Figueroa y Santos en Vega Baja—los quiero muchísimo y les doy gracias por todo el apoyo y el amor que brindan. Abuela Santo, te amo. My titi Carmen and the Otero family have always supported me with words and actions. Vanessa is always in our hearts. Alana, you are brilliant and I am so thankful for you. Titi Yeye, papi's favorite sister, you are fierce and thank you for the memories and stories you share with me. My love and thanks to my incredible in-laws, the Peters family (Mom, Dad, Yejide, Kamau, Aleah, Azikiwe, Tamique, Alain and Samira, Michael Davis, and Grandma Laverne), who have encouraged me since we met over a dozen years ago and have come to be some of the people I hold most dear in the world.

My parents made this life possible. From the barriada Morales in Caguas and el alto de Cuba in Vega Baja in Puerto Rico, my mami and papi made a life for themselves and for their four children and survived more than I can ever know. Lo he dicho y siempre lo diré: vinieron sin nada y nos dieron todo. Faltan palabras para poder darles las gracias. Yo siempre sere la nena de Marcelino Santos-Figueroa. Papi cuanto te extraño, amor de mis amores, sangre de mi alma.

Tacuma, you've changed my life and fill my days with possibility, laughter, and joy. Your brilliance, generosity, and ethics are unmatched. You have seen me through this project and beyond, with a loving care that cannot be named. Thank you for standing alongside me each step of the way. I love you and I am so grateful to be your partner in this world. This is always.

NOTE ON LANGUAGE AND TRANSLATION

The works I examine in this manuscript are written in English and Spanish, and Spanglish. There are also instances where Fang, Ndowe, and other languages from Equatorial Guinea appear. All translations are my own unless otherwise noted. When quoting from works that are untranslated or that require linguistic context, I provide an English translation after the quotation in the original language. Many of the endnotes offer additional context, suggested readings, and related commentary. Please note these as alternative dialogues or directions that inform the work at hand. Very few novels from Equatorial Guinea have been translated into English. I have incorporated some of these translated texts throughout the book, but I rely mostly on the original Castilian versions for my close readings. The rationale behind this is as follows: while there "ain't nothing like the real thing," I want to ensure that the writers who have worked so tirelessly to gain a wide readership by getting their works published in Spanish and later translated to English are seen. I hope that reading this book inspires readers to pick up these works in whatever language is best for them.

PREFACE

How do we map relations? About twenty miles off the coast of West Africa lies the island of Bioko, one of the most important insular territories of Equatorial Guinea, the only Spanish-speaking nation-state in sub-Saharan Africa. There, in the capital city of Malabo, a salt-whipped bronzed plaque reads: "En memoria a los cubanos deportados en el siglo XIX a la isla de Fernando Po / 28 de mayo de 1869 / Embajada de Cuba en Guinea Ecuatorial." This plaque, dedicated to the memory of Cubans deported to Fernando Pó, Bioko's colonial-era name, marks an important and understudied history between Hispanophone Africa and the Hispanophone Caribbean.

In 1845, the Spanish Crown's Royal Order 13 saw to it that emancipated slaves from Cuba—Blacks and mulattos—be deported to the island of Fernando Po to labor in the newly solidified colony of Spanish Guinea.[1] By

Fig. 1. Cuban deportee memorial in Malabo, Bioko, Equatorial Guinea.

1865, these emancipados had been joined by political activists and dissidents from Cuba, Puerto Rico, and the Philippines who were "disappeared" from their homes and deported to Bioko's penal colony. It was not, however, until thirty years later, in 1898, when Spain lost the Spanish-American War and by extension Puerto Rico, Cuba, and the Philippines—its last remaining colonies in the Americas and the Pacific—that Spain turned its full imperial attention to its remaining African colonies. In "Rethinking the Archive," Benita Sampedro Vizcaya notes: "In the aftermath of 1898, when Spain lost what remained of its credibility as a global force and imperial anxieties passed through one of their most critical phases, the scramble for Africa by the European powers left little to appropriate. Equatorial Guinea would become, along with Morocco, the essential locus for covering the economic and psychological trauma and contributing to the formation of a public imperial imaginary."[2] The shift that left Puerto Rico, Cuba, and the Philippines in the imperial hands of the United States likewise ushered in an age of renewed colonial interest, extraction, and exploitation in Spanish Guinea, as it was then known.[3]

While each of these Caribbean island nations faced different political outcomes under U.S. imperial rule and later independence, protectorate, or commonwealth statuses, 1898 marks an important political, social, and

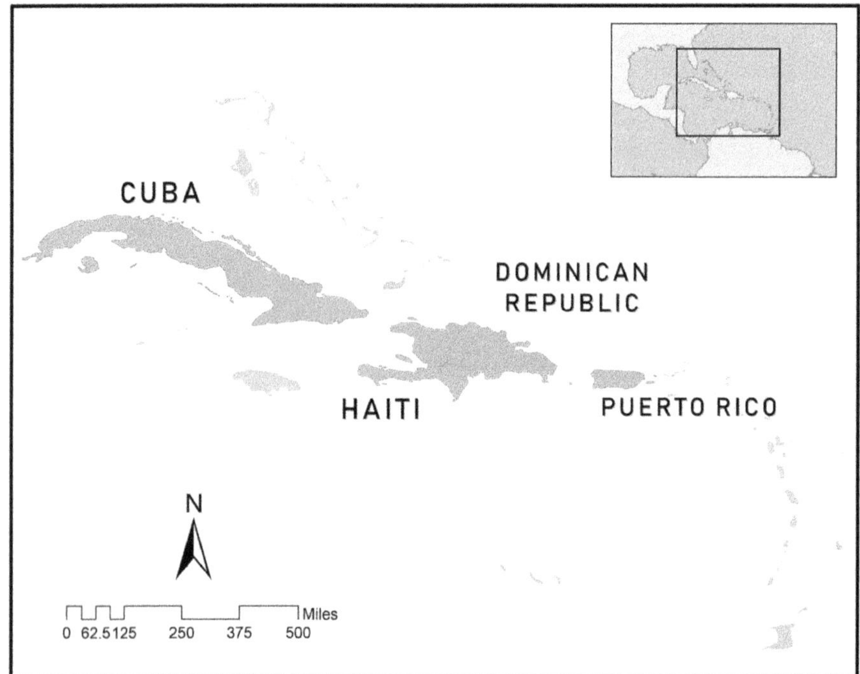

Fig. 2. Cuba, Puerto Rico, and the Dominican Republic.

economic shift that bears on contemporary realities. I would be remiss if I failed to note that the year 1898 had a significant impact on the place from which I am writing, the state of Michigan, which is on the ancestral, traditional, and contemporary lands of the Anishinaabeg—the Three Fires Confederacy of the Ojibwe, Odawa, and Potawatami peoples.[4] As legal scholars Wenona Singel and Matthew Fletcher explain, the Burt Lake Anishinaabeg resistance to forcible removal in 1898 was followed by continued harassment in 1899, and culminated in the violent "burn out" of the Indian Village on Burt Lake in 1900. Notwithstanding these forceful histories and ongoing forms of dispossession, "Indian and Indian tribes have never forgotten their sacred homelands, and continuously seek to restore their lands."[5] Colonial legacies of dispossession and violence go far beyond and before 1898. Thus, while this book focuses on the Hispanophone Afro-Atlantic, I understand these histories as overlapping with the forceful removal, dispossession, and other forms of oppression faced by Indigenous, Black, and people of color around the globe. These are the palimpsests of oppression and resistance to which we must bear witness.

In the case of the Spanish-speaking Caribbean and Spanish-speaking Africa, it is not only the legacy of Spanish colonial rule that connects these islands but also histories of war, dictatorship, migration, and defiance. The histories, and very often the imaginaries, of these islands and their diasporas often overlap in generative and complex ways. Spanish Guinea did not become Equatorial Guinea until it was administratively decolonized in 1968. Thus, as Spain shifted from fascism to democracy after 1975, Equatorial Guinea shifted from colonial rule to a fifty-year-long autocratic government.[6] In 1968 Equatoguineans elected their first president, Francisco Macías Nguema. By 1970, Macías had made Equatorial Guinea a single-party state, and within six months he had declared himself president for life. Effectively a dictatorship, his repressive rule saw the deaths of thousands of Equatoguineans and political dissidents, the displacement of the Bubi (the autochthones of the island of Bioko, which is central to political power), the severing of political ties with Spain and the West, and the ousting of anyone who had been educated under Spanish colonial rule. Many of those young students, like authors Remei Sipi Mayo and Donato Ndongo Bidyogo, were unable to return to Equatorial Guinea, and watched the nation transition from colony to democracy to dictatorship from their exile in Spain.

These oppressive maneuvers drove a surge of Equatoguineans into exile in Spain and led others to migrate to the neighboring nations of Gabon and Cameroon. Those who survived and remained in Equatorial Guinea suffered from malnutrition, state-sponsored terror, and coercive treatment from paramilitary and state power representatives—what Achille Mbembe has called "private indirect government."[7] This ethnic and ideological cleansing was intended to purge any political opposition, and to remove the memory of colonial-era rule. Macías went so far as to outlaw the word "intellectual."[8]

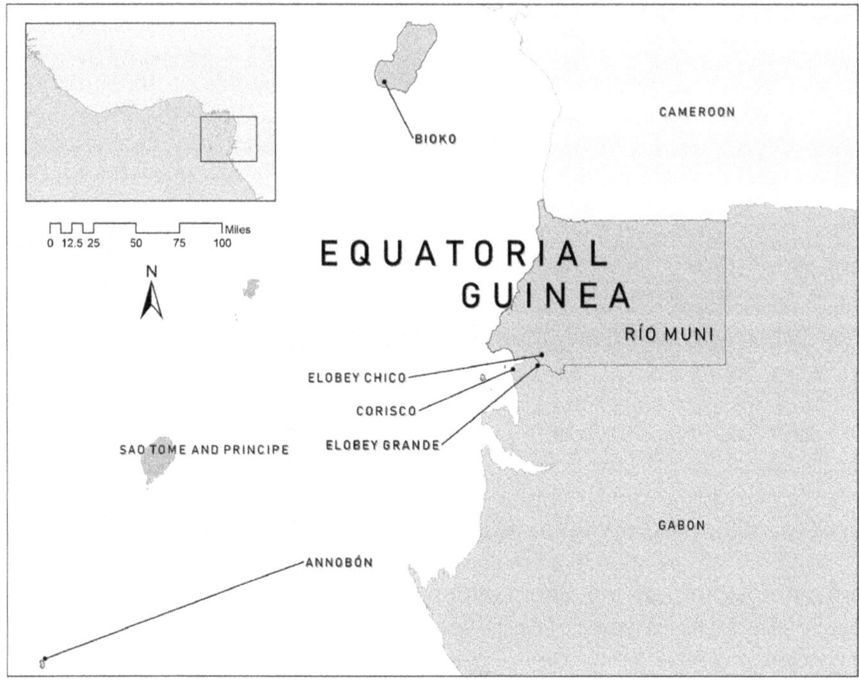

Fig. 3. Equatorial Guinea.

During this time, many writers and teachers (among others) fled the country and were unable to return. The years of Macías's reign have been called the "years of silence," referencing both the silencing of writers and intellectuals and the extensive and demoralizing political and social silencing of the people of Equatorial Guinea. As such, literary poetics written from exile, as Benita Sampedro Vizcaya argues, "was one of the most forceful forms of resistance during the years of silence, especially under Francisco Macías Nguema."[9]

In August 1979 Teodoro Obiang, Macías's nephew and lieutenant, led a coup d'état, overthrowing his uncle and sentencing him to death by firing squad. Obiang became the second president of Equatorial Guinea and remains in power today. Obiang is now the longest-serving dictator in Africa, and the world's second-longest-serving political leader. His regime, though seen as less repressive than Macías's before him, remains an oppressive, ethnocentric, and autocratic rule with no free press, radio, or other outlets. The discovery of offshore oil reserves in the 1990s ensured Equatorial Guinea's rise on the global stage. Contemporarily, it is considered one of the wealthiest nations on the continent of Africa.[10] But the wealth from the oil boom is distributed extremely unequally; the majority of the population lives in destitute poverty, many without access to clean water. The oil boom and subsequent financial windfall further complicate the nation's human rights violations, in light of the Equatoguinean government's relationship with international oil corporations and countries like the United States, which has consumed more than one-third of Equatoguinean oil. Furthermore, there are currently hundreds of Cuban medical doctors, professors, and others working in Equatorial Guinea as part of international political and solidarity efforts between their countries.[11]

Due to the repressive political climate within Equatorial Guinea, resistance movements, much of the country's oppositional thought, and literary poetics that address postcolonial corruption, cultural resurgences, and liberatory strivings are produced in exile and diaspora in Spain.[12] The literary corpus of Equatorial Guinea falls primarily into the categories of colonial literature and contemporary works of poetry, drama, fiction, short stories, essays, music, and other artistic expressions. Contemporary works by Equatoguineans who were born in or came of age in Spain reveal their struggles with racial and ethnic belonging and their complex ties to a homeland made impossible by dictatorship and coloniality. These literatures also reflect affective and material relationships with other immigrants, African, Caribbean, and otherwise, in Spain.[13] The literature and cultural production of Equatorial Guinea, while preoccupied with the homeland, political economies, interethnic relations, and the everyday injustices of private indirect government, are likewise diasporic and transnational in their focus. As Marvin Lewis argues, "the capital of Equatorial Guinean literature" is in "the heart of every Guinean, whether in Spain, in France, or in Equatorial Guinea," because after the successive dictatorships, "a dislocation of the literary frontier is verified, and each author remains 'wherever he best finds himself,' from wherever he writes for his country."[14] Overall, however, Equatoguinean literatures written in diaspora and exile represent a broad range of concerns that are fundamentally linked in many ways to the literary corpus of Latinx Caribbean peoples in exile and diaspora. It bears mentioning that these literatures are rarely put into relation to each other.

On the other side of the Atlantic, the 1960s would also usher in a new era for Latinx Caribbean peoples in the Americas. For example, by 1963 over 215,000 elite and middle-class Cubans had fled Cuba after the 1959 revolution. Given the status of special refugees and aid in the form of U.S. subsidies, these Cuban exiles joined earlier waves of Cuban immigrants to the United States and necessarily transformed the cultural landscape of southern Florida.[15] During this same time and for decades afterward, Cuba underwent political, social, and cultural changes and suffered an embargo that would see it pitted as a political showcase vis-à-vis Puerto Rico.[16] Cuban migration to the United States would exponentially increase later in the twentieth century, as other middle-class Cubans in the 1970s, Marielitos in the 1980s, Balseros in the 1990s, and continuing waves of migration in the 2000s left the island by the thousands.

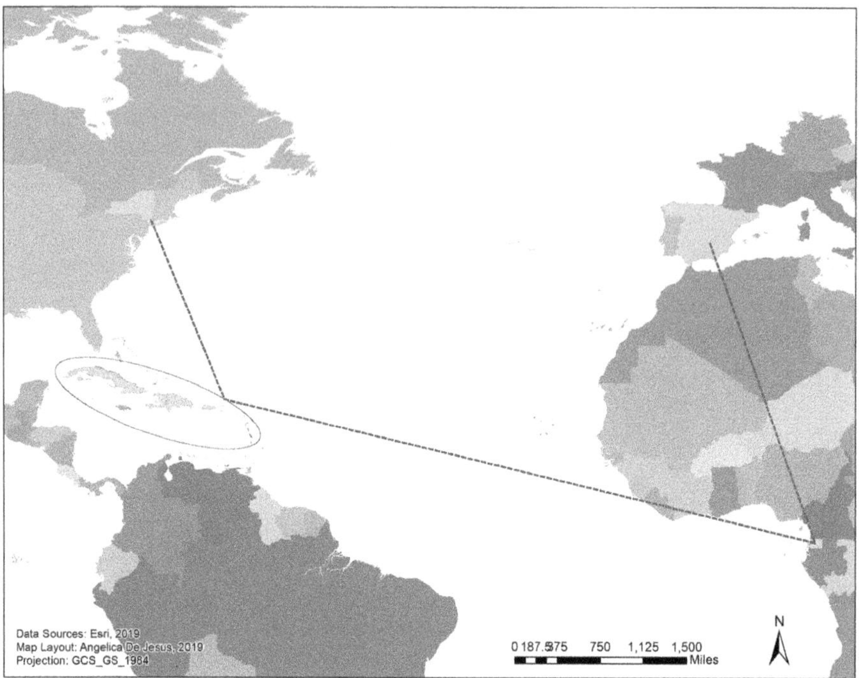

Fig. 4. "Let the Geographies Sink In": Afro-Atlantic Hispanophone Diasporas: Latinx Caribbean migration to the United States (New York highlighted) and Equatorial Guinean migration to Spain (Madrid highlighted).

Likewise, though a significant number of Puerto Ricans had been immigrating to the United States since the early twentieth century, dispossession and occupation after the Spanish-American War, coupled with efforts to rapidly industrialize the island through capitalist designs for a whiter middle class, meant that by 1960 there were over 600,000 Puerto Ricans living in New York City and hundreds of thousands more in Chicago, Michigan, Ohio, Pennsylvania, and other locales throughout the continental United States and Hawaii. Puerto Rican immigrants were seen as a source of cheap labor and worked on rural farms and in factories in densely populated urban centers.[17] Waves of migration steadily increased throughout the latter half of the twentieth century, an era marked in Puerto Rico by economic depressions and deindustrialization driven by corruption, corporate tax evasion, ongoing dispossession, and the island's colonial (or commonwealth) status vis-à-vis the United States. The island's current fiscal crisis, due to the odious debt Puerto Rico has "accrued"—upwards of seventy billion dollars—can be tied to its commonwealth status and has propelled another wave of population dispersal which rivals that of the twentieth century. The year 2015 marked a historic moment in Puerto Rican migration history: there were officially more

Puerto Ricans living in the United States than on the island. The onslaught of Hurricane Irma and then of Hurricane María in September 2017 destroyed much of the island's infrastructure, leaving millions without electricity, running water, or access to basic goods. FEMA and the U.S. and Puerto Rican governments' massive mishandling of recovery efforts after Hurricane María made for an unnatural yet predictable disaster that counted over 4,000 dead in its wake. It has also led tens of thousands to flee the island to cities like Orlando, Florida.[18]

The 1960s also proved to be a critical decade in the history of the Dominican Republic, as Rafael Trujillo's more than thirty-year rule came to an end with his assassination in 1961. In 1963, the democratically elected president Juan Bosch was overthrown after just two years in power. In 1966, after almost two years of military rule, Joaquín Balaguer was elected president. His twelve-year presidency, predicated on political repression, was reprised throughout the twentieth century, as he was reelected in 1986, 1990, and 1994. Thus, between 1961 and 1986, over 400,000 Dominicans fled to the United States, while another 44,000 migrated to the neighboring island of Puerto Rico. Political and economic instability likewise drove Dominican immigration to the United States throughout the 1990s and 2000s. A 2014 study from the CUNY Center for Latin American, Caribbean, and Latino Studies found that Dominicans had become the single largest foreign-born immigrant group in New York City.[19]

The decades following the 1960s saw a surge in literary poetics, arts, and musical genres in the diasporic populations of these nations. For example, the Nuyorican Poets Movement of the 1960s and 1970s radically changed the literary landscape of Latinx and U.S. literature and aesthetics. These groundbreaking decades saw working-poor and immigrant populations reflect their experiences as colonial subjects, immigrants, and racialized peoples in new and syncretic forms. This era also saw the formation of radical political Latinx organizations, neighborhood associations and grassroots activism, and, facilitated by bilingual education programs, an influx of Latinxs to colleges and universities. This growing number of people of color in the university system and their demands to see Eurocentric education decolonized and transformed led them to create new fields of thought that took seriously the knowledges, contributions, and cultural productions of people of color in the United States and the Third World. These new fields would not be like the area studies programs before them, which were often funded by and linked to U.S. military intelligence efforts, but rather, sought to transform Eurocentric knowledge production writ large.

In 1968 and 1969 the Third World Liberation Front, a coalition of Black, Latinx, and Pilipino student groups at San Francisco State University and the University of California at Berkeley, led the longest student strike in U.S. history. Their demand to decolonize the white supremacist curriculum and other structures within higher education led to the formation of ethnic studies,

African American studies, Native American studies, Puerto Rican and Chicano studies, Latino studies, Asian American studies, Women's and Gender studies, and other such fields all over the United States. While this is by no means an exhaustive history, I do hope to mark some of the relations between migration, political resistance, and the movements that sought to transform knowledge practices. While I am wary of engaging in teleological narratives that flatten these dynamic histories and decolonizing projects, I am nevertheless committed to offering some of the important overviews and linkages that make this book possible.

With regard to Equatorial Guinea, the scholarship of these critical historical crossings resides primarily in the field of Hispanic studies and to a lesser extent in African studies, with Ibrahim K. Sundiata and Benita Sampedro Vizcaya underscoring the importance of the nineteenth-century deportations to penal colonies and Michael Ugarte, Elisa Rizo, and others engaging the salience of Equatoguinean literatures.[20] Furthermore, linguistics and sociology scholarship tracks the varieties of Spanish, including linguistic borrowings from Antillean Spanish, in the language practices of Equatorial Guinea.[21] In *Decolonizing Diasporas*, I aim to expand the ways we map these crossings between Spanish-speaking Africa and the Spanish-speaking Caribbean through a sustained meditation on their diasporic and exilic poetics. As Katherine McKittrick argues in *Demonic Grounds*, "Geographies of domination, from transatlantic slavery and beyond, hold in them the marking and the contestation of old and new social hierarchies."[22] Thus, I contend that putting into relation the preoccupations and reflections that emerge in post-1960s literary and cultural productions offers us a radical remapping of Afro-Atlantic Hispanophone subjects. This kind of relational project sees an often-ignored corpus of work as sites through which we can indict oppression, resist domination, and imagine decolonizing strategies. In mapping these imaginaries across these bodies of literature, I have found that, although distinct, they reflect similar preoccupations, experiences, and liberatory strivings. And although the historical, contemporary, literary, and ontological relations between Equatorial Guinea and the Hispanophone Caribbean islands—Cuba, Puerto Rico, and the Dominican Republic—are rarely discussed in the context of Black, Latinx, and Hispanophone studies, I believe that such a study offers critical implications for these fields.

The connections between these poetics are not imagined. For example, we find intertextual dedications lauding Negrismo, a Cuban precursor to the Negritude movement, in the poetry of Equatorial Guinea.[23] One example is a 1993 poem published in the literary journal *El Patio*, a Hispano-Guinean cultural magazine. In it, the Equatoguinean poet and critic Carlos Nsue Otong offers an elegy to Nicolás Guillén, one of the foremost Afro-Cuban poets and political activists of the late twentieth century. Nsue Otong writes:

Quisiera tejer mi palabra / con esta emoción que me embarga
y hacerla volar presurosa / a Cuba, mitad africana.
Guillén Nicolás, compañero: / labré con mi canto corona,
Maestro, Cantor y Poeta / salud a tu egregia persona.
Robé el acento africano, / poeta soñé en la noche
y era canto pregonero / al ritmo sonoro del bronce.
Recibe mis versos, Guillén, / mi ritmo, mi metro, mi rima
nativos del África madre / en viaje allá por Antillas.[24]

I wish to weave my word / with this emotion that overcomes me
and make it fly swiftly / to Cuba, half African.
Guillén Nicolás, comrade: / I crafted with my highest song,
Teacher, Singer and Poet, / a greeting to your eminent persona.
I stole the African accent, / I dreamed of a poet in the night
and it was the people's song / set to the sonorous rhythm of bronze.
Receive my verses Guillén / my rhythm, my meter, my rhyme
natives of Mother Africa / en route over there through the Antilles.

Here, Nsue Otong praises Guillén's lyrical virtuosity, establishing a link to his African ancestry, "nativos del África madre," and broadly hails Afro-Caribbean peoples as being "en viaje allá por Antillas." Through this elegy, Nsue Otong contends that Cuba is "mitad africana," and pleads that Guillén receive his poetic verses, "mi ritmo, mi metro, mi rima." What, then, do we make of this ode, of this "viaje," and of these long historical and contemporary poetic crossings between Equatorial Guinea, the Hispanophone Caribbean, and their diasporas? What can a mapping of these relations illuminate?

Decolonizing
Diasporas

Introduction

Relations

> Peoples do not live on exception.
> Relation is not made up of things that are foreign
> but of shared knowledge.
>
> —Édouard Glissant, *Poetics of Relation*

Decolonizing Diasporas makes a critical move toward engaging the relations between Equatorial Guinea, comprised of five islands and a small continental swathe, and the Latinx Caribbean islands of Cuba, Puerto Rico, and the Dominican Republic, through a study of their diasporic and exilic literary productions. Rather than an exhaustive linguistic, historical, or sociopolitical study, *Decolonizing Diasporas* is suggestive in its remapping of diasporic Afro-Atlantic literary and cultural aesthetics. Each chapter builds on a particular theme that emerges as a shared preoccupation within the analyzed works. In it, I critically engage eleven novels, a series of visual/sonic works, poetry, essays, and a short story. Through this undertaking, *Decolonizing Diasporas* engages topics such as the intimacies of colonial domination and erotic freedom practices; the act of faithful witnessing; the phenomena of dispossession, or what I call destierro; the possibilities of a reparation of the imagination; and visions of Black futurities as apocalypsos. In conceiving this project, my aim is to render legible what these texts offer to subjects who resist ongoing forms of colonialism, as intellectuals, as post/colonial subjects under coloniality, as organizers and activists, and as peoples who necessarily document often-unacknowledged sets of histories. By studying diasporic Afro-Puerto Rican, Afro-Dominican, and Afro-Cuban literary texts and cultural productions in relation to those emerging from Equatorial Guinea and its diaspora, I track the relationship between Afro-Atlantic Hispanophone subjects. I argue that these multilingual and insurgent works push the boundaries of decolonial thought by offering radical perspectives from the underside of the Afro-diaspora.

This project of relationality across Afro-Atlantic Hispanophone diasporas is made possible through the work of decolonial thinkers and decolonial and women of color feminists, who have continually framed literature as a critical space in which to create coalitions and relations across difference, to imagine radical liberatory futurities, and to reimage the human. These thinkers, including Audre Lorde, Michelle Cliff, Sylvia Wynter, Nelson Maldonado-Torres, Yolanda Martínez-San Miguel, Chela Sandoval, Vanessa Valdés, and Laura E. Pérez, take seriously the cultural productions of those rendered invisible by coloniality. As part of this tradition, I propose that we see the works of the Afro-Atlantic Hispanophone diaspora as archives of indictment and as liberatory discourses that fashion and imagine what I call "worlds/otherwise" (the subject of chapter 5). *Decolonizing Diasporas* maps decolonial poetics through a sustained engagement with the multiple perspectives, experiences, histories, and lived realities of different peoples living under various conditions of colonialism (including settler colonialism, coloniality, and manifold modes of domination and extraction) as well as the radical resistance and imaginations they use to counter these structures of oppression.

In using the term "Afro-Atlantic" I am necessarily hailing the term "the Black Atlantic," which Paul Gilroy defines as a "rhizomorphic, fractal structure of the transcultural international formation." What Gilroy coined "the Black Atlantic world" includes the "historical conjunction—the stereophony, bilingual, or bifocal cultural forms originated by, but no longer the exclusive property of, blacks dispersed with the structures of feeling, producing, communicating, and remembering that I have heuristically called the black Atlantic world."[1] Gilroy urges cultural historians to use the Atlantic as an analytic beyond metaphor, and to consider it "one single, complex unit of analysis in this discussion of the modern world and use it to produce an explicitly transnational and intercultural perspective."[2] The use of the term "Hispanophone" in relation to the Afro-Atlantic is not to demarcate solely Spanish/Castilian language cultural productions, but rather to engage the complexities within the field of global Hispanophone studies. In their introduction to the special issue on "Global Hispanophone Studies" of the *Journal of Spanish Cultural Studies*, Adolfo Campoy-Cubillo and Benita Sampedro Vizcaya argue that using the term "Hispanophone" is an "invitation to branch out beyond the traditional archives of Hispanism, engaging with some of the dispersed geographies, cultural and linguistic traditions . . . It is also a determination to break away from the overarching Iberian/Latin American binary and to embrace other communities, histories, experiences and repertoires."[3] Throughout this book I use the term "Hispanophone" to signify the political and linguistic geographies of the Afro-Latinx and Equatoguinean diaspora in a way that is not restricted by linguistic borders, points of origin, or distant homelands. In fact, the examination of these Afro-Atlantic Hispanophone cultural productions in relation to one another complicates language practices because they are written in Spanish, English, and Spanglish as well as French, Yoruba, and various Indigenous languages such as Ndowe, Fang, and so on.

In engaging what has ostensibly been one of the most important concepts of the twentieth century, I am also calling attention to what M. Jacqui

Alexander calls "the Crossing," which alludes to the told and untold histories of the Middle Passage and pushes us to consider the relations that emerge in the wake of these histories of modernity. The "Crossing" is likewise a pedagogy that disrupts the binaries inherent to modernity and "interrupt[s] inherited boundaries of geography, nation, episteme, and identity that distort vision [and] enable an understanding of the dialectics of history, enough to assist in navigating the terms of learning and the fundamentally pedagogic imperative at its heart: the imperative of making the world in which we live intelligible to ourselves and to each other."[4]

In his landmark book *Poetics of Relation*, Édouard Glissant traces the possibilities of relationality, beginning with the Middle Passage and the endless crossings of the Atlantic. Enslavement, a "debasement more eternal than apocalypse," is but the beginning of relations, and Glissant aptly centers the Caribbean as a site through which to examine the multiple and overlapping ways that modernity connects and disconnects peoples across the globe. For Glissant, the effects of the abyss—the ship, the ocean, and life at the "edges of a nonworld"—are intergenerational and shared experiences that "made us, the descendants, one people among others." As such, he contends that "peoples do not live on exception. Relation is not made up of things that are foreign but of shared knowledge. This experience of the abyss can now be said to be the best element of exchange."[5] Living in the chasm of the abyss and its aftermath requires ways of reckoning. For Glissant, poetry and poetics become a technology that bears witness to the known and unknown terrors that we live and share. Relations are thus political and require both a reckoning with the *longue durée* of our histories as well as a commitment to seeing relations and disjunctures across the Black Atlantic and across the world.

Throughout *Decolonizing Diasporas*, I use the term "Afro-Atlantic" rather than "Black Atlantic" as a way to call attention to how "Afro" as a prefix has been used throughout the Caribbean and Latin America to signal or claim afrodescendencia, or Afro-descendance. As Agustín Laó-Montes notes, "['Afro'] has been used on the southern side of the American hemisphere since at least the early twentieth century," and using this term would "allow us to analyze the differences and particularities, as well as the articulations and common ground of the manifold histories of the African diaspora in the Americas."[6] Joseba Gabilondo argues that the term "Hispanic Atlantic" is a useful vector of analysis when considering historical and contemporary migrations to Spain from Latin America and Africa, as well as Spain's enormous economic and political investments in Latin America (second only to those of the United States). Gabilondo argues that this "two-way flow of capital and bodies across the Atlantic brings to the fore a host of political and historical problems that have not been fully addressed by either Latin Americanists or Hispanists." This "underscores a new reading of modernity that goes back to the Spanish colonization of the Americas."[7] I add the prefix

"Afro" to the term "Hispanic Atlantic" in order to more directly address the ways that Atlantic modernities are contingent upon forms of racialization and domination that are most often expressed through modes of anti-Blackness. Using the prefix "Afro" also allows for Africa to be central to the configurations of Atlantic circuits, especially in light of my focus on Caribbean and African islands and their diasporas.[8]

My emphasis on diasporic perspectives is also purposeful, as this concept helps to fracture national, regional, and racial cartographies.[9] Laó-Montes argues that theorizing Afro-diasporic perspectives "can allow us to rethink self, memory, culture, and power beyond the confines of the nation as a unit of analysis (and the dominant form of political community), and to develop a politics of decolonization beyond mere nationalism."[10] This is not only true of Afro-Latinx Caribbean literature, but is also an important node within Equatoguinean literature. Marvin Lewis notes that after national independence and two successive dictatorships that saw the exile of over a third of the country's population, "the capital of Equatorial Guinean literature was now neither Santa Isabel (Malabo) nor Madrid, but rather the heart of every Guinean, whether in Spain, in France, or in Equatorial Guinea. Because from that moment on, a dislocation of the literary frontier is verified, and each author remains 'wherever he best finds himself,' from wherever he writes for his country."[11]

While anthropologists were some of the earliest to discuss theories of diaspora, cultural and literary theorists have offered invaluable dimensions to diaspora studies. In fact, Kim Butler argues that "much of diaspora experience is unwritten: it is inscribed in the creative arts, material culture, and oral traditions."[12] As such, I start with the imaginary, looking at diasporic cultural works in relation to one another as a way to expand what we can know about diaspora studies. Diaspora is likewise a literary contact zone.[13] Building on the work of Yolanda Martínez-San Miguel and Marisel Moreno, I see diasporic literary and cultural productions that "reflect on the postcolonial and neocolonial cultural exchanges" and "address the continuities that can be observed between the literature" of homelands and diasporas.[14] Samantha Pinto's concept of 'difficult diasporas' dislocates conceptual notions of belonging, dispersal, and furtive returns, while subverting the notion of linearity and of being able to trace oneself or others back to points of origin or homelands.[15] Diaspora as an analytic reveals structures, relationships, and phenomena that are instrumental to understanding modernity. Antonio Benítez-Rojo's foundational study argues: "If someone had to define, at once, the meta-archipelago's historical novel and its folk narrative, using just two words, these would be, unquestionably: *revealer* (to reveal and re-veil in Spanish) *violencia*."[16] I contend that these diasporic Afro-Atlantic Hispanophone literatures reveal not only violence, but also insurgent forms of resistance and the radical potential of Afro-futurities.

The Peripheral

Building on the works of Silvio Torres Saillant and Ramona Hernández, in *Decolonizing Diasporas* I argue that the aesthetic productions of these Hispanophone Afro-Atlantic subjects are "peripheral," or better yet, "peripheralized," and are situated at the far extremes of already marginalized peoples, nations, and histories.[17] I am particularly interested in how a sustained meditation on peripheralized literatures allows us to glimpse often-ignored sets of knowledges and experiences, and offers a radical remapping of diasporic Afro-Atlantic Hispanophone cultural productions. I conjure a "periphery" here to highlight the ways in which both Afro-Latinx and Afro-Hispanic literature and cultural productions remain at the edges, or the periphery, of already marginalized texts and experiences.

For example, if African literature is marginalized in relation to literary Eurocentricity, then Equatorial Guinea, surrounded by Anglophone, Francophone, and Lusophone nation-states and literature, stands alone as the only Spanish-language literature in sub-Saharan Africa. Although much Equatoguinean literature is produced in exile in Spain, these literary works are not necessarily considered part of the Spanish canon. When examined, Equatoguinean literature is often discussed as a reflection of a colonial past or as a signifier of the legacy of Spanish democracy. Benita Sampedro Vizcaya has argued that "it is particularly unsettling to note that, in the construction of (trans-)Atlantic paradigms from the Spanish and Latin American standpoints, Africa, and its multiple intersections with both Europe and the Americas, has frequently been absent. If and when Africa actually makes an appearance, it is often under the (useful but nonetheless limited) rubrics of migration, diaspora, or creolization."[18] In these contexts, the literature, narratives, and experimental works produced by Equatoguineans represent the periphery of the margin. I believe that Latinx Caribbean literature is similarly positioned.

In the United States, we find Latinx literature juxtaposed to canonical and popular Anglo texts but rarely taken seriously as sources of study, and continually subordinated by white supremacist markets and logics. The works produced by Afro-Latinx writers are often overlooked both in the Caribbean and in the United States. Petra Rivera-Rideau posits that "Puerto Rico and the Dominican Republic, along with many other Afro-Latino American and Afro-Latino populations, have often been left out of conceptualizations of the African diaspora, despite the presence of substantial African-descended populations, histories of black resistance, and African-based cultural practices there."[19] In Rafael Pérez-Torres's study of Chicano poetics, he argues that Latinx literature (and, I would add, Afro-Latinx literature) traverses "the gaps . . . [and] bridges between numerous cultural sites" and is an accounting of the "discontinuities of history and power."[20] However, even with the international recognition of Afro-Latinx writers such as Piri Thomas, Junot

Díaz, and Mayra Santos Febres, the work of Afro-Latinx Caribbean writers is underrepresented overall and often remains unacknowledged. Although more recently, critical approaches to Afro- and Indigenous Latinidades are becoming more visible in Latinx studies, with a turn away from ideologies of mestizaje and notions of "la gran familia," Afro-Latinx literature and scholarship has remained peripheralized and much more work needs to be done.[21]

Decolonizing Diasporas joins the challenge posed by Latinx Caribbean scholars, whose work rejects notions of a Latinidad based on social and political racial hierarchies founded on mestizaje and anti-Black discourses on the islands and in the diaspora.[22] A recent cultural and sociological turn to Afro-Latin America has seen an increase in the study and critical documentation of Afro-descendants' cultural work and activist organizing.[23] Several important edited volumes and collections published in the 2000s also represent some of the few works that have carved out a space to discuss Afro-Latinidad and Afro-descendancy.[24] Many of these works interrogate how colonial Spanish forms of anti-Blackness in the Caribbean and Latin America, and Anglo forms of anti-Blackness in the United States, have undermined the ways in which Afro-Latinxs belong in/to these spaces. In building on these works, I look towards mapping critical cartographies of Afro-Atlantic Hispanophone subjects in exile and diaspora through a relational framework that uses their resistance writings as a point of departure.

And yet this project does not intend to argue for the inclusion of Equatoguinean literary studies into a U.S. Latinx Caribbean framework, or for relegating it to the Hispanist canon. Rather, *Decolonizing Diasporas* offers another way of radically remapping Afro-Diaspora studies and the Afro-Atlantic writ large, with Equatorial Guinea and Afro-Latinxs as central thinkers, actors, and anticolonial and decolonizing agitators. In this way, the critical cartographies offered in *Decolonizing Diasporas* mark new inroads for Black, Latinx, and Hispanic studies through a sustained engagement with the decolonizing poetics of the peripheralized Afro-Atlantic subjects who are often absent from our discourses.

A radical relational remapping of Afro-Latinx and Afro-Hispanic aesthetics, and by extension their histories, also transforms some of the more dominant tropes within Black studies, for which the central discourses often reside in African American or Anglo contexts. As Laó-Montes notes, "In the hegemonic Anglophone world there is a tendency to marginalize Afro-Latinos from the historical memory and cultural-political mappings of the African diaspora."[25] This remapping also challenges Latinx studies wherein tropes of mestizaje and ethnic/national belonging often circumvent critical discussions about Afro-Indigeneity and racialized Blackness. And finally, in Hispanic studies, the study of Hispanophone Africa is not usually discussed in relation to the Caribbean or Latin America.[26] Thus, the project of mapping Equatoguinean and Afro-Latinx Caribbean literary imaginaries is a critical cartographic practice that exemplifies what Glissant aptly named a "poetics of relation."

The long-established sociocultural ties between Latinx Caribbean and Black peoples in the United States requires a rearticulation of Black studies and Latinx studies.[27] Likewise, decolonial thought from Caribbean and extended Caribbean contexts must engage with the decolonial thought from Indigenous thinkers living and resisting in settler colonial contexts. In taking seriously this critical cartographic practice, one can then see a similar phenomenon in the context of the Equatoguinean exilic population in Spain. The literature of Equatoguineans necessarily speaks to preoccupations in sub-Saharan Africa as well as their lived experiences in the diaspora. These texts engage different kinds of African migration to Europe, and reveal distinct forms of domination and oppression faced within Equatorial Guinea under dictatorship, and anti-Black and anti-African racism in Europe.[28]

Decolonizing Diasporas is imbued with these politics, and while fleshing out each of these ties is beyond the scope of this book, I am clear about the stakes and limits of this project. Without bearing witness to these interrelated and overlapping histories and political imperatives, we risk playing into the dynamics of domination that seek to fracture peoples across axes of difference. I follow Alexander Weheliye's succinct endorsement of relationality: "Relationality provides a productive model for critical inquiry and political action because it reveals the global and systemic dimensions of racialized, sexualized, and gendered subjugation, while not losing sight of the many ways political violence has given rise to ongoing practices of freedom within various traditions of the oppressed." I take seriously Weheliye's call to "design novel assemblages of relation," a call that women of color and ethnic studies scholars have long practiced in their scholarship and activist work.[29]

Relating the Hispanophone Caribbean with Equatorial Guinea elucidates how colonial intervention, revolutionary actions, dictatorial rule, and first-world corporate interests are manifested within the lives and imaginaries of post/colonial Afro-Atlantic subjects. However, rather than solely building this work around erasures or absences, I am interested in what kinds of insurgent worldviews surface when we link diasporic Afro-Atlantic Hispanophone Caribbean and sub-Saharan Africa to the works of Black, Indigenous, and women of color thinkers, and see what they can offer to the realm of decolonial thought. Through this study I show how these poetics elucidate how, tucked in the periphery, Afro-Atlantic works indict the intimacy of dictatorship and occupation, engage in philosophies of witnessing which reject colonial politics of recognition, articulate new forms of finding homes amid a world circumscribed by destierro, reimagine reparations beyond positivism, and offer meditations on futurities or worlds/otherwise.

Critical Cartographies of Racialization

The writers and artists I engage here offer ways to critically remap an often-unacknowledged set of Afro-Atlantic texts. I engage in a methodology of relationality born through my training in comparative ethnic studies. My methodological approach to this work further troubles the impression that Afro-diasporic peoples can be placed into stark comparisons. Keith Feldman argues, for example, that the genealogy of comparison offered by comparative ethnic studies "reveals the tension among the coalitional imaginaries of race radical insurgency, sociological approaches to minority difference, and the proliferating terms of inclusion on offer from the U.S. state and the academy."[30] I contend that Afro-Puerto Rican, Afro-Dominican, Afro-Cuban, and Equatoguinean peoples, who shoulder 500 years of distinct historical, colonial, and cultural contexts and lived experiences, cannot be put into a simple comparison or a framework of comparativity.

Thus, while *Decolonizing Diasporas* is a meditation on the relations between and contributions of diasporic Afro-Atlantic Hispanophone subjects, it also underscores their disparate material histories and distinct lived experiences under ongoing forms of colonialism, including coloniality and settler colonialism. I understand coloniality as the continuation of colonial practices, ideologies, and structures long after nations have undergone administrative decolonization—what Nelson Maldonado-Torres refers to as "long-standing patterns of power that emerged as a result of colonialism, that define culture, labor, intersubjective relations, and knowledge production well beyond the strict limits of colonial administrations."[31] Lisa Lowe contends that settler colonialism is also an ongoing project. "What we might identify as residual within the histories of settler or colonial capitalism," she argues, "does not disappear. To the contrary, it persists and endures, even if less legible within the obfuscations of the new dominant."[32] Ongoing colonialism or coloniality is then a systematic process of racialized dispossession. Jodi Byrd acknowledges Glen Coulthard in noting that "colonialism endures . . . as 'a form of structured dispossession' of Indigenous peoples and lands that exists within the usury regimes that ensure financialization as the fulfillment of accumulation."[33] Thus, throughout *Decolonizing Diasporas* I critically link these histories of Black and Indigenous dispossession, especially as they pertain to diasporic politics in the United States. These politics are part of the decolonial turn, which Maldonado-Torres argues is "about making visible the invisible and about analyzing the mechanisms that produce such invisibility or distorted visibility," and "takes the colonized as . . . a source for inquiry into problems created by modernity and forms that may adequately respond to these problems."[34] While I engage in decolonial thought and theory, I agree with Barbara Christian that there is no monolithic theory for the "multiplicity of experiences," especially for Black peoples in the modern world.[35]

Furthermore, I track other forms of material relations through the literary and cultural imagination, and through the vectors of Afro-descendancy and scripts of Blackness.[36] If, as Christina Sharpe argues, "anti-Blackness is total climate," then my meditation on the Afro-Atlantic begins with the fact that the vastly different racial and ethnic ideologies in the Latinx Caribbean and sub-Saharan Hispanophone Africa, and their diasporas, cannot be collapsed into simple racial classification systems.[37] The move to label all of these subjects as Black peoples, without a nuanced understanding of the stakes and limits of what that means in each of their homelands and diasporic contexts, would produce violent cartographies that flatten and distort their subjective experiences. While comparativity on the axis of racialized Blackness would be a more easily consumable project within certain binary racial frameworks, this project requires nuance and specificity. To reduce the complexity of Black life is to erase subjectivity and enact generic violence over and against multivalent forms of oppression and resistance. I have tried, to the best of my ability, to complicate facile notions of race, ethnic belonging, and racialization in my analyses.

In *Decolonizing Diasporas*, I outline and pay close attention to what I am calling critical cartographies of racialization. Following Katherine McKittrick's contention that "human geography needs some philosophical attention," the concept of critical cartographies of racialization helps us to hold space for different ways that anti-Blackness and the colonial difference imbue former colonies and contemporary metropoles.[38] This relational cartography of racialization for Afro-diasporic and exilic peoples outlines the unfixed racial and ethnic ontological and phenomenological experiences that emerge when moving across spatial and temporal locales. While these practices of racialization manifest differently for Black Puerto Ricans, Cubans, Dominicans, and for Equatoguineans, it is precisely in thinking about the ways that they diverge and overlap that we better understand the forms of anti-Blackness endemic to modernity. Anti-Blackness and anti-Indigeneity are critically intertwined and are central conceits of the colonial difference, of coloniality, and of ongoing settler colonial projects. Understanding the complexity of these discourses and their material impacts across the Afro-Atlantic is central to understanding what Fanon calls the "lived experience of the black."[39]

Critical cartographies of racialization help us to unpack and understand how Afro-descendant peoples are racialized in divergent ways, depending on their ethnic or national citizenship, location and ability to move or travel, class status, phenotype, and other factors. In tracking what Chandra Talpade Mohanty and Katherine McKittrick each call "cartographies of struggle," the concept of critical cartographies of racialization simultaneously attends to shifting subjective experiences and the seeming permanence of racism and anti-Blackness endemic to the modern world.[40] These shifting rules of race and racialization, often concealed or unspoken, surface in the experiences of

Caribbean and extended Caribbean contexts. In Latinx Caribbean frameworks, we see an adherence to centuries-old ideologies of mestizaje that underscore the importance of mixed-race ethnicity underpinning cultural nationalism.[41] Such ideologies, championed through centuries of Spanish colonial rule, casta systems, and sociopolitical codes, have been robustly internalized. The concept of mestizaje, however, relegates both Blackness and Indigeneity to backwards moves within national imaginaries and nation-building projects that seek to move towards whiteness.

Therefore, the insistence on Latinidad as mestizaje, a triumphant and vigorous mixing of "three races" to produce a unifying ethnicity in which we are "all mixed"—café con leche, unos más café, otros más leche—holds the same underlying structures of anti-Blackness and anti-Indigeneity as Anglo and U.S. racial hierarchies based on hypodescent. Latinx Caribbean peoples in diaspora exist within a violent set of demands stemming from competing forces of racialization. Within the national imaginary of the Latinx Caribbean—and perhaps within one's own kinship network and community—being Puerto Rican or Cuban or Dominican might eclipse racial categories, even as this ethnic and national identification enables covert and overt forms of anti-Blackness.[42] While in the Hispanophone Caribbean, race is not based on binaries but rather on "different color spectrums," Afro-Latinx Caribbean peoples living in diaspora in the United States find themselves racialized according to ever-shifting rules and regulations.[43] Often this means negotiating between Spanish and Anglo colonial notions of race: scripts that demand "bettering the race" or those that quantify race through vectors of blood quantum or hypodescent, better known as the "one-drop rule."

While one drop of "Black" blood can mean that an Afro-Dominican is categorized as Black in the United States, this is not necessarily the case in the Caribbean, where there exists a plethora of racial categories that create distance between Afro-descendants and binary ideologies of Blackness.[44] Even within these acutely narrow social structures, there exist choices in self-identification and self-naming. For example, "Afro-Latinidad" has become an important political term and cultural framework throughout Latin America, the Caribbean, and the United States and has historically and contemporarily given space for Latinx peoples of African descent to identify and organize politically as such.[45] Both Anglo and Latinx ideologies of race and racialization continue to demarcate social, economic, and political stratification for Black populations across the Americas and the Caribbean. However, my engagement with these literary corpora offers me a discursive space to reflect on the constant negotiation of race and the subjective experience of Blackness. The texts discussed in this book become sites that document and destabilize processes of racialization that attempt to circumscribe Afro-Latinx subjects into disparate—but equally anti-Black and anti-Indigenous—matrices of race.

These racializing categories are further complicated by gender and sex. Angela Jorge's foundational 1979 essay, "The Black Puerto Rican Woman in Contemporary Society," argues that there are critical distinctions among Black Puerto Rican women on the island and the first, second, and third generations in diaspora in the United States. These differences "are the result of their ability or inability to cope with the racism that confronts them."[46] Jorge contends that Afro-Puerto Rican women's choices with respect to marriage—for example, having an African American partner—can in effect exclude them from Puerto Ricanness or acceptable forms of belonging.[47] This example reveals both anti-Blackness across diasporic contexts as well as the tenuousness of belonging for Afro-Puerto Rican women in the diaspora. Jorge underscores that a series of factors including partnerships, physical appearance, and so on can shape how race, racialization, and belonging impact Afro-Latinx subjects, especially women, femmes, and those living in diaspora.

For Equatoguineans, the realities of anti-Blackness, particularly for those living or exiled in Spain, are salient. Remei Sipi Mayo's *Inmigración y género* examines these racialized experiences through an intersectional methodology.[48] Sipi Mayo outlines the distinct experiences that propel women from the African continent to Spain, and underscores the kinds of racialization and "quotidian violence" experienced by Black women and femmes in diaspora and exile. She explains that "La Mirada," the reductive "gaze" through which immigrant women are often seen, is a kind of quotidian violence that often circumscribes their experiences:

> Es aquella que surge del exterior o sea de la sociedad receptora, de aquellas miradas que ante mujeres procedentes de escenarios humanos diferentes tienden o pretenden encasillarnos, reduciendonos a estereotipos y aplicándonos prejuicios como, por ejemplo, los referidos a considerar que por ser de un determinado origen, somos prostitutas, trabajadoras del servicio doméstico y un largo, en ocasiones, etc. Intentando borrar saberes y riquezas que algunas trajimos y los que aprendimos aquí como maestras, escritoras, dinamizadoras de grupos, mediadoras interculturales, etc.[49]

> It is that [look] which emerges from the outside or from the receiving society, those views that tend or portend to frame us, women from different human scenarios, reducing us to stereotypes and applying prejudices such as, for example, [considering] that by being of a certain origin, we are prostitutes, domestic workers and so on, sometimes, etc. Trying to erase the knowledge and wealth that we brought with us and learned here as teachers, writers, group promoters, intercultural mediators, etc.

For Sipi Mayo, the violence of La Mirada is a way to categorize or reduce African and Afro-descended women to stereotypes, and subject them to prejudice and discrimination. Under this mirada, Black women from Equatorial Guinea and the Caribbean are seen as prostitutes or domestic workers, while the kinds of rich knowledges and skills they bring from their homelands, or even the resources or education they acquired in exile or diaspora, are minimized or rendered invisible.

Similarly, Michael Ugarte's *Africans in Europe* maps how racial otherness, exemplified by Black skin, is a marker of outsider status in Spain. In recounting the experiences of the Equatoguinean author and critic Donato Ndongo Bidyogo, Ugarte recalls that Donato's career as a journalist was marked by his Black skin without regard to his skill, his subjective experience as a Spanish colonial subject, his language, or his ethnicity.[50] In Wynterian terms, the history of Equatoguinean colonial subjecthood does not successfully select Afro-Hispanics into the world of Man.[51] As inhabitants of a former Spanish colony with a longer history of overlapping colonialisms, Equatoguineans have "internal and external obstacles related to ethnicity, identity, place and displacement, dislocation and migration, language, violence, and politics." Lewis argues that these dynamics are "better understood when discussed in relation to Equatorial Guinea's colonial past."[52]

Paying close attention to the critical cartographies of racialization allows us to bear witness to both anti-Black racism in Spain and different forms of racialization at play in Equatorial Guinea. A closer study of history shows that ethnicity and belonging in Equatorial Guinea are circumscribed by hierarchy and political exclusion. The aftermath of independence saw the rise of dictatorial regimes, first that of Francisco Macías Nguema (1968–79) and later of Teodoro Obiang Mbasogo (1979–present), which accelerated social and political upheavals that led to the killing, incarceration, or exile of over one-third of the Equatoguinean population. Equatorial Guinea is comprised of several Bantu ethnic groups, including Fang, Bubi, Combe, Bujebas, and Ndowe, as well as Annoboneses and Fernandinos. Contemporary Indigenous writers represent and write about different islands and regions within Equatorial Guinea, such as Annobón, Corisco, Bioko, and Río Muni, and while they are "unified politically on the surface under Spanish colonialism and becoming one 'nation' with independence, most of the writers still maintain their unique ethnic identities and interrogate what it means to be Equatorial Guinean."[53] Thus, inter-ethnic divisions become a primary site of identification within Equatorial Guinea and cannot be summarily transferred to facile notions of Blackness or racialization.

While these groups can arguably all be categorized as "Black," especially within diasporic locales, these ethnic differences, as well as their perceived and real proximity to political power in Equatorial Guinea, engender oppression, suppression, and exploitation within and among citizens of the same nation-state. For example, in the twentieth century there was and continues to be a demonstrable struggle between ethnic groups in Equatorial Guinea. The historian Marvin Lewis notes that "the tension between the Bubi and the dominant Fang, viewed as occupiers of Bioko by the Bubi, is palpable." Lewis contends that this tension is also seen in the Annobónese and the Playero cultures, which see the legacy of the Spanish empire in the ethnic hierarchies that remain in Equatorial Guinea after administrative decolonization because it was the "colonizers who enforced Fang hegemony over the other ethnic groups and perpetrated divisions that remain evident today."[54] Furthermore, there are other dynamics at play, including multiple and overlapping colonialisms (Portuguese, British, Spanish), dictatorial regimes (Macías Nguema and Obiang Mbasogo), and a form of inter-ethnic settler colonialism that took hold in the aftermath of independence. The primacy of the Fang ethnic group, to which the two successive dictators belong, has led to a social, economic, and political reality that thrives on exploitation, neglect, and inequality. As Donato Ndongo argues, the most intimate parts of peoples' lives are affected by this kind of ethnic politicization. Igor Cusack, for example, contends that "the Fang are made up of various close-knit clans and since independence the country has been ruled by one such clan from a 'locality' called Mongomo." This is suggestive of Ndongo's claim that those who have any economic, social, or political opportunities in Equatorial Guinea are "appointed by the finger of the dictator" or rather, are selected within a select network of family, loyalists, or political allies.[55]

Critical cartographies of racialization can help us track how racialization shifts from Equatorial Guinea to Spain and underscores how these forms of racialization are related and yet distinct from Afro-Cuban, Puerto Rican, and Dominican peoples' experiences of race and ethnicity, both in their homelands and in diaspora. And while Puerto Rico, the Dominican Republic, and Cuba are intimately tied historically, linguistically, and regionally, they too are marked by distinct yet related histories of occupation, colonialism, revolution, and diaspora.

Finally, critical cartographies of racialization can also hold space for differences across the Afro-Atlantic and its diasporas, thereby expanding how we conceive of both the Afro-Atlantic and Afro-diasporas, writ large. Equatorial Guinea, for example, has a long history of Portuguese, British, and Spanish colonization that includes Nigerian coolie labor, Spanish fascism, successive dictatorships, and mass exile. The linguistic practices in Equatorial Guinea are also dynamically different than those of the Latinx Caribbean; Equatoguineans speak a variety of Indigenous and creole languages, and while the lingua franca is Spanish, other official languages include French and Portuguese. In engaging different sets of literatures throughout each chapter, I complicate the idea that Afro-Puerto Rican, Cuban, and Dominican literature can be easily put into relation without accounting for differing forms of racialization. I also contend that the literature of Equatorial Guinea cannot be read as a homogenous corpus, because that would elide the sociocultural rifts within and beyond the borders of that nation. Thus, *Decolonizing Diasporas* enacts a relational decolonial feminist mapping along axes of racialization and difference.

In this way, the histories of the Latinx Caribbean, Equatorial Guinea, and their diasporas are necessarily tied to so many other intersecting histories of colonization, migration, and radical liberatory movements. It is in this spirit of a critical and decolonial ethnic studies which seeks to put in relation the histories, lived experiences, and philosophies of peoples who resist white supremacy, cis heteropatriarchy, and capitalist accumulation that I usher in this project of mapping the contributions of Afro-Latinx and Afro-Hispanic Atlantic literatures. Rather than a project that uses the lens of decolonial theory to interpret or analyze the texts, I aim to see what these texts offer to decolonial thought and to track how they propel our decolonizing politics toward more radical and liberatory futures. If we take these works seriously and approach them through critical methodologies and an ethical praxis, we bear witness to how these diasporas are necessarily decolonizing forces that provide new and creative forms with which to resist coloniality and domination.

Crossing Again: Women of Color Feminisms and Decolonial Thought

Decolonial and women of color feminist thought offer us a methodology of relationality through which to engage these works. The project of women of color feminisms, as articulated by the Combahee River Collective, Audre Lorde, Wendy Rose, Barbara Smith, Aurora Levins Morales, Gloria Anzaldúa, Cherríe Moraga, M. Jacqui Alexander, Michelle Cliff, and others is one in which relations across difference and complex coalition-building are the stepping-stones to fashioning new futures that do not rely on hierarchies of domination. In their 1977 statement, the Combahee River Collective declared that they not only understood oppression to be interlocking, but also that Black feminist thought and organizing could combat the oppressions which women of color faced:

> [We] are actively committed to struggling against racial, sexual, heterosexual, and class oppression, and see as our particular task the development of integrated analysis and practice based upon the fact that the major systems of oppression are interlocking. . . . As Black women we see Black feminism as the logical political movement to combat the manifold and simultaneous oppressions that all women of color face.[56]

This collective of visionary African American and Afro-Caribbean lesbian feminists articulated a politics of relationality that has resounded in the work and organizing of women of color feminists in the decades since it was published.

This labor of relationality is difficult and requires a praxis of witnessing fueled by love and fury. In "Age, Race, Class, and Sex: Women Redefining Difference," Audre Lorde tells us that "the Future of our earth may depend upon the ability of all women to identify and develop new definitions of power and new patterns of relating across difference." She argues that "we have no patterns for relating across our human differences as equals," and because of this we stand to be fractured from one another and ourselves. This project of relations is a "lifetime pursuit," one that women of color feminists have kept alive as a politics and praxis.[57] It is a methodology of complex coalition-building, of learning each other's histories, of understanding why difference fragments communities in search of liberation. As Chandra Mohanty argues, "It is not color or sex that constructs the ground for these struggles. Rather it is the way we think about race, class, gender—the political links we choose to make among and between struggles."[58]

Aurora Levins Morales posits that "like it or not, our liberation is bound up with that of every other being on the planet," and anything else "is unaffordable."[59] Thus, the critical work of decolonial and women of color feminists fuels this project. Angelique Nixon, for example, argues that Michelle Cliff's literary poetics "critique racist, patriarchal, and homophobic structures while also making readers recognize the ways in which we participate in these structures." For Nixon, Cliff's work exemplifies "revolutionary and feminist" ethics because "it is passionate in its embrace of difference and (re)writing of Caribbean histories grounded in Caribbean women's experiences."[60] It is in this spirit of complex coalition-building, across often incommensurable differences and grounded in silenced and overlooked experiences, histories, and subjectivities of women of color, that I craft this project which meditates on literary poetics and cultural productions. For, as Lorde reminds us, "the literatures of all women of Color recreate the textures of our lives."[61]

Decolonial thought is suggestive as a framework, as a body of work, and as a political practice that looks to arts, poetics, and musical inspiration for its resistance and liberation work. The genealogy of decolonial thought to which I am referring is particularly generative because it finds its *longue durée* in the modern colonial project beginning in the late Middle Ages. Because I work across locales in the Caribbean and Africa, this temporality is key. This temporal framework offers an important perspective that is often overlooked in our quests to problematize categories which attempt to suffocate and limit our lives. Taking the fifteenth century's imperial/colonial project into account as a foundational violence, along with historical and spatial specificity, makes the ideological and structural reach of colonialism and coloniality visible. This then illuminates the dimensions of what Ngũgĩ wa Thiong'o deftly refers to as the "cultural bomb."[62] In locating modernity, colonialism (in its myriad forms), and coloniality as the problem, decoloniality bears witness to the humanity of the *damné* (condemned) and the value of their epistemologies, cosmologies, and lived experiences.

Following Laura E. Pérez's contention that "a decolonizing politics must introduce, engage, and circulate previously unseen marginalized and stigmatized notions of 'spirituality,' 'philosophy,' 'gender,' 'sexuality,' 'art,' or any other category of knowledge and existence," I aim to relate the literary corpora of often-overlooked Afro-Atlantic diasporic peoples, and trace both the preoccupations and the liberatory practices that dot the horizons of their decolonial imaginaries.[63] This decolonial feminist imperative rejects the dehumanization endemic to the colonial project that emerged in the long sixteenth century. Furthermore, decolonial feminist approaches rebut the colonial difference, or the creation of systems that categorize difference into hierarchies of humanity and nonhumanity.[64] Instead, decolonial and women of color feminists, such as María Lugones and Xhercis Méndez, have offered new ways of reimagining the human and a new ethics for relationships across difference.[65]

Thus if, as Maldonado-Torres argues, decolonization encompasses a "process of undoing colonial reality and its multiple hierarchies of power as a whole," then decolonization is necessarily both an embodied practice and a radical political project.[66] For example, Maldonado-Torres says that decolonizing projects are "grounded on the histories, lived experiences, and ethico-political imperatives of colonized peoples, as well as on their desires for open human interrelationality at the intimate erotic and public levels."[67] Centering the ways in which these diasporic subjects subvert and resist modernity and coloniality through their poetics and cultural productions is part of the aesthetic inquiry of the decolonial turn, or "an epistemic, practical, aesthetic, emotional, and oftentimes spiritual repositioning of the modern/colonial subject by virtue of which modernity, and not the colonized subject . . . appears as a problem."[68] *Decolonizing Diasporas* argues that these Afro-Atlantic writers offer ways of imagining new worldviews that unsettle and dismantle the logics of modernity/coloniality.

One fundamental aspect of this project is what Maldonado-Torres has called the "decolonial attitude," or a subjective disposition towards knowledge which demands an ethics that takes seriously the contributions, practices, knowledges, and experiences of those who have been systematically oppressed, disenfranchised, and silenced.[69] If, as Juan Flores argues, "Diasporic experiences—African in the Caribbean, and Caribbean in the imperial metropoles—have the effect of relativizing and de-essentializing, and of course de-territorializing, the traditional national construct and its hegemonies," then centering these works allows for a close examination of how the shared experiences and critical differences of Afro-Atlantic Hispanophone subjects can help us map resistance to the unfinished project of Western modernity and coloniality.[70]

Decolonizing Diasporas contributes to decolonial Caribbean discourses, and is in dialogue with African decolonial discourses that take into account the *longue durée* of the colonial project, understand colonial intervention as foundational violence and settler colonialism as an ongoing project, and name the contemporary effects of coloniality on the lived experiences of peoples resisting on its underside.[71] In addition, I see this project as the result of having engaged the work of scholars who have written about the Caribbean and its contributions to thinking about modernity and decolonization; scholars such as Sylvia Wynter, Derek Walcott, Kamau Brathwaite, Audre Lorde, Aimé Césaire, Yolanda Martínez-San Miguel, Frantz Fanon, Xhercis Méndez, Nelson Maldonado-Torres, Édouard Glissant, Ramón Grosfoguel, Lorgia García-Peña, Jessica Marie Johnson, Tacuma Peters, Antonio Benítez-Rojo, Vanessa Valdés, and M. Jacqui Alexander (to name a few).

By contributing to the study of both Caribbean and African decolonial poetics, this project frames decolonial politics and relational praxes as important lenses through which to understand Afro-Atlantic diasporas. *Decolonizing Diasporas* develops a decolonial feminist analysis that illuminates what these literary and sonic/visual works can offer to the theorization, politics, and practices of decoloniality. Furthermore, the discursive possibilities enabled by the disciplines of ethnic studies and decolonial and women of color feminist thought have facilitated the discursive moves undertaken in *Decolonizing Diasporas*. In fact, without such epistemological foundations, this project would not be possible.

Decolonizing Diasporas also recognizes the challenges and contributions brought to the fore by Indigenous, Native American, and First Nations feminist activists, scholars, and thinkers' decolonizing and resurgence projects, including Leanne Simpson, Kim Anderson, Cheryl Suzack, Dory Nason, and Danika Seltzman-Medak. Thus, *Decolonizing Diasporas* exists within the unyielding matrices of chattel slavery and Indigenous dispossession, across Abya Yala and Turtle Island. Disabused of objectivity, this text is articulated from the position of an Afro-Puerto Rican colonial subject thrust into diaspora onto settled, contested, and unceded territories. In this way, the overlapping histories of dispossession, destierro, and diaspora are rendered visible, and can speak to one another in relation to each other, rather than solely in relation to structures of domination.

Such a project would create the scaffolding for complex coalition-building, a practice that women of color and decolonial feminist thinkers have long practiced.[72] In focusing on literary poetics, I take up the mission that Sylvia Wynter has laid before us in "The Ceremony Must Be Found after Humanism." Wynter posits that it is the "literary humanities which should be the umbrella site for the transdisciplinary realization of a science of human systems."[73] Thus, literature, poetics, and the *studia humanitatis* are at the forefront of the project of radically remapping the human. *Decolonizing Diasporas* is both a signifier and a verb, and looks to the imaginary as a source of possibility.

On the Archipelago

Throughout *Decolonizing Diasporas*, I mark some of the relational preoccupations, thematics, and frameworks that dot the horizons of the Afro-Atlantic Hispanophone archipelago. I mobilize the term "archipelago" strategically in relation to what I see as an archipelagic turn in Latinx studies and the attention to islands in African studies. As Sampedro Vizcaya notes, "The recognition of islands as discursive spaces of textual production, and as privileged spaces for the articulation of a critical perspective, continues to be very limited in contemporary approaches to empire and imperial violence."[74] In the case of this project, thinking in and across island terms is crucial. Equatorial Guinea is comprised of five islands and a small continental swathe, while Cuba, Puerto Rico, and the Dominican Republic are all islands that are part of the Caribbean meta-archipelago (and each island is made up of their own archipelagos, i.e., several island formations). They also symbolize a larger Caribbean imaginary in which the migrations to metropolitan locations such as New York, Orlando, Chicago, and Miami represent an extended Caribbean. My focus on the archipelago is not only about the islands themselves, but also about the sea. In the context of Oceania, Epeli Hau'ofa challenges colonial cartographies that see the Pacific archipelago as "islands in the sea" through an oceanic epistemology which sees the archipelago as a "sea of islands," thereby centering the sea as part of Pacific identity formation.[75] Latinx studies, and in particular the study of Latinx Caribbean poetics, has long imagined the diaspora in the United States—especially locations such as New York City, Chicago, and Miami—as archipelagic extensions of the Caribbean.[76] As Rebeca Hey-Colón argues, "For many, New York City has become a member of the extended diasporic family, but we must not forget that this place in the north is also an island; the Hudson laps at its shores."[77] In the context of Latinx Caribbean cultural studies, Hey-Colón notes that "the protean sea has the capacity to surpass physical boundaries, promoting the fashioning of a regional identity rather than a national one. . . . Latino/a writers that incorporate the sea into their work fashion new spaces for identity and relation(ships) to emerge, and the possibilities are as limitless as they are abundant."[78]

One example of this is Joshua Jelly-Schapiro and Rebecca Solnit's book *Nonstop Metropolis: A New York City Atlas*, which offers dozens of alternative cartographies of New York City that challenge the reader to see and understand the southern islands of New York State in novel ways. The chapter titled "Archipelago: The Caribbean's Far North" includes a map by the cartographer Molly Roy, designed by Lia Tjandra, and an essay by Gaiutra Bahadur called "Of Islands and Other Mothers," which overlays the Caribbean islands and New York City's islands as one archipelago (see figure 5). In reflecting on her cartographic rendering, Bahadur asks, "Had maternal fierceness somehow forged a chain to connect us across the divisive waters of race and religion and history? Was this then, at last, our Caribbean archipelago?"[79] Bahadur's archipelago is anchored by kinship ties and bound by discourses, histories, religion, and race. McKittrick argues that "geography, then, materially and discursively extends to cover three-dimensional spaces and place, the physical landscape and infrastructures, geographic imaginations, the practice of mapping, exploring, and seeing, and social relations in and across space."[80] This radical reimagining of the material and geographic through a consideration of affective ties to space dovetails with diasporic patterns, and offers us a new way to map human geography that is both tangible and ephemeral. This discursive movida, or heretical move, challenges us to see the effects of insularity, the limits of thinking from a continental perspective, and at the very least offers us a visual mapping of the impact of Caribbean migrations to New York.

Martínez-San Miguel and Michelle Stephens have argued that archipelagic thinking necessarily "interrogate[s] epistemologies, ways of reading and thinking and methodologies, informed implicitly or explicitly by more continental paradigms and perspectives."[81] While Archipelagic studies has long-established discourses in Oceania and Pacific Island studies, thinking about Archipelagic American studies is a recent turn. This is reflected in both the journal *American Quarterly*'s 2015 special issue on "Pacific Currents," and in the publication of the 2017 collection *Archipelagic American Studies*, edited by Brian Russell Roberts and Michelle Ann Stephens.[82] Both of these generative and timely collections help to expand how we conceive of archipelagic formations, extended archipelagos, and what Craig Santos Perez calls "imperial terripelagos."[83]

Central to *Decolonizing Diasporas* are the ways in which discourses from the periphery, from small places, from islands and their diasporas, offer transformative approaches to thinking about modernity and its discontents. Those who stand to witness the machinations of power and domination from afar have much to offer us and our collective liberation. In this book, I trace relations by hailing distant and recent crossings. I propose a radical mapping of new diasporic relations linked through material and cultural productions, through historical crossings, through archives of the sea, and through archipelagic thinking. This methodology sees Afro-Atlantic Hispanophone islands as always already and necessarily related and in relation. Studying these nations and nation-states from archipelagic and diasporic perspectives shifts dominant continental discourses towards the potentiality within the Afro-Atlantic Hispanophone archipelago. In doing so, I read these historical crossings as palimpsests that engage the influences of the Spanish Empire as well as relationships to the British Empire and U.S. imperialism. I also consider the impact of relations with Francophone, Lusophone, and Anglophone nations and nation-states, which is particularly salient for the Dominican Republic and Equatorial Guinea, as well as contemporary ties to the United States.

This context notwithstanding, I also attend to diasporas springing forth from these islands, which punctuate this cartography like so many waves on the sea. Read as a palimpsest, these movements allow us to bear witness to traces of earlier movements and experiences, to the long legacies of the sea, of the Crossing; to mark relations between difference; and to weave stories pried from survival. Vanessa Pérez-Rosario argues that

Fig. 5. "Archipelago" by Joshua Jelly-Schapiro and Rebecca Solnit, from *Nonstop Metropolis: A New York City Atlas* (University of California Press, 2016); cartography by Molly Roy, design by Lia Tjandra. Reproduced by permission of Joshua Jelly-Schapiro.

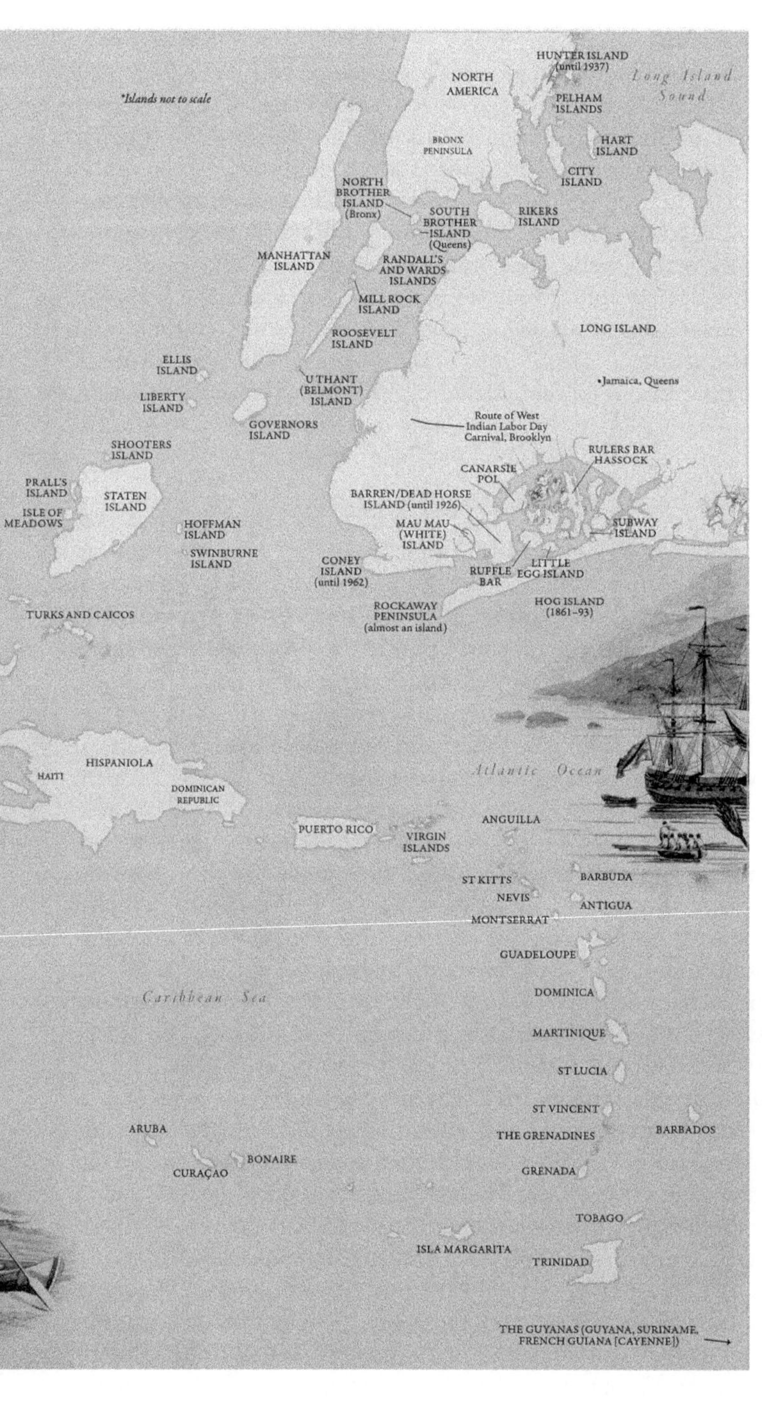
*Islands not to scale
HUNTER ISLAND (until 1937)
NORTH AMERICA
Long Island Sound
PELHAM ISLANDS
BRONX PENINSULA
HART ISLAND
CITY ISLAND
NORTH BROTHER ISLAND (Bronx)
SOUTH BROTHER ISLAND (Queens)
RIKERS ISLAND
MANHATTAN ISLAND
RANDALL'S AND WARDS ISLANDS
MILL ROCK ISLAND
LONG ISLAND
ROOSEVELT ISLAND
ELLIS ISLAND
U THANT (BELMONT) ISLAND
•Jamaica, Queens
LIBERTY ISLAND
GOVERNORS ISLAND
Route of West Indian Labor Day Carnival, Brooklyn
SHOOTERS ISLAND
RULERS BAR HASSOCK
CANARSIE POL
PRALL'S ISLAND
STATEN ISLAND
BARREN/DEAD HORSE ISLAND (until 1926)
ISLE OF MEADOWS
HOFFMAN ISLAND
MAU MAU (WHITE) ISLAND
SUBWAY ISLAND
SWINBURNE ISLAND
CONEY ISLAND (until 1962)
RUFFLE BAR
LITTLE EGG ISLAND
ROCKAWAY PENINSULA (almost an island)
HOG ISLAND (1861–93)
TURKS AND CAICOS
HISPANIOLA
HAITI
DOMINICAN REPUBLIC
Atlantic Ocean
PUERTO RICO
VIRGIN ISLANDS
ANGUILLA
ST KITTS
BARBUDA
NEVIS
ANTIGUA
MONTSERRAT
GUADELOUPE
Caribbean Sea
DOMINICA
MARTINIQUE
ST LUCIA
ST VINCENT
ARUBA
THE GRENADINES
BARBADOS
BONAIRE
CURAÇAO
GRENADA
TOBAGO
ISLA MARGARITA
TRINIDAD
THE GUYANAS (GUYANA, SURINAME, FRENCH GUIANA [CAYENNE])

"foregrounding the sea decenters cities such as Miami and New York and resituates them as extensions of the Caribbean archipelago. Contemporary Latino writers and artists use the image of the sea to illustrate the fragility and fluidity of identity constructs in transnational relations."[84] The sea is present and prescient in each chapter of this book, hailing relations and possibilities as well as marking distance and impossibilities. It is for this reason that I end this book with a meditation on the sea as material and immaterial history. Hey-Colón asserts that "the sea's propensity to exalt the sensorial aspects of literature [creates] an amorphous link to healing, trauma, and ultimately transformation."[85] *Decolonizing Diasporas* hails longer forms of archipelagic and diasporic relations, including the transatlantic slave trade, emancipation, and anticolonial struggles, and makes possible a linking of contemporary archipelagic and decolonizing imaginaries.

On Ethics and Methodologies

While *Decolonizing Diasporas* focuses on a small aspect of Afro-Atlantic Hispanophone and diasporic thought and politics, it prods at larger questions of national and ethnic belonging, and racialization and resistance. Global Hispanophone scholars are continually remapping the field of Hispanic studies in light of colonial legacies and Spanish-language practices, and are in many ways refashioning the Hispanist archive to include African, Filipino, and Asian literatures.[86] Outside of Hispanic studies, however, there is rarely sustained engagement with Equatoguinean literature. This project, then, is an attempt to engage and relate across these fields from the position of ethnic studies, and to see what these works can offer decolonial thought. This engagement with and practice of relationality also requires contending with my position as a subject of the world's oldest colony, and a subject who, through the systematic dispossession of ancestral lands and overlapping diasporic processes, directly and indirectly participates in the ongoing settler colonial projects of the United States.

While anchored in relationality and shared peripherality, this project is also deeply invested in recognizing and attending to the irreconcilable differences of the Afro-Latinx Caribbean and Equatoguinean diasporas. Taking these differences seriously is central to both the project of decoloniality and to women of color theorizing. However, there must be critical care in relational projects of this type. Thus, I make space for what is incommensurable across the experiences of Afro-Latinx Caribbean and Equatoguinean diasporic subjects. This is crucial since race and Indigeneity, modes of racialization and ethnicity, or forms of colonization and resistance are not reducible to one another. Sampedro Vizcaya references Ian Baucom to note: "Incommensurability can be both daunting and paralyzing. The task would rather be to 'attend to a series of moments in which an array of African, Caribbean,

North American, South American, or West European cultural, narrative, literary, historical, and ideological practices converge.' "[87] Following Keith Feldman, I contend that the practice of being in relation in Afro-Atlantic worlds and world-making processes is "both an ethics and the fashioning of a phenomenology." As such, "the conditions of possibility for relation are the foundational worldings that are made in conquest and enslavement."[88] If these heterogeneous, overlapping, and irreconcilable diasporas are understood as somehow in relation, as vectors of knowledge for one another, then we are engaging in decolonial acts, traversing centuries, unrooting colonial structures and attitudes, and creating a constellation of radical hope and creativity that can fashion our futures.

Such a project, if taken seriously, would not only trouble tightly circumscribed narratives of Blackness, but would also bear witness to how Indigenous knowledges and practices continually unsettle and resist settler colonialism and coloniality. *Decolonizing Diasporas* must put its own title into practice. It must recognize the kinds of coloniality afoot within Indigenous African contexts and their diasporas, while also contending with the fact that Afro-Caribbean Latinx peoples in diaspora are often colonial or postcolonial subjects living on lands marred by Indigenous dispossession, the afterlives of slavery, and differing forms of racialization, sociopolitical exclusion, domination, and racism—what Ruth Wilson Gilmore defines as the "state-sanctioned or extralegal production and exploitation of a group-differentiated vulnerability to premature death."[89]

These tense and tender relations evoke Eve Tuck and K. Wayne Yang's assertion that the incommensurability of these realities, under differing yet overlapping forms of colonial subjugation, can lead to distinct liberatory projects.[90] However, rather than turn decolonization into an "empty signifier to be filled with any track towards liberation," *Decolonizing Diasporas* points towards practices, politics, and reflections of liberation as articulated and imagined by these diasporic Afro-Atlantic authors.[91] In particular, the emphasized preoccupations reflect divergent approaches and histories to similar circumstances of oppression and domination—specifically processes of dispossession and domination that expel Afro-Hispanophone subjects into diaspora and exile. Thus, this is an examination of the varied liberatory strivings that rip the seams of foundational histories, and of the practices and fashioning of radical futures that do not rely on assimilation, dispossession, or coloniality.

Rather than a neatly corseted study of the links between Afro-Cuban, Afro-Puerto Rican, Afro-Dominican, and Equatoguinean writers and thinkers, *Decolonizing Diasporas* marks some of the preoccupations that emerge in these texts, and reads them against the grain of coloniality and towards a decolonizing politic, with a decolonial attitude.[92] I take on a decolonial attitude and engage in a methodological and political practice that illuminates what these diasporic and exilic authors and texts offer and disrupt within colonial and decolonial imaginaries, even as it is often difficult, dangerous, or deadly to do so.

My transdisciplinary training in ethnic studies enables me to take an approach that prioritizes the contributions of literary and historical studies, women of color feminisms and feminist philosophy, and decolonial and critical theory. Thus, while *Decolonizing Diasporas* focuses on literary, sonic, and visual cultural productions, I utilize an ethnic studies methodology to see how sociopolitical, cultural, philosophical, and theoretical issues are taken up and expanded within the works. The literatures of people of color and women are a prime site of analysis for radical and decolonizing work. As Barbara Christian famously declared, "People of color have always theorized," and this theorizing is "often in narrative forms, in the stories we create, in riddles and proverbs, in the play with language, because dynamic rather than fixed ideas seem more to our liking." I heed Christian's advice and center the ways that literature is "not an occasion for discourse among critics," but rather a "necessary nourishment for their people and one way by which they come to understand their lives better."[93] In *Decolonizing Diasporas*, I follow the concepts and language that the works themselves offer and, by remaining "open to the intricacies of the intersection of language, class, race, and gender in their literature," have, in the words of Christian, "discover(ed) what language I might use."[94] Thus in each chapter of *Decolonizing Diasporas* I develop a central theme from within the literatures studied in that chapter; by following these works, I conceptualize how each novel engages with each theme and I analyze the distinct ways that each preoccupation is approached within these literary traditions.

Decolonizing Diasporas meditates on literary and cultural works articulated from different parts of the Afro-Atlantic world, representing unfixed and ever-shifting loci of enunciation. I argue that this condition of destierro, of being ripped forcibly from the earth, exiled, or dispersed, is a precondition of modern/colonial and settler colonial projects, which have made diaspora and exile a living reality for billions of people. In light of these long histories of domination, literary poetics and art become forces that challenge structures of power, and challenge us to imagine different modalities of being. Nancy Morejón argues that Caribbean poetics are a cultural and political tool. "The poetry of the Caribbean or, better yet, its poetics," she writes, "multilingual and plural, multiple and one, challenges us by being faithful to the origins that created it."[95] Afro-Caribbean poetics traverse regional, linguistic, and generic boundaries, speak of home, destierro, and other impossible spaces while carrying within them un/traced, un/spoken, and intersecting histories.

Afro-Latinx and Afro-Hispanic cultural productions emerge from unfixed loci of enunciation and across ontological modes of non-being and non-belonging. This begs the question, where does the study of these Afro-descendants belong? *Decolonizing Diasporas* proposes that a meditation on these peripheralized Afro-Atlantic texts calls for a rearticulation of Latinx studies, Hispanophone studies, and Black and diaspora studies. This project engages in a dialectical practice of reading these texts with a decolonial attitude, while recognizing and articulating what new tools they offer to the study of Afro-diasporas, the field of decoloniality, and projects that envision liberatory futures.

This practice of traversing borders and boundaries which have been built through modernity and its violent processes is necessarily fraught with tensions, and compels us to recall Gloria Anzaldúa's conjured image of the U.S.–Mexican border as "*una herida abierta* [an open wound] where the Third World grates against the first and bleeds." Anzaldúa tells us: "Before a scab forms it hemorrhages again, the lifeblood of two worlds merges to form a third country—a border culture."[96] We can think of the sea as a vast and fluid border, as a site of "colonial convergence" and resistance.[97] The sea appears, and while it is both seen and unseen in each chapter, its presence makes possible these works and this meditation. In the contexts of the literatures outlined in this text, I pose that the lifeblood of these worlds takes the shape of decolonizing diasporas—radical Afro-diasporic imaginaries that subvert coloniality and usher in new ways of knowing and being, and interrogate and excavate location and dislocation.

Each of the chapters in this book represents a love letter to the imaginations of the Hispanophone Afro-Atlantic. In each chapter I read a collection of literary texts and cultural productions linked by a thematic relation. The book develops in the form of a sequence, with each chapter building on the previous one, and each chapter underscoring a particular theme undertaken by the authors and artists in distinct ways. I take seriously Christian's call for literary criticism that is "promotion as well as understanding, a response to the writer to whom there is often no response, to folk who need the writing as much as they need anything."[98] Thus, the chapters of *Decolonizing Diasporas* continually accentuate the potentiality of these literary poetics to radically change our liberation practices and ourselves.

Routes: Chapter Breakdown

In chapter 1, "Intimacies," I examine how experiences of dictatorship, military occupation, and the coloniality of gender, respectively, impact intimate, kinship, and communal relations in Juan Tomás Ávila Laurel's *By Night the Mountain Burns* (*Arde el monte de noche*), Trifonia Melibea Obono's *La bastarda*, and Nelly Rosario's *Song of the Water Saints*. I develop the concept of the intimacies of coloniality in order to trace how these novels reveal the ways that structural domination shapes everyday intimate practices, including access to sustenance, sociality, and sexual desire. While erotic desire is central to thinking about intimacy, I attempt to expand the intimacies of coloniality to include kinship ties, everyday needs, and communal violence. In turning from the more dominant analyses of dictatorial regimes, which often narrate power from a bird's-eye view, I instead look at the ways that autocratic power, sexual exploitation, and varying degrees of sociopolitical neglect likewise intimately impact the lives of those living under postcolonial and dictatorial regimes.

Analyzing the often-invisible impact that dictatorship has on reproductive labor, food insecurity, sexual economies, and the psyche underscores the insidiousness and intergenerational effects of domination. I contend that the three novels offer a distinct perspective on the intimacies of coloniality and center the oft-obscured subjectivities of Afro-femmes and lesbians, showing how erotic freedoms emerge and travel in relation to, against, and outside of social and political domination. While these erotic and corporeal freedoms are often severely punished, the authors frame what historian Jessica Marie Johnson calls "Black femme freedom" and what Nadia Celis Salgado argues is "conciencia corporal" (corporeal consciousness) as central to surviving within oppressive regimes. For example, in two of the novels, *Song of the Water Saints* and *La bastarda*, both authored by women writers, petit and grand marronage emerge as sites of freedom for Black women and femmes, even as they come up against systems of domination for which their gendered and racialized bodies are prime sites for regulation and control. In *By Night the Mountain Burns* we see the intimate and community-wide impacts of isolation, hunger, and foreign resource exploitation as experienced on the island of Annobón, the most remote island of Equatorial Guinea. I end the chapter by arguing that these texts demand a particular labor from the reader, which is to bear witness to the interstitial effects of domination, and to take note of how erotic freedoms emerging from Afro-femme subjects challenge the intimacies of coloniality. In this way, "Intimacies" opens a discursive space to engage the following questions: If these literatures demand witnesses, who has seen this? How can we be faithful witnesses to the visible and invisible effects of coloniality? These critical questions are the arc of chapter 2.

Chapter 2, "Witnessing," utilizes decolonial feminist philosopher María Lugones's concept of "faithful witnessing" as a point of departure to think about the ethics, possibilities, and limits of recognition. For Lugones, faithful witnessing is an act of aligning oneself with oppressed peoples against the grain of power. This act is one not only of seeing, but also supporting, the narratives of peoples, recognizing their lives and stories to be true despite their lack of institutional endorsement. I propose that faithful witnessing—bearing witness to the known and unknowable effects of colonialism, coloniality, and domination—is a critical element of the decolonial attitude. Through a close reading of Donato Ndongo's *Shadows of Your Black Memory* (*Las tinieblas de tu memoria negra*) and Junot Díaz's *The Brief Wondrous Life of Oscar Wao*, I build on the concept of faithful witnessing as a decolonial alternative to Eurocentric philosophical notions of recognition. This chapter opens a space to think about the ethics of bearing witness, and examines how faithful witnessing reveals the machinations of coloniality and gendered violence. I propose that faithful witnessing is what happens when one does not collude with oppressive structures, and I argue that one of the most critical phenomena to which we must be faithful witnesses is the condition of destierro—the kinds of dispossession endemic to colonial/modernity that are expanded upon in chapter 3.

Chapter 3, "Destierro," is a meditation on exile and memory. Here, I develop the concept of destierro, the phenomenon of being ripped forcefully from the earth, as a violent precondition of modernity, colonialism, and settler colonialism. This chapter offers decolonial feminist readings of *El dictador de Corisco* by Juan Tomás Ávila Laurel and Loida Maritza Pérez's *Geographies of Home*. These texts engender critical discourses on destierro related to the suppression of memories and cosmologies, and the political and metaphysical realities of alienation. I argue that destierro is a violent act that is likewise a site for resistance. This form of exile is endemic to modernity's unquenchable hunger to consume and exploit, and thus compels Black, Indigenous, and Afro-Indigenous peoples to rise and make claims against it. I trouble the permanence of destierro, and open a discursive space to reimagine reparations outside of modern capitalist frameworks. I continue this line of thinking in the following chapter where destierro is taken up as a potential space to develop practices of decolonial love and a reparation of the imagination.

Chapter 4, "Reparations," examines how these narratives imagine reparations beyond the material. I begin by historicizing reparations as the concept pertains to radical Black thinkers in U.S. and Caribbean contexts. Using the work of Christina Olivares, Robin Kelley, and Chela Sandoval, I read Ernesto Quiñonez's *Bodega Dreams*, Junot Díaz's *The Brief Wondrous Life of Oscar Wao*, and Joaquín Mbomío Bacheng's *Matinga, sangre en la selva*. I argue that within these works, decolonial love is part of imagining nonmaterial reparations. These works bring forth and demand what I call a "reparation of the imagination." I understand this type of reparation as being sustained by remembering practices; grafting and culling our pasts and conjuring radical futures. I conclude by considering the kinds of radical futurities that a reparation of the imagination makes possible.

Chapter 5, "Apocalypso," examines the futurities that emerge from the Afro-Atlantic Hispanophone diaspora by tracing how decolonial love and resistance are conjured through the imagining of possible futures. Because the science of transforming the human is not only about historicizing how Man has come to overrepresent himself as the human, but also about mapping and imagining new ways of being human in the present and the future, the preoccupation with futurities and imagining other possibilities beyond coloniality is central to decolonial poetics, practices, and politics.[99] This chapter uses Michelle Cliff's treatise on apocalypso as a point of departure to examine how Afro-Atlantic authors and artists trouble tropes of racialized Blackness, conjure apocalyptic worlds, and center Santería and Lucumí as Afro-Atlantic religious syncretisms which represent acts of decolonial love and make space for the present-past and for Black futures.

The chapter examines the eponymous debut album and video images of the Afro-Cuban French singers Ibeyi, and Daniel José Older's novel *Shadowshaper*. I argue that these works trouble colonial notions of temporality, cosmology, and spirituality, and underscore the ways that the past and present are likewise the stuff of futurities. I then analyze Junot Díaz's short story "Monstro" and Juan Tomás Ávila Laurel's futuristic novel *Panga Rilene*, elucidating how these texts conjure apocalyptic worlds and further Afro-futurist discourses. Rather than imagine utopian liberation or dystopian futures, the writers that I study in this chapter imagine apocalypsos and what I am calling "worlds/otherwise" taking root in the ruptures between modernity and coloniality, and being forged by the collision of domination and resistance. Thus, the chapter maps how diasporic Afro-Atlantic Hispanophone writers and artists create worlds/otherwise. Many of these futurities rely on intimacies and transgenerational kinship ties, thus recalling the book's first chapter on intimacies and likewise shifting toward the book's coda which is a necessary meditation on the sea, the Atlantic, and waters beyond.

The coda, "Sea," acts as a conclusion for *Decolonizing Diasporas*. It is a brief reflection on how decoloniality and radical relationality in diasporic contexts open a space for further relational, archipelagic, and transatlantic projects. I conclude with a meditation on the sea, and examine how writers and artists imagine possibilities for racialized subjects in destierro. I discuss Raquel Ilombe del Pozo Epita's poetry in *Ceiba II* and undertake an analysis of Aracelis Girmay's *The Black Maria* and María Magdalena Campos-Pons's image, "De las dos aguas." The coda traces how Afro-Hispanic and Afro-Latinx literary poetics and art remap geographies of the human by offering alternative ways to consider the intimacy of violence, the act of witnessing faithfully, the impossibility of destierro, reparations as decolonial love, and present futurities. I offer methodological interventions at the intersections of Black, Latinx, and Hispanic studies, with radical women of color and decolonial feminist thought at the fore.

In engaging these topics, *Decolonizing Diasporas* addresses the following questions: What are the critical perspectives and challenges offered by peripheralized Black literature? How can we map beyond geographical and material locations/dislocations and towards a mapping of the imaginary? What if relations across difference in Afro-Atlantic Hispanophone diasporas became additional vectors of analyses that help us complicate and interrogate contemporary discourses on race, sex, gender, sexuality, diaspora, belonging, decoloniality, and liberation?

This project, then, offers a lens through which to read peripheralized Afro-diasporas in a different way, not only from the perspective of the underside, but from an approach that sees difference as consequential, and the Afro-Atlantic Hispanophone diaspora as a palimpsest, as an archive of overlapping histories and incommensurable differences. *Decolonizing Diasporas* marks the literary and cultural preoccupations of Afro-Atlantic Hispanophone subjects who produce within and far from their homelands. These writers and artists speak across spatial, temporal, and linguistic planes to indict and recite the weight of five centuries of resistance to domination. These voices, too often silenced, too often siloed, are read alongside each other throughout this text, a methodology that offers another layer to the palimpsest of the Afro-Atlantic.

Chapter 1

Intimacies

> Our erotic knowledge empowers us, becomes a lens through which we scrutinize all aspects of our existence, forcing us to evaluate those aspects honestly in terms of their relative meaning within our lives.
>
> —Audre Lorde, *Sister Outsider*

The playwright leaned over and gritted, "[Es] la sombra que nos acompaña," it is the shadow that accompanies us. There, in the capital city of Malabo in Equatorial Guinea, near the end of our interview, the writer acted out an informal and dangerous gesture by confiding in me, in a public place, about the corporeal and affective impact of dictatorship.[1] The shadow that is always present, that always follows, is also the shadow that bites, "muerde," like being scorched by the sun, he continued. This audacious public disclosure was a way to convey the near-omnipresent power of dictatorship, the command of structural domination, and the dominance of sociopolitical repression in Equatorial Guinea. The playwright's turn of phrase revealed the ways in which the reach of the Obiang regime's domination is continually present in both public and intimate arenas of Equatoguinean life. These intimate moments of corporeal, epistemological, and ontological domination can be understood as the effects of the intimacies of coloniality which are part of larger social, political, and ideological structures that continually attempt to circumscribe Black life in, and beyond, the colony. The intimate impacts of coloniality are varied and are nationally and perhaps even regionally specific. However, they include the brutal impacts of colonization, postcolonial dictatorships, occupation, and the forms of coloniality that affect the intimate and everyday lives of the *damné*, or those condemned to the underside of coloniality. While these forms of domination occur over the course of different historical moments, at many points overlapping, they are to be understood as interrelated yet distinct apparatuses of power that can and should be put into relation in order to track how these structures of power operate and impact the most intimate parts of people's lives. If, as Ann Stoler argues, "matters of the intimate are critical sites for the consolidation of colonial power,

. . . management of those domains provides a strong pulse on how relations of empire are exercised, and . . . affairs of the intimate are strategic for empire-driven states," then looking to the remnants of those structures, the intimacies of coloniality, deserve consideration and a space for theorization.[2]

In this chapter I examine how erotic and corporeal freedom emerge in the face of the intimate impacts of dictatorship, occupation, and the coloniality of gender in the work of three diasporic Afro-Atlantic Hispanophone authors: Juan Tomás Ávila Laurel's *Arde el monte de noche* (2009; translated into English in 2014 as *By Night the Mountain Burns*), Nelly Rosario's *Song of the Water Saints* (2002), and Trifonia Melibea Obono's *La bastarda* (2016; translated into English in 2018 as *La Bastarda*). I understand coloniality as the ongoing forms and structures of unfreedom that remain and multiply within nations, nation-states, and communities despite past processes of administrative decolonization and irrespective of postcolonial status. Thus, the remarks of the aforementioned playwright reveal new possibilities within the practice of reading against the grain of coloniality: reading for the corporeal impacts of domination. This dialogue, alongside my discussions with other Equatoguinean authors and editors such as Donato Ndongo and Remei Sipi Mayo, makes clear that the literary poetics of Afro-Atlantic subjects demand witnesses.

Christina Sharpe's meditation on what she calls "monstrous intimacies" is key to the arc of this chapter. She argues that "[thinking] about monstrous intimacies post-slavery means examining those subjectivities constituted from transatlantic slavery onward and connected, then as now, by the everyday mundane horrors."[3] I am interested, then, in the ways that these literary works offer intergenerational retellings of often-obscured histories of violence and resistance, and the ways that they reveal the intimacies of power and its impact on people's everyday lives and worldviews.

Similarly, my examination of these Afro-Atlantic literatures reveals new methods in the tracking and fashioning of femme subjectivities, and the impact of structural domination on the intimate lives of women, girls, femmes, and their kin and communities. When using the terms "femme" and "femmes" in this book, I am referring to bodies that are categorized as women or feminine, or which alternately perform femininity, with or without adhering to cis-centered ways of being and knowing. Though there is a critical debate within feminist politics, one productive position contends that ethical feminist practices should consider the "concurrent trans histories" that exist alongside the historicized experiences of working-class (often white) lesbians; that is, take seriously the femme identities of trans women, feminine-presenting drag queens, and non-binary femme-presenting people. B. B. Buchanan argues that "femininity, as a form of expression, is denigrated and devalued on all bodies; no matter an individual's self-identification. . . . Femmes aren't constructed as femmes because of self-identification either, but about the connotation of difference and lesser status which marks all feminine performance."[4] In building a femme framework, Macarena Gómez-Barris forms what she calls a "decolonial queer femme" methodology that challenges the colonial normative of knowledge extraction and instead builds from women of color feminisms and practices of relationality: "like women of color feminisms that analyze through a relational field of multiplicity, I situate the theory and praxis of de-linking from the colonial as refusing to see from a singular frame of analysis, standpoint, interpretation, or experience. What I am calling a 'decolonial queer femme' method valorizes nonnormative embodied femininity as sources of knowing and perceiving."[5] In the novels that I examine in this chapter, the bodies of women and femmes become sites of resistance and knowing, and in some instances, they trouble colonial patriarchal gender arrangements by traversing corporeal boundaries of sexual dimorphism. Thus, reaching for relations across the Afro-Atlantic alongside the axis of the intimacies of coloniality makes it possible to map how this broader corpus of indictment—including fiction, nonfiction essays, journalism, sonic/visual performances, and political demonstrations—represents an archive of the known and the unseen effects of colonialism and coloniality, including dictatorship, occupation, and gendered and sexual violence. It likewise locates and indicts the intimacies of coloniality.

I open this book with a meditation on intimacies for three reasons. The first is because the role and subjective position of women, girls, femmes, and queer colonized subjects are often relegated to liminal spaces when discussing the violence endemic to colonialism and coloniality. Jafari Allen contends that "*Erotic subjectivity*—deeper understandings and compulsions of the body and soul—simultaneously embodying and invoking sex and death—works toward not only transgressing but transcending and finally transforming hegemonies of global capital, the state, and of bourgeois, limited, and limiting notions of gender sexuality, or blackness."[6] This chapter centers the movements, resistance, and freedoms that these Black femme subjects undertake in the face of ongoing forms of political, structural, and gender violence that impact the intimate dimensions of their lives. Second, I am interested in reading how three very different texts from arguably peripheralized Afro-Atlantic diasporas take up questions of belonging, refusal, and fugitivity in distinct yet related ways. Finally, the structure of this book is both thematic and sequential. In opening with "Intimacies," I hope to show the robust potentiality of the literary works from the Afro-Atlantic Hispanophone diaspora before moving on to the successive arguments of chapters 2 through 5.

To be clear, while I am reading these texts to better understand how ongoing forms of inequality and violent power structures reach into the most intimate parts of the lives of Afro-Atlantic subjects, these novels likewise showcase the rich heterogeneity of this literary corpus. These literary texts not only offer new ways of understanding human phenomena, but they also provide imaginative possibilities for freedom practices and resistance to violence and colonialism. As Régine Michelle Jean-Charles argues, "The prominence of articulations of violence in Africa and the diaspora has long been related to slavery and colonialism. Yet, given the explicitly sexed and gendered manifestations of violence in today's global age, most of these theories fail to unpack the dynamics of sex and gender in the occurrence and representation of violence."[7] This chapter on the intimacies of coloniality builds on the work of Jean-Charles, Sharpe, Mimi Sheller, Donette Francis, and others who have created rich discourses on racialized gender, sexuality, and sex as they pertain to citizenship, belonging, and the erotic. I look to Dominican and Equatoguinean literature as sites through which to further theorize intimacy, tracking the role of dictatorship, occupation, and the coloniality of gender in ontological experiences of disparate diasporic Afro-Atlantic communities from the Caribbean and sub-Saharan Africa. My reading of these novels through the lens of women of color feminist, decolonial, and ethnic studies is but one way to approach these works. I begin this meditation by outlining the intimate impacts of dictatorship, occupation, and the coloniality of gender and follow with an examination of the three novels by Ávila Laurel, Rosario, and Obono. I conclude with a discussion of what it means to bear witness to the ways that these novels challenge dictatorial, imperial, and phenomenological power structures, and prompt the reader to consider faithful witnessing as a reading practice that is both necessary and demanded by the texts.

Intimate Impacts

The preoccupation with dictatorship, occupation, and coloniality and the need to mark it, name it, document its actions, subvert it, and topple it are pressing political concerns in Afro-Atlantic literatures. In these contexts, literatures work to uncover the machinations of power by making visible what is often dangerous to utter in public (and even intimate or private) spaces.[8] As Donette Francis argues in *Fictions of Feminine Citizenship*, in these novels, "the presentness of the past calls for tracing out imperial circuits of desire, which shows that empire's operating logic in colonial theaters was equally about regulating intimacy as it was about disciplining populations through military force."[9] Literature becomes a witness to the unbearable reach of sociopolitical repression by exposing its innermost machinations and thus revealing the normalization of domination and the absurdities of power. Key to this chapter is the way in which these works divulge how dictatorship, occupation, and the coloniality of gender become intimate parts of the lives of the *damné*. Within these works, erotic or sexual, corporeal, and subjective freedoms become sites of possibility, but also a critical lens. The resulting narratives reveal how domination from afar is felt within the realm of the intimate, the everyday, and the erotic. I argue that these texts not only document how the intimate nature of dictatorship, occupation, and the coloniality of gender dictates how Afro-Atlantic and Afro-femme subjects live and die, but they also track the development of ravenous personal quests for corporeal and erotic freedom. Finally, these literary works underscore how the effects of domination influence families across generations and migrations.

I include occupation and the coloniality of gender in this chapter alongside dictatorship because while dictatorship is an important trope in Dominican and Equatoguinean literature, the often-obscured occupation of the Dominican Republic and Equatorial Guinea by the United States and Spain, respectively, are both precursors to structures of coloniality, in its various iterations, and dictatorship. Reading for the impact of these distinct but interconnected sociopolitical events allows me to track relations across subjects in Afro-Atlantic literatures. Each of these three works emerging from Equatoguinean and Dominican diasporas—Ávila Laurel's *By Night the Mountain Burns*, Rosario's *Song of the Water Saints*, and Obono's *La bastarda*—reveal and indict the intimate impacts of dictatorship, occupation, and ultimately the machinations of coloniality through different vectors.

The intimacies of coloniality that I track here are the physical, erotic, spiritual, cosmological, edificial, and emotional forms of domination and extraction that affect the lives of those living under coloniality or ongoing forms of colonialism and imperial exploitation. While these literatures are heterogeneous (Ávila Laurel writes from the Annobonese experience, Obono writes from a Fang perspective, and Rosario's work emerges from a diasporic Afro-Dominican positionality), reading them in relation exposes shared experiences. In short, the novels illustrate how these insidious intimacies affect everyday practices, limit access to sustenance, shape sociality, and circumscribe sexual desire. They center the oft-obscured subjectivities of Afro-femmes, women, and girls, and likewise indicate how erotic freedoms emerge and travel in relation to, against, and outside of dictatorship, occupation, and the coloniality of gender. In doing so, the novels underscore how erotic freedoms and corporeal consciousness can arise as forms of resistance to the lived experiences under and long after dictatorship and occupation.

I build this analysis and the concept of the intimacies of coloniality through an engagement with Nadia Celis Salgado's concept of "la conciencia corporal" (corporeal consciousness) and Jessica Marie Johnson's conceptualization of "Black femme freedom."[10] Following these works allows for an analysis of how Black femmes in Caribbean diasporic and Afro-Hispanic contexts produce forms of liberation through bodily acts that resist the corporeal and epistemological enclosures of coloniality. Building on the work of women of color thinkers such as Mimi Sheller and Audre Lorde, Celis Salgado contends, "El saber anclado en el 'cuerpo vivido' es origen y producto de lo que a lo largo de este libro denomino la 'conciencia corporal' " ("The knowledge anchored in the 'lived body' is the origin and product of what I call 'corporeal consciousness' throughout this book").[11] Ephemeral acts, gestures, and practices allow for the "cuerpo vivido," the lived body, to buttress and traverse the limitations of heteropatriarchy and infantilization as well as occupation and dictatorship.

The theorization of this corporeal consciousness is developed through an understanding of the "condición *encarnada* que las escritoras estudiadas atribuyen al proceso de hacerse mujeres y el uso del cuerpo como sitio de resistencia son características comunes en variedad de autoras contemporáneas del Gran Caribe y su diáspora" (the "incarnate condition that the women writers studied attribute to the process of becoming women and the use of the body as a site of resistance are common characteristics in a variety of contemporary authors of the Greater Caribbean and its diaspora").[12] Here it is important to note the use of the word "encarnada," flesh (but literally meat), as a site of resistance, and the ways that this theme emerges throughout the literature of women of color in the Caribbean basin.[13] Furthermore, Celis Salgado argues, "Las niñas son sujetos de deseo y no solo objectos del mismo" ("Girls are subjects of desire and not just objects of it"), and acknowledging this means that we understand their bodies, minds, and desires as complex and purposeful entities in search of autonomy.[14] The works by the Caribbean writers that Celis Salgado analyzes "ponen en evidencia el deseo activo de las niñas, manifiesto en las sensaciones, movimientos e interacciones con el entorno y con otros cuerpos, en la presencia de pulsiones sexuales, en su curiosidad intelectual y en la búsqueda de la autonomía" (The stories analyzed "show the active desire of girls, manifested in the sensations, movements and interactions with the environment and other bodies, in the presence of sexual drives, in their intellectual curiosity and in the search for autonomy").[15]

Celis Salgado's theory of corporeal consciousness dovetails with Jessica Marie Johnson's concept of Black femme freedom. For Johnson, the Black women of the New Orleans Atlantic world "moved beyond the fractional flesh of la traversée and the container of the manumission act" through their freedom practices, manipulation of legal systems, and quotidian kinship practices, forged outside of their conscripted positions as Black enslaved or formerly enslaved women. In her book *Wicked Flesh: Black Women, Intimacy, and Freedom in the Atlantic World*, Johnson argues:

> [Black femme freedom] points to the deeply feminine, feminized, and femme practices of freedom engaged in by women and girls of African descent. In the practice of refusal, whether in rejected labor demands or sexual advances, and even refusal to concede to officials in manumission disputes, black women and girls claimed ownership over themselves. . . . Black femme freedoms emerged in these interstices as black women exploited every tool at their disposal on behalf of themselves and their kin.[16]

These "feminine, feminized, and femme practices" are intrinsically tied to a corporeal consciousness or a knowing body whose contours burst towards freedom practices over and against public and intimate forms of domination. In the novels I analyze in this chapter, I see Black femme freedom and corporeal consciousness as erotic resistance and refusals of the intimacies of dictatorship and occupation.

Reading the works of Juan Tomás Ávila Laurel, Nelly Rosario, and Trifonia Melibea Obono in relation uncovers a common preoccupation. Rather than constructing what has been aptly called "the dictator novel," these writers approach dictatorial domination and imperial occupation from the periphery, and thus reveal the phenomena of the intimacies of dictatorship and occupation.[17] Ávila Laurel's *By Night the Mountain Burns* takes us to Annobón, one of Equatorial Guinea's most remote islands, furthest away from the coast of the continental swathe of Rio Muni and the capital city, Malabo, on the island of Bioko. Annobón is where the nameless protagonist recounts his childhood among his family and community, and in doing so shares the disastrous consequences of living both too close and too far from the seat of power. Rosario's *Song of the Water Saints* centers the lives of four generations of Afro-Dominican girls and women on the Caribbean island and in diaspora in New York City. In this novel, the 1916–24 U.S. occupation of the Dominican Republic and, later, Rafael Trujillo's U.S.-backed dictatorship are represented as ever-present shadows, as vectors of intimate violence, and as catalysts that shape the psyche and kinship and erotic practices of each woman. Obono's *La bastarda* is known as the first LGBTQ novel in the Equatoguinean literary corpus. Through the narrative of the protagonist Okomo, Obono elucidates how the coloniality of gender, including homophobia, within Fang communities leads to social, familial, and political exclusion.[18] Rather than a tragedy, however, Okomo, who is caught within matrices of desire, obligation, and conscription, ultimately chooses erotic freedom and queer communal living in the forests outside of her Fang community.

Each of these works demands that we witness something distinct about the intimacies of coloniality. For Ávila Laurel, *By Night the Mountains Burns* demands attending to power's reach, the decisions made from afar that impact an isolated community, and bearing witness to how political isolation begets illness, malnutrition, and a form of erotic violence that leaves an indelible mark on the social history of a place and its people. For Rosario, *Song of the Water Saints* acts as a balm and a spell and depicts Black femme erotic freedoms as linked to both the United States' military occupation of the Dominican Republic and later the dictatorship of Rafael Trujillo. The erotic practices and corporeal consciousness evoked by the novel's Afro-Dominican femme characters point to the emergence of liberatory spiritual connections across generations. Finally, Obono's *La bastarda* demands that we acknowledge the imperiled lives of women, girls, queer, and gender-nonconforming peoples in Equatorial Guinea, and that we bear witness to how erotic freedoms make possible corporeal liberation, even in spaces constrained by the coloniality of gender, including heteropatriarchy, misogyny, compulsory heterosexuality, homophobia, and other affective impossibilities. Overall, reading these texts in relation evinces the interconnections between racialized modes of intimacy, demonstrating that gender, sexuality, and women's corporeal and erotic practices are not private affairs, but sociopolitical matters that do not escape power structures.[19] Domination, in this case dictatorship, occupation, and the coloniality of gender, produces uncanny intimacies that articulate and perpetuate anti-Blackness under the heel of coloniality.

Living in the Dark

In *By Night the Mountain Burns* (2014), the English translation of Juan Tomás Ávila Laurel's novel *Arde el monte de noche* (2009), the protagonist muses that "to be in the dark is to turn your back on life" (184). In the original, *Arde el monte de noche*, Ávila Laurel writes, "En realidad vivir en la oscuridad es hacerlo de espaldas a la historia," which, when directly translated, evokes a sentiment of "living with one's back to *history*" (158). It is here that I would like to begin a close reading of Ávila Laurel's narrative of a tiny Atlantic Ocean island. I turn towards an analysis of what the novel offers us: intimate stories and small histories from below. *By Night the Mountain Burns* is a recounting of a childhood on the island of Annobón in Equatorial Guinea during the 1970s, a particularly calamitous era in the island's history. Throughout the novel, the narrator confides that he is tormented by the extreme darkness of the night, which is catalyzed by the absence of kerosene to fuel the lamps. As the story unfolds, we come to understand that the lack of kerosene and the all-encompassing darkness are related to larger structures of political indifference; the plunge into darkness is manufactured by a dictatorship that creates the conditions for isolation, desperation, and eventually death. For the narrator, this fear of the dark is matched only by his fear of the moonlight, which illuminates and emphasizes the contours of the unlit nights.[20] One can read this fear as evocative of the novel's arc: the (dark) catastrophe of isolation is destructive, yet shedding (moon)light on the collective actions of those living under such conditions is far more devastating.

In writing this novel, Ávila Laurel makes a purposeful turn away from replicating foundational narratives of colonial Hispanophone Africa, avoiding what could have easily been a pastoral. Instead, the author emphasizes the role of literature as history through a fictionalized retelling of his childhood on the island of Annobón. Thenesoya Vidina Martín de la Nuez argues that Ávila Laurel's writing represents a form wherein "ficción e historia se dan la mano . . . abriendo con ello una nueva etapa de la literatura guineoecuatoriana centrada en la re-creación de un mundo, de una realidad hasta ahora silenciada" ("fiction and history go hand in hand . . . thus opening a new stage of Equatoguinean literature centered on the re-creation of a world, of a reality hitherto silenced").[21] Annobón is an important locale in the colonial history of Equatorial Guinea, and a strategic point of departure through which to engage complex histories of overlapping colonization and dictatorship. The

Portuguese reached the island, originally thought to be inhabited by pygmies, in 1473 on New Year's Day (hence, it was named after the Portuguese phrase *ano bom*, meaning "good year"). They swiftly colonized it and brought primarily Angolan people to live and labor on the island. Annobón passed to Spain in 1778 through the Treaty of El Pardo, which also granted Spain control of parts of the Guinea coast and of the island of Fernando Po (now Bioko, the center of governmental power in current Equatorial Guinea).[22] Annobón's inhabitants are of Angolan descent, with very little evidence of Portuguese or Spanish intermixing (unlike other Equatoguinean islands such as Corisco or neighboring island nations like São Tome and Príncipe). Annobón's geographical location as the furthest island from the Equatoguinean mainland and its proximity to the Portuguese-speaking São Tome and Príncipe has facilitated the island's cultural and linguistic ties with Portugal. There was fierce opposition to Spanish rule in Annobón; though Spanish is the "official" language used for education, government, and administration, the population cleaves linguistically to a form of Portuguese creole, Falá d'Ambô, as the lingua franca.

We see this linguistic difference surface in the novel as the narrator recounts his disdain for the Spanish language and practices. His disidentification with Spanish, "a language that was not my own," is critical here, and shows the tense relationship between religion, linguistic practices, and colonial education (101). The realities of religious colonization and the ensuing cultural and ideological clashes are central themes in the novel. Thus, the historical and linguistic palimpsest that Ávila Laurel offers evokes a history of Annobón that is intimate, remote, and yet tied to larger arbitrary political and economic arrangements. Key to contextualizing Annobón is the long history of colonial religiosity, a Catholicism that is arguably an archaic sixteenth-century variety. This is echoed in the novel, as religious figures or "sacristanes" become part of a mysterious backdrop to the misery endured by the inhabitants of Annobón.[23]

The island of Annobón is of strategic importance to Equatorial Guinea because its ownership extends Equatoguinean maritime territory beyond the islands of São Tomé and Príncipe. As with their fierce rejection of Spanish colonization, the populace of Annobón spurned subsequent post-independence Equatoguinean dictatorships. This led to periodic isolation of the cruelest kind. For example, the cholera outbreak of 1976 decimated the island's population, but Macias Nguema refused international aid.[24] Furthermore, in 1993 Obiang expelled foreigners, including humanitarian organizations, and in doing so completely isolated the island. Ensuing revolts led to executions.[25] In this context, it is also important to note that there is evidence of large-scale dumping of toxic waste and ecological devastation on the island, which is the subject of some of the works by the Annobonese author Francisco Zamora Loboch.[26] Coloniality, as we see it represented in the Equatoguinean novel, is the product of a dual process of colonization and succeeding dictatorships. First, colonialism choked the nation's people and resources, hierarchized difference (colonial difference), and only allowed "advancement" by way of assimilation (a process accessible only to a small number of elites). Then, Macias Nguema's dictatorship rejected all vestiges of colonization in an attempt to recapture a sense of African authenticity. He eradicated all ties to Europe and the West while simultaneously engaging in social and political practices that violated Equatoguineans' human rights—especially those not of Fang descent and those who opposed the political silencing. The country's first dictator, Macias, and its second and current dictator, Obiang, reproduced colonialist and capitalist structures rooted in racism and dehumanization. Sociopolitical, geographic, and economic isolation limits the people's access to movement and educational and nutritional resources. There is severe suppression of oppositional political parties, no free press, and a strict policing of novels, books, and other materials critical of the Obiang regime. Coloniality in the political context of Equatorial Guinea helps us to map how dictatorship can be authored by the logics of colonialism and white supremacy, even in the absence of white bodies. We can thus understand dictatorship as a form of unfreedom that begets a domination that does not produce social death, but rather an intimacy that is both violent and violating.

However, *By Night the Mountain Burns* decenters the dictatorial regime and shifts to an examination of both ordinary and extraordinary everyday experiences on the island of Annobón. The sea and the collective are central to the narrative, and we read about a cooperative community that reaps benefits and suffers calamity together on a nearly forgotten island in the Atlantic Ocean. Ineke Phaf-Rheinberger argues that "Annobón is indissolubly linked to the sea; it is the storehouse and carrier of spiritual power and the information medium," and these ties to the sea are underscored throughout the novel.[27] The terrors that strike Annobón in the novel come in quick succession: the theft of fish by commercial fishing vessels, a devastating fire that ruins the community's primary crops, an outbreak of cholera that kills hundreds, the public communal murder and sodomy of a woman suspected of invoking an elder's death, the disappearance and hauntological arrival of seven fishermen, and the death of an infant from the exploitative conditions created by the dictatorship's neglect and greed. Recounted by the eyes of an unnamed child, *By Night the Mountain Burns* is a fictionalized intimate history of what happens to a community at the shores of indifference.

This story of survival and seeking an existence while lacking the most basic necessities in one of the richest nations on the African continent documents how the lives and histories of Annobón's inhabitants seem to matter only to themselves. The feeling of the collective opens the novel, as the first lines are lyrics from a traditional call-and-response song, sung as the entire community collaborates in the creation of a new canoe. The trees felled for the canoe belong to the women in the community; they are the owners and stewards of the lands and plantations. Any man who will dedicate his life to fishing, the subsistence economy, must ask permission from a woman to fell a tree from her land. He must then enlist other community members to help drag the tree to the shore in order to carve it into a canoe. A rite of passage, the creation of a new canoe, entails laborious efforts, a "simple but meaningful song" that urges collective work, a celebration marked by the sharing of root vegetable soup prepared by groups of women (8). The collective also closes the novel, as again the community gathers together to build another canoe, comfort an injured mother, and bury an infant who was not thought to be hearty enough for life in the tropics. The survival of the collective in the face of isolation is the crux of the narrative, and each story that Ávila Laurel recounts is contingent on many people, voices, and perspectives. This palimpsest of stories is also a reflection of the history of Annobón.

Because fishing is the major subsistence industry of Annobón, the narrator emphasizes the importance of fishing in his explanation of the island's physical and social geography: "I should mention that the island is African and that the people who live on the island are black, every last one of them. And that it's surrounded by the Atlantic Ocean. Totally surrounded. The black people I speak of live on a sliver of land that pokes out of the murky waters" (8). The narrator repeatedly tells the reader that "on our Atlantic Ocean island, if you didn't fish, or get fish to eat, you didn't eat" (35). Thus, when the dictator of the nation-state leases out Annobón's famously abundant seas to be plundered by outsiders, the island's inhabitants are thrust into the throes of hunger. In the novel, Annobón is intimately impacted by this deal between two governmental powers that lie far from those directly affected. As sailors in giant ships ransack the fish around the island, Annobonese fishermen row in their canoes to protest and bargain for fish and goods. The men frequently fail in their quest for fish and basic necessities, and more often than not return instead with liquor and cigarettes. Soon the fishermen begin to paddle towards any "little stick on the thin line of the horizon" in order to chase down ships and demand fish for their village (275). This becomes a common practice that culminates in tragedy near the end of the novel, as eight fishermen launch out to sea and paddle towards what they think is a ship. When only one returns, the village of San Xuan mourns their loss, for the impact of the seven fishermen's disappearance is felt in the lives and livelihoods of those left grieving them. Their deaths illustrate the direct and indirect impact of outsourcing Annobón's fishing waters. We also learn that their deaths are foreshadowed by a woman named Sabina when she is followed by a group of men who "smelled strongly of sea water" (255). These apparitions are men from the village that eerily trail her to her plantation. Sabina declares that these men were "deads . . . telling her to warn everyone that something bad was going to happen on the island" (256). Their forewarning of the eventual disappearance of the seven men at sea makes the narrator question the "deads" themselves, for "what is the point of the deads" if they could not "prevent the catastrophe from happening?" (261). In asking this question, the narrator turns the cosmology of ancestral veneration and spiritual guidance on its head. This complicates a question posed by the scholar and critic Tamara Butler, who asks, "What do we owe the dead?"[28] Instead, the novel's narrator demands to know what the deads owe to the living. We can see how the intimacies of coloniality, and in particular a dictatorship imposing power from afar, impact the food security, safety, and livelihoods and likewise affect the very lives, beliefs, and practices of those on the island.

As the constant pillaging of the seas sinks the island further into hunger, a famine takes hold, exacerbated by an accidental fire caused by two sisters that ravages the plantations and decimates the crops alongside the mountain. Ávila Laurel depicts a palpable famine and underscores how the women of Annobón are those most exposed to the direct and indirect impacts of the intimacies of dictatorship. For example, the sailors on the big ships begin to offer better goods in exchange for access to young women from Annobón. These women, knowing that simple items like kerosene for light, matches for fires, soap for bathing, and clothing for wear are critical everyday needs, sacrifice their bodies to the ships that have been contracted to steal the fish from their island's waters. The abuse and rape of these women becomes invisible and normalized, and the product of these exploitative intimate relations comes to a tragic end in the last parts of the novel.

The experience of women under forms of colonial and postcolonial domination is a central theme in the work of Ávila Laurel. His first novel, *La carga*, critiques the oppression of the colonized and the precarious position of Equatoguinean women; in particular the burden of carrying unwanted pregnancies by white men.[29] The last part of *By Night the Mountain Burns* concerns the pregnancy of one of the sisters who caused the fire. These sisters are orphans tasked with farming their plantation, and one of them gives birth to a baby boy fathered by a sailor from one of the international ships. Her desolation in the wake of the death of her "white" baby, who is supposedly not physiologically able to withstand the tropics, is one of the final tragedies of the novel. While the child was most likely undernourished due to his mother's lack of access to food, the community is convinced that the whiteness of the child led to his death. The narrator considers: "The sickness could have been caused by any number of things: a hard life, the sun, mosquitoes, the fact that the child's mother had no one in the world but a sister. What's more, the child was white and I don't think white people are born to lead such hard lives" (247). In the process of procuring medicine for her child, the mother is caught in a collective event: the creation of a new canoe. The mother joins the community because, as the narrator tells us, "there are lots of things you do collectively on our island," and "she didn't like to ignore customs, nor did she think it necessary to do so now" even as her child was on the brink of death (244, 249).

Later, it is revealed that while the woman "pulled the half-built canoe," the child "was already dead" (249). What the community mistook for sweat on her face was actually "tears of hurt, for her terrible misfortune" (249). That evening, when she finally boards a canoe to a large village with her godfather and her dead infant, the canoeman is puzzled by the boat's weight and the slowness of what is usually a quick journey to the larger village. The narrator confides that the mother and godfather indeed knew "what was obstructing them, what made him feel as though his hands were tied . . . for the fact of the matter was there was a dead person aboard the canoe. And it was no ordinary thing to transport a dead person. . . . Everybody knew the deads weighed more than alives" (249). The narrator offers us a moment to consider the intimacy of the rower carrying the dead and the weight of transporting a mourning mother, a lifeless child, and a knowing godfather.

The outbreak of cholera is another calamity in the novel. The lack of access to basic medical care and the general malaise and malnutrition exacerbate the effects of the disease. The narrator laments: "Nobody ate, either because there was nothing to eat or because everything tasted bitter from the tears that ran down everyone's face in furrows from their eyes. It was a terrible time, truly the worst time in the history of the island" (111). The narrator tracks the deaths of over 150 women, men, and children in the community. The text marks these deaths by recounting the ceremonial proceedings, but also by marking the dead with the symbol of a cross:

This paratextual image is likewise a haptic element, forcing the reader to both read, feel, and witness the sites of the cemetery. Tina Campt defines the haptic as "multiple forms of touch which . . . create alternative modalities for understanding the archival temporalities of images."[30] The crosses are symbols that allow us to track what has heretofore gone unregistered in the historical record: the tragic deaths of hundreds of people on an African Atlantic island, and the callous intimacy of those losses. One hundred fifty-two crosses cut across the page as the narrator tells us of the continual death assailing the residents of the small island. "Some crosses," he continues, "were accompanied by the handwriting done by those who knew how to write" (111). The narrator then calls out those whose names appear on the crosses, compelling the reader to name in silence or aloud the lives torn from Annobón during the cholera outbreak:

> Mené Jachiga, Mamentu Lavna, Pudu Kenente, Maguntín Jambab'u, Toiñ Yaya, Pudu Toñia, Madalam'u Tómene, Pudu Gadjin's, Masamentu Áveve, Jodán Tómbôbô, Majosán Ánjala Pet'u, Fidel Tompet'u, Madosel Menfoi, Chit'e Zete Doix, Nando Guesa Ngaiñ, Mápudu Chipa Longo, Saan'e Sámene, Xancus'u Menenov,

> Menembo Jalafund'u, Ximá Dancut and his three sons; Manel'a Vepanu, Saana Tábôbô, Mafidel Ménkichi, Mené Ze Palm'a, Pilinguitu Menfoi, Masantu Jadôl'o, Magutín Bichil, Menembofi Dadot, Santo Sadot, Mafidel Dadot, Másamentu Fadoliga, Mal'e Púluv, Menesamentu Guesangaiñ, Fidel Dadalán, Zetoiñ Padjil, Mafide'l Padjil, Yahií Padjil, Ndeza Liguilía, Rosal Tombal'b, Nando Lem'u Bass'u, Tusantu Dosal'u, Màmentu Jonofund'u, Majosán Zanja Gôôd'ô, Chigol Zampet'u, Mal'e Bojô Longô, Gutín Pendê Mozso, Chiit'e Masamentu, Joodán Pendê, Mangutín Pendé, Ximé Jambuk'ú, Doszal Sámpete, Fiip'a Tonchiip'a, Gutín Tonfiip'a, Madozee Menfoi, Majolé Ntelacul, Menembô, Fídiligu'I, Gutín Lamabas'u, Jodán Menpix'i, Yahií Jázuga, Pudul Legaváan, Madalam'u Maapendê, Toiñ Babadjí'an, Mené Jandija, Mápudu'l Jandjía, Madalam'u Awacul'u, Quilit'u Menedoix, Menembofi Japiz'a, Fidel Sana Jodán, Tayayô Meendjing'u, Nguzal'u Tómene, Mámentu Chipafend'e, Szebel'u Teszalicu, Ndêêsa Jonoxinc'u, Jodán Chiipagaiñ, Menembofi Límapeet'u. All were lowered into the ground to the *Padre's* Latin. (111–12)

The seventy-five names plus the three nameless sons represent some of the adults who died as a result of the cholera outbreak. The names of children do not appear, and the narrator recalls the "thick and fast" deaths that led to hasty burials without funerals, crosses, or names. While these are not the actual names of the people who died during the cholera outbreak, these fictionalized names represent the real deaths that occurred on Annobón during this tragic time. According to the author, these names should be taken as a reflection of history itself. The fact that the names are fictionalized "no altera ninguna realidad, porque otros nombres reales hubo" ("does not alter any reality, because there were other real names").[31] What Ávila Laurel offers us through his use of symbols (crosses) as paratext, followed by a practice of naming, is the possibility of experiencing haptic alterity. We are forced to reckon with the intimacy of naming the dead, the tactility of touching the page, the feeling of the names moving through our mouths, the sounds of new naming arrangements spilling across the page.[32] We also see and feel the dissonance of these names and these bodies being lowered into the ground in the "*Padre's* Latin," a language peripheral to the people themselves. In reading the names, the author demands that we create space for the lives of those who died and accompany Annobón in its historical grief.[33] Saying the names of the dead and recalling the countless unnamed dead are part of a remembrance ritual that the novel labors to produce.[34] Readers cannot turn their backs on this death or on the intimacies of these histories of violence and death on Ávila Laurel's Atlantic Ocean island. We can also think about this in relation to contemporary Black political movements such as #SayHerName and #BlackLivesMatter which underscore the value of Black life, the impact of Black death, and the need to call forth the names of those who have been murdered by state-sanctioned, extralegal, and intimate violence. Memory, remembrance, and rememory are produced and reproduced as acts of resistance through these naming practices, which traverse the Atlantic and cross temporal and spatial dimensions.

Most traumatizing to the narrator is the public beating and killing of the woman accused of causing the death of a spiritual elder. This scene is recounted over and again in the narrative. Early in the novel, as the narrator offers an overview of the island, he notes that there are certain littoral practices that are viewed as natural and others that are viewed as vile:

> Apart from [catching crabs or relieving one's belly], there were some people who went to the beach at night to commit a shameful act and they would have fingers pointed at them the next day and be called wicked. . . . These people were always women, usually older women, and when it started to be said that a particular woman went by herself to the beach at night, our grandmother would tell us never to walk past the door of her house, for that woman had acquired the ability to send objects into any child that went naked before her. (20–21)

This early context foreshadows the violent attack, death, and intimate violation of the woman for having practiced a form of corporeal freedom—bathing in the sea at night. The narrator explains that the woman was a she-devil and "when everyone else slept in their beds at night, she started to feel suffocating heats, she took off her clothes, opened the door to her house and ran down to the beach to bathe in the sea" (147). In this context, the intimate practice of bathing one's body in littoral spaces, albeit alone, is considered an affront to communal standards. This practice, thinly veiled as unorthodox erotic behavior, was shrouded in potential witchcraft, thus transforming the night travels of these women into unthinkable evil habits. We can read the woman's bathing as a sign of her wickedness, as a side effect of possible menopause, or as a practice of freedom that removes the yoke of intimate domination on an isolated island crushed by hunger, death, and dictatorship.

The traumatizing scene in which the woman is pulled from her home and chased to the church, violated with a stick, and beaten to death—all in public view—is a breaking point for the narrator (140–53). This communal act of violence is continually revisited throughout the novel. The narrator understands the act as a form of intimate violence at the hands of the community, which neither the woman nor her husband or children could prevent. Furthermore, with the final egregious action of penetrating her sex organs with a stick, the intimate nature of this violence becomes a violating erotic act. "Looking back," the narrator says, "I see or understand that the incident and the cholera were part of the same sickness. And the cure of that sickness was beyond the reach of our adults, for it was a sickness that was greater than them and so it was able to dominate them" (116). He then situates the violent event in geographical as well as affective terms: "And on that island out in the middle of the Atlantic Ocean, nasty episodes unfortunately had to be explained somehow; something had to satisfy people's need for a cause. Living so far away from everything else gave us a particular way of feeling. Of seeing or thinking" (116). The reader thus witnesses the woman's murder as a collective action fueled by isolation, suspicion, and shared suffering. Each time the narrator retells the story of this woman's murder he poses rhetorical questions about the inaction of the community, implicating all of the island's inhabitants.[35] And yet, as Marvin Lewis notes, in Ávila Laurel's work there is an alternate "worldview at work by which the population uses internal cultural beliefs to make a challenging existence more bearable and more meaningful."[36] The intimate relationships between the collective are complicated as both communal acts of good or complicit acts against good.

The novel ends with a depiction of the rower who ferried the grieving mother—the narrator imagines him going out to fish in the sea. The narrator fears for the rower's life, knowing that if the fisherman sees a stick on the horizon (a possible ship), he will paddle towards its light and conceivably perish like the men who disappeared. Yet, however enticing and dangerous that potential light on the horizon may be, it is the dark that circumscribes Ávila Laurel's carefully constructed novel. *By Night the Mountain Burns* is a text produced on the underside of foundational colonial and dictatorial history. Phaf-Rheinberger argues that the narrative's long form and constant repetition of these stories are ways of painting the "picture of the island's monotonous quotidian routine," and that "Avila Laurel structures his novel as one long narrative without division into chapters . . . constantly repeating the same issues, such as hunger, lack of sanitary conditions, and the absence of the men," which "gradually [give] more insight into the dynamics on the island's society."[37] Ávila Laurel's snippet of Annobón's history is stitched against the grain of coloniality and postcolonial dictatorship and violence. In the final pages of the novel, the narrator indicts the reader's ignorance of the intimate impact of these histories and denounces history itself, noting, "If this story becomes known it will be because of some white people" (270). The novel is revealed to be a collection of the narrator's childhood memories for an oral history project of white researchers, which suggests a deeper indictment of the academy and scholarly research as a form of colonial knowledge accumulation. The narrator ventures to guess that the novel's readers do not know anything about Annobón and as such, we too live in the dark with our "backs turned to history." Ávila Laurel's work and much of the Equatoguinean tradition demonstrate that history and chronology won't save us, especially if that history is disciplined and constructed to elide, minimize, or reduce our histories to footnotes in the foundational myths of modernity. Listening to and reading these counter-narratives with a decolonial attitude is of vital importance. The decolonial attitude, as Nelson Maldonado-Torres argues, is a subjective disposition towards knowledge beyond the ethics of war and towards an ethical position that validates the experiences of those who are deemed insignificant. In her work on intimacies in colonial and imperial contexts, Ann Laura Stoler argues that "to study the intimate is not to turn away from structures of dominance, but to relocate their conditions of possibility and relations and forces of production."[38] While this chapter is specifically attuned to forms of coloniality in postcolonial and dictatorial contexts, Stoler's perspective is pertinent—the intimate allows us to bear witness to the machinations of power, both structural and interpersonal, in new ways that shift relations of power. Ávila Laurel makes clear that the intimate chronicles of a small Atlantic Ocean island, the stories of Annobón and its people, are Black histories, Atlantic histories, which chronicle the impacts of the intimacies of coloniality.

Lucías

"Todo el mundo sabe que lo peor que hay en el mundo es una mujer lucía."[39] So begins Mayra Santos-Febres's *Sobre piel y papel*, a collection of feminist essays on the condition of Afro-Puerto Rican women, with sections on the labia (erotic), the skin (race), and paper (writing). And because everyone knows that the worst thing to be in the world is a showy woman, a rebellious woman, a nonconforming woman, a queer woman, a promiscuous woman, a fighting woman, a woman undedicated to the domestic—in short, a "lucía"—I use Santos Febres's words as a point of departure in my meditation on the intimacies of occupation and dictatorship in Nelly Rosario's debut novel, *Song of the Water Saints* (2002). Many of the women and girls in the novel represent different dimensions of lucías who tap into the erotic, and use their deepest knowledge as rebellion against domination. As Donette Francis has argued, Caribbean women's literature is an apt site through which we can unpack the "archives of intimacy," through which women's corporeal desires and epistemologies challenge imperial, patriarchal, and misogynistic histories of the Caribbean and its diasporas.[40]

Graciela, the protagonist in *Song of the Water Saints*, is a hungry and free-willed Afro-Dominican woman, "born with the hot leg" like her "maroon grandpai," but born under a different set of oppressions. Graciela's narrative, anchored in the aftermath of the transatlantic slave trade, begins in 1916 at the advent of the United States' military occupation of the Dominican Republic (1916–24). This occupation, the subsequent U.S.-backed dictatorship of Rafael Trujillo (1930–61), and her progeny's thrust into diaspora in 1987 become the palimpsestic backdrop to the novel. Rosario traces the lives of four generations of women and girls in the Dominican Republic and New York, beginning with Graciela. She is a woman who finds no satisfaction in the suffocating life under U.S. occupation. As Mónica Ayuso argues, Graciela is an "'unlettered,' restless black woman whose life is enmeshed in the U.S. presence on the Dominican Republic."[41] Graciela's daughter Mercedes (b. ca. 1918–19), traumatized by her mother's absence, cleaves to God and country while Mercedes's own daughter Amalfi (b. 1961), rebellious and independent, becomes a single mother to Leila (b. ca. 1984) who, having inherited the spirit of her great-grandmother Graciela, comes of age in New York during the 1990s.

In Rosario's work, we see how the intimacies of coloniality, entrenched through occupation and later dictatorship, engender a rage and resistance that propel erotic freedom and corporeal consciousness among Afro-femme subjects on another Atlantic Ocean island. In *Borders of Dominicanidad*, Lorgia García-Peña argues that Dominican novels written in diaspora are "textos montados," or "possessed texts," which offer the "possibility of finding a more complete version of the truth through the embodied memory of silenced histories." Following García-Peña's proposition that "when a land is occupied, so are its inhabitants," I argue that Graciela's quest for erotic and corporeal freedom is rooted over and against the colonial and postcolonial imperial projects of occupation that seek to stifle the lives, imaginations, and possibilities of Afro-Indigenous peoples in general, and women, girls, and femmes in particular.[42] While Rebeca Hey-Colón argues that Graciela's "yearning for freedom clashes violently with her social, economic, and gendered reality," Mimi Sheller contends that "practices of embodied freedom continue to inform the contemporary national, racial, and sexual geographies that arose out of post-slavery transitions in state power."[43] As such, tracing the corporeal consciousness and the Black femme freedom practices of this novel offers us an opportunity to see the intimate impact of colonial and imperial powers as they affect the lives of those most vulnerable to the whims of their dictates. In doing so, we also bear witness to how their forms of fugitivity and resistance map out possibilities for liberation.

Because the novel traverses histories of occupation and the dictatorship of Rafael Trujillo, it is important to note the dovetailing of powers that stifle the possibilities of corporeal liberation for women. Dixa Ramírez's *Colonial Phantoms* elegantly surveys the impact of nationalism and resistance on the bodies of women, noting that "Trujillo entered the homes of all of his constituents both literally with his person and figuratively through his government officials and spies."[44] I contend that Trujillo and the United States' occupation that preceded him also produced fear and domination over the intimate lives and imaginaries of Dominican subjects. In spite of this, Rosario weaves a narrative wherein Black femme freedom creates imperfect sites of possibility and liberation, but at a cost.

The opening scene of the novel portrays fourteen-year-old Graciela with her fifteen-year-old lover Silvio, convinced by the promise of pesos to pose for an erotic photograph that will become a postcard displaying Dominicans' exotic and animalistic sexuality to Western consumers. Victoria Chevalier reads this ekphrasis, or the narrative description of the postcard as artifact and image, as concomitant with the colonial imperial gaze. According to Chevalier, this scene links "the imperial gaze represented by West's photography to the physical and cultural violence that the U.S. military occupation enacts upon the Dominican Republic," which "reinforces the relation between vision and empire so thoroughly apparent in the photograph-postcard the audience encounters in the margins of the novel."[45] The photographer, Peter West, leads Graciela and Silvio to a warehouse where he "kneaded their bodies," forcing them to mimic his hapless erotic gestures and covering them in mud (10–11). After wrapping his fingers around Silvio's penis and wedging his thumb "into the humid mound between Graciela's thighs," Peter West tosses pesos at Silvio. Silvio attempts to destroy the camera equipment and hoards the money, refusing to give Graciela her share. Despite Silvio's attempt to destroy the camera, the couple is "immortalized" as primitive, hypersexual, and exotic objects of desire in a photograph that becomes a widely circulated postcard (12). Citing Suzanne Stewart, Chevalier discusses the postcard as a way to track the "intimacy of distance," a transaction of exotic locales when "sent from one person to another."[46] Omaris Z. Zamora argues that this encounter with Peter West violates Graciela's erotic agency and is cause "for the dispiriting violence that creates a transient subjectivity in search of re-establishing its own power."[47] In turn, I contend that at this tender age Graciela develops a differential corporeal consciousness—one that puts erotic desire, corporeal knowledge, and an unquenchable lust for liberation at the forefront of her personhood. If, as Audre Lorde argues, "the erotic is the nurturer or nursemaid of all our deepest knowledge," then Graciela's erotic knowledge leads her to engage in Black femme freedom practices throughout the short span of her life.[48] Indeed, her dissatisfaction with the violence, fear, and suffocation of the United States' occupation leads her to tap into dimensions of liberation provided by erotic practices and the eschewing of domesticity and deference.

Graciela comes face-to-face with the barbaric arc of the United States' military occupation in the form of a singular and foundational violence. On her way out of the market, she is stopped by a "swan woman" holding linens atop her head, who warns Graciela that her mother is waiting for her to return home and to be careful with the yanqui-men on the road:

> Tall uniformed men in hats shaped like gumdrops sat on the roadside. Graciela squatted in the dense grass to see how the fearless swan woman would move safely past them. The yanqui-men's rifles and giant bodies confirmed stories that had already filtered into the city from the eastern mountains: suspected gavillero rebels gutted like Christmas piglets; women left spread-eagled right before their fathers and husbands; children with eardrums drilled by bullets. Graciela had folded these stories into the back of her memory when she snuck about the city outskirts with Silvio. The yanqui-man in the warehouse

> seemed frail now, his black box and clammy hands no match for the long rifles aimed at the swan woman. "Run, you Negro wench!" The soldier's shout was high pitched and was followed by a chorus of whistles. A pop resounded. Through the blades of grass, Graciela could see the white bundle continue down the road in a steady path. The woman held her head high as if the bundle could stretch her above the hats. Another pop and Graciela saw the woman drop to the ground. Some already had their shirts pulled out of their pants. (14–15)

Francis argues that this scene "[juxtaposes] how military occupation instills a pervasive sense of fear in the daily life of the city's inhabitants."[49] Graciela's witnessing of the woman's brutal attack, perhaps her murder, and the systematic rape of her mortally wounded body is followed by her encounter with yet another group of yanqui-men and their interpreter in her home; they are torturing her mother in front of her younger brother, Fausto. Indeed, someone directed the soldiers to search the home for weapons, and Graciela walks into the sight of "Mai knelt by a soldier whose fists entangled in her hair and had undone the cloth rollers" (14). The kneeling position in this passage alongside the soldier's fist entangled in Mai's hair produces a psychosexual scene reminiscent of forcible fellatio. This moment of terror and the juxtaposition of the knees and fists alongside the mundane sight of undone cloth rollers underscore how these forms of gender violence and political torture easily fall into historical erasure. The interpreter then turns his attention to Graciela, shoving her against the cold hearth and jamming his fingers into her face. Only when she offers to tell the troops where her father keeps his secret stash of cane rum do the soldiers stand down—but not before exhibiting their power over peasant citizens like Graciela and her family. Occupation is indeed an intimate affair, and the soldier who shoved Graciela against the hearth leaves only after one more act of violence. He "clamped Graciela's nose and held it until there was blood, which he wiped against her blouse. Now you've got my aquiline nose, he said, then sucked the rest of her blood from his fingers," after which he and the other soldiers "rinsed their hands in the family's barrel of fresh rainwater" (15). Here we witness two violent practices that bear on the intimate lives of others. First, the clamping of Graciela's nose, a form of racial disciplining, resonates as a diasporic echo—one that is part of white supremacist discourses that seek to shape and police the phenotypes and features of non-white peoples. This brief moment of violence as racial disciplining has diasporic reverberations, an experience that traverses the Black Atlantic and its descendants—here we not only see the intimacies of coloniality, but also the intimacies of colonial Blackness as part of imperial efforts to discipline, punish, and police Black peoples, Black bodies, and Black life. Second is the haptic alteration of intimate space, the rinsing of bloodied hands in the drinking water of the family, which effectively contaminates what is to be consumed. Following Campt, a close reading of these scenes allows us to see the relationship between the "quiet, the quotidian, and the everyday practices of refusal enacted and inherited by dispossessed subjects."[50]

In this scene and throughout the novel, Rosario employs the word "hearth" to refer to the kitchen, cooking quarters, or the centermost part of the home, thus highlighting the intimacy of such spaces where families gather to cook, sustain their bodies, and share in the products of their labor. These interstitial spaces, the intimacies of the carnal, the domestic, and the everyday, are stitched together to accentuate the always violent presence of occupation. Indeed, Stoler asks us to consider the intimate nature of such domination: "On what grounds has 'intimacy' become shorthand for domestic relations, affections, child care, and sex but used less often to refer . . . to other forms of bodily exposure . . . that open to embodied and affective injuries of a different intensity . . . ?"[51] Rather than geographical or spatial military directives, this scene and those like it allow us to see the United States' occupation of the Dominican Republic through its impact on the bodies and intimate lives of Black women and femmes.

In one afternoon, Graciela is digitally penetrated by a yanqui photographer who aspires to create erotic postcards of exotic and lustful Dominican couples; witnesses the possible murder and rape of a neighbor; and confronts yanqui-men in the hearth of her home violating her mother. In fact, Francis argues that Rosario "links sexual invasion as a constitutive part of the military project, which then extends to the formation of a sexual self."[52] Rather than terror, Graciela realizes that the "overeager display of barbarism" fuels in her "more anger than fear" (15). This anger against occupation and domination is the anchor with which Graciela steadies herself throughout the novel. In García-Peña's reading, Rosario allows the reader to bear witness to the "silenced histories of violence against black women during the occupation through the occupied female body."[53] We see the intimacies of colonial Blackness and the direct impacts of these scenes in the hearth of the home and the violence upon the bodies of Black women and girls throughout Graciela's life trajectory. Rather than becoming a God-fearing housewife and dutiful mother, Graciela eschews all ideologies of domesticity and femininity, rejecting reproductive labor in search of fulfilling her own yearnings. Her abandonment of domestic duties leads neighbors to joke that Graciela's hearth is "colder than a witch's breath" (22). Zamora contends that "Graciela defies all parts of this 'womanhood' and turns it on its head: never grounded in her 'home' duties, never truly a consumer, but not a provider either."[54] Suffering hunger and pangs of abandonment after Silvio accepts a job fishing at sea for months at a time, Graciela takes to her hammock and imagines herself in the "cirrus ships in the sky," remembering that even as a child she had wanted to "ride ships" (24–25). Rather than being bound by her sex, station, and race, Graciela's subjectivity is defined by her unwavering desire to be free, to travel, and to be intimately fulfilled.

Graciela's imagination and desire to escape can be seen in the stories her parents' friends tell about her childhood, and particularly in Graciela's memories of seeing a globe in a convent at the age of four (46, 25–28). As a child in the convent, Graciela understands herself for the first time as "a speck rising from the globe's surface" (26). She asks, "How much bigger could the world be when the head of a tiny animal was her whole world?" (27). In an interview, Rosario notes that mapping is central to *Song of the Water Saints*, and this scene is especially meaningful. It is in this moment that "Graciela looks at the globe and starts trying to figure out the proportion of her life to the rest of the world." Rosario argues that this is a "shocking revelation when you realize your entire universe is a speck; it's mapped as a speck somewhere. And it makes you question what the size of your domain is. What is the size of you?"[55] The freedoms that Graciela takes in the face of the intimacies of colonial Blackness manifest as a desire to escape and to live a bigger life, freedoms that are deemed impossible given the terms under which she lives as a woman, widow, and mother.

Throughout the course of the novel, Graciela abandons her home—a form of petit marronage that Neil Roberts defines as "individual fugitive acts of truancy."[56] When she escapes from her suffocating life, she leaves her daughter to be cared for by her nonchalant lover, Casimiro. After Graciela absconds, she first takes another lover, Eli, a European man from "Germany-france" who was drawn to the island by erotic photographs of its exotic beauties (64–65). Eli brings Graciela to a brothel, orders her a bath with lavender and herbs, and it is understood that their sexual interaction infects her with syphilis. While Graciela tries to "own some of the pleasure," she later realizes that "men were no more free, for all their mobility," and she considers the ridiculousness of having "expected Silvio, Casimiro, or even the fool beside her to hand her a world that was not theirs to give" (79–80). Chevalier argues that "Eli and Graciela are mutually desirous of experience; one has the gendered, racial, social privilege, and capital to acquire racialized sexual pleasure, the other is bound to the island, despite her attempts to explore her own world."[57] It is precisely because Graciela yearns for erotic freedom and for liberation from the intimacies of occupation that she tries and fails to find satisfaction in sexual encounters with Eli and, later, with other men in her community. Lorde argues that the "erotic is a measure between the beginnings of our sense of self and the chaos of our strongest feelings," and that "it is an internal sense of satisfaction to which, once we have experienced it, we know we can aspire"; over and over again throughout the novel Graciela attempts to achieve the erotic freedom that would allow her to live bigger than what is possible for poor Black women and femmes in the Dominican Republic under the U.S. occupation.[58]

After escaping the brothel, Graciela takes a job as a domestic servant for an elite Dominican family, where she learns about the racial and domestic insecurities of the island's upper class. She eventually flees their home after being accused by the wife of sleeping with her husband and being threatened by the husband after he suspects that she has stolen his watch. Her final journey is to a convent, a return to the space where she first laid eyes on a globe, a moment that revealed her place in the world. She confides in a nun, Sol Elisa, that she had "waited on a long line to get born. Pushed the weaker souls aside," underscoring her prescience and absolute impatience for living (151). Graciela begins to feel the symptoms of late-stage syphilis, including feverish visions of an approaching military man who transforms into a demon—premonitions of Trujillo's impending dictatorship (171). She also has vivid dreams, a rememory of enslavement, marronage, and furtive freedoms:

> In one, rats chewed at the calluses of Graciela's heels. She tore through dense forest, her heels further ripping on thorns and exposed tree roots. Fear of rats, then of running guardias, then of slave-hunters with dogs. Above her the sky was India ink, punctured by a bright white crack of light. Graciela came upon a mammoth coral reef flanked by coconut trees. The cluster of coral came together to form a pair of lips, from which came a heartbeat. She climbed the coral and slid deep into the cave's center. (152–53)

This scene, which flashes back to territorial escape and terror, culminates in the discovery of a safe cluster of coral near the sea, depicted in sensual detail as having "two lips" and a "heartbeat." Graciela slips "deep" into the center of the cave, calling forth images of entering a woman's body and underscoring histories of femme freedom practices while also conjuring her ancestral connection to fugitivity and marronage practices; recalling her maroon grandpai.

This is by no means the only scene in the book that evokes histories of enslavement. For example, in an early scene, Graciela spits and curses, "¡Thief!" into the sea after one of Silvio's many departures: "She spat her bitterness into the water . . . whose depths contained jewelry unhooked from the wrists of the wealthy, whole bodies of metal sea animals with fractured waists, and hundreds of ball-and-chained bodies trapped in white coral" (31). Here Rosario intimately ties together the complex histories of the transatlantic slave trade: the riches gained by exploitation, the ships lost at sea, and most devastating, the innumerable bodies trapped in the depths below. Thus, Rosario's novel engages in what Édouard Glissant calls the poetics of relation. For Glissant, literary poetics become a technology that bears witness to the terrors that our ancestors withstood. They are an aesthetic way to approximate the unknown that we live and share as Afro-descendants in the matrix of modernity. Rosario weaves these histories into the fabric of the everyday and exceptional lives of Dominican women and girls. Important to note is her use of punctuation in this scene and throughout the novel, which troubles the divide between English and Spanish language practices by including inverted exclamation points and question marks. The effect is subtle, but a careful reader will note what Frances Aparicio calls a "subversive signifier" that "tropicalizes" the English language of the text.[59]

Graciela's search for freedom leads her to danger and eventually to death as a result of syphilis. As Zamora argues, "Graciela's subjectivity as an individual is one formed by her incessant 'search' for the intimacy and adventure that will fulfill her."[60] Rosario depicts Graciela dying with "a map of the world on her face," which Eliana Castro argues is a "(trans)figurative and disfiguring record of her tribulations."[61] Yet, while her excesses are radically rejected by her daughter Mercedes, they are later seen in the tempestuous decisions made by her granddaughter Amalfi, and are most broadly reflected in the patterns of behavior embodied by her great-granddaughter, Leila. The erotic and corporeal freedoms that Graciela asserts are the same desires that her daughter Mercedes attempts to suppress. Mercedes's rejection of Graciela's reckless abandon and desire for freedoms heretofore denied to women and girls, especially Afro-descended peasants, causes Mercedes to cleave to domesticity and religiosity for safe harbor. Graciela's syphilitic death ensures that Mercedes rejects her mother's spirit of freedom. However, Mercedes does not lack but rather restrains her desire for intimate and corporeal freedom as a way to show her reverence for her Christian God. In one scene, Mercedes confides, "Young as she was, she suffered plenty for Him. Suppressed her natural urges, like bathing in the rain, in a thunderstorm, where she was born, kept her hair from flying loose about her face the way she wanted. Tried not to let the new attention from men put a tremble on her lips. But those simple desires required hard bargaining with Him" (162). This refusal to give in to her urges is likewise tied to her fantasy of being a descendant of "royal white blood," a story she conjured by revering a stolen wedding photograph of an elite handsome couple from her mother's stint as a domestic worker.[62]

Tracking Mercedes's rampant anti-Haitianismo is important within the context of tracing the intimacies of colonial Blackness. In her 2010 thesis "'A Border Is a Veil Not Many People Can Wear,'" Megan Adams offers a generous and critical reading of Mercedes's deep-seated antagonism against and outright bloodthirst for Haitians and Dominicans of Haitian descent.[63] Mercedes bears witness to the infamous "Parsley Massacre" of 1937 in which "drunken Dominican soldiers, on orders from Trujillo, took their machetes and built a dam of human bodies in the western Dajabón River" (181). This death sentence was predicated on the subjects' ability to pronounce the rolling consonant *r* in the word *perejil* (parsley), leading to the deaths of thousands of Haitians, Dominicans, and Dominicans of Haitian descent. As Ayuso has argued, the infamous Parsley Massacre has become a symbol of "the atrocities of the Trujillo years."[64] Mercedes's fear morphs into a smart-tongued disidentification with Blackness and staunch support for Trujillo's dictatorship. Her modest kiosk has not one, but two portraits of "El Generalisimo Doctor Rafael Leónidas Trujillo Molina, Benefactor de la Patria y Padre de la Patria Nueva" (187). I contend that paying close attention to these scenes allows us to see how the racialized and gendered machinations of the intimacies of coloniality impact racial and ethnic relations in the Dominican Republic.

Furthermore, *Song of the Water Saints* allows us to trace the love and resentment between mothers and daughters as a form of intimacy across four generations. Just as Mercedes resented Graciela for leaving, so too does Leila resent her mother Amalfi for choosing to stay in the Dominican Republic, even as the entire family migrated to New York in the 1980s. Leila's exploration of her sexuality and her desire for corporeal and erotic freedom at the age of fourteen become the focus of the final arc of the novel. Like her great-grandmother Graciela, with whom she seems to communicate in a trance-like realm, Leila finds that sex does not necessarily offer erotic or corporeal satisfaction. Her precocious pursuit of Miguel—the married superintendent of her building who is more than ten years her senior—quickly turns into pedophilic grooming. Miguel's manipulations culminate in raping and threatening Leila. As she heals from this traumatic event, the truth of which she hides from even her closest friends, she begins to dream a patchwork of images:

> [Two] copulating lizards . . . cumulonimbus clouds shaped like ships . . . small brown hands paring an apple . . . the map of the world on a face . . . La Virgen de Altagracia without a face . . . a peppermint stick inside a coffee cup . . . lavender tangled in pubic hair . . . a hatbox . . . mercury stained skin . . . an uncombed baby under a chair . . . a thorned and bleeding plaster heart. (238)

Leila's dreams are glimpses into her great-grandmother Graciela's life and memories. Her desire for freedom is mediated through Graciela's spirit, which she feels fluttering in her chest. Graciela whispers to her, "[Waited] on a long line to get born. Still, life dealt me a shit deal. Don't listen to whoever invents magics about me. Always tried to live what I wanted. Never pretended to be a good woman. Never tried to be a bad one. Just lived what I wanted. . . . Make something better of it than me" (242). This scene is a revelation and a healing balm as Graciela is able to communicate to her great-granddaughter Leila through this intimate patchwork of dreams and offers her crucial advice about embodying freedom and corporeal control. Hey-Colón contends that Leila and Graciela's healing "can only take place through movement, when waters (and bodies) can flow freely again" (19). This is made possible only through "the family migration to the United States and Leila's integration of her great-grandmother's past into her present and her future."[65] Through these embodied memories, Leila is able to build the resolve to return home to her grandparents with a new sense of corporeal consciousness.

Graciela's erotic freedom, while punished by the limits of filial love and the reach of venereal disease, offered her the possibility of living and knowing beyond what was permitted under the intimacies of colonial Blackness. As Chevalier argues, "This is Graciela's entire feminist quest throughout the novel, to 'feel beyond' the limitations of her life and experience as she understands them to be."[66] Her crystalline visions on her deathbed about the impending dictatorship, and later, her communion with her great-granddaughter Leila, illustrate the power of being in touch with erotic knowledge. "Sex," Omise'eke Natasha Tinsley argues, "is almost as omnipresent in black Atlantic storytelling as salt water on an island."[67] In *Song of the Water Saints*, sex and the erotic are central to understanding the history of a nation and its diaspora. As Lorde notes, the erotic is "an assertion of the lifeforce of women; of that creative energy empowered, the knowledge and use of which we are now reclaiming in our language, our history, our dancing, our loving, our work, our lives."[68] Graciela's corporeal consciousness and search for erotic freedom over and against the intimacies of coloniality are precisely the powers that allow her spirit to communicate with her great-granddaughter more than seventy years after her death. The Black femme freedom practices illustrated in the novel represent one form of resistance to systems of heteropatriarchy, occupation, domination, and dictatorship that follows these generations of women and girls from the island to the diaspora. Santos-Febres argues that women who dare to be lucías, know that to be lucía is both a simulacrum and a weapon, "es atrevimiento necesario para imaginarse un mundo diferente" (17; "it's a daring that is necessary to imagine a different world"). Graciela's visionary liberation and her deep knowledge anchored in the erotic—which she shares with her great-granddaughter Leila—is likewise a labor that helps her to, in the words of her daughter Mercedes, "nudge humanity just a little further forward" (194).

Bastarda Yo, Lesbiana

Trifonia Melibea Obono's 2016 novel *La bastarda* (translated into English in 2018 as *La Bastarda*) is the first LGBTQ novel in the Equatoguinean literary corpus. The novel underscores the double standard within Fang marriage and partnering practices which, following Xhercis Méndez's reading of Julieta Paredes's *Hilando Fino* (2008), represents the "doble entronque" (double juncture) of European bourgeois colonial patriarchy and patriarchal Indigenous practices.[69] *La bastarda* reveals that in a postcolonial Catholic nation under a repressive dictatorship, Fang practices of hierarchical polygamy, patriarchal structures, misogyny, and homophobia create a society where same-sex-loving women, girls, and femmes are both invisible and impossible subjects.[70] In fact, Luis Melgar Valero's introduction to *La bastarda* informs us that in the Fang language "no existe ninguna palabra para designer una mujer lesbiana. La mujer lesbiana, simplemente no existe en la mente fang" (14; "There is no word to designate a lesbian woman. The lesbian woman simply does not exist in the Fang mind").[71] While Melgar Valero is not a speaker of Fang, the idea of a lack of a word for lesbian in the Fang language is echoed throughout the novel by various characters and leads many of them to denounce this form of same-sex desire as an impossibility: a lesbian simply cannot exist. Because languages change and expand over time and space, Obono's narrative may be offering readers this impossibility as both a metaphor and/or a material reality. In either case, it is over and against a worldview that devalues same-sex love between women that Obono crafts *La bastarda*, making space to imagine other ways of being, knowing, and loving. Parker Brookie argues that "Okomo unravels traditional Fang society through the perspective of the queer and female subject."[72] By centering the search for erotic and corporeal consciousness, Obono adds to the Black femme queer archive which calls attention to and seeks to dismantle compulsory heterosexuality, patriarchy, and normative power. Following Tinsley, *La bastarda* is a literary text that is a "queer, unconventional, and imaginative archive of the black Atlantic."[73] In focusing on the protagonist's practice of Black femme freedom in the face of racialized homophobia and cultural traditions, the author makes space for erotic and "disruptive possibilities for black womanhood to emerge" through practices of subversion, fugitivity, and ultimately marronage—the process of extricating oneself from enslavement through absconding and the creation of new communities outside of colonial orders.[74] The novel is written in the voice of a young girl, coming of age and coming to better understand her position within and outside of her community. At first childlike, the protagonist's narrative voice builds with rage and rebellion, offering the reader a stunning portrait of what it means to come into one's corporeal consciousness through acts of resistance and the erotic. The form of the novel itself reflects a political insurgency in its economy (under 100 pages) and its forceful and quick-paced narrative structure—the reader senses that this story must be told expeditiously.

The protagonist, Okomo, is a sixteen-year-old orphan. Her unmarried mother died in childbirth and her father has not recognized her due to Fang cultural traditions that upon birth relegate Okomo to her maternal family. She is raised to understand that according to Fang practice, she is the daughter and kin of every Fang adult man. As a result, Okomo belongs to every man and yet is recognized as the daughter of no man at all, "la hija de ningún varón" (32). She is in essence and in effect a bastard daughter, which causes her deep anguish and prompts her incessant search for her biological father. This relentless search is seen as a transgression, and she is punished by the head of her family, her grandfather Osá, for refusing to adhere to tradition. Her reprimand includes having to tend to her grandfather's feet and toenails while listening to him recount the long history of the tribe. His pedantic speech irritates Okomo: "Estaba hastiada de escuchar las aventuras de los fundadores de nuestra tribu, hombres valientes de los que debería sentirme orgullosa" (33–34; "I was so sick and tired of listening to the adventures of our tribe's founders, brave men who I was supposed to be proud of," 3). Her reticence is mirrored by the reactions of other women in the home, who also listen to Osá wax poetic about the great men of the Fang community and their bravery in establishing new communities in the uninhabited forests.

Within her polygamous Fang family, Okomo contends with the relationships between her grandfather's wives, including that of her own grandmother Ada and her rival—the youngest and newest wife who goes unnamed in the novel (a sign of her position within the family). Each of the women is dutiful yet rebellious, often condemning traditions that restrict their ability to act freely. The phrase "¡Maldita tradición!" uttered by the new wife becomes an echo heard throughout the novel as they each struggle to gain corporeal and erotic freedom from the constriction of heteronormative Fang practices. Okomo learns that the only reason she is considered an orphan is because her father had not completed the dowry payment for her mother at the time of her birth. Because her parents had broken the hard-and-fast rules of marriage within the Fang community, their relationship was considered adultery, with her father as a "desgraciado" ("scoundrel" or "disgraceful man") and her mother as a "soltera fang" (32; "unmarried Fang woman," 2).

The frustration with women's roles, the intimate impacts of gender domination, and the coloniality of gender in the Fang family surface in the experiences of the other women in the novel as well. For example, even as the second wife is doted on by Osá, she is irritated by having to play a subservient role to the first wife, Ada. Ada, having lost her preferred status, goes to great efforts to entice her husband Osá to return to their marriage bed, not for love, but to gain the power that is bestowed upon her for being in his favor. Despite her attempts to win his affections by purchasing spells, Ada rebels against her own growing invisibility with every fiber of her being by subverting power relations throughout the home. For example, as Osá drones on about the greatness of the male Fang lineage, Ada interrupts him, demanding that Okomo ask Osá about the lack of women in his stories: "Si en nuestra tribu no existían mujeres, porque Osá no las enumeraba entre el colectivo de heroes" (36; "If there were any women in our tribe since he had failed to mention any in his collection of heroes," 6). The absence of women in his stories and in Fang kin histories is palpable, as is the absence of women in the "casa de la palabra," the palaver house or house of the word, where men gather and make binding decisions over the entire community's public and private affairs.

Okomo detests the ways in which her life choices, desires, and possibilities are circumscribed by Fang cis-gender heteropatriarchy and misogyny. Okomo's transgressions are linked to her relationship with her gay uncle, tío Marcelo, whom his family and community call "hombre-mujer" or "fam e mina" (man-woman), showing the existence of a terminology to denote a homosexual man. Because he refuses to reproduce with the wives to whom he has been assigned, and because he fails to fulfill his duty to impregnate the wife of his infertile cousin, tío Marcelo is seen as the reason for the failing crops and is summarily ousted by the community. His house is burned to the ground and he flees to the forest to live with his friend Restituta, a disabled sex worker, and his lover Jesusín. His escape and refusal to be recruited into the scripts of heteropatriarchy and tradition can be read as a form of grand marronage, what Neil Roberts calls the "creation of communities of freedom outside the parameters" of Fang society (10). For Roberts, maroons are "heretical, non-state actors" who "construct a clandestine series of hidden transcripts in opposition to the zones of governance and appropriation intrinsic to existing state regimes of slavery (5)." They do so by "cultivating freedom on their own terms with a demarcated social space that allows the enactment of subversive speech acts, gestures, and social practices antithetical to the ideas of enslaving agents (5)." [75] Tío Marcelo engages in "grand marronage" even as it is dangerous and perhaps deadly to do so.

In the wake of tío Marcelo's narrow escape, Okomo refuses to denounce him and instead begins to question the limits of what makes a male-bodied person a "man" in the eyes of the Fang community. Soon after, Okomo is given a task that takes her through the forest on the outskirts of her community, and there she encounters a group of three mysterious girls—Dina, Pilar, and Linda—who give her a letter from tío Marcelo explaining his escape to the forest and his long-standing friendship with these young women. Dina, Pilar, and Linda confide in Okomo that they are both proud of and grateful for Marcelo: "Se había convertido en el ejemplo a seguir al atreverse a deasfiar al Consejo de Ancianos de la tribu" (62; "He had become an example for them to follow in having dared to challenge the Council of Elders of the tribe," 32). Marcelo's queer corporeal resistance and physical defection from the community offer a possibility and a path to freedom that inspire these young women who were his friends and confidants. Over the course of their friendship, Marcelo and the girls kept each other's secrets about their illicit activities in the forest.

While Okomo is at first reticent, Dina, Pilar, and Linda entice her into joining their "club de la indecencia" ("club of indecency") and having group sex in the Fang forest. The girls assuage her fears, telling her: "Estás en el bosque: el bosque Fang es un entorno libre. Ahora eres libre" (57, 65; "You're in the forest–the Fang forest is a free space. Now you're free," 35). Drawing the forest as a space of both temptation and liberation, Obono offers the possibility of freedom for her queer femme Fang characters. This sexual encounter is indeed liberating for Okomo: "Me estaba gustando y por primera vez en mi vida me sentía sexualmente libre" (65; "I was enjoying it, and for the first time in my life, I felt sexually free," 35). Here, queer intimacies between women and girls act as both erotic experiences and a delving into corporeal knowledge. Aligned with Lorde's assertion that "once we begin to feel deeply all the aspects of our lives, we begin to demand from ourselves and from our life-pursuits that they feel in accordance with that joy which we know ourselves to be capable of," Okomo's erotic encounter awakens her. Okomo realizes that her attraction to women is not new, but rather a deeper feeling that she had shunned. "Our erotic knowledge empowers us, becomes a lens through which we scrutinize all aspects of our existence," argues Lorde, "forcing us to evaluate those aspects honestly in terms of their relative meaning within our lives."[76] It is here that Okomo begins to further question her grandparents' insistence that she find a wealthy man to marry, and during her encounter with the indecency club, new intimate (im)possibilities take shape.

Although the indecency club has a pact to only engage in group sex, Okomo falls in love with Dina and is publicly outed by Linda and Pilar when they find out about Dina and Okomo's affair. Okomo's "indecent" behavior marks her as an excessive and impossible member of the Fang community, and the four young women are summarily punished for going against Fang practices. Okomo recounts the punishments suffered by her lovers. Linda's father sells her to pay off his gambling debts, a form of bride-price that the men in the town rush to agree to in the Casa de la Palabra. Dina is hastily married to her sister's widower and is sent away to help raise her three nieces. Pilar "no volvió a salir de su casa" ("wasn't allowed to leave her house anymore," 76), and when she finally reemerges in the community, is found to be pregnant by incest (103–5). It is revealed that Pilar had been raped by her father for years and that he murdered her mother when she discovered this abuse. Okomo's sentence is months in the making, and during that time she is never left alone. She is forced to stay away from her friends and from her uncle, the "hombre-mujer." She laments that her voice is silenced, "mi voz se apagó" ("my voice died out," 77), or is extinguished (105). Okomo thus tracks how the shared intimacy and sexual pleasure among four women incur corporeal punishments, including losses of self-determination, of bodily control, and ultimately of her own voice.

Part of Okomo's punishment is to engage in domestic labor in the family home. Any complaint or objection is met with pointed criticism of her sexual deviance, as evidenced in her grandmother's indictment during an argument over the retrieval of pots from the stove. According to Fang custom, women do not feel heat on their hands, and so handling hot pots directly from the flame without a dishcloth is considered a hyper-feminine and laudable act. When Okomo refuses to comply with this practice, her grandmother alleges that she has "tocado cosas peores con las manos" (106; "touched worse things with your hands," 77). Touching a vulva, Ada continues, is the most disgusting thing Okomo can do: "¡Qué asco! No existe nada más asqueroso en la vida que tocar aquello. . . . Solo los hombres la tocan, las mujeres no. La tradición se respeta y tú la has violado junto a estas tres muchachas indecentes" (106; "How disgusting! There is nothing more disgusting in life than touching that. . . . Only men can touch it, not women. Tradition must be respected, and you have violated it with those three indecent girls," 78). Women's bodies and genitals become "asqueroso," disgusting organs to be touched only by men for their sexual pleasure, or for reproduction. However, Okomo has experienced sexual pleasure, and as Ondo Edzodzomo argues, "La experiencia amorosa en el bosque entre Pilar, Dina, Linda y Okomo permite afirmar que el sexo sirve solo para procurar placer" ("The experience of love in the forest between Pilar, Dina, Linda and Okomo allows us to affirm that sex serves only to procure pleasure").[77] The fact that Okomo's grandparents and even tío Marcelo declare that there exists no word for "lesbian" in Fang can be tied to the impossibility of women's sexual desire, erotic intimacy, or corporeal consciousness outside of heteronormative arrangements. If indeed the erotic is off-limits for women and girls, then the idea that they would find pleasure, knowledge, and sexual satisfaction with one another and in groups is an unfathomable act and an offense within a worldview that sees vulvas as repellant organs.

Okomo's punishment is slightly alleviated when her extended family finds her a boyfriend nicknamed Pequeño, and she resigns herself to going with him on walks to the river, forests, and other places. One afternoon in the forest, Pequeño attempts to sexually assault her: "De repente me agarró los brazos por la espalada e introdijo sus dedos en mis genitales de manera agresiva, mientras yo intentaba zafarme" (107; "Suddenly he pulled my arms behind my back and jammed his fingers between my legs. I tried to escape . . ." 79). After Okomo fights him off, he confesses that he was simply fulfilling her grandmother's order; she had demanded that he confirm that Okomo is sexually attracted to men (107). Here we can see an example of how consent can also carry the violence of anti-Blackness, because in Okomo's case we can see how Black women and femmes are not protected under the kind of consent wherein those closest to them affirm and require their violation.

Okomo decides to leave her community after this assault, and she finds her father with the help of tío Marcelo's advice. She discovers him in a neighboring town, confronts him, and asks to be part of his family. When he turns her away and demands that she return to the home of her mother's kin, Okomo realizes that her grandparents were right: "Sólo era eso, una bastarda" (116; "I was just a bastarda," 88). She leaves, but rather than return to her community, she heads to the forest to reunite with tío Marcelo, Jesusín, Restituta, and Dina, Pilar, and Linda, who have managed to evade their punishments and abscond, the group creating a queer commune of sorts. For Okomo, these five people are "la única familia que la vida me había dado" (116; "the only family that life had given me," 88). There in the Fang forest, Okomo is reunited with Dina, and the two travel deeper into the forest to enjoy each other's bodies: "Las dos nos adentramos en el interior del bosque para pasarlo bien" (116; "Right away, the two of us went deep into the woods to be alone together," 88). This final scene of the novel again frames the forest as a place of escape and potential liberation, especially for those on the periphery of social and cultural traditions: "El bosque de mi pueblo constituía el único refugio de las personas que no econtraban sitio en la tradición fang como yo:

como hija de una soltera. Bastarda yo, una mujer fang; bastarda yo, la hija de una soltera fang; bastarda yo, lesbiana" (116; "The forest was the only refuge for those who had no place in Fang tradition, like me. I'm a bastarda, a Fang woman; I'm a bastarda, daughter of an unmarried Fang woman; I'm a bastarda, a lesbian," 88). The group's fugitive movida to the forest can be read as what Roberts calls "sociogenic marronage," or the "supreme ideal of freedom," which "denotes a revolutionary process of naming and attaining individual and collective agency, non-sovereignty, liberation, constitutionalism, and the cultivation of a community that aligns civil society with political society."[78] This scene is foreshadowed by Okomo's grandfather Osa's stories about the great Fang founders who established communities in the forests. Tío Marcelo and his partner along with Okomo, Dina, Linda, and Pilar venture into the uninhabited forest and establish a new Fang community, thereby potentially becoming a new lineage in the Fang ethnic group.

While it is important to underscore the forest as refuge and as the beginning of a maroon community of queer Fang kin and lovers, we must consider the concept and space of the forest within the longer history and cultural traditions of the Fang. The Fang forest has long been understood as a place of solidarity between women, a space where they give birth, where men do not often enter except to hunt, and as land that offer sustenance to entire communities. In the Fang language there are multiple words for "forest," but because the novel is written in Spanish and later translated to English, readers are not privy to the precise words for forest that would be deployed in such contexts. As such, non-Fang readers are left with the unknown, and this is perhaps one of the most powerful linguistic decolonial moves made in *La bastarda*. Obono offers a critical narrative that can only be truly understood by those situated within the Fang and Equatoguinean contexts.

The novel ends with the words "bastarda yo, lesbiana" ("I'm a bastarda, a lesbian"), and with Okomo forward-facing and conscious of what she means and how she matters within the context of the Fang world. This final utterance is likewise an indictment of Fang practices that erase and elide women both in their oral histories and in their cultural traditions. She pronounces herself "lesbiana" and "bastarda" in an act of witnessing her own positionality and identity, and in a refusal to adhere to heterosexist and patriarchal norms that cast queer subjects as outside of personhood. For Okomo and her kin, "freedom is not a place; it is a state of being."[79] The queer kinship that she helps to engender evokes longer histories of Black queer Atlantics that have no fixed beginnings or ends. The collective that Okomo joins in the forest can be read as an extension of Fang cultural practices and relations in/to the forest or even as a queer utopian commune. However, the ending of the novel is abrupt and unresolved, since the group is engaging in a daring and dangerous fugitive practice which can potentially incur the wrath of the extended Fang community. As Johnson argues in *Wicked Flesh*, "[in] the practice of women loving each other, black women and girls, sometimes in broader community of men and children of color, stepped into the fray on each others' behalf."[80] Okomo's erotic freedom in the face of the intimacies of coloniality, including the coloniality of gender, heteropatriarchy, misogyny, compulsory heterosexuality, homophobia, and other forms of domination, ushers in a space to develop and trust her corporeal consciousness, one that helps her to imagine other ways of being that are rooted in ontological freedom, erotic desire, and the body.

Sites of Freedom

By Night the Mountain Burns, *Song of the Water Saints*, and *La bastarda* each illustrate how the machinations of power impact the intimate lives and subjective experiences of colonized peoples, particularly Black women, girls, and femmes. The insidiousness of occupation, dictatorship, and coloniality is subtly revealed through characters' attempts to understand and subvert orders of knowledge, gender, and power. Each of the authors demands that readers bear witness to the everyday forms of domination, visceral restlessness, and radical isolation that exist within communities racked by occupation and dictatorship. The narratives expose dictatorship as unfreedom, occupation as coercion, and the intimacies of coloniality as impossibilities. In doing so, the novels point to the ways that these forms of domination are public and manipulative, but also intimate and invasive; they reside in the consciousness of those who have experienced them and those who come after.

While Ávila Laurel documents the "deads" and the tragedy of indifference, he also indicts the collective murder of a woman who sought to break free from communal mores. Rosario's novel offers the possibility of Black femme freedom beyond the politics of respectability and beyond the limits put on Black women's lives across four generations. Graciela's corporeal consciousness becomes a form of petit marronage, which allows her to fulfill her deepest desires to be free and, later, make spiritual connections to her great-granddaughter. Okomo's rebellion, the awakening of her erotic desire, and her decision to abscond to the forest to form a queer kinship collective of oustcasts breaks new ground in both the literary corpus of Equatorial Guinea and in tracking the queer Afro-Atlantic imagination. Okomo's corporeal consciousness is also a form of marronage, a site of freedom and possibility that is likewise bounded, surrounded, and is attempting to undermine heteropatriarchal and homophobic Fang cultural practices.

What work does literature do in laying out the machinations of power? Of bearing witness to the unbearable? By engaging these texts in this first chapter, I hope to create a discursive space to consider the literatures of diasporic Afro-Atlantic Hispanophone writers as archives of indictment. The novels studied in this chapter bust wide open the potential sites of resistance in the diasporic cultural productions of the Afro-Atlantic. This is a collective project that requires both storytellers and those who bear witness to these stories. Indeed, what is the labor and the demand of archives of indictment? If these texts are filled to the brim with rich histories, robust concepts, and complex imaginings of resistance and fugitivity, how can we bear witness to them? Indeed, who sees this? Just as Graciela and Okomo demand to be seen, the nameless narrator of *By Night the Mountain Burns* demands that readers refuse to turn their backs on history. Such an immense task requires an ethical imagination, a faithful witnessing beyond colonial ways of knowing and being, and this is precisely the subject of the next chapter.

Chapter 2

Witnessing

> Hey, World—here I am . . . I'm here, and I want recognition, whatever that mudder-fuckin word means.
>
> —Piri Thomas, *Down These Mean Streets*

"Who has seen this?" This is the question that lê thi diem thúy asks in her debut novel, *The Gangster We Are All Looking For*. lê's novel, about a Vietnamese refugee family haunted by war and the drowning death of their son, is narrated by a nameless young protagonist. In one passage, she explains the exterior optics of her home in southern California: "It is hot and dusty where we live. Some people think it's dirty but they don't know much about us." She goes on to describe their "gardens full of lemongrass, mint, cilantro, and basil." While passersby may see "the pigeons pecking at the day-old rice and the skinny cats and dogs sitting in the skinny shade of skinny trees," they miss the beauty of "the berries that we pick," and the staircase that her father lovingly built from her bedroom window to the backyard. Indeed, she asks, "Who has seen this?"[1]

I teach lê's novel whenever I have the opportunity to explore its well-worn themes of migration, displacement, nation, and identity through the perspectives of postwar Vietnamese refugees in the United States. This passage in particular has prompted one of my favorite assignments, in which students are tasked with formulating a creative project in any medium that reflects something about their kin or community that they know or see but others do not. The "who has seen this?" project, inspired by this tender and unnerving novel, has produced pieces that offer powerful sociopolitical commentary and reveal intimate portraits of kinship and labor that often go unseen in places like the university classroom. This unassuming experimental text has likewise propelled my meditation on faithful witnessing in forums ranging from ethnic studies courses to English critical theory seminars. It was in thinking about the ways we bear witness to the lives, struggles, and oppression reflected in texts such as these that I began to construct a methodology shaped by the ethical task of witnessing faithfully within and across relations.

Another example of faithful witnessing can be seen in Piri Thomas's groundbreaking book *Down These Mean Streets* (1967), which offers a glimpse into the life of an Afro-Puerto Rican man coming of age from the 1930s to the 1960s.[2] Thomas's work has been the source of some of the richest scholarship in Latinx studies, particularly with respect to race, gender, class, and color.[3] Many scholars have examined Thomas's identity formation and positionality in his debut autobiographical novel in order to consider the histories of Puerto Ricans and Black Puerto Ricans in the United States.[4] Still others have analyzed Thomas's work through the lenses of psychoanalysis, linguistics, racial formation, and geography.[5] Such scholarship has laid the groundwork for much of Afro-Latinx studies today. While this chapter does not engage *Down These Mean Streets* as a primary text, I use this foundational text as a point of departure for my meditation on witnessing. It is the narrator Piri's prologue on being recognized by his father, by New York, by his community, and by the world that is most striking to me in this regard. In the film *The World of Piri Thomas* (1968), Gordon Parks offers us a stunning and heartbreaking view of the places and people that young Piri and the author Thomas were speaking to and with.[6] Parks's film allows us to glimpse some of the lived experiences of Puerto Rican and African American communities in New York City in the late 1960s, and through its snippets of sights and sounds, bears witness to the ways that their lives were often only seen by one another. An elite and mostly white New York City is presented in sharp juxtaposition to both Spanish Harlem and Harlem. The lives that are deeply entangled through historical and political forces of migration, disenfranchisement, and exploitation seemed (and continue to seem) to exist in different worlds, never meeting. I am interested in how the labor of witnessing is undertaken, not only by Thomas and Parks but also by writers, poets, and people living always in recognition of each other's humanity even amid the structures and practices of coloniality that elide their struggles and deny their lived experiences. In this chapter, I examine this form of recognition as witnessing, building on the work of women of color feminist thinkers and philosophers who have uncovered different ways of seeing and knowing that do not require recognition from elites, whites, or otherwise enfranchised people, but rather see the most value from within each other.

Peppered with "gutter language" and predicated on contentions with racial and ethnic identity, *Down These Mean Streets* opens with a prologue—young Piri hollering from the rooftop of his Spanish Harlem tenement: "I want recognition."[7] In the text, Thomas offers the reader the opportunity to bear witness to the humanity and lived experiences of working-poor, racialized, and immigrant communities from the Great Depression through the civil rights era. What Thomas's Piri demands of us, the reader, is to see him against the grain of powerful tropes that cast Puerto Ricans and other racialized and oppressed groups as pathological peoples suffering from a culture of poverty.[8] Much of the radical post-1960s "coming-to-consciousness" literature by U.S. Latinxs and people of color makes similar demands on the readers: to witness and recognize the hostility of heteropatriarchy and white supremacy, the aftermath of colonization and migration, and the humanity and lived experiences of their subjects.[9] Yet, how can we read resistance in these texts? Is it possible to bear witness to what the authors offer or to what the characters narrate (and often demand)?

In this chapter, I use the examples of lê and Thomas as a point of departure to argue that Junot Díaz's *The Brief Wondrous Life of Oscar Wao* and Donato Ndongo's *Shadows of Your Black Memory*, products of distinct literary traditions and published twenty years apart, engage in what the Latina feminist philosopher María Lugones calls "faithful witnessing."[10] Faithful witnessing is a political act that aligns itself within feminist and decolonial epistemologies. The act of faithful witnessing, as demonstrated by the novels' narrators, allows us to understand shifts in the structure of power and resistance to domination, particularly the domination of women of color, femme, and queer bodies. My effort to build on the decolonial feminist philosophical concept of faithful witnessing as a decolonizing practice is part of a larger political project of engaging the work of women of color as tools that guide us toward liberation. In examining these works, I also aim to illustrate how literary poetics labor to reveal faithful witnesses who work against the grain of dominant narratives and against erasure.

Carolyn Forché's edited anthology *Against Forgetting: Twentieth-Century Poetry of Witness* (1993) offers an opportunity to read poems that emerged from some of the most unthinkable political and social catastrophes, such as the Holocaust, the Armenian genocide, and South African apartheid. The collection posits that poetry, in whole and in snippets, is "evidence of what occurred."[11] Considering poetry as a method of evidencing, as a way of bearing witness, is nothing short of revolutionary, for it brings to the surface the economy of the form as a kind of documentation and it bridges the individual to the collective.[12] Forché further contends that "the poem might be our only evidence that an event occurred: it exists for us as the sole trace of an occurrence."[13] I telegraph poetry to the labor of poetics and consider the ways that fiction and poetry have acted as vessels through which to tell "othered" histories, silenced histories, and stories of survival and resistance. Oral and written storytelling is a labor which keeps alive that which ought not to be forgotten, the stories that Aimé Césaire argues "are not to be so easily disposed of."[14] As Audre Lorde reminds us in her poem "Sisters in Arms," one of the most important tasks we have in the battle against oppression is to "fight side by side," documenting "our dead behind us" and ushering in the possibilities of futurities beyond the death knell of colonialism through a "ritual of healing."[15]

In *Pilgrimages/Peregrinajes: Theorizing Coalition against Multiple Oppressions* (2003), María Lugones describes the act of "faithful witnessing" as a method of collaborating with those who are silenced. This concept is both a political act and a feminist philosophical approach that aligns itself with women of color and decolonial epistemologies. Lugones deploys faithful witnessing as a strategy through which oppressed peoples form coalitions in order to combat multiple and systematic oppressions.[16] In what follows, I provide a context for the concept of faithful witnessing and offer some examples in two novels from the Afro-Latinx and Afro-Hispanic tradition: Junot Díaz's *The Brief Wondrous Life of Oscar Wao* and Donato Ndongo's *Shadows of Your Black Memory*. In doing so, I argue that just as Thomas's narrative is responding to the sociopolitical struggles of Latinxs and Afro-Latinxs in the civil rights era, Ndongo and Díaz are responding to experiences of religious colonization in the twentieth century and coloniality and gender violence in the twenty-first century, respectively. The concept of faithful witnessing is a useful tool through which to analyze these texts and read resistance in postcolonial and decolonial narratives. Furthermore, the practice of faithful witnessing is one that oppressed and colonized peoples have deployed since time immemorial as a method of bearing witness to each other's humanity even as they faced myriad forms of violence. The texts analyzed in this chapter mark ways of tracking narratives of indictment, and offer an opportunity for readers to read against the grain of foundational histories that often erase the lived experiences and perspectives of those most directly affected by colonialism, coloniality, and anti-Blackness. By examining the literary works produced by Afro-Atlantic Hispanophone diasporic subjects written in English, Spanish, and Spanglish, as faithful witnesses, we align ourselves with insurgent worldviews that offer new ways to understand decolonization as project and practice.

Framing Faithful Witnessing

Witnessing as a concept has a long history within feminist, philosophical, decolonial, religious, and juridical debates. For example, in *Witnessing Beyond Recognition*, Kelly Oliver develops a theory of subjectivity whose cornerstone is the very act of witnessing. Oliver contends that the Hegelian master-slave dialectic can leave the oppressed unrecognized, needing or desiring only what their dominators can provide.[17] The act of witnessing then enables unrecognized subjects to demand that their oppression be seen beyond the dynamics of agonistic recognition.

Oliver argues that victims of unthinkable oppressions, such as enslavement or the Holocaust, "do not merely articulate a demand to be recognized or to be seen. Rather, they witness to pathos beyond recognition."[18] In the context of colonization and coloniality, Nelson Maldonado-Torres asserts that "the demand for liberation is also a demand for recognition," and this is a twofold ethical act of giving and demanding.[19] In *Decolonizing Methodologies*, Linda Tuhiwai Smith also highlights the importance of "witnessing," "claiming," and "*testimonio*" as ways in which Indigenous and colonized peoples can "make claims and assertions about [our] rights and dues."[20] Smith names claiming and testimony as central to the act of witnessing; testimonies, she argues, are vehicles through which "the voice of a 'witness' is accorded space and protection."[21] I am attentive to the articulation of the witnesses' protected space and to the ways in which witnessing in literature could provide safe spaces to reflect on and indict violence, particularly the violence endemic to colonization and coloniality.[22]

As Oliver's concept of witnessing goes beyond agonistic Hegelian recognition, Lugones's concept of faithful witnessing, as a decolonial practice, goes beyond colonial epistemologies. Faithful witnessing, as a decolonial feminist tool, makes visible the often-unseen consequences of the coloniality of power, knowledge, and gender.[23] Coloniality is not only tied to colonialism or racial classification, but rather is "an encompassing phenomenon, since it is one of the axes of the system of power and as such it permeates all control of sexual access, collective authority, labor, subjectivity/intersubjectivity and the production of knowledge from within these intersubjective relations."[24] Lugones theorizes witnessing by centering the struggles of women of color. She understands witnessing as a praxis of epistemic pilgrimaging against physical and metaphysical domination. This no doubt is dangerous in a real-world sense, since witnessing threatens dominant powers and established scripts. "To witness faithfully," Lugones explains, "one must be able to sense resistance, to interpret behavior as resistant even when it is dangerous, when that interpretation places one psychologically against common sense, or when one is moved to act in collision with common sense, with oppression."[25] She posits that in order to see resistance, one must be able to see domination, which itself is a subversive act. It is in the act of perceiving resistance to oppression "in [its] complex interconnections," or beyond the colonial difference that "fragment[s] people categorically," that we can locate one another as "possible companions in resistance."[26] Faithful witnessing puts the viewer in the path of danger, but also conveys meaning against the grain of domination. This act offers a view from below, from within the matrices of oppression, and recognizes multiple forms of resistance.[27]

Popular conceptions of witnessing define the act as a kind of bearing witness to types of truth, as in "eye-witnesses to historical facts or accuracy."[28] Yet, it also has religious connotations: "Witnessing has both the juridical connotations of seeing with one's own eyes and the religious or now political connotations of testifying to that which cannot be seen, or *bearing witness*."[29] It is this dual meaning which underscores my reading of *Shadows of Your Black Memory* through a faithful witnessing framework. The juridical and religious meanings of witnessing provide a space through which to analyze Ndongo's narrative of one community's experience with religious and political colonization in (Spanish) Equatorial Guinea.

Lugones further argues that faithful witnessing challenges singular narratives or dominant perspectives, and in doing so takes subjects away from singular interpretations of truth, knowledge, and rights. Instead, faithful witnessing moves subjects toward a polysensical approach, one which understands that there are many worlds, and which sees/reads many perspectives, particularly the perspectives of those who are dehumanized or rendered invisible. One way that literature conveys these multiple narratives is through the use of multiple narrators, or multiple perspectives of the same moments or experiences. An example of this is the way that Díaz provides multiple and competing narratives in *The Brief Wondrous Life of Oscar Wao*. Díaz's characters bear witness to the physical, historical, and psychosocial violence of coloniality.

A polysensical approach, akin to Chela Sandoval's concept of differential consciousness, is aligned with a decolonial ethics that looks to different forms of knowing and being as a practice and as politic. According to Sandoval, "Differential consciousness has also been defined by Anzaldúa as the workings of the 'soul,' and by Audre Lorde when she describes the 'erotic' as a place where 'our deepest knowledges' are found."[30] Similarly, in his 2011 essay "Decolonizing Post-Colonial Studies and Paradigms of Political-Economy," Ramón Grosfoguel argues: "A truly universal decolonial perspective cannot be based on an abstract universal (one particular that raises itself as a universal global design), but would have to be the result of the critical dialogue between diverse critical epistemic/ethical/political projects towards a pluriversal as opposed to a universal world." He contends that the decolonization of knowledge requires that we "take seriously the epistemic perspective/cosmologies/insights of critical thinkers from the Global South thinking from and with subalternized racial/ethnic/sexual spaces and bodies."[31] Faithful witnessing as a radical and ethical decolonial practice rejects universal narratives and instead privileges the perspectives, cosmologies, and insights of peoples on the underside of coloniality and ongoing settler colonialism.

Lugones refers to two distinct perspectives: a view from above and a view from below. There is "the bird's-eye view—the perspective from up high . . . the analysis of life and history. There is the pedestrian view—the perspective from inside the midst of people, from inside the layers of relations and institutions and practices."[32] The view from above represents an assumptive view invested in vestiges of history and the mechanisms of oppression, whereas the view from below negotiates oppression through relational practices. For Lugones, the pedestrian view is one that understands internal and external meaning; one that, because it sees relations from up close, can provide ways of seeing and resisting erasure and indifference to oppression.

Faithful witnessing offers a lens through which to recognize the assertion of humanity and dignity in moments when these would otherwise be unseen or ignored. The concept of faithful witnessing has been used in ethnographic research with specific attention to LGBTQ youth of color. Cindy Cruz's "LGBTQ Street Youth Talk Back: A Meditation on Resistance and Witnessing" offers faithful witnessing as a framework for understanding those who bear the weight of interlocking oppressions. She posits that employing faithful witnessing in ethnographic work acts as recognition of the "rejection of this radical othering that often happens in social science research."[33] It is what happens when a person is not complicit with the powers that dehumanize others. In this way, Cruz's study shows how faithful witnessing offers an "opening for critical and decolonizing ways to position ourselves as researchers of color, in standpoints that help us *recognize these gestures of resistance*."[34] It is in the faithful witnessing of moments of resistance, failure, deception, triumph, violence, love, and small histories that one actively participates in the affirmation of other voices and the substantiation of other truths. Without this kind of recognition, histories are erased, silenced, and ultimately invalidated as human experiences.

In *Specters of the Atlantic* (2005), Ian Baucom argues that "to 'witness' . . . is to regard something that appears both in the guise of the event and in the form of the series, to see what we see as if we are seeing again what we are seeing for the first time, to encounter history as déjà vu."[35] Here Baucom attends to the historical hauntological interrogation of the *Zong* massacre (1781), noting the limits of Hegelian justice and turning to Caribbean poetics as a space of reckoning. Namely, he examines how both Glissant's conceptualization of poetics of relation and Derek Walcott's poem "The Sea Is History" take up the *Zong* massacre—not in name, but in the guise of the poetic form. Glissant and Walcott bear witness to the event and recognize the narrative as a constitutive part of the history of the Caribbean, of the sea, and in relation to their own being. Their poetics make it possible for readers to become faithful witnesses to the guise of the event—a massacre of enslaved peoples on the high seas—and to the form of the historical series—a massacre of Black bodies in a watery grave containing countless others, modernity pulling bodies into and across the sea, slavery and its afterlife.

Baucom cites and counters Fred D'Aguiar's line, "The past is laid to rest when it is told," with an imagined response from Glissant: "The past is laid to rest when it is related."[36] The Glissantian relation, Baucom argues, "is not about forgetting but about living on within the abysmal."[37] I posit that the narratives told and retold over generations are never laid to rest, but rather are conjured over and again, seeking faithful witnesses. To be a faithful witness means to align oneself with these stories, to be haunted by the remnants, to be stirred by the irreconcilable, and to keep those histories alive. A polysensical position would posit incommensurable views such as "The past is never laid to rest," or "The past demands faithful witnesses," or, in fact, "The past rests only when it devours those who deny it." To be a faithful witness, then, one must see the guise of the event and the form of the series—that is, a faithful witness must see past the appearance to the true nature of the event, and then must identify it as a pattern; or rather, as part of a long history of such oppression and domination. Faithful witnessing is always already part of the ethical actions of a decolonizing politic.

In reading *Shadows of Your Black Memory* and *The Brief Wondrous Life of Oscar Wao* as narratives that act as faithful witnesses to coloniality, I take up women of color theorizing and the decolonial attitude. Faithful witnessing takes seriously the knowledge of those who have historically been silenced, cast as ahistorical subjects, or considered insignificant.[38] The decolonial attitude sustains a "new ethics beyond coloniality" and is an "expression of an ethical subjectivity that defines and positions itself in a way that promotes decolonization and re-imagines human relationships."[39] Thus, I engage the fiction produced by Afro-Atlantic writers, and read these works against the grain of power and towards a decolonial praxis.

Witnessing Cosmologies Collide

Donato Ndongo's novel *Shadows of Your Black Memory* (2007) is perhaps the best-known literary text translated to English in the Equatoguinean canon. (It was published in Spanish as *Las tinieblas de tu memoria negra* in 1987.) The novel is at once a fictional account of Spanish colonization in Equatorial Guinea and the narrative of a particular subject: an Equatoguinean in exile who witnessed the political transitions of both Equatorial Guinea and Spain during the late 1960s. As Michael Ugarte has noted about Ndongo's unique position as a Spanish writer and journalist in the 1970s: "He was strange: a colonial subject of flesh and bone—we needn't forget his skin. . . . Writing from the subject position of a black man is uncommon, if not completely absent, in the annals of Spanish literature."[40] *Shadows* tells the story of a boy being raised within two cultures: his Fang community, of which his uncle is one of the most respected elders, and that of the Spanish Catholic missionaries, of whom he is a student. The text, written as a retrospective account from the vantage point of adulthood, articulates the contact between the two worlds, each fighting to survive the other. The narrator's uncle, Tío Abeso, is the community's leader but his brother, the narrator's father, seems to embrace Catholicism and the sweeping changes being made in the Spanish colonial regime. Throughout the text, Tío Abeso and the Spanish priest, Father Ortiz, battle for the young narrator's loyalty. They each see him as a vessel through which their respective worldviews will either uphold or subvert the new colonial order. Esther Sánchez-Pardo argues that rather than solely a work of fiction, *Shadows of Your Black Memory* is a "compelling memoir, the story of a boy coming of age over the background of the last years of Spain's colonial rule over Guinea. From the perspective of a grown-up man living in Spain, the memories are themselves an exploration of how he arrived at the land that paradoxically has become an object of anxiety as well as the possibility to fulfill his emancipatory project."[41] In fact, Susan Martin-Márquez contends that such literary works are more than just histories or memoirs, but rather are texts that offer the possibility of bearing witness to the histories of resistant colonial subjects. "While Spanish Africanist texts are preoccupied with mobilizing the colonies and the colonized in the construction of Spanish national identity," she argues, "*Tinieblas* [*Shadows*] emphasizes that now it is the Guineans' turn to construct their own nation—with and against Spain and Spaniards."[42]

The boy, a witness to the debates between his uncle and the missionary priest, begins to see the ways in which Tío Abeso is fighting not only Father Ortiz but also what Ngũgĩ wa Thiong'o deftly describes as colonialism's "cultural bomb." In *Decolonising the Mind*, Ngũgĩ argues that this cultural bomb effectively annihilates people's "belief in their names, in their language, in their environment, in their heritage of struggle, in their unity, in their capacities and ultimately in themselves." Furthermore, it fosters disidentification and cultivates a sentiment of ahistoricity: "It makes them see their past as one wasteland of non-achievement and it makes them want to distance themselves from that wasteland."[43] As Martin-Márquez so aptly notes, Ndongo's use of "polyphonic interior monologues" exposes how his indoctrination into Catholic religiosity collides with the worldview and the humanity of his Fang community: "The narrator's thoughts are permeated with the xenophobic discourses repeated ad nauseam in the Spanish colonial world, from the patriotic Falangist hymns sung by the children every morning before the flag outside the school, to the imperialist history textbooks recited aloud in class, to the hate-infused 'religious' lessons imparted by Don Ramón and Father Ortiz."[44] Throughout Ndongo's narrative, there are moments when the boy rejects and disidentifies with his own extended family and community, seeing them as "dimwitted" and "savage" (59).[45] In one instance, while alongside the priest on his conversion mission, the boy notes:

> With the priest I asked myself if all those dirty smelly blacks, no matter that they were dressed in their Sunday best, if those poor folks devoured by mosquitos, reduced to a hypnotic, irreversible state by dysentery and malaria, always looking lethargic, dazed, submissive, if only those men, women, and children, so dimwitted, so attached to the savage nature surrounding them, were worthy of the immense goodness I was trying to bring them as I offered the possibility of a new life, eternal life, amen, *per omnia secula seculorem*, trying to rid them of their idolatry and elevating them to the supreme category of civilized beings. (59)

Here the narrator exemplifies one of the effects of the cultural bomb that "makes them want to identify with that which is furthest removed from themselves. . . . It even plants serious doubts about the moral rightness of struggle. Possibilities of triumph or victory are seen as remote, ridiculous dreams."[46] In fact, the boy thinks that his uncle's rejection of Catholicism and the Spanish occupiers is a contempt born out of ignorance. Tío Abeso, he recounts, "saw no advantage at all in making friends with the white occupiers; and that was the origin of his contempt of those who were ignorant of your people, a contempt you thought was spite" (84–85). It is through the narrator's retrospective that we bear witness to these colliding cosmologies.

The novel begins in Spain with the narrator, now an adult, approaching an old and decrepit Reverend Father, informing him of his choice to abandon his studies and return to Equatorial Guinea. The narrator confesses that he had known for a very long time that it was not his call to be a priest: "I had this feeling some time ago, but I doubted, I fought with myself, I asked for guidance. And because my soul can no longer endure such a conflict, it's time to put an end to it" (11). He describes a feeling of strength, an ancestral power that drives and speaks through him: "It wasn't difficult for me to say this; the fear was no longer in me, and it was as if ancestral powers were speaking for me. The moon had become radiant" (11). The moon's radiance signals his relief in this scene and foreshadows his coming-of-age ceremony held in resplendent moonlight. Of this moment he writes, "The moon glowed above, a big moon, round, smiling, and guiding you to the dwelling of the dead, the center of your beginnings and your power" (137–38). While in that scene the moonlight was leading him to the resting place of his ancestors, he still chose to leave Equatorial Guinea to become a priest. Now, with his resolve to return home, he feels that the ancestral strengths are renewed within him. This is the first sign of what is to come in the novel, a consistent battle between the promises and mystic rituals of Catholicism and the beliefs and ceremonies of his community.

The readers are spectators to the narrator's indoctrination into these competing worldviews. Early in the narrative, the boy is chosen to be Father Ortiz's companion and to assist him as translator as he preaches to different members of the community (many of whom are the boy's extended family members): "Yes, you assisted him and in all the villages you instructed the black savages to rid themselves of totemic symbols, lances, arrows dipped in poison, masks, wood figurines, bronze effigies, and drums while you spoke of the wrath of God against those who kept the devil inside, and Father Ortiz took all those things away to burn them, or so he said" (23). The boy, proud of his status as an altar boy and assistant to the priest, takes seriously the task of conveying the damnation that people would earn by rejecting Father Ortiz's admonitions. His instruction, in both the church and at the Catholic school with his pedantic teacher, Don Ramón, creates a dichotomous reality with his life at home as the nephew of a respected community leader. His school experiences read like pages from critical anticolonial narratives on colonial education, and reveal how youth were trained to speak in Spanish, taught Spanish history, and punished for any sign of speaking their indigenous languages:

> [When] Don Ramón asked you what you were your little voice stood out clearly: all of us together are Spaniards by the grace of God!

> And why are we Spanish? Intoned Don Ramón, and your clear voice again stood out: we are Spaniards blessed for having been born in a country called Spain. And with Don Ramón's facile explanations you accepted the inexorable and inextricable absurdity of successive centuries: Spaniards had come to save you from anarchy because your ancestors were heathens, barbarians, cannibals, idolaters, who kept cadavers in their dwellings, vestiges of savagery that you censored along with Father Ortiz. (22–23)

In the presence of Don Ramón and under the influence of Father Ortiz, the boy takes on the Spanish missionaries' colonial attitude and perspective. He begins to see his own people and his family as fetishistic and uncivilized, and looks to Spain and Christianity as beacons of civility and progress.

The boy constantly negotiates his beliefs and practices, at one point daydreaming about his future as an adult man in the tribe: "I'd be able to go hunting with Tío Abeso. . . . I'd sit down with the elders in the meeting house and no one would be able to say, hey you kid, don't bother your elders" (32–33). These musings of hunting and sitting with the elders go on until his initiation ceremony begins. The boy's ecstasy culminates when Tío Abeso falls into a trance and recites the names of the familial ancestors, their nomadic history to the point of settlement, and finally acknowledges the boy as "a legitimate descendant of the ancestors and a bona fide member of the tribe" (35–36). The boy soon realizes that he is no ordinary member, but rather one who is consecrated to carry on the tribe's traditions and collective memory. The continuing ceremony takes place over five weeks, and the boy witnesses and retells each ritual in detail. It is during this time that he undergoes moonlit walks with his uncle, has his foreskin cut, and encounters the spirit of his grandfather standing on a crocodile on the riverbanks. These sacred moments he experiences at the age of six are bookended by earlier religious incidents. Thus, the chapter is literally situated between his cursing the tribe at Father Ortiz's side, and his memories of internalizing the catechism and reenacting the ceremonies he witnesses in church at the age of eight. The boy, straddling two worlds, never wavers from faithfully witnessing, and speaks honestly, even matter-of-factly, about their competing realities. He bears witness to the shifts within his family and community, and the Church's assault on Fang cosmology. He does so retrospectively, acknowledging that the political and religious oppressions as well as the resistance practices are intermeshed with one another. Though he admires the Church officials, he does not hide or underplay their disdain for his community. However, he continually equivocates about whether he could ever live the life of a peasant farmer like his father, going on "day after day, always, back and forth" (96). In comparison, a prospective life in the priesthood appeals to him.

In one of the most riveting moments of the novel, the boy bears witness to a debate between Tío Abeso and Father Ortiz. While Father Ortiz never loses hope of converting Tío Abeso to Christianity, Tío Abeso maintains his acts of resistance with the goal of getting rid of Father Ortiz and the missionaries:

> He would call my uncle a blasphemer and tell him he would go to hell. And with infinite patience Tío Abeso answered that at the moment they were not in a territory of the white man's tribe, that *he* hadn't gone to the other man's tribe trying to convert everyone to his belief, and he told the priest there was no reason for him to be angry, and he asked him whether he could give me any idea how to find that place where I will burn, and whether he has been there. (86–87)

Tío Abeso and Father Ortiz, with the boy as translator, go on to discuss matters of polygamy, medicine, law, land, and the worship of ancestral and religious figures. In this debate, Tío Abeso argues that Fang traditions are no stranger than Father Ortiz's cosmological beliefs, questioning whether Father Ortiz has seen any of the transcendental planes of which he preaches. Father Ortiz, whose definitive mission is to convert Tío Abeso, retorts by calling him a blasphemer, an idol worshiper, and a licentious adulterer (85–93).

When asked by Father Ortiz about the fact that the tribe has no books with which to record their history, Tío Abeso states:

> We don't read books. We know our tradition because the eldest member passes it on to the young so that when he too is old, he will in turn impart the tradition to his young. This is how we have always lived. You say you have brought medicine, but you found medicine here too. You say you have brought peace, but you were the ones who incited war. And tell me, don't the tribes of white people fight among themselves? The only problem I see with you is that you want us to give up our customs and trust your ancestors. And that can't be. I can't tell the member of another tribe to honor the figure of Motulu Mbenga, because it means nothing to him. (92)

While his uncle is angry and saddened by having to fight for the survival of their ancient traditions, the priest is conflicted, feeling that Tío Abeso is, on the one hand, an exceptional man, and on the other, feeling frustrated at his inability to convert him.

At this critical moment, the boy translates between Father Ortiz, who does not speak Fang, and Tío Abeso, who does not speak Spanish. When Father Ortiz realizes that Tío Abeso is besting him, he regrets that the boy is listening: "The priest kept looking at me because I should not have heard such things, but he couldn't have communicated with my uncle if I hadn't been there. I was indispensable, a necessary drive to accomplish his apostolic mission" (92). Through this act of translation, the boy witnesses what each of these men believes to be true and is caught between two worldviews that are diametrically opposed. Because the boy is the only one who can facilitate the communication between the Spanish missionaries and the Fang community, he embodies the constant and contentious negotiations of colonial rule and Indigenous struggles against oppressive impositions. As he recounts the debate between them, he apprises the reader of the unspoken sentiments in the room. He notes, "I was observing the last splendors of a world that was disappearing forever, and another very different one was arriving; I couldn't embrace either one" (93).

Although he comes to acknowledge that Tío Abeso was the only person enacting a forceful resistance in the name of the tribe, "the one who refused to capitulate, the one who wanted to keep the torch burning; he was the light that your generation was dimming little by little," the boy's internal conflict leads him to pursue the priesthood in Spain (24). Through his careful and faithful retelling of his family history and his own experiences, the boy acknowledges his family and community's humanity. While he understands that colonial religiosity could not eradicate his family ties, he also recognizes that Tío Abeso's sole resistance could not prevent the realities of colonial devastation in Equatorial Guinea. Near the end of the novel, as the boy undergoes a ritual ceremony, once again under the moonlight, he comes to consciousness, thinking: "And despite your brief thirteen years you were convinced that although you would one day cross the ocean and go beyond, you would always have the spirit of the tribe within you, the blood of the tribe, you would always hear the tribe whispering to you" (143). The boy confronts the reality of being torn between his role as a member of his family and Fang community and his potential future in the Church. He realizes that the Fang kinship ties and the cosmologies were planted deep within him.

The novel ends with a confession: Tío Abeso and the boy's father had encouraged his studies with the missionaries while teaching him their family history and bringing him into the Fang community through various rites of passage. The boy's father was an initial link to the Church; in allowing his son to become an altar boy and the priest's companion, he was engaging in methods of resistance: infiltrating the space of the occupiers, learning their worldviews and practices, and thereby becoming able to better navigate forms of resistance to colonial rule.

> And my father too was looking at me lovingly, and then I understood his role. He had never been on their side, he was the link between the tribe and the occupiers, someone has to negotiate, someone has to talk to them to figure out how they should be treated, what foods they like and what bothers them, how they fornicate and how many cigarettes they smoke a day; someone should be with them to spy on them from the inside; the tribe must store information on their movements and their ideas. (126)

After this revelation, and in a seeming narrative twist that complicates simplistic accounts of consciousness and resistance to domination, the boy asks permission to travel to Spain to become a priest. His eventual return as an adult is a key moment, another coming-to-consciousness, which compels him to do what is dangerous—to recount his family story and become a faithful witness to the violence of religious colonization.

In this way, *Shadows of Your Black Memory* rejects teleology and instead offers a view from within the overwhelming conflict the boy faces, a view from below. He narrates the double consciousness that has shaped his worldview, with special attention to the multivalent resistance of Tío Abeso and the strategic positionality of his father. The boy's experience is evocative of what Ngũgĩ calls a contemporary postcolonial struggle, "an imperialist tradition on one hand, and a resistance tradition on the other."[47] And though the narrator engages both worldviews, often taking on Father Ortiz's dehumanizing perspective, he does not vacillate in his faithful witnessing of these internal and external conflicts. In doing so, he attests to the cosmological shifts, and retrospectively indicts himself and the Church in the hegemonic colonial process. His adult perspective serves as a challenge to the occupier's history of the colonizing process by going beyond colonial epistemologies and challenging the misguided ideologies that cast his familial Fang community and Equatoguineans as ahistorical peoples. In this context, faithful witnessing allows the narrator to offer a fragment of this story while referencing the occupation of Fang territories in Spanish Guinea and later Equatorial Guinea, and providing the context for his choice to leave and his eventual choice to return. Sánchez-Pardo argues that "[creatively] these texts are also monuments to the lost histories of their ancestors in Africa, they (re)build community, bear witness, and engage audiences in an almost utopian effort."[48] But while in *Shadows of Your Black Memory*, faithful witnessing takes the form of indicting colonial religiosity, in *The Brief Wondrous Life of Oscar Wao*, faithful witnessing reveals the violent dimensions of the coloniality of gender.

A Witness to Coloniality

Since Junot Díaz's *The Brief Wondrous Life of Oscar Wao* (2007) is a particularly Caribbean and diasporic novel, a transnational and decolonial reading of this text is fitting. The novel strategically marks the first European contact with the Caribbean as the advent of a centuries-long curse, the "fukú," and makes visible the effects of coloniality in the Dominican Republic and in diaspora.[49] Violence, private indirect government, and heteropatriarchal structures all make appearances in the novel, and most of their powers are wielded over women's, femme, and queer bodies.[50] The characters and the reader(s) witness how the power structures of coloniality reach across spatial and generic bounds.

Though some reviewers argue that Díaz's work replicates and venerates heteropatriarchal normativity and misogyny, I posit that Díaz's writing allows the reader to bear witness to the ways in which coloniality exerts power over and commits violence upon bodies deemed to be insignificant.[51] Discussing Díaz's work makes it necessary to discuss the 2018 allegations against him, many of which were brought forth by women of color writers. These accusations of bullying, aggressive sexual advances, and shaming were made in the wake of Díaz's revelation of being a survivor of childhood sexual abuse.[52] The accusations made by former partners and writers add a critical dimension to how we read Díaz's work, and how we link the impact of his work and actions to the bodies and lives of women of color. There have been a great number of blog posts, think pieces, open letters, and essays on the topic. One I would like to highlight here is Aya de Leon's "Reconciling Rage and Compassion: The Unfolding #MeToo Moment for Junot Díaz," wherein she asks, "Can we hold the complex reality that Junot Díaz is both a #MeToo survivor and a perpetrator?" De Leon underscores the complexities of wanting accountability and holding space for humanity and healing: "I want to hold Junot accountable, but I also want to hold up his humanity and push him to be a better leader in this conversation. In the past, he has called himself writing about toxic masculinity. He has also acted it out, and pushed back hard on women who challenged him."[53] I believe that Díaz's work does the important labor of bearing witness to how misogyny, gender violence, and patriarchy are formed and perpetuated. His actions, however, further reveal deeply entrenched forms of domination. My engagement with his work is informed by the many truths that have been shared by and about the author. In what follows, I argue that Díaz's narrative offers an opportunity to faithfully witness the founding violence of colonization via the traveling curse (the fukú), the legitimization of violence through Trujillo's dictatorial rule, and the normalization of gender violence across temporal and spatial planes.[54]

In a 2014 interview, Díaz engaged critiques about the racism and apparent misogyny of his fictional characters and asked readers to consider the following question: "If Yunior is simply an objectifying misogynist, then why is he so preoccupied with bearing witness to the transnational rape culture that women are victimized by?"[55] *The Brief Wondrous Life of Oscar Wao* has multiple faithful witnesses in the form of its narrators: the primary narrator Yunior; two sections narrated by Oscar de Léon's sister, Lola; the ever-present footnote narrator, who offers historical context, humorous and tragic counterpoints, and enhances the story arc overall; and Oscar's narration, which is presented through his final letter. Yunior's adult retrospective narrative, however, is the main line through which we hear the stories of Oscar and his family. As Dixa Ramírez notes, *The Brief Wondrous Life of Oscar Wao* acts as an undoing of histories of great men often told about the Caribbean and the Americas and instead offers a polyvocal, often acerbic and rhizomatic retelling from the perspective of Black diasporic subjects.

"Rather than a teleological retelling of Caribbean or even Dominican history," Ramírez argues, "the novel's narration is nonlinear and multivocal. More directly, it testifies to the violence of these major historical actors. In so doing, it critiques the authoritarian leadership of men like Trujillo and Balaguer, who repeat the 'spirit of Columbus,' and, as such, reinscribe the wounds of the Spanish conquest on an already traumatized region."[56] Like the nameless narrator in *Shadows of Your Black Memory*, Yunior's perspective is key to hearing the polysensical truths and relations within the de León family. However, unlike the narrator in *Shadows of Your Black Memory*, Yunior is in a seemingly peripheral position, as he is not a member of the immediate family, but rather a witness to their stories as Oscar's best friend and as an occasional, mostly unfaithful, lover of Oscar's sister, Lola.

In many ways, Yunior is both within and outside the story, and yet he refers to himself as a "faithful watcher," a phrase that conjures both the fantastic and the philosophical. The ability of the text to traverse genres, provide a multiplicity of narratives, and trouble familial, colonial, and postcolonial histories while indicting coloniality and imagining futurities outside of the material makes it a decolonial text.[57] Monica Hanna contends that "Yunior self-consciously struggles and experiments with *how* best to accomplish his task because in the process of his research, as he attempts to uncover both the story of the family and the history of the nation, he is continually confronted with silences, gaps, and 'páginas en blanco' left by the Trujillo regime."[58] Rather than follow a singular narrative that centers solely his own perspective, Yunior's position as a faithful watcher is about documenting the many threads of the de León family's histories and Dominican national and diasporic experiences, fully cognizant of his place within and outside of them. This undermining of singular narratives is also a form of faithful witnessing against the grain of oppression. *The Brief Wondrous Life of Oscar Wao* destabilizes dominant tropes of heteromasculinity by revealing how it binds the male characters emotionally and psychologically. The novel also serves as a faithful witness to and critic of thirty years of dictatorship and state-sponsored terror on women's, femme, and queer bodies.

The novel tells the story of Oscar de León, a hopeless antihero who does not fit into the mold of Dominican masculinity: "He had none of the Higher Powers of your typical Dominican male, couldn't have pulled a girl if his life depended on it" (19–20). Oscar's life is narrated through an analysis of his family history, of Trujillo's dictatorship in the Dominican Republic, and of diaspora to the United States. The fukú is the catalyst for the story and is associated with European imperial expansion:

> They say it came from Africa, carried in the screams of the enslaved; that it was the death bane of the Tainos, uttered just as one world perished and another began; that it was a demon drawn into Creation through the nightmare door that was cracked open in the Antilles.

> Fukú americanus, or more colloquially, fukú—generally a curse or doom of some kind; specifically the Curse and the Doom of the New World. (1)

The colonial project is indicted as the fukú's accelerant, and in the narrative, the key to unraveling the de León fukú lies in tracing it back to founding violence and dictatorship. The narrator explains that "no matter what its name or provenance, it is believed that the arrival of Europeans on Hispaniola unleashed fukú on the world, and we've all been in the shit ever since" (1).

An early footnote in the novel introduces the reader to El General Rafael Trujillo, the Dominican Republic's thirty-year-long dictator who controlled almost every part of the nation's "political, cultural, social, and economic life through a potent (and familiar) mixture of violence, intimidation, massacre, rape, co-optation, and terror; treated the country like it was a plantation and he was the master" (2). The narratives of Oscar's mother, Belicia, violently thrust into diaspora, and his sister, Lola, shuffled back and forth between the United States and the island, are critical to understanding the fukú to which Oscar falls victim. Each of these characters' narrative arcs is central to the critique of the kinds of violence engendered by coloniality and dictatorship: that of singular authority. As Jennifer Harford Vargas points out, Díaz's text "displaces the dictator from the center of the narrative and redistributes attention to those subjects at the bottom of the hierarchy or at the margins of power." As such, the novel "exchanges a dictator-centric character-system for a character-system centered on marginalized subjects."[59] Díaz resists the traditional structure of the novel by writing in multiple and conflicting narrative voices and in doing so, offers a polysensical approach. Furthermore, the competing familial, political, and historical narratives battle teleology and contest foundational histories. By faithfully witnessing sites of interpersonal and state-sponsored violence and resistance to that violence, the novel challenges heteropatriarchy and coloniality, and it defies the everyday violence faced by Belicia, Lola, Oscar, Ybón, and many other named and unnamed characters. The narrators witness what is understood to be secretive: the family curse and its history; what is deadly: resistance to Trujillo and existing power structures; and what is silenced: the violence wielded against women's, femme, and queer bodies.

Many critical and literary analyses focus on Oscar's apparent masculine deficiencies, his "queer" body, and the equally impossible and homoerotic relationship with Yunior.[60] Although these offer necessary and judicious readings of the text, I want to shift the focus from Oscar's queer masculinity (or what Elena Machado Saéz calls his "queer Otherness"), lack of hypersexual prowess, and what he "loses" (sexual and romantic relationships) to what he gains from being on the sidelines: witnessing the sexual, psychosocial, and physical violence enacted on the bodies of women.[61] As Aishih Wehbe-Herrera argues, "The lack of identification and performance of hegemonic masculinity is immediately related to the undervalued world of the feminine and the queer, which is the *raison d'être* of Oscar's nickname."[62] Oscar's position as a romantic ne'er-do-well allows him to gain proximity to potential love interests who are often involved in abusive relationships.[63] In this way, experiences of gendered and racialized violence, particularly in relation to women's, femme, and queer bodies, emerge as central to the narrative.

Most of the women Oscar encounters are steadily subjected to physical, sexual, and emotional abuse. Oscar's queer otherness allows him to witness intimate forms of violence that would otherwise go unseen, unheard, or unmarked. Oscar documents his neighbor Maritza's tumultuous relationship: "Maritza was a girl who seemed to delight in getting slapped around by her boyfriends . . . being pushed down onto the sidewalk" (18). Soon it becomes clear that Maritza is not alone, but rather all of the women in the novel, and Oscar's own queer body, are subjected to threats, violence, and torture. The novel, which is about diaspora, intimate ties with terror, and the enduring legacy of colonialism, is simultaneously an account of the everyday nature and normalization of gender violence and bodily terror.

The often-gruesome details of violent acts are central to the text and serve as documentation of commonplace brutality. In another instance, Ana, one of Oscar's teenage love interests, confides in Oscar about her relationship, telling him how her boyfriend Manny "smacked her, Manny kicked her, Manny called her a fat twat, Manny cheated on her" (44). Even Oscar is featured as an aggressor in one of these violent bouts, as Yunior recounts how he targeted and destroyed the room of his college crush, Jenni, when he finds her with another man (187). Yunior too acts as a faithful witness, loyally conveying Oscar's experience, although he also emerges as one of the emotionally abusive men in Oscar's accounts. In fact, Yunior tells us, "success, after all, loves a witness, but failure can't exist without one" (149). Díaz's text highlights how domination—be it dictatorship or other forms of sociopolitical power—desires *silent* and fearful spectators. The narrative points to and offers multiple ways to faithfully witness the failures of coloniality from the perspective of those on the underside of postcolonial dictatorial regimes.

The reader also bears witness to the unspeakable, Lola's rape, which she mentions only once as "when that thing happened" (57). Belicia's seemingly unloving treatment of her daughter Lola is one of the ways we can see how foundational violence permeates her most intimate family relations: "You don't know what it's like to grow up with a mother who never said a positive thing in her life, not about her children or the world, who was always suspicious, always tearing you down and splitting your dreams straight down the seams" (56). Lola laments her tense relationship with her mother: "She was that kind of mother: who makes you doubt yourself, who would wipe you out if you let her. . . . For a long time I let her say what she wanted about me, and what was worse, for a long time I believed her" (56). This strained relationship with her mother, alongside the sexual and bodily violence she witnesses in her relationships and within her family, makes Lola critical of violence as a normal state of family and social relations (324). Belicia refuses to bear witness to her daughter's rape, and this refusal extends to Lola, who forces herself to forget: "I finally told her what he had done, she told me to shut my mouth and stop crying, and I did exactly that, I shut my mouth and clenched my legs, and my mind, and within a year I could not have told you what that neighbor looked like, or even his name" (57). Belicia cannot bear witness to her own trauma and refuses to be a faithful witness to Lola, even as she loves her daughter fiercely. Here Díaz complicates the act of witnessing, as Belicia's refusal to bear witness to Lola's rape reflects her inability to confront her own experience of sexual and psychosocial violence.

We can also read this scene within the context of the intimacies of coloniality and the disproportionate effects of gendered and sexual violence faced by Black women, girls, and femmes in colonial and postcolonial contexts. In considering these realities, the writer Edwidge Danticat is empathetic with the ways that mothers may discipline their daughters against bearing witness for fear of more severe repercussions: "A slap, like the one given to the daughter who must not speak against the evil she witnesses, to silence her and protect her from greater injuries."[64] We can never know the precise reason for Belicia's refusal to bear witness to Lola's rape, but in unraveling her own story Lola is a faithful witness to her mother's lived experience—showing a form of intergenerational reckoning with these histories of violence and corporeal dispossession.

Central to the narrative is Belicia's history with her boyfriend, known only as the Gangster. This relationship and its brutal aftermath led to her escape from the Dominican Republic under the threat of death. Belicia meets the Gangster at a nightclub, and Yunior's narrative reports, "Santo Domingo was to popola what Switzerland was to chocolate. And there was something about the binding, selling, and degradation of women that brought out the best in the Gangster" (121). Perhaps the most brutal of all the violent acts in the novel is committed against sixteen-year-old Belicia. Unbeknownst to her, the Gangster is married to Trujillo's sister, and Belicia is to suffer the consequences of the Gangster's philandering. She is kidnapped and mercilessly beaten in a cane field, a prominent backdrop in the novel, and the place where Oscar is executed at its end. The vicious attack on Belicia causes a miscarriage and extensive bodily damage. Yunior briefly recaps the beating and her wounds:

> How she survived I'll never know. They beat her like she was a slave, like she was a dog. . . . Damage inflicted: her clavicle, chicken boned; her right humerus, a triple fracture (she would never again have much strength in that arm); five ribs, broken; left kidney, bruised; liver, bruised; right lung, collapsed; front teeth blown out. About 167 points in damage . . . I suspect there was [a rape or two]. (147)

Belicia's beating in the cane field is a recurring image in the novel; its retelling becomes a reminder to the reader that violence against women is not scaled down through time, but rather exacerbated through state-sanctioned mechanisms. It does not stay on the island, but is replicated and travels with and within the diaspora.[65]

Díaz's narrative acts as a witness to Belicia's beating by locating it as the guise of the event and, later, in the form of the series, when the imagery and violence are repeated on Oscar's body. By enumerating the violation against Belicia's body (and the wounds on Oscar's), Díaz conjures Hortense Spiller's concept of the hieroglyphics of the flesh. Spillers cites colonial reports of enslavement, highlighting the "anatomical specification of rupture, of altered human tissue, [that] take on the objective description of laboratory prose—eyes beaten out, backs, skulls branded, a left jaw, a right ankle, punctured, teeth missing, as the calculated work of irons whips chains, knives, the canine patrol, the bullet." Spillers argues that while these "undecipherable" hieroglyphics come to be "hidden to the cultural seeing by skin color" (particularly those that make up the state apparatus and uphold domination), these hieroglyphics are in fact cultural texts that mark the body, whose flesh carries one "to the frontiers of survival."[66] There is power in bearing witness to these hieroglyphics of the flesh; Belicia's scars conjure the wounds of slavery and foundational violence and call for us to be faithful witnesses to a long and unbroken line of violence that exists alongside contemporary forms of domination, suppression, and gendered and racialized violence.[67] Spillers tells us that "the familiarity of this narrative does nothing to appease the hunger for recorded memory, nor does the persistence of the repeated rob these well-known, oft-told events of their power, even now, to startle. In a very real sense, every writing as revision makes the discovery all over again."[68] Thus, every faithful witness in the novel—Yunior, Lola, and the ever-present footnote narrator—sees the guise and locates the series over and again.

Belicia's massive back scar, "as vast and inconsolable as the sea," a product of her time as a "criada" (a child servant afforded a status approximating enslavement), is a constant reminder of how violence is wielded against the bodies of girls. Her scar, a prominent image in the novel, is also deeply connected to the founding violence of the slave ship, the tortures of slavery, and their permanence. Jennifer Vargas argues that the scene in which the scar is shown, with Belicia's "bra slung around her waist like a sail" (51), "calls forth a slave ship in the Middle Passage."[69] In a scene where Lola faces her mother's scars and breasts, feeling the cancerous tumor that will eventually kill her, Lola is also bearing witness to a much longer history of sexual and physical violence, medical experimentation, the whip, the cage, the torture, the miscarriage, the rape, and the hand of dictatorship that created the conditions for all of this, the hand of the imperial forces that placed Trujillo in power, colonialism and coloniality. Lola becomes a faithful witness through the corporeal presence of her mother, physically touching the hieroglyphics of the flesh. Lola thus engages in a haptic alteration of her own future through grappling with her mother's keloid flesh, breasts, and the cancerous "knot" that grows within her. "You change too," Lola says about herself in reflecting on this moment with her mother. "Not right away, but it happens. And it's in that bathroom where it all begins. Where you begin" (54).

In a transnational twist of fate, Oscar finds himself the victim of physical violence at the hands of "Third World Cops" (291). His last love interest, Ybón Pimentel, a retired sex worker, is the girlfriend of a high-ranking police officer in the Dominican Republic. The similarity to Belicia's experience with the Gangster cannot be understated, and in fact, the repetition of these circumstances of love and violence calls forth Antonio Benítez Rojo's concept of the "repeating island" whose echoing arcs are both archipelagic and transnational.[70] Whereas the ensuing violence against Oscar is front and center, the violence and brutality against Ybón takes place behind the reader's gaze. In a brief retrospective, the narrator informs us, "Of course the captain had beaten the shit out of [Ybón] too, of course she had two black eyes (he'd also put his .44 Magnum in her vagina and asked her who she *really* loved)" (304). In the final chapters of the novel, after Oscar returns to the Dominican Republic to be with Ybón, they are caught together and Oscar is summarily executed in the cane fields. Wehbe-Herrera contends that "Oscar's conscious misidentification with hegemonic masculinity is violently censored in a world in which gender, racial, sexual, and ethnic differences are systematically condemned, paying with his life for it."[71] That this foreshadowed finale ends with Oscar's death, rather than Ybón's, is important to note because even as Oscar is represented as a queer masculine subject and is killed as a result, in the contemporary Dominican Republic it is often women and femmes who are the victims of rampant misogyny and heteromasculinity. As Maja Horn notes, "While in Diaz's novel this leads to Oscar's death, in the Dominican Republic more often this results in the murder of the woman involved; such femicides by jealous partners in fact constitute a widely recognized and ongoing crisis in the country."[72] After Oscar's execution, Ybón is only briefly mentioned as "dancing" again at another nightclub in the city (323). With Oscar dead, Yunior's faithful witnessing and his reading of Oscar's journals, papers, and letters are the only documentation of the love and tragedy that have transpired.

In *The Brief Wondrous Life of Oscar Wao*, the faithful witnesses spare no detail about the precipitous violence and the danger in telling what is supposed to remain unseen and unspoken. From Oscar's battle with love, depression, and weight loss to Lola's abusive relationships, to their mother Belicia's enduring trauma with the scars to match, the narrators' faithful witnessing validates the lived experiences of these characters, following them from the Caribbean to the United States and back. Lugones tells us that faithful witnessing is an act against oppression on the side of resistance, an act that though dangerous, can build coalitions between oppressed peoples and validate non-dominant truths and experiences. The writing and reading of literature, then, is one way in which historical, present, and future possibilities can be imagined and offer lenses through which to witness resistance. *The Brief Wondrous Life of Oscar Wao* is an example of a fictional text that resides in the interstices of history, narrated with a decolonizing imperative. The novel's plot is intimately tied to the history of the Dominican Republic, the stories of Oscar's mother and sister, and the forces of diaspora. Faithful witnessing offers a lens for reading decolonial imaginaries, spaces where the coloniality of power, gender, and knowledge are countered and confronted.

So Much Unheard

Because the coloniality of power produces and reproduces foundational dehumanizing violence, most kinds of historical, structural, and gender violence are masked in the hubbub of the everyday. These forms of domination mask themselves, obfuscate themselves, in an effort to confound those who seek to indict them. Faithful witnessing as reading practice allows us to see dehumanizing colonial violence and coloniality, and acts of resistance to these forms of oppression, even in retrospect. Literary poetics can be radical discursive spaces that allow us to be faithful witnesses to histories and truths that may have gone untold, unnoticed, and silenced. As the writer Juan Tomás Ávila Laurel notes, "I only want my work to incite questions and interest in the topic. So much is unheard."[73] Ávila Laurel is referring to the sociopolitical content of work by Equatoguinean writers, who often use literary fiction to speak about the harsh realities of political oppression, exile, and resistance.

In *Shadows of Your Black Memory* and *The Brief Wondrous Life of Oscar Wao*, faithful witnessing does not function as an act of observing, but rather is often a seconding and thirding of unrecognized (hi)stories. Faithful witnessing, then, is not only useful in reading Díaz and Ndongo, but can also be helpful in decolonial readings of other Afro-Atlantic authors and resistance writers of color. Literatures that incorporate and traverse the boundaries of fiction and history are critical to the development of decolonizing strategies. Reading these texts with a decolonial attitude opens discursive spaces for reading and witnessing resistance, and for decolonial theorizing. History as it needs to be done after 1492 necessitates faithful witnesses because the present and the past demand redemption from the imperial colonial project of the last five centuries. We are fixed in an ethical relationship in the present that requires faithful witnessing. If we are looking to our pasts, to our futures, and to our present moments, it is our responsibility not to collude with those who have stripped others of their humanity by denying their voices, intellects, histories, or freedoms. The nameless narrator in *Shadows of Your Black Memory* and the multiple narrators in *The Brief Wondrous Life of*

Oscar Wao exemplify a refusal of the dominant form of chronicling—beyond colonial epistemologies. Faithful witnessing, in this context, destabilizes foundational and singular narratives intended to silence, recognizes resistance to oppression, and privileges perspectives from below. If faithful witnessing is a decolonizing strategy, then its ethics demand that we reckon with the foundational violence of colonial modernity. As such, we must bear faithful witness to the forms of forcible dispossession that are endemic to colonial and imperial projects. The following chapter engages precisely this topic, offering the term "destierro" as a decolonial concept which attends to the long histories of exile, diaspora, and colonial dispossession.

Chapter 3

Destierro

> Rocks hold memory. Land holds memory. . . .
> Water always remembers.
>
> —M. Jacqui Alexander, *Pedagogies of Crossing*

In the novel *Days of Awe*, Achy Obejas's protagonist explains: "In English, destierro always converts to exile. But it is not quite the same thing. Exile is exilio, a state of asylum. But destierro is something else entirely: it's banishment, with all its accompanying and impotent anguish. Literally, it means to be uprooted, to be violently torn from the earth."[1] Literary writers and theorists in exile and diaspora have long expressed an interest in understanding the phenomenology of exile and diaspora. Literatures on Black internationalism, for example, have provided invaluable analyses of the experience and cultural productions of migrating, exiled, and displaced Afro-descendants across long historical and global contexts.[2] In this chapter, I transition from examining the possibilities of faithful witnessing to discussing how diasporic Afro-Latinx and Equatoguinean literatures meditate on overlapping forms of dispossession. These forms become critical to conceiving of real and imagined concepts of home, belonging, diaspora, and exile. I contend that one of the most important ethical questions to which we must attend is how destierro, or exile, diaspora, and the palimpsest of dispossession intersect and shape much of the lives of Afro-descended peoples. Here I examine how the concept of destierro can be used to articulate ontological dimensions of exile and diaspora through an examination of Loida Maritza Pérez's *Geographies of Home* and Juan Tomás Ávila Laurel's *El dictador de Corisco*.[3] These novels underscore the differing ways in which diasporic Afro-Atlantic Hispanophone subjects experience destierro and resist the physical and metaphysical experiences of being "violently torn from the earth."

In offering the term "destierro," I aim to call attention to the impossibilities of home in decolonial contexts.[4] While exile and diaspora are rich discursive spaces in postcolonial literature and theory, they have remained critical yet undeveloped in decolonial thought. In this chapter, I first examine some of the tropes of exile in postcolonial thought that undergird this meditation, and then I offer and expound on the decolonial concept of destierro that emerges from within Latinx literature. I then engage in close readings of the two diasporic Afro-Atlantic novels by Ávila Laurel and Pérez to show how each of them unearths new ways of thinking about destierro as overlapping forms of dispossession, including attempts to cut peoples away from their land, bodies, memories, and spiritual practices. I argue that "destierro" is a term that can capture the complex and multiple forms of dispossession and impossibilities of home for Afro- and Indigenous-descended peoples in the modern world.[5] Thinking about and through destierro within and beyond the *longue durée* of the modern colonial project allows us to further push decolonial thought towards liberatory practices, and map different forms of dispossession across intersecting identities.

Postcolonial Exile

Studies of exile in postcolonial contexts often lead us to the prolific work of Edward Said. While I center decolonial and woman of color feminist thought in this project, I must also note that postcolonial thought, and particularly meditations on exile, have been formative in my development of the concept of destierro in decolonial contexts. Yolanda Martínez-San Miguel has noted that the term "'postcolonialism' has not been a relevant notion for thinking about the political situation of Puerto Rico, and the same term has very limited political or theoretical resonance in Martinique. In some of these cases, terms such as 'decolonization,' 'neocolonialism,' or even 'postmodernity' seem more useful for understanding local political and cultural discourses."[6] While postcolonial thought is rooted in a different temporal and spatial context—eighteenth-century British colonialism in the Indian subcontinent and Africa—this theoretical field has been a boon to many writers and thinkers who contend with the afterlives of colonialism and slavery across the world and within the context of the long sixteenth century. While there have been polemical debates on what constitutes the difference between decolonial and postcolonial projects and critiques, I see these tools for analyzing historical and contemporary phenomena as mutually enriching. Thus, in many ways my development of destierro as a decolonial conceptual framework dovetails with foundational postcolonial works on exile.[7]

Exile, Said tells us, is comprised of "various forms of dislocation."[8] We can think of the punctuating and documenting functions of epistolary form, the indefinite sentence of exile, and the vaivén and the "ni de aquí ni de allá" of Latinx Caribbean migration as conditions that beg meditation. When I speak of "vaivén," I am referring to the move or sway of a population that constantly migrates (in circular migration or otherwise) to and from a homeland. The word "vaivén" literally translates as "to go and return" or "fluctuation," but is also a way to refer to what Jorge Duany calls a "nation on the move," or a migration that is "best visualized as a transient and pendulous flow, rather than as a permanent, irrevocable, one-way relocation of people."[9] Thus, vaivén is necessarily tied to the colloquialism "ni de aquí ni de allá," which gestures toward the impossibilities of belonging, of being from "neither here nor there." These two phrases, which are common parlance in Latinx communities, especially within Latinx Caribbean and even Mexican/Chicano borderland spaces, become an important way to mark location and dislocation, and unveil the ways that lived experiences of migration or exile, ushered in by varying forms of dispossession, intergenerationally affect subjects, language, and memory.[10] This can also be seen in the case of Equatorial Guinea. The writers Remei Sipi Mayo and Trifonia Melibea Obono have discussed the ways in which their subjectivities as migrants have shaped the ways that they connect to Equatorial Guinea and to Spain. "Me he dado cuenta hace tiempo que se puede tener dos o más sentidos de pertenencia o identidad," says Sipi Mayo, "pues en Barcelona yo pongo a hibernar mi identidad bubi, que despliego y pongo en juego en Rebola, y cuando para la gente en Rebola soy la barcelonesa, para la de mi barrio de Gracia en Barcelona soy la rebolana" ("I have realized for a long time that you can have two or more senses of belonging or identity, because in Barcelona I put my Bubi identity to hibernate, which I display and put into play in Rebola, and when for people in Rebola I am the Barcelonan, in my neighborhood of Gracia in Barcelona, I am the Rebolana").[11]

The writings of exiled subjects open discursive spaces for contending with exilic conditions and imagining other ways to live within the impossibility of home and homelands. Said tells us that exile is "the unhealable rift forced between a human being and a native place, between the self and its true home: its essential sadness can never be surmounted. . . . The achievements of exile are permanently undermined by the loss of something left behind forever."[12] As an exilic writer, Said's work takes on both the mundane aspects of exile and the broader implications of its lived realities. In his reflections on postcolonial Africa and exile, Paul Tiyambe Zeleza argues that while exile "remains difficult to define as a concept and a condition," the "causes, contexts, courses, constitution, and consequences of exile and the exilic life and identity are so complex and varied that they cannot but have multiple referents."[13] Being able to hold multiple and complex realities, such as the rooted desire to return to an often-impossible homeland, the complex relationship to anti-Black and anti-Indigenous nation-states, and the desire for liberation from a matrix circumscribed by these violences, becomes central to exilic poetics and cultural productions.

In *Reflections on Exile* (2001), Said writes of the exiled subject as a bane to the nationalist yearnings of his or her host nation.[14] The exiled subject is perpetually outside; that is, outside both the homeland and the host nation's community. This is what Said calls "a perilous state of not-belonging."[15] He correlates the not-belonging position of the exiled subject to Pierre Bourdieu's concept of the *habitus*, which links the practice of habit with the act of inhabitance. Thus, the practice of living and being outside of the national collective is understood as an inferior existence. This solidification of the inside/outside binary, of belonging and not-belonging, further bolsters the foundational myths of the nation. Paul Zeleza argues: "Said seeks the validation of exile not in his own eventual return to the homeland but in the freedom inherent in the very condition of exile."[16] In postcolonial contexts, the condition of exile has both inherent freedoms and burdens of not-belonging, and this constant negotiation within tenuous positions offers a third space: a critical voice that writes from a position of difference.

Postcolonial scholars have long argued that exile has increasingly become the lived reality of more and more people, and because of this it can be represented by multiple conditions. I contend that exile overlaps with forms of exclusion, othering, and capitalist excising, including those surviving as refugees, asylum seekers, dispossessed immigrants, and others at the precipice of precarity. Each of these conditions has distinct origins of departure and different manifestations, illustrating Zeleza's point that "exile is a metonym for various forms of dislocation from a physical and psychic homeland." Perhaps it is in this inherent dissonance, this incommensurability, that the possibility of the relationality of these "various forms of dislocation" emerges.[17]

If, as Said claims, the position of exile is one constituted by moments of solitude and dislocation, then the very act of writing in exile—which connects the exilic writer to the reader and to others—begets an ethical relationship built in exile. In writing, the exiled subject opens a discursive space for examining the ontological and phenomenological experiences of exile while also imagining other ways to live within and beyond exile. Azade Seyhan suggests that "literary expressions of contemporary sociopolitical formations offer critical insights into the manifold meanings of history and take us to galaxies of experience where no theory has gone before."[18] The exiled subject is not one, but many, and in the act of writing and giving a space for protagonists and characters to expound on exile, writers give weight and importance to the varied experiences of exiled subjects. Seyhan says that the narratives, imagined or not, draw from history and the past: "In narrative, we may be able to redress forcibly forgotten experiences, allow the silences of history to come to word, and imagine alternative scripts of the past. Our understanding of the present is invariably predicated on actual or imagined links to, or ruptures from, a recalled past."[19] Links to the past, though ruptured, are critical to understanding the present. This understanding of temporal and spatial connectedness within postcolonial thought is also central to decolonial projects.

Diasporic Afro-Atlantic Hispanophone literary and cultural productions take seriously the experiences of those condemned to exile in the modern world.[20] What is more, these works offer human praxes and reveal possibilities for resistance within oppressive political structures and authoritarian kinship networks. I contend that these texts, emerging from within a distinct spatial and temporal locale, bear on decolonial thought. Building from the conceptual and theoretical contributions on exile in postcolonial thought has allowed me to develop a framework for thinking about overlapping dispossessions, exile, and diaspora as destierro. The concept of destierro is likewise a methodology that takes seriously the centrality of fifteenth-century modernity and colonialism within decolonial thought. Destierro as a decolonial concept offers us a way to think through exile and diaspora in longer colonial historical and relational contexts while also prioritizing the various and overlapping forms of dispossession that supervene when peoples are displaced and dispersed onto unceded and settled territories.

On Destierro and Relations

The *longue durée* of colonialism leaves a palimpsest of dispossession and genocide in its wake. If modern capitalism is the accumulation of land, resources, and labor, to the extent that it enables the accumulation of capital, then the act of tearing peoples away from their land and land-based practices is the central component of capitalist world-systems, particularly as they developed in the fifteenth century. While Zeleza argues that exile is "exceedingly common in modern Africa, indeed in the world at large, so much that it could even be seen as one of the major characteristics of the twentieth century," I contend that for Indigenous peoples facing genocide and dispossession on Abya Yala and Turtle Island, for enslaved African subjects forcibly removed from their lands, and generations of their descendants, destierro has taken multivalent forms since the long sixteenth century.[21] Jodi Byrd contends that "[dispossession] in North America . . . depends on the ongoing colonization of Indigenous lands as the transformation of those lands into property, but more, it depends on reproducing the propertied relations through which dispossession itself occurs and then reenacting those relations subsequently upon settlers and arrivants over time as a generative process that ensures that the original colonization of Indigenous lands remains unassailable, natural, rational, and necessary as the condition of possibility for all other dispossessions to come."[22] I argue that imagining destierro as a palimpsest of centuries of overlapping histories, lived experiences, ties to land and land-based practices, and multiple movements (forced and voluntary migrations) by dispossessed peoples onto dispossessed lands allows us to be faithful witnesses to the layers and forms of being forcibly ripped from the land while also seeing the resurgence of those land-based practices and resistance to dispossession.

Destierro can become a decolonizing tool if, in calling attention to how it is a constitutive part of exile and diaspora, it also focuses on the long legacies of self-determination by peoples on the underside of modernity. Holding this dialectic central to understanding the phenomenological, ontological, and epistemological experience of destierro is critical if we are concerned with not only documenting suffering, but also with marking, holding, and remembering resistance. Black and Indigenous marronage, literary poetics, art practices, and communal, tribal, political, and cultural organizing—such as Idle No More, #NoDAPL, #BlackLivesMatter, American Indian Movement, Young Lords Organization, Black Panther Party, Chicano Movement, MOVE, The Black School, Colectivo Ilé—are some examples of these forms of resistance that emerge amidst and against destierro. These forms of organizing and activism call attention to some of the structures of destierro, which are often made invisible by nativist and settler colonial trappings. In "Land as Pedagogy," Leanne Betasamosake Simpson argues that while the settler colonial project attempts to sever ties to Indigenous (specifically Nishnaabeg) spiritual and ancestral knowledge, it is critical to maintain, recuperate, and expand ties to land as practice. She argues that understanding land as pedagogy subverts the logics of "colonial permanence" and bolsters Indigenous knowledge and practices of sovereignty.[23] Simpson contends that "within a Nishnaabeg epistemology, spiritual knowledge is a tremendous, ubiquitous source of wisdom that is the core of every system in the physical world. The implicate order provides the stories that answer all of our questions. The way we are taught to access that knowledge is by being open to that kind of knowledge and by being engaged in a way of living that generates a close, personal relationship with our ancestors and relations in the spirit world through ceremony, dreams, visions and stories."[24]

The term "destierro" includes exile, dispossession of land, removal, contestation, multi-diasporas, and other forms of being ripped from land, land-based practices, and communal and socioeconomic resources. These conditions, to which Afro- and Indigenous-descendant peoples are subjected, are phenomena birthed by modernity, and intersect across temporal and spatial planes in ways that intimately tie them to the histories and experiences of other peoples on the underside of coloniality. In order to understand the ontological impacts of destierro, it is imperative to have a critical and relational understanding of its processes and its impacts.

The works of women of color feminist thinkers are necessary theoretical and practical tools that aid our understanding of the complexities of destierro in relational contexts. That is, their works—political, personal, and poetic—have made clear the stakes and difficulties of working in relation to other oppressed peoples more broadly, and within our own racial/ethnic relations.[25] In *Pedagogies of Crossing* (2005), M. Jacqui Alexander challenges us to continue the difficult work of relating across difference: "If we continue and meet eye to eye, black women born in this country, black women from different parts of the continent and from different linguistic and cultural inheritances of the Caribbean, Latin America, Asia, and the Pacific who experience and define themselves as black . . . there is nothing that can replace the unborrowed truths that lie at the junction of the particularity of our experiences and our confrontation with history."[26] Here, Alexander calls attention to the relationships between Black women across the diaspora. Such a meeting would produce a confrontation with the divergent experiences of women of color, and would generate a confrontation with history itself. Alexander goes on to ask: "What kinds of conversations do we, as black women of the diaspora, need to have that will end these 'wasteful errors of recognition'? Do we know the terms of our different migrations? Each others' work histories? Our different yearnings?"[27] This kind of move toward relationality is both a radical practice and a fertile ground for solidarity.

Alexander takes up concerns with exile, diaspora, and destierro and how peoples in exile/diaspora "have grown up metabolizing exile, feeding on its main by-products—alienation and separation."[28] She asks us to think specifically about the problematic of being "African American and exiled on the spot where one is born. To be Caribbean and exiled on foreign soil producing a longing so deep that the site of neglect is reminiscent of beauty."[29] Here, Alexander underscores the ontological and phenomenological aspects of being exiled in multigenerational contexts, a form of destierro, and how the effects of feeding on "alienation and separation" as a birthright engender a forceful bout of nostalgia and unwavering longing—even amid the edificial, political, and social ruins of our homelands.[30]

In these contexts, destierro can be understood as processes of gendered racialization and dehumanization that are contingent upon the dispossession or tearing-away of a person or peoples from land. For decolonial political projects and discursive analyses, this term requires a reckoning with the *longue durée* of modern colonial knowledge systems and a faithful witnessing to how the longing for, and act of, remembering home/lands are acts of resistance. This is particularly powerful in the context of coloniality, which requires forgetting and erasure. Thus, in times and places where we are encouraged and even given metaphorical cookies for forgetting, it is rebellion to remember, to tell stories about land and land-based practices, and to make claims to home/lands in the face of dispossession. Likewise, it is heresy to claim that the land remembers you: "Rocks hold memory. Land holds memory," and water, Alexander tells us, "will call you by your ancient name, and you will answer because you will not have forgotten. Water always remembers."[31] Thus, I propose that resistance to destierro through decolonial land and knowledge practices undermines the processes of coloniality, settler colonialism, and neocolonialism which attempt to further sever our connection to the land and systematically othered knowledge.[32] If we are to take seriously diasporic subjectivities, then we must also see how they intersect with and resist settler colonialism as an ongoing project.[33] The archive of destierro can be found in these narratives which force us to be faithful witnesses to varying forms of dispossession. Divergent forms of destierro appear across the literary poetics of the Latinx Caribbean and Equatoguinean diasporas.

Loida Maritza Pérez's *Geographies of Home* (1999) is a meditation on a Dominican family in New York City. Pérez's protagonist, Iliana, is a young woman who has just left a hostile university environment in order to return home to support her family as they contend with sexual and domestic violence, poverty, and mental illness. Iliana struggles with her discovery that the home she has returned to after college is a hotbed of racism and degradation, unwelcoming and circumscribed by a denial fueled by heteropatriarchy and conservative Judeo-Christian religious mores. In *Geographies of Home*, Pérez illustrates destierro as a failure to find home even among family. The rejection of Blackness and the contention with different forms of religious spirituality become central to understanding how destierro takes form. The symptoms of destierro can be seen in the deep resentments, mental illness, and depression exhibited across Pérez's cast of characters. Furthermore, the novel is centered on Afro-Dominican experiences, particularly on Afro-Dominican femme identity formation in the diaspora. The literature written from these subjective experiences transforms dominant tropes of exile and diaspora, and shows different dimensions of destierro as experienced by Black and femme characters who are likewise othered racially and linguistically.

Juan Tomás Ávila Laurel's *El dictador de Corisco* (2014) is written from the perspective of a woman named Malela, a mother of two sons and a lifelong resident of Corisco, one of the five Equatoguinean islands. *El dictador de Corisco* is tied to Spanish colonialism, the dictatorial rule of Macias and Obiang, and the arbitrary abuses of power that become part and parcel of Equatoguinean life. While one of Malela's sons carries on an affair with a white tourist, her other son, upset by the changes occurring on the island, declares himself to be the new dictator of Corisco. Dictatorial abuses coupled with the collective power of memory lead the family to destierro, as they are torn away from the land and island they love. Here, exile is shown as an unwanted reality propelled by despotic power and ecological destruction. The ongoing forms of structural political and gender violence endemic to colonization—the coloniality of gender and power that are represented as repetitive acts of violence—become the backdrop as the protagonist and her two sons struggle to endure and remember traumatic events that have befallen their community. The novel's discussion of the ecological impacts of dictatorial violence, greed, and neglect likewise underscores the kinds of ties to land and the ways in which the characters faithfully witness against the grain of dictatorial scripts.[34] *El dictador de Corisco* points to dual forms of destruction and dispossession: the actual tearing-away of land and resources, and destierro which forces peoples to leave their lands.

At the core of these literary works are the acts of remembering histories and knowledges that subvert domination; a practice of faithful witnessing that is dangerous and potentially deadly. Exhuming these memories is an act of subversion, and in both of these novels the characters resist domination by going back to practices or knowledges that were previously foreclosed or forbidden.

Corporeal

Pérez's novel *Geographies of Home* opens dramatically as the protagonist's grandmother, Bienvenida, lies on her deathbed summoning her youngest daughter, Aurelia, through her metaphysical powers. Aurelia, in an act of rebellion and denial, has negated her filial responsibilities and refused to attend to her mother as she faces death. Aurelia wakes to a jarring sensation and witnesses a black cat running across the room. Just after she tastes "a bitter scent of freshly cut grass," she doubles up in pain as the cat reemerges (ix). Aurelia notices that the scent and bitter taste that engender the pain are "familiar as the dirt she craved since the onset of her pregnancy" (ix). Her mother's death and sudden apparition as the black cat bring on the onset of Aurelia's labor pains; her child is to be the protagonist of the novel, Iliana, the youngest of thirteen children born to Aurelia and her husband, Papito.

This juxtaposition of life and death, the desire for consuming grass or dirt, and the reckoning of divergent spiritual practices are central to Pérez's narrative. The novel questions familial ties and underscores how destierro shapes relationships and knowledge practices. The women in the novel, all Afro-Dominican, navigate the reconfigurations of home and belonging as they are unmoored from their homes, foundational beliefs, and their families. While the novel juggles several primary and secondary characters—Iliana has twelve siblings, eight of whom appear in the novel—I will briefly discuss just four of these characters: Iliana, her mother Bienvenida, and her two sisters, Marina and Rebecca. In doing so, I track Afro-diasporic feminist epistemologies and knowledge practices, and the deep-seated practices of gender violence, including the coloniality of gender, which impact how destierro takes shape for Afro-diasporic women. Likewise, these characters' desires, resistance, and struggles offer an understanding of destierro as tied to the land, to spiritual belief systems, and to the Black femme body. Throughout the novel, we see how the repudiation of Blackness—revealed in the radical rejection of Afro-syncretic ritual practices, and by extension a refusal of Black identity—leads to physical and metaphysical destierro. Pérez offers us a glimpse into the lives of a sprawling Afro-Dominican family contending with the effects of destierro, including crushing poverty, Judeo-Christian mores, and rampant gender and sexual violence.

We meet Iliana, a first-generation college student, in the first chapter as she gazes at the word "NIGGER" written on her dorm room message board (1). This act of blatant racism and intimidation foreshadows her family's conflicted relationship with their own racialized Blackness. While Iliana had imagined that the university would be a haven from her religiously conservative home, she quickly realizes that she is left unmoored by the racism and isolation of life in rural upstate New York. At school she finds herself in a kind of social isolation and has but one friend, a white-passing queer Latino man named Ed. Disillusioned with her institution and her liminal place in it,

Iliana resolves to leave her elite university and return home to New York City to be with her family.

In returning home, Iliana is at once faced with the dysfunctions of her family and plagued by feelings of obligation. Raised in a strict Seventh Day Adventist household, Iliana is fearful of her undisclosed and possibly queer sexuality, and is often taken aback by how her body is read by others. Lastly, she is coming to consciousness about her family's anti-Blackness, which is reflected in her sister Marina's racist delusions and her mother's battle against her intergenerational connections to Afro-Dominican ritual practice. Iliana's lack of attention to her appearance and lack of feminine performativity incites a violent backlash from her family and culminates in a sexual assault at the hands of her sister Marina, who suffers from delusions marked by uncontrollable rage.

The rejection of Afro-Dominican syncretism is tied to a larger rejection of familial histories, legacies of slavery, the intergenerational trauma of the Trujillo regime, sociostructurally-enabled anti-Blackness, and the confines of heteropatriarchy. The confluence of these histories—autocratic repression and the rejection of ritual practice—underscore Aurelia and Iliana's alienation from their identities as Black Afro-Atlantic women. This refusal magnifies their feelings of destierro; they do not feel at home in New York or even in their own bodies. We first see the denunciation of Afro-Dominican ritual practice with Aurelia, who rejects the "gifts" of telepathic communication, metaphysical powers, and the ability to "see the invisible," all of which were given to her by her mother Bienvenida (134). A young Aurelia blamed the "sight" for the death of her brother and vowed to distance herself from her mother's spiritual practices (134). Thus, she rejected her mother, to the point of refusing to be at her deathbed, and married Papito, a Seventh Day Adventist who demands that his family adhere to conservative Christian traditions. In her reading of feminist subjectivity and Afro-syncretic practices in the novel, Vanessa Valdés argues that Aurelia's rejection of her spiritual inheritance provided "an opportunity for misogyny to flourish in what is to be their communal refuge, that is to say, their home."[35] Valdés contends that the engagement with this unnamed matrilineal spiritual practice "allows for an appreciation of that whole self rather than an accommodation of the self to fit into the patriarchal norms."[36] However, Aurelia finds herself at a constant crossroads, shrouding her rejection of Afro-Dominican syncretism in a feigned religious fervor to please her husband. Only Iliana knows of the Sabbath-affected illnesses wherein Iliana and Aurelia dance merengue alone in the house (134). Just as Iliana is torn between a life outside of her parents' home and her deep desire to return there, Aurelia is torn between the strict religious mores that her husband demands they follow and her own familial history and spiritual/metaphysical powers. Though nascent in her, Iliana too has these powers of communication, for it was her birth that occurred on the night her grandmother died. While Iliana too rejects her mother's uncanny ability to metaphysically communicate with others, she slowly begins to question the strict Protestant religious philosophies with which she was raised.

We learn in the novel that Bienvenida attempts to give Aurelia the tools of the family practice, but her daughter closes her ears and heart to the gifts: "She wanted no more of such a legacy. . . . She heard her mother's voice but did not listen to the words" (2–3). Aurelia abandons the "gifts, including the quilt and shawl, at the base of a palm tree beside the road," but comes to regret her decision to "[run] from her heritage as if the past had the power to transform her into a pillar of salt" (135). Aurelia, facing her daughter Marina's physical, emotional, and mental deterioration, the sudden return of an independent Iliana, and the abuse and malnutrition of her three grandchildren at the hands of her daughter Rebecca and her husband Pasión, pleads for Bienvenida's guidance: "She longed for the counsel of one who had been long dead." Aurelia believes that her mother left her cursed with a "legacy of woe," but, resolved to save at least one of her daughters, she considers how to use the other gifts her mother gave her (295).

Aurelia employs her exceptional abilities to bring on the death of her son-in-law, Pasión, who abuses her daughter Rebecca and their two young children. Fearful that Rebecca will return to Pasión and risk the lives of her grandchildren, Aurelia resorts to using her powers for what she believes is a just cause: "With her hands busy, she was able to concentrate on the task for which plucking the chickens was a guise" (254). As Aurelia plucks the feathers from dead boiled chickens, she conjures the image of Pasión feeding his flock on his rooftop coop. She compels the hundreds of chickens to create a flurry of feathers, and "sailed toward him on the feathers, depriving him of breath" (256). Valdés posits that in this act, "Aurelia reclaims not only her voice but also her willingness to act."[37] Pasión's death is not mentioned again, and the reader does not know if his corpse is discovered. But what is clear is that Aurelia's return to her familial beliefs is her first step toward reclaiming her spiritual identity, protecting her family, and finding a home within herself.[38] In fact, Valdés contends that within the novel the idea of home "is defined by one's cultivation of a holistic sense of self, a recuperation of that which was lost in the transit of exile. These characters develop a sense of home by engaging in spiritual systems that have survived for millennia. For these daughters, home is a processor healing broken psyches."[39] For both Valdés and Lyn Di Iorio Sandín, the fact that this spiritual practice remains unnamed throughout the novel is evocative of "Aurelia's repression of it."[40] In recovering her power and using her embodied spiritual knowledge, Aurelia challenges the permanence of destierro.

Aurelia recalls her mother's explanation of the gifts in the sack which she left at the base of the palm tree: "A fistful of the earth to which we return to nourish those who follow" (134). This earth that Aurelia was intended to carry was a gift that would anchor her to her homeland, to sacred knowledges, and to the generations before and after her. Leaving it behind leaves her and her daughters wanting. Eating earth, then, is a signifier for a yearning for grounding or mooring, an understanding of past histories and spiritual practices. Aurelia's metaphysical destierro has led her to reconsider her conception of home: "Only now did she understand that she should have yearned not for a geographical site but for a frame of mind able to accommodate any place as home" (137). Jill Toliver Richardson argues that in this act of rejecting her spiritual legacy, "Aurelia rejects her mother's lessons and withholds this integral part of her inheritance from her daughters, which leaves them ill-equipped to navigate the American landscape."[41] Aurelia comes to terms with her dystopian perspective and realizes that a physical geographical home is an impossibility. She cannot return, but she would "hold herself accountable" for making possible some kind of fulfillment for herself and her children (137).

I trace Aurelia's gift—that is, the practices that connect her to a familial home and histories, buried and forgotten under a palm tree in the Dominican Republic—to the recurring image of the desire to eat dirt and grass. Many of the women in the novel, especially those who are prepubescent or pregnant, express a craving to consume earth, dirt, land. In fact, destierro is tied to women's bodies and to the development of their erotic selves.[42] In one scene, Rebecca recalls her teen years in the Dominican Republic, when she would sneak out of the house to a quiet place and masturbate while chewing on grass: "The movement of her hands massaging the tender flesh between her thighs; the bitter taste of a blade of grass tucked between her teeth" (205). Rebecca finds pleasure in the erotic and finds solace in this grounded pleasure even as she is torn by feelings of abandonment. After leaving her grandmother's home in the Dominican Republic at the age of eight, Rebecca is left unmoored in the diaspora. Rebecca's destierro is then multifold, emotional and physical. As a child in the Dominican Republic and as a woman in the United States, Rebecca is unfulfilled. Married to the abusive Pasión, who beats, starves, and rapes her, she quickly loses her sense of place and realizes that she cannot care for her children. She is depicted as a lost woman who is transfixed by the desire for stability. Her longing for foundation can be traced to those sexual excesses on the land and her insatiable desire to consume grass. For these desterradas, eating the earth is a connection to land and landlessness. The medical term for eating dirt, grass, mud, and other nonnutritive substances is "pica," and it has roots in Caribbean slave history; it is a practice that has been documented, pathologized, and condemned by plantation owners and doctors.[43]

Rebecca's craving to consume earth is descriptive of her life with Pasión, which is circumscribed by emotional, sexual, and physical violence. It also evokes the loss of her grandmother Bienvenida, by whom she was raised and nurtured in the Dominican Republic. In tracing the relationship of these women to the land, Pérez shows how they have been torn from it through spiritual and physical dispossession. As Simpson argues, "being tied to land also means being tied to an unwritten, unseen history of resistance."[44] Pérez traces destierro through matrilineal lines, making femme bodies central to connections to the land and home. The distinct forms of destierro that Aurelia, Rebecca, and Iliana feel, and their connections to Bienvenida, have corporeal undertones. The novel frames a space to engage how Black women's bodies and their "deepest and nonrational knowledge" are critical for understanding destierro as an ontological phenomenon (53).[45]

Geographies of Home also traces how destierro likewise produces psychological and physical distress. Marina, Iliana's older sister, is battling her own demons and insecurities, and spirals into a deep psychosis as the novel progresses. Marina's mental and emotional decline is central to the narrative arc, and her visions and sexual hallucinations become focused on her sister Iliana. Myriam J. A. Chancy argues that the novel seeks to "represent . . . multiplicity through sexuality and in defiance of patriarchal power structures."[46] Rather than present gender role reversals as a radical challenge, Pérez weaves a complex narrative that points to the erotic and racialized femme body as volatile defiance. Chancy argues that racial self-loathing and the "lesbian phallus" are central to understanding Pérez's female characters, their identities and sexualities.

Marina, who is described as having "wide lips and kinky hair," yearns not only to be white-passing, but also to become the wife of a white or light-skinned man. While such men have propositioned her, none have asked to marry her, and she hits a breaking point when sexually belittled by one of the lawyers for whom she works (97, 190). Marina's psychological breakdown, marked by delusions and uncontrollable rage, is tied to her own desire for whiteness and its trappings: heteronormativity, middle-class aspirations, and a distancing from her own Blackness through an attempt at "marrying-up" or "bettering the race."[47] Dissatisfied with her life, Marina disassociates from her family mentally and emotionally. Her mental illness is marked by frequent hallucinations and a deeply racialized sexual trauma. In one scene, Marina rails against an imagined sexual assailant and declares, "No flat-nosed, wide lipped nigger would claim her soul. No savage with beads dangling from his neck" (17). Triggered by failed assimilation attempts and alienated from her own body, her erotic imagination becomes circumscribed by white supremacy, cis-heteropatriarchy, experiences of being sexually devalued, and fears of being racialized as Black and poor.

Marina's mental illness is thus embodied, and Pérez articulates the changes in her body as a marker of her declining mental health. Alexander reminds us that much of what we remember and what we know is embodied: "[Violence] can also become embodied, that violation of sex and spirit. Assimilation is another kind of violation that can be embodied, assimilating alienation, one's own as well as others."[48] Marina's body odor, rapid weight gain, and unruly hair become embodied markers of her state of mind. Chancy argues that "Marina's mind, rather than her body, is contaminated—filled with both racial and sexual loathing. Does her personal memory fail her here, or does it give shape to a cultural memory of miscegenation, racial fear, and the trauma of the rapes of enslaved African women, women of whom she issues?"[49] Chancy links Marina's mind to a longer cultural memory that likewise points to a long history of the violation of Black women. Whatever the case, Marina's racist and self-loathing behavior is represented as physical convulsions, belief in spiritual anointment, and a deep distrust of her family.

Furthermore, Marina becomes obsessed with the possibility that Iliana may have a hidden or inverted penis. Marina's fear and loathing of Iliana's Blackness, queerness, and gender nonconformity have made her a target of Marina's suspicions. These suspicions are exacerbated when she meets Iliana's queer friend Ed. Marina has difficulty reading his queer body as something other than femme or non-masculine. For her, Ed's queerness underscores Iliana's masculinity vis-à-vis the idea of white middle-class womanhood that Marina has imagined as normative. In order to better observe Iliana, Marina stops taking her medication and begins to carefully study her sister's hands, walk, clothing, facial structure, and presentation: "Iliana's body—with its meager breasts, long arms and massive hands, thin legs and knobby knees—had appeared as lean as a prepubescent girl's and more so like a boy's. Her gait, when she headed into the bathroom, had been the exaggerated walk of a man imitating a woman" (276). Marina decides to bring Iliana's "secret" (hidden or inverted penis) into the open by sexually assaulting her sister while she sleeps. In the moment of violence, Iliana thinks of herself beyond flesh and body: "She was far more than the sum of her spilled blood and her flesh that had been pierced, she was the breath seeping from her lips, the heart resounding in her chest, the anima enabling her to perceive" (287). However, when Marina attacks her for a second time, Iliana loses all sense of calm. She realizes that Marina's actions are not solely the actions of someone who is ill, but rather stem from denial, deep hatred, and perhaps jealously of Iliana's ability to move through the world independently (290). She becomes enraged upon seeing Marina's look of satisfaction at having penetrated her body, gratified by the idea that she has taken something vital from Iliana. Thus, Marina's destierro and fear of sexual violence lead her to violate her sister's body as a way to ground her delusions and disillusions.

Iliana, nauseated at the events that have transpired and recognizing how deeply in denial her parents are about Marina's condition, steels herself against her sister's attempt to tear her away from her very own body (291). Iliana flees and cannot face returning home. She begins to hate the very blood that flows through her veins and contemplates suicide. Echoing Obejas's *Days of Awe*, Iliana realizes that this destierro will kill her. When she returns home the following day, she is confronted and slapped by her father Papito. It is then that she becomes fully conscious that her father's narrow religious beliefs and the home he has created based on those beliefs have no place for her or her body. She is left with no home or safety or foundational beliefs to which to adhere.

In Pérez's novel, destierro is not a form of exile that is overtly linked to the nation. Instead, she provides a rich terrain through which to understand the various ontological dimensions of non-being produced by anti-Blackness and the coloniality of gender. Coloniality and dispossession, in their myriad forms, are present in every aspect of the family's destierro. The family's members try and fail to adhere to conservative religiosity and attempts at assimilation. Iliana's body is the final limit. Though she is left desterrada in multiple ways, she refuses to be torn from her body. Valdés contends that this critical moment is one in which Iliana "cultivates a sense of wholeness" and looks to her own deepest knowledge as a "guide for living."[50] This is the decolonizing moment in *Geographies of Home*, the reclamation of their corporeal and ritual knowledge for both Iliana and her mother Aurelia.

The themes in *Geographies of Home* trouble the idea of home as a spatial location. Iliana is forced to choose a life beyond the obligations she feels to her mother, father, and siblings; "she felt as displaced out in the world as in her parents' house, she had made the decision to return and to re-establish a connection with her family so that . . . she would have comforting memories of home propping her up and lending her the courage to confront the prejudices she had encountered" (312). Iliana decides that she can no longer interact with her family, nor imagine thriving in a world without "the only home she knew" (312). There is no neat ending for Iliana; her destierro, like that of her parents and siblings, is a part of her own experience as an Afro-Latina immigrant in the United States. Her desire to belong somewhere and find fulfillment is also the desire of many of the other characters in *Geographies of Home*. As C. Christina Lam argues, "Fiction, far from providing mere escapism, works to transmit the horror of traumatic experiences so that it can be accessed and acknowledged by the reader who, in turn, becomes a potential witness."[51] This novel, comprised of Afro-Latinx characters and authored by an Afro-Latina writer, speaks to an often-unspoken set of questions about Afro-Latinx immigrant families regarding race, spirituality, and sexuality. Iliana's embrace of familial destierro and rejection of corporeal destierro underscore the complex negotiations of racialized, sexualized, and marginalized immigrant subjects. Contending with destierro allows for many of the characters to reimagine their relationships to embodied knowledges and practices, and radically redefine home.

Memorial

In his novel *El dictador de Corisco* (2014; *The Dictator of Corisco*), Juan Tomás Ávila Laurel fictionalizes little-known histories of Equatorial Guinea's island of Corisco. By examining the political impossibilities of dictatorship, the novel underscores the danger of memory in a nation where dictatorship and autocracy followed colonialism and fascism. As Benita Sampedro

Vizcaya has noted, memory and forgetting are powerful practices that emerge in the wake of colonialism and dictatorship. In her article "Routes to Ruins," Sampedro Vizcaya tells of an event that all the inhabitants of Corisco of a certain age (over seventy years old) recall: a horrible and uncontrollable fire caused by a priest, Father Andrés Bravo, who quickly escaped the island and never returned.[52] While the memory of this fire lives on, the details have been forgotten, and Sampedro Vizcaya argues that the "brutal repression and exploitation in the decades following the event helped to shape the politics of forgetting; new forms of repression in the present day generate a combination of amnesia and nostalgia closely associated with political disempowerment."[53] In crafting this narrative, Ávila Laurel offers a searing critique of the machinations of dictatorial power, ecological destruction masked as transnational collaboration, and memory as both a salve and a curse.

El dictator de Corisco introduces us to a Benga family, Malela and her two sons, Primero and Segundo.[54] While in *Geographies of Home* the characters face psychological and emotional destierro in the diaspora after their own experiences under the Trujillo regime, in *El dictador*, Malela and her sons experience destierro as the perpetual threat of death and/or displacement as a result of colonial and then despotic rule. For Malela, Primero, and Segundo, Corisco becomes an impossible home because of the long-standing excesses of dictatorial power and the ecological destruction of the island brought on by modernization.

The novel engages matters that are important to understanding the contemporary social and political realities affecting Equatorial Guinea. The novel's backdrop includes living among the physical and emotional ruins left by colonialism; the educational, social, and welfare neglect of the postcolonial authoritarian government; the suppressed histories of ethnic cleansing during Macias Nguema's dictatorship; and the destruction of ecological sites without regard for Indigenous populations. Sampedro Vizcaya's "Routes to Ruin" interrogates the affective, edificial, and historical archives across some of the more distant islands of Equatorial Guinea, including the island of Corisco, which is located approximately thirty miles southwest of Equatorial Guinea's continental swathe. She notes that the "ghost-like villages and vacuumed-like empty islands can be as eloquent about the past as archives. . . . They speak of the politics and experience of abandonment, and they are 'endowed with a capacity to penetrate our sensibility' . . . and eventually move us to action—that other data may lack."[55]

El dictador de Corisco takes place amid these ruins left by colonial and industrial processing facilities, and highlights the absurd repetition of destructive political practices. The neglect is further emphasized by the history of genocide, and thus creates a state of precarity. Ruth Wilson Gilmore's definition of racism as "state-sanctioned or extralegal production and exploitation of group-differentiated vulnerability to premature death" holds for the case of Equatorial Guinea, and more specifically for the picture of Corisco that Ávila Laurel paints for us.[56] This is because the ethnic groups that comprise the population of Equatorial Guinea, including the Bubi and Ndowe, represent an ethnic underclass in relation to the Fang ruling class (the dictator and his extended family and cronies) since the transition from colony to dictatorship.[57]

The kinds of ecological, sociopolitical, and economic devastation faced by some of the more peripheral islands and smaller ethnic groups, however, leave witnesses in their wake. Sampedro Vizcaya argues that "the places—or, rather, spaces—in which we encountered the women and the men of Elobey, Corisco, and Cabo San Juan bear continued witness to the experience of large-scale exile, migration, depopulation, alienation, dispossession, illness, alcoholism, and deprivation of educational and health resources."[58] *El dictador* is a form of witnessing and acts as an indictment against the dispossession and destierro that eventually force Malela and her sons to escape.

We first encounter Malela as she watches a white tourist from Holland, Anika/Anita, enter her town. Anika/Anita's arrival puts into motion a set of events in Corisco that forces Malela to recall some of the most painful colonial and dictatorial histories that have been strategically forgotten by the elders. News of Anika's arrival incites Malela to smoke her pipe, which, in the narrative, is unheard of for a woman in Corisco, especially after the departure of the white commercial factory owners in the late 1960s. Malela's pipe-smoking floods her with memories about her youth, and she laments the fact that she never married even though she was from a prominent family. She discloses that because she was constantly visited by white suitors, no one from her community approached her for marriage. Though her parents followed Ndowe traditions and indeed wanted her to marry into the community, Malela was perceived as belonging to the white colonizers.

> Las constantes visitas que le hacían los dueños de factorías hicieron que todas las familias creyeran que su vida pertenecía a los blancos, por lo que ya no sería bien visto que ningún hombre de aquellas familias la quisiera para el y para su familia. Se pensaba en aquellos tiempos que los mares estaban llenos de peces y en que la echada de una red daba para alimentar varias bocas, que una mujer que había sido tan visitada ya no podia ser de ningún sitio. Estaba en medio del pueblo siendo mirada por todos como si nadie la quisiera reconocer como alguien de la comunidad. (6)

> The constant visits made to her by the owners of factories made all the families believe that her life belonged to the whites, so it would not be well seen that any man from those families would want her for themselves or their families. It was thought at that time that the seas were full of fish and that the pitch of a single net was enough to feed several mouths and that a woman who had been visited so much

> could no longer be from any place. She was in the middle of the town being seen by everyone as an outsider, as if no one wanted to recognize her as part of the community.

Malela lived amidst her people, and yet they saw her as someone they did not want to recognize as part of their community. Malela's proximity to colonial-era white men, by virtue of being desired, marked her as an outsider and left her desterrada from certain forms of kinship and community ties.[59]

Sampedro Vizcaya's research resonates once again, as she notes that the "dark past" of colonization "is characterized not least by gender exploitation." In her interviews with Equatoguinean elders, Sampedro Vizcaya underscores the forms of gendered subjugation and exploitation that women in Corisco face:

> Life stories unveiled, in interviews with women in their sixties and seventies, are threaded through with the image of the *corisqueñas* as an inexhaustible harem of concubines, *miningas* in the local colonial parlance. Their stories speak of miscegenation, of children that grew up without ever meeting their (white) fathers, of women eternally at the disposal of their capricious European partners, personal experiences of subjugation.[60]

These tacitly understood practices of gender exploitation are the backdrop for Malela's peripheral experience within her community. Though she was never officially outcast, she is barred from the community by *congosa*, or gossip, as if she no longer belonged to any place. However, Malela is a keeper of much of the community's oral histories, especially of events that have been long suppressed and forgotten. It is her peripheral position that enables her to keep this historical memory that many others—those who live day-to-day within the community as full members—do not know or remember. In this way, Malela as desterrada, as someone living on her own land but ripped away from community, is key to keeping alive what others have let die.

One example of this periphery as destierro is that Malela's community remains baffled about the origins of her two children. In questioning the parentage, birth, and appearance of her two sons, the community underscores that Malela is not part of natal kinship or child-rearing practices in her community. Thus, many community members ask what kind of power has intervened to occlude her life: "¿Quien había metido su mano en la vida de Malela para que los hechos de su vida parecieran haber ocurrido en un tiempo en que nadie del pueblo lo daba por cierto?" (8; "Who had put their hand in the life of Malela in such a way that the facts of her life seemed to have occurred in a time that none of the people could be certain of?"). This trope of memory and forgetting is tied to the larger histories of trauma and forgetting in the novel, and it is likewise an indictment of the reader. Ávila

Laurel's question haunts the reader, for we too are reading about a time, space, and nation whose histories go unknown and unmarked. The conjuring of memory in the novel is also a conjuring or coming to consciousness for the reader.

The story of Malela and her sons is intimately tied to the dictatorship of motodu Don Francisco (i.e., Macías Nguema) and the later rule of motodu Obiang.[61] Malela recalls the era right after independence, when Don Francisco took power, expelled all Europeans from Equatorial Guinea, and sent into exile all those who had any intellectual, social, and economic relations with them. The factory owners of Corisco were expelled their factories and homes, never to return while Don Francisco exerted power over Equatorial Guinea's island territories. In some ways, the histories of Equatorial Guinea after colonialism mirror much of what we know about the formations of domination and dispossession in ongoing settler colonial projects.[62] Malela's retelling of this history points to Don Francisco's fear as reason for his distrust and violent rule: "Como Don Francisco no conocía el mar ni había tenido un trato profundo con los blancos, los temía mucho, y desde su puesto de motodu luchó para borrar las huellas que dejaron, dondequiera que estuvieran las mismas" (9–10; "Since Don Francisco did not know the sea nor had ever had any deep relationship with the whites, he feared them very much and from his position as motodu he fought to erase the fingerprint that they left, wherever they may have been"). Don Francisco's distrust of white people becomes his distrust of the inhabitants of Corisco, who had the longest history of relations with Europeans.

Motodu Don Francisco aimed to eliminate anyone who had had any relationship with whites, and dictated that after "gloriosa evacuación de los blancos de los territorios nacionales, era considerado un delito de alta traición que hubiera un grupo de hombres, un pueblo entero, que tuviera a los blancos en el recuerdo" (14; after "the glorious evacuation of the whites from the national territories, it was considered a crime of high treason that there be a group of men or an entire population that had the whites in their memory"). The expulsion of the whites occurred in tandem with the destruction of any village or peoples who at any time had had economic, social, or educational connections to the whites. Malela's island, with its many factories, was a prime example of a territory that had had too much contact with whites and was thus tainted. The safety of its people, however, was guaranteed by the presence of their dignified "ekambi" (chief), and by the fact that in order to reach Corisco, Don Francisco would need to embark on a sea voyage. It is implied here that because Don Francisco was part of the Fang ethnic group and from the continental swathe, he feared the ocean. Corisco's insularity kept it further away from, yet still under the heel of, an all-dominating power. Malela's conjuring of the past at the opening of the novel and her memory of the plantation owners and their post-independence departure would be considered high treason.

Malela's position as an outsider and as a desterrada allows her to remember one of the most violent episodes of motodu Don Francisco's regime. She painfully recalls the destruction of an entire Ndowe village by Don Francisco's military. Families were killed, their homes burned to the ground, and young girls taken to the woods and violated. Of the latter, Malela recalls:

> Las mujeres jóvenes que tenían Buena Mirada y no habían tenido hijos, un hecho decidido por Dios, fueron apartadas y obligadas a acompañar al bosque a los mismos que cometieron aquella cosa terrible con su pueblo. En los bosques, y sin nadie que las defendiera, sufrieron tanto que cuando regresaron al sitio de sus casas quemadas no pudieron hablar. (14)
>
> The young women who were of good looks and did not have children, a fact decided by God, were taken aside and forced to accompany to the woods those very same men that had committed that terrible thing to their people. In the woods, and with no one to defend them, they suffered so much that when they returned to their burned homes they could no longer speak.

Ávila Laurel's choice to make Malela recall this painful event in detail highlights the significance of memory in historical trauma. That it appears in a literary text and not in archives or history texts emphasizes the role of literature as a discursive strategy with heretical and decolonizing potential. This destruction of the Ndowe community is one of the few documented events of the era that propelled a great number of Equatoguineans into exile beginning in 1969. In fact, Francisco Macías Nguema's reign resulted in the execution, imprisonment, or exile of more than one-third of the nation's population, and his tactical ethnic cleansing was directed at groups such as the Bubi and the Ndowe, particularly those located in the island territories. These kinds of overtly violent pacification tactics were meant to show Macías Nguema's authority and ensure obedience from the Ndowe and other non-dominant ethnic groups that were indigenous to the islands off the coast of the continental swathe. These strategies were part and parcel of the brutality of the regime, whose soldiers so brutalized the bodies of their victims that mourners could not identify their dead. Moreover, these strategies mirrored the kinds of foundational violence within Spanish colonial imperial projects. The coloniality of power reveals itself in the ways that a "postcolonial" nation can enact the same forms of physical, structural, and ideological domination and violence.

Malela's community suffers a great loss when their ekambi dies. His death is especially distressing because his son, who is to be his successor, is abroad. They fear that he will not hear of his father's death in time for his burial or that he will have difficulty reentering the country. Anxiously they wait for the inevitable; motodu Don Francisco hears news of the ekambi's death and sends militants to investigate. Since the motodu could use any excuse of disloyalty or omission to finally wipe them out of existence, the entire community engages in open celebrations and food preparations in order to convince the visitors that all is normal. Throughout the days-long visit, the body of the ekambi rots in the woods, a disgraceful decomposition unworthy of his status. The villagers, though putting on a façade of happiness and subservience to the militants, are in mourning, so much so that Malela recalls "el llanto en las gargantas de la gente" (21; "the rising cries in the throats of the people"). In the end, the militants leave loaded with goats, foodstuffs, and excessive gifts that they have demanded. The village is traumatized not only by the loss of the ekambi and their inability to bury him properly, but also because of the angst of their prolonged act of subterfuge. They have been removed or desterradas from both their grief and their bodies. Malela notes later in the novel that this event is never spoken of again. It becomes a suppressed memory, one that the elders do not want to pass along to their children, and it foreshadows the novel's tragic ending.

This relationship with the past is made material by the constant presence of colonial-era ruins, which engender conflicting memories. The dictatorial regimes' disregard further dislocates the present by allowing blight and disrepair to overrun the neglected island. "Ruins of the old regime," Sampedro Vizcaya notes, "are a shattered mirror of colonial production, power, modernity, and subjugation." The ruins reflect or act as mirrors for the tyranny and manipulation of the postcolonial regimes. These mirrored ruins also reveal a kind of memory play, what Sampedro Vizcaya calls "a combination of amnesia and nostalgia closely associated with political disempowerment."[63] However, Malela's conjuring of the past is not circumscribed solely by the destruction of the Ndowe community and its constant fear of reprisals. Rather, Malela thinks about the past colonial legacies of imperial violence while also thinking about the realities inflicted by the present dictator, motodu Teodoro Obiang.

The novel closely reflects reality in that the fictional motodu Teodoro overthrows his uncle, the fictional motodu Don Francisco. Motodu Teodoro practices a sustained negligence and disregard which results in the island lapsing into ruin. But Motodu Teodoro later sees the island as an opportunity to increase his wealth by attracting affluent white tourists to bask in its beauty: "Ese descubrir de las maravillas ocultas de la tierra de Malela hizo que el siguiente motodu hablara con el ekambi de otro lejano país" (25–26; "This discovery of the occult marvels of Malela's land made the next motodu speak with the ekambi of another far away"). After discovering the marvelous beauty of Malela's island, the motodu speaks with the ekambi of another faraway nation, and they decide to "desecar un hermoso lago que había en la zona oeste de aquella tierra recién descubierta por los que habían hablado con ellos" (25–26; "drain a beautiful lake that was on the west side of that land recently discovered by those they had spoken to"). Motodu Teodoro contracts foreign laborers to drain and fill the large lake on the western side of the island in order to lay a landing strip so that wealthy foreigners can easily access Corisco. It is within this matrix of occurrences that Anita/Anika, the tourist and catalyst of the novel, appears.

Ávila Laurel's narrative centers on the destruction of this lake and the devastation it brings. This is a deliberate discussion of the airport actually built on the island of Corisco in 2011, which extends the entire length of the island from north to south.[64] In an ecocritical turn, Ávila Laurel reveals the draining's environmental impact. He stresses that in making this choice to destroy the largest source of fresh water on the island, the motodu had no regard for the people's needs:

> Lo primero que había que hacer era decir a las mujeres del pueblo que desde aquella fecha tenían que saber que lo más importante en el pueblo no eran sus plantaciones para que la gente tuviera que comer con el pescado que traían los hombres, sino la obra de la pista de los ricos de otros países. Entonces si alguna plantación se econtraba dentro del terreno elegido por los capataces musulmanes, las mujeres tenían que alegrarse pues podían favorecer los planes del que estaba en la silla renunciando a las mismas. (26)
>
> The first thing that needed to be done was to tell the women of the community that from that date forward they needed to know that the most important thing in the country was not their plantations that served for people to eat the fish that the men brought, but rather, the work of the landing strip for the rich men from other countries. So if any plantation was found in the area chosen by the muslim foremen, the women needed to rejoice because they could favor the plans of the very one sitting on the throne that was damning them.

Developing the airport served motodu Obiang's plans, but it left families in the area in destierro, literally ripped away from their plantations and displaced.

The arbitrariness of the motodu's plans and power can be seen in the decision to forge ahead even when the project's foremen realize that the lake is much too difficult to seal. Not to be deterred, when filling the lake with dirt and trees proves ineffective, they spend excessive amounts of money securing rocks from a neighboring nation in order to fill the basin and displace the water. Malela laments that the foreign engineers may do so good a job that no one will remember there was ever a large, beautiful lake on the island (55). This ecological violence mirrors other kinds of violence that the motodu arbitrarily inflicts without any regard for human life.

Segundo, Malela's second son, living under motodu Teodoro's regime, becomes enraged at the destruction of the lake and the island's ecosystem.

He comes to believe that he can solve the political dilemma by becoming the new dictator of Corisco:

> Aquí caeremos de culo cuando esto se convierta en otro Sahara porque estos salvajes están protegidos por el kalashnikov de Bob Denard. Y nadie lo quiere ver; solo abriremos la boca cuando estemos con el agua aquí. Pero no me voy a callar. Aquí hay que hacer algo antes de que estos mamelucos se lleven todas las ceibas y nos dejen sus viejos catapilas. Nadie quiere hacer nada y como soy un muana mboka, voy a defender mi pueblo. Aquí hay que montar una verdadera dictadura y yo voy a ser el dictador de Corisco. (30)
>
> Here we will fall on our asses when this becomes another Sahara because these savages are protected by Bob Denard's kalashnikov. And nobody wants to see it; we will only open our mouth when we are up to here with water. But I'm not going to shut up. Here something must be done before these crazies take all the ceibas and leave us their old Caterpilars (machines). Nobody wants to do anything and since I am a muana mboka, I am going to defend my town. We need to mount a true dictatorship here and I am going to be the dictator of Corisco.

Here, the Ndowe phrase "muana mboka" (or "mwana mboka" or "mwa mboka") is key. It refers to a young person or youth who is essentially of the earth or the land—"un joven esencialmente de la tierra." In this moment Segundo emphasizes his connection to the land, and his emotional and political commitments to protecting it by any means necessary. He tells his mother and brother, "Aquí hay que montar una verdadera dictadura," and declares, "Yo voy a ser el dictador de Corisco" (30). His dictatorship would defend his community from the inevitable: the island's ceiba trees surrounding the lake, which had been uprooted to facilitate the draining, will be replaced by more ruins: the abandoned construction vehicles.

The narrative arc of the novel, a critique of the dictatorship, closely resembles the work of another Annobonese writer, Francisco Zamora Loboch, whose poem "Vamos a matar al tirano" ("We Are Going to Kill the Tyrant") is likewise a cry for the eradication of dictatorship and tyranny. In it, the speaker asks his mother to give him "esa vieja lanza / que usó el padre" ("that old spear / that the father used") for he is going to "matar al tirano" ("kill the tyrant").[65] Similar to Segundo's claim that he is a muana mboka, the speaker of the poem states, "pertenezco a un pueblo de revueltas / observa mi hechura / de escaramuzas y levantamientos / mi pulso no temblara," ("I belong to a people of revolts / observe my workmanship / skirmishes and uprisings / my pulse will not tremble"), making clear his resolve to join a long history of his nation's resistance to tyranny. The poem conjures the long history of Annobonese resistance to colonial rule and dictatorship, histories that often remain untold but are nevertheless alive in the memories of the people.[66] The poem ends with the declaration "ya no habrá más tiranos / nunca más dictadores / sobre mi pueblo, sobre tu miseria / sobre tu miedo" ("there will be no more tyrants / never more dictators / over my people, over your misery / over your fear"), which resembles but is likewise incommensurable with Segundo's announcement that he will become the dictator of Corisco. While Zamora Loboch's poem proclaims that there will no longer be tyrants or dictators after him, Segundo appoints himself a dictator, seemingly the only form of power that he can replicate.

For Ávila Laurel, the narrative underscores an ignorance about the modalities and functions of power. Because Segundo does not know how power works, he believes that he can arbitrarily declare himself a dictator and that he will prevail in changing the abuses in Corisco.[67] Segundo's declaration opens a floodgate of memories, as Malela recalls the last time someone declared himself a dictator. She understands the power behind Segundo's utterances, and thinks about the repercussions and reactions her son would receive from the elders for even daring to utter the word 'dictator': "Y fue después de aquellos hechos, y durante los mismos, los que conocían las palabras dijeron que todo aquello podía ocurrir porque lo que imperaba era una dictatura. Como aquello se decía en voz tan baja que parecía una confidencia, la gente aprendió que era una palabra que no se podía soltar así por así" (30; "And it was after those events and during them that those that knew the words said that all of that could happen because what propelled it was a dictatorship. Since that was said in such a low voice that sounded like a secret, the people learned that it was a word that could not be set free at whim"). Segundo goes on to reveal that he knows a history which has been long forgotten: "Como no montemos una dictadura para expulsarlos, acabaremos envueltos en la red como sardinas o como la cabra que llevaban los militares el día en que estaba pudriéndose en el bosque el ekambi" (31; "Since we won't enact a dictatorship, we will end up tangled in a net like sardines or like the goat that the militants carried the day that the ekambi was rotting in the woods"). In uttering these words Segundo recalls a history that he should not have known, remembering the visit of motudu Teodoro's militants after the death of the ekambi. Malela closes her eyes and crosses herself.

> Aquel hijo suyo había mencionado los aspectos de una historia muy triste, y dura, en la vida del pueblo, pero que el no debería haber debido conocer porque cuando ocurrieron aquellos hechos era un niño y porque nunca quisieron los mayores que se contara como si fuera un cuento de su tradición. De hecho era así un secreto que quisieron guardar los mayores para que quedara en la memoria oculta del pueblo. (31)

> That son of hers had mentioned the details of a very sad and difficult history in the life of the community, but one which he should not have known because when they occurred he was a child and because the elders did not want it to be told as an oral history of their tradition. As a matter of fact, it was a secret that the elders wanted to keep so that it would become a suppressed (occult) memory of the people.

Though the community elders have attempted to suppress this history, Segundo invokes it at the very same moment that he declares his petit dictatorship. This act of remembering and retelling is a decolonizing act, one that indicts violence through a practice of listening and conjuring the past. Segundo's remembering, however, mirrors another kind of repetition—that of coloniality. That is, while remembering these histories, he also declares himself a dictator, therein repeating the cycle of political repression. However, Malela is aware of the layers of danger that her family is facing.

For Segundo, this dictatorship is not a fantasy, but a plan he would like to put into action. Day after day he traverses the island until he discovers something unbelievably grim. In a forgotten coastal quarter, he finds a community of people, descendants of the servants of the colonial settlers who left in the late 1960s. This group of survivors made homes for themselves from littoral caves previously used for preparing and burying dead bodies. Segundo finds that in addition to taking shelter in these mausoleums, they reside amid mass open-air graves with bodies in various states of decomposition. It is this news of what Segundo has discovered on the forgotten edges of the island, along with Primero's illicit affair with Anita/Anika, that cements Malela's decision to escape from Corisco.[68]

Malela's decision to go into exile is tied to the fact that her sons are repeating many different aspects of histories that they do not know. Primero's affair with Anika and the possibility that it could encourage congosa is eerily similar to the community's attitude when Malela was visited by, or "belonged" to, white plantation owners. Segundo's desire to become a dictator is an act of repetition that can bring on brutal forms of violence; his imagined regime, though intended to help the communities of Corisco, takes the very same approach as the dictatorial regimes that have ruled Equatorial Guinea since 1968. The destruction of the lake to build an airport that would welcome the same kinds of foreigners who were expelled decades before is an act of violence and displacement—one that arrives on top of the long-standing neglect exemplified by blight, ruin, and the extreme isolation of the servants' descendants on the other side of the island.

Malela finally chooses another kind of destierro for her family, but the emotional toll is more than she bargains for. As they board the ship to leave Corisco, Malela and her sons take a final look at the island: "Abandonaban la tierra donde habían vivido siempre y desde lejos veían que estaba rodeada de agua por todas partes. El sol se ponía, y en la penumbra no dejo que de los ojos de Malela caín unas gotas de lágrima" (55–56; "They abandoned the land where they had always lived and from afar they saw that it was surrounded by water on all sides. The sun set and in the shadows of light you could not see that out of Malela's eyes tears fell"). For the first time, the family sees Corisco from afar, and the reader feels the pang of their decision to abandon their home for a future life in destierro. Her sons feel Malela's devastation as well. Primero sits next to his mother, blinking rapidly, while Segundo stands up and walks to the edge of the ship: "Quería ver cómo se perdía su tierra al salir de ella por el mar. Su espíritu inquieto le llevó a mirar todo lo que se podía ver. . . . El sol se había metido, pero la noche cercana, con sus negros brazos sobre la aguas, tenía cosas que mostrar. Por esto se levanto de donde estaba su familia. Salío solo" (56; "[He] wanted to see how his land was lost as they left by sea. His spirit, restless, took him to survey all that could be seen. . . . The sun had set, but the night was near, with its black arms over the waters, had things to show. This is why he stood away from where his family was seated. He went alone"). This moment, when the setting sun and the night skylights dance on the water, is circumscribed by Segundo's melancholy over leaving Corisco indefinitely. Ávila Laurel tells us that he went alone, "salío solo," and Segundo does not return. The next morning, Malela realizes that Segundo has vanished. Perhaps he leapt overboard to his death, or has disappeared in a rejection of destierro and towards some other possible life. Malela and Primero, however, are never to see Segundo again, and so it seems that this young keeper of memories, this mwa mboka, could not endure destierro.

El dictador de Corisco is a novel about memory—about the act of forgetting and the dangerous, even deadly, act of remembering. The novel indicts the arbitrariness of power, the liminalities of dictatorship, and the indefinite repetition of tragic histories. For Malela, Primero, and Segundo, Corisco has become an impossibility, and the novel builds to this moment of choosing destierro as an act of resistance against the kinds of removal and dispossession occurring on their lands. In this narrative, destierro is not only being removed from resources, land, memories, and histories, but is also an act that refuses to capitulate to a regime which demands ahistoricity and subservience. Malela chooses the destierro that she does not know over the destierro that she knows intimately.

Remembering Destierro

In writing these narratives the authors undertake a decolonizing task, one that examines, subverts, and complicates forms of destierro.[69] In *Geographies of Home*, destierro is rooted in the rejection of ritual practice and an adherence to heteropatriarchy and anti-Blackness.[70] It is this aversion to Blackness, a product of anti-Black racism rooted in the modern colonial project, that poisons the home, the psyche, and in the end leads to Iliana's sexual assault at her sister's hands. Furthermore, Aurelia's rejection of Afro-syncretic beliefs exiles her from her own innermost knowledge. It is only by recovering these practices and accepting these histories that Aurelia begins to reconceive her familial history and tries to address the trauma her daughters have suffered. Iliana, like her mother Aurelia, begins to reimagine home outside of a geographical location, and comes to a corporeal consciousness.[71]

In *El dictador de Corisco* Malela and Segundo are vessels for long-forgotten memories, which is dangerous in a nation where remembering can be considered an act of high treason. While the principal problems in the novel seem to revolve around the draining of the lake, other critical issues also come into view. Segundo's encounters with people living among open-air graves and Primero's sexual affair with Anika/Anita propel the family into destierro. However, the novel centers the act of remembering in spite of and against power. It is in the rejection of forgetting that Malela is able to imagine a life outside of Corisco. Not only are Malela and Primero devastated by the loss of their home, they also suffer the tragic loss of Segundo, the son who had declared himself the dictator of Corisco. *El dictador de Corisco* illustrates how the act of remembering trauma, of speaking its unnamable name, is a kind of decolonial love. It is speaking and writing truths and histories that have been left tacitly unspoken. Through writing narratives such as *Geographies of Home* and *El dictador de Corisco*, these authors show an acute understanding of destierro and dispossession that severs them from a homeland. While the novels' plots remain unresolved or unknown, we are left in the ethical position to take seriously what they have posited. The question remains: how can we attend to the ways in which modernity tears peoples from their roots and dispossesses them through varying forms of destierro? The condition of destierro demands reparations. Yet, does an ethical reparation exist for the condition of living in destierro in the face of overlapping and often incommensurable dispossession? The following chapter takes up these questions and tracks how diasporic Afro-Atlantic Hispanophone authors consider the question of reparations in decolonial contexts, and offer ways to think about a reparation of the imagination through acts of decolonial love and resistance.

Chapter 4

Reparations

> Love is the unremitting, love is the unrelenting work, what sustains and blooms all of us in your blinded & bound times.
>
> —Christina Olivares, "Letter"

In 2013, the Caribbean Community (CARICOM) instituted several National Committees on Reparations and a Reparations Commission in order to "establish the moral, ethical and legal case for the payment of reparations by the former colonial European countries, to the nations and peoples of the Caribbean Community, for native genocide, the transatlantic slave trade and a racialized system of chattel slavery."[1] Citing crimes against humanity that disenfranchised the victims of colonial genocide and slavery, as well as their descendants, the commission brought forth a lawsuit against the United Kingdom, the Netherlands, and France to begin a "reparatory dialogue to address the living legacies of these crimes."[2] This demand, like others, is part of a long history of oppressed peoples wrestling with the aftermath of imperial violence, slavery, and degradation. At its center, the CARICOM lawsuit emphasizes what theories of decoloniality have long underscored: that the ideological structures, orders, and legacies of colonialism subsist, even after colonial administrations have ceased to exist in full.[3] These structuring processes, or what Aníbal Quijano calls the "coloniality-of-power," are central to how I analyze struggles for reparations in the modern/colonial world.[4] In *Black Skin, White Masks*, Frantz Fanon meditates on anticolonial struggles and what he calls "a double process" of inferiority. For Fanon, the anticolonial struggle must be waged on two interrelated levels: the objective and the subjective, or addressing both the colonial administration and its ideology.[5] The proof of the need for this dual process can be seen in the failure of the political decolonization projects that reached their apex in the 1950s and 1960s.[6] These projects largely focused on transforming colonial administrations, but were unwilling or incapable of transforming the ideologies and practices undergirding colonialism. Contemporary calls for reparations must not only contend with past evils and the current social and political injustices that stem from those evils, but must also transform or attempt to dismantle coloniality itself; any reparation that does not address coloniality and settler colonialism is a failed reparation.

In the last chapter, I outlined the concept of destierro as a methodological and praxical approach to mapping and subverting overlapping forms of dispossession for Afro- and Indigenous-descended peoples in the modern world. Destierro demands material reparations, as well as decolonizing reparations which are unquantifiable. In attending to the difficulties of decolonizing the subjective and ideological aspects of coloniality and ongoing forms of colonialism, I argue that literary narratives offer discursive spaces through which to imagine and reimagine the possibilities of decolonial reparations as amends that are both material and immaterial.[7] In this chapter, I take up the works of Equatoguinean, Puerto Rican, Dominican, and Cuban writers and poets in order to meditate on literature's ability to reimagine reparations in ways that do not reinscribe colonial power relations. I first examine and contribute to discourses of decolonial love and reparations in the work of Christina Olivares, Chela Sandoval, Audre Lorde, and Nelson Maldonado-Torres. I use the concepts of decolonial love and the reparation of the imagination as frameworks for engaging these texts, and I propose that at the center of a decolonial reparation is decolonial love. I then examine how Ernesto Quiñonez's *Bodega Dreams*, Joaquín Mbomío Bacheng's *Matinga, sangre en la selva*, and Junot Díaz's *The Brief Wondrous Life of Oscar Wao* conceive of reparations as decolonial love which posits a reparation of the self and a reconciliation of community as integral parts of imagining decolonial futurities.[8] I contend that the reparations they propose are a reparation of the imagination fueled by decolonial love that goes beyond colonial and settler logics.

Decolonial Love and Reparations of the Imagination

The work of the queer Cuban poet Christina Olivares is the source of this chapter's epigraph. Her essay "Letter," written for *About Place Journal* in 2015, posits an intergenerational reparation of "futures imagined differently."[9] In it, Olivares underscores how essential love is in sustaining humanity, kinship, and community in the wake of colonialism, dispossession, and enslavement. The letter is written to human ancestors on Earth in the year 2015 from the perspective of future generations in some unknown time (also on Earth). The letter details the transformation of the Earth, humanity, and language practices, and offers possibilities of love within difference, as it is experienced by these future generations. Throughout the letter, the narrator acknowledges the limits of fear, difference, and the "historical trauma of self hatred, born of other historical traumas" that ancestors experience in the present. As such, the message is imbued with understanding and empathy as well as an unrelenting plea for the ancestors to keep working towards futures and keep practicing love in their trying times. "Imagine the tremendous love within us for you," the author writes. "Imagine you are laying down your body in the dusk of humanity in order to evolve into what sings your praise. You, alive. You, my deepest and most complete authentic loved beloved home AND origin." I am interested in the ways that "Letter" enacts a form of reparation of the imagination through decolonial love. Woven throughout the piece is the fact that language, particularly English, is not enough to traverse the "gaps between the tenderness I'd like to communicate to you and my ability to do so using this instrument." In "Letter," future generations of humans have found the ability to speak many oral and physical languages, to transcend differences among humans and between human and nonhuman animals. "Love," Olivares writes, "is the unremitting, love is the unrelenting work, what sustains and blooms all of us in your blinded & bound times."

Olivares's "Letter" troubles temporality by simultaneously being a document of the past and of the present, and one written from an imagined future beyond the colonial present. It imagines a human and, in fact, a global reparation that is not based on sociopolitical economies, material transactions, or apologies, but is rather bound in interrelationality. The letter documents that differences continue to exist, but "fear of difference, which is false and was outdated and eventually worked itself out, is nearly gone." "We evolve," the letter continues, "we become a we. . . . But also: we are not unified. We fight. We are aroused by this but not that. So. We are DIFFERENT FROM ONE ANOTHER. But more also: we look different. We taste different. We act different. Our values are different. We are still us but we are more us, each. We did not become all the same *and therefore* it worked. We never became the same. Imagine a human world built of differences that does not prompt colonization and slavery." Rather than a utopian future based on sameness, conformity, and hierarchy, these reparations are based on an ethics of valuing differences, and the notion that the decolonizing and justice-oriented work of the present is valuable to the future. "The earth will not end soon, and neither will you," the letter urges. "Do not be afraid of the work. The work pushes forward, relentless and perfect, despite and instead of and within you. Have babies, have lots of babies. Feed them and love them, practice love, overflow with love. Babies and babies and babies. Some of you resist making more children because you are afraid to bring them into this world. That fear makes sense; the decision born from it is pragmatic and of love. But if you are compelled otherwise, bring the babies." Olivares's "Letter," then, is about bringing forth generations secure in the radical knowledge that other worlds and futures outside of our own imagining are possible.

Central to imagining decolonial reparations in modern/colonial and settler colonial contexts is the concept of decolonial love. Decolonial love, Chela Sandoval argues, is a technology for social and political transformation, which is achieved through "a shared practice of hermeneutics of love in the postmodern world."[10] This struggle is in turn fueled by the "decolonial praxis of love," which Sandoval defines as an "attraction . . . and relation carved out of and in spite of difference."[11] She theorizes decolonial love as a transformative political tool that demands the recognition of humanity and affinity across difference. She argues that U.S. Third World feminisms represent the creation of theoretical and methodological approaches that "clear the way for new modes of conceptualizing social movement, identity, and difference."[12] This relation, carved out of and in spite of difference, is central to women of color feminist thought. Audre Lorde understands difference as a "dynamic human force" that "enriches" rather than destroys.[13] To be able to create an affinity or political love that is rooted in the desire for and action towards the liberation of others is difficult and necessary labor, as discussed in the previous chapter on destierro. Olivares's "Letter," then, is part of this radical imagination that builds on an ethics of love and a promise of futurity based on women of color thought, specifically the work of Octavia Butler, who is named in "Letter" as a prophet of possibilities to come.

Decolonial love serves as a rupture in systems of coloniality and ongoing settler colonialism which fragment humans by creating hierarchies of difference. Lorde reminds us that imagining new ways of relations is critical, since "[the] old patterns, no matter how cleverly rearranged to imitate progress, still condemn us to cosmetically altered repetitions of the same old exchanges, the same old guilt, hatred, recrimination, lamentation, and suspicion." The "future of our earth," argues Lorde, depends on developing relations across difference.[14]

Maldonado-Torres's Fanonian meditations advance the idea that the oppressed, or subaltern, subject is best understood as the *damné* who, under the weight of the coloniality-of-power, has the potential to "advance the unfinished project of decolonization." He contends that this condemned political subject "'cries out in horror' in the face of the . . . modern/colonial 'death-world' and aspires—through the decolonial praxis of love . . . through an ethic of the liberation of life . . . and through a decolonizing and liberatory politics inspired by the 'decolonial attitude'—to create a transmodern world 'in which many worlds fit' and where the global dictatorship of capital, property, and coloniality no longer reigns."[15] This decolonial perspective enables the condemned political subject to struggle for liberation in the modern/colonial system while continuing to imagine other kinds of worlds and futurities. Maldonado-Torres suggests that this attraction, kinship, or affinity "goes together here with non-indifference and responsibility, both of which presuppose listening to the cry of the condemned."[16] This non-indifference means a willingness to take action, a kind of move that is "no longer defined by the hand-that-takes but rather by receptive generosity and what Sandoval has aptly rendered as de-colonial love."[17]

Olivares, Sandoval, and Maldonado-Torres's radical and complex understanding of kinship and love recognizes "alliance[s] and affection across lines of difference," whether of the body or outside the body.[18] Decolonial love is part of what fuels the work of decolonization as a political and social project. Maldonado-Torres considers decolonial love to be "the humanizing task of building a world in which genuine ethical relations become the norm and not the exception."[19] It is an integral part of imagining decolonial futurities because it imagines a world in which ethical relationships beyond coloniality are built in spite of the impositions of the colonial difference.

I argue that decolonial love is a practice that bears witness to the past while looking towards a transformative and reparative future by unraveling coloniality, the matrix of power that is manifested in our contemporary conceptions of power, gender, and bodies.[20] Decolonial love, then, necessitates acts of faithful witnessing and ethical actions in the face of visible and invisible domination. Recognizing the violence of dehumanization is necessary for forging ethical relationships based on love and affinity. Bearing witness to violence in the past and in the present is central to achieving a decolonial reparation. Practices of decolonial love can be found across communities of color in creative, political, social, and cultural forms, and act as reparative forces beyond the scope of capitalist accumulation.

Furthermore, decolonial love as an ethical reparation can forge relationships that foster dialogue and action around the irreconcilability of reparations in North American contexts. Two examples are the difficult dialogues surrounding the calls for reparations for the descendants of enslaved Africans, and Indigenous demands for the rematriation of lands stolen by the politics and practices of the United States and Canada's ongoing settler colonial project. The 2015 Critical Ethnic Studies Conference in Toronto engaged such discussions at panels, most notably at the closing plenary session.[21] One speaker recalled an organizing meeting with Black and Indigenous community members in which one person was said to have declared, "You can have the mule but the forty acres are ours." Yet another example can be found in the story that Joanne Barker recounts about an Occupy Wall Street community organizing meeting in Oakland that resulted in anti-Indigenous sentiments. "The most severe expression of this hostility," Barker notes, "occurred when a man who identified himself to me as a 'member of the Black community' accused me of having a 'hidden agenda' to move 'Indians' into the 'family homes of Black people' that the banks had foreclosed on" (23).[22] These statements highlight the tensions within the discourse of liberation for people of color who are fractured by colonial difference and incommensurable yet often overlapping experiences of dispossession, enslavement, and ongoing forms of oppression.

The rhetorical promise of Black reparations as potential land accumulation is part of settler colonial logics that have historically parceled out land over and against the continued dispossession of Indigenous peoples and communities. As Eve Tuck and K. Wayne Yang argue:

> Breaking the settler colonial triad, in direct terms, means repatriating land to sovereign Native tribes and nations, abolition of slavery in its contemporary forms, and the dismantling of the imperial metropole.

> Decolonization "here" is intimately connected to anti-imperialism elsewhere. However, decolonial struggles here/there are not parallel, not shared equally, nor do they bring neat closure to the concerns of all involved—particularly not for settlers. Decolonization is not equivocal to other anti-colonial struggles. It is incommensurable.[23]

This incommensurability can be illustrated by "The Case for Reparations" (2014), Ta-Nehisi Coates's overview of reparations in African American contexts.[24] In Coates's narrative, the injustices are both tangible and state-sanctioned. His poetic and searing use of the word "plunder," however, leaves an absence in its wake. The plunder of Black bodies, wealth, property, families, dreams, and lives was made possible by another form of plunder—Indigenous genocide and dispossession. Coates fails to address Indigenous dispossession; and whether this is the result of ignorance of converging histories or disregard for these realities, we must interrogate what it means to continue to evoke racial reparations without a critical and ethical relationality. We must also examine what it means to equate reparations exclusively through positivistic models. What are the pitfalls of equating historic and systemic racialization, plunder, and dispossession with monetary value?

My goal in discussing these complex and problematic schemas is to illustrate how swiftly we can find ourselves at the crossroads of incommensurable strivings for reparations and liberation, especially if we fail to think in critical and relational ways. Thinking in decolonizing contexts forces us to imagine other forms of reparation that do not rely on the recognition of white cis heteropatriarchal power; do not require the exchange of capital as a primary means of relation or recognition; and begin from a place of shared humanity, a belief in the Sacred, and a shared ethics of decolonial love. We must also undertake the task of imagining what a reparation of the imagination can do for communities that dwell on the underside of modern/colonial and settler colonial projects. This is precisely what Olivares does, asking humans in the present to keep "having babies," to have hope in future generations.

The kinds of reparations that coalitions like CARICOM demand seek to undermine the processes of formal colonialism and ongoing forms of imperialism in the Caribbean. They account for historical and political wrongdoing, and these discourses are relevant in other colonial contexts as well. While North American reparations, which are often reduced to official apologies or monetary payouts, often overdetermine reparations discourse, we must be careful not to collapse discussions of reparations in the (post)colonial Caribbean with settler colonial North American contexts. Though in Equatorial Guinea there may not be an open political arena to discuss reparations for ethnic minorities such as the Bubi, Benga, and Annobonese, for the forced exile of Guineans during Macias's regime, or for the widespread oppression and poverty during the Obiang regime, there exists in literary poetics a reparation of the imagination that indicts the ongoing effects of colonial and dictatorial rule. Equatoguinean authors recover histories of resistance, cosmologies, and mythologies that seek to repair broken kinship ties and subvert fascism and dictatorship. When taken together across these contexts, the Equatoguinean and Afro-Latinx diasporic texts in this chapter act as a reparative force, a form of decolonial love, which inspires new ways of knowing that inform and transform our political demands for reparations.

On Reparations in Relation

Afro-Atlantic literatures often reimagine foundational concepts such as power, gender, and bodies. They primarily accomplish this work through attention to the changes in apparatus and ideologies of power that mark the shift between colonial and postcolonial moments. These reimaginings of well-worn themes and tropes also include a commitment to a notion of reparations. I argue that these narratives challenge popular notions of reparations as simple acts of government policy. Instead, the texts explore the possibilities of reparations as the result of acts of interrogating the links between bodies and violence, redefining relations across difference, and the achievement of decolonial love.

How should we conceive of the term "reparations"? What are the ways in which it has been historically deployed? The term "reparation" stems from the Latin *reparare*, meaning to "restore" or "repair," and is also derived from the Old French *reparacion*, referencing acts of repair or restoration. It first appears in the late fourteenth century as "reconciliation," yet its contemporary meaning as "compensation for war damages owed by the aggressor" can be traced to 1919–21 in reference to France's claims for war reparations from Germany after World War I.[25] The term "reparations" has historically complex usages and meanings, including in Latin, where it was used in the context of restitution. The *Oxford English Dictionary* defines "reparation" as both "a healing, especially of an injury," and "the action of making amends for a wrong or harm done by providing payment or other assistance to the wronged party; an instance of this. Also: payment or assistance given in compensation for such a wrong; an example of this" (among other definitions).[26] While the term "reparation" as defined by these hegemonic institutions does not encompass other and oppositional understandings and usages of the word, we can use these as points of departure to better track popular conceptions of reparations. For example, the latter definition offered by the *OED* is often the first that comes to mind when discussing reparations, especially within Indigenous and Black communities.[27] In *Freedom Dreams: The Black Radical Imagination* (2003), Robin Kelley provides a historical overview of reparations for U.S. Black communities, from the end of the Civil War with the promise of "no less than forty acres" to the political organizing of radical groups such as the National Coalition of Blacks for Reparations in

America, the Black Radical Congress, the Student Nonviolent Coordinating Committee, the Black Panthers, the Black Economic Development Conference, and a plethora of other radical groups. Kelley suggests that if we think of reparations as part of a broad strategy to radically transform society, then the ongoing struggle for reparations holds enormous promise for revitalizing movements for social justice, including redistributing wealth, creating a democratic and caring public culture, and exposing the ways that capitalism and slavery produced massive inequalities that persist into the present.[28]

For Kelley, these movements start with a radical vision of justice and social reorganization, one that must begin with imaginings of what could be after one recognizes what has been. Economic reparations are both ethically and morally justified, yet ending the process at monetary attainment would leave unreconciled the psychological and psychosocial effects of colonialism, and the systems of dehumanization that have endured. As Staceyann Chin notes in the context of CARICOM's lawsuit, "People need an apology, they need acknowledgement of what happened, and they need the acknowledgement of how it has affected them generation after generation after generation."[29] Material reparations, then, must go in tandem with a decolonial reparation, reparations which have a commitment to transforming both the ideologies and structures of coloniality.

The Afro-diasporic and Afro-exilic writers read in this chapter imagine reparations as part of future transformations. However, these texts are not bound by the idea of reparations solely as monetary gains, a formal apology, an official policy, or a solemn promise.[30] Reparations are reimagined as actions based on relations across difference; a recognition of structural, gendered, and intergenerational violence and a move away from its normalization; and as decolonial love. I pose that these conceptions of reparations are decolonial because they traverse the oft-used positivistic calculation of debts or apologies owed, and instead engage in intergenerational and collective acts of love and demand an understanding of (and an accounting for) the *longue durée* of colonialism and contemporary forms of coloniality.

Quiñonez's *Bodega Dreams*, Díaz's *The Brief Wondrous Life of Oscar Wao*, and Mbomío Bacheng's *Matinga, sangre en la selva* are novels that stage opportunities to envision reparations within and beyond material gains. While each text speaks to notions of reparations and futurities, they do so in dynamically different ways. I argue that these writers imagine the future of their communities through radical (re)definitions of social and political concepts. Theories of decoloniality show how these novels reimagine reparations as a radical transformation of communities and as an attempt to repair broken societies, histories, and identities that have been destroyed by colonialism and the coloniality-of-power.

These novels undertake a decolonizing approach to reparations by thinking beyond capitalist frameworks and engaging what I call a "reparation of the imagination." In doing so, they reveal the machinations of power, bodies and nations wracked by violence, and how communities coalesce at crossroads of liberation. Across these texts is a commitment to investigating and enacting ways through which to practice decolonial love and (re)imagine decolonial futurities.

Reparations on Our Own Terms

Ernesto Quiñonez's *Bodega Dreams* (2000) frames reparations as a project that propels community liberation. I would be remiss to exclude *Bodega Dreams* from a discussion of Afro-Latinx and Afro-Puerto Rican reparations because it is one of the few diasporic Puerto Rican novels that explicitly addresses the topic. Furthermore, the novel centers on a historic Afro-Boricua community: El Barrio, also known as Spanish Harlem or East Harlem. While the author is not Afro-Puerto Rican, he is of Puerto Rican and Ecuadorian descent, and the novel includes tropes and practices that are important to mapping Afro-Puerto Rican aesthetics within literary contexts.[31] The crux of *Bodega Dreams* is one man's attempt to foment community-wide reparations in El Barrio via neoliberal logics that rely on real estate schemes and middle-class aspirations. The novel has been the source of numerous scholarly analyses, from its Gatsby-like arc to more nuanced critiques of its neoliberal market aesthetics, religious symbolism, and linguistic style.[32] Arlene Dávila, for example, argues that *Bodega Dreams* represents "the ultimate neoliberal novel." She contends that Quiñonez has "expressed publicly his wish for an empowered Latino middle class to combat gentrification," even though the "feasibility of such a dream is quickly fading" due to rising rents, and investors and speculators who have attempted to take over the housing market.[33]

The novel focuses on Spanish Harlem and the dreams of activist-turned-hustler Willie Bodega, whose covert scheme seeks to fund and create an educated class of people born and raised in El Barrio who will return to live and own properties in their community. For Bodega, this is a way to circumvent the neoliberal politics that are gentrifying Spanish Harlem by creating a community-based form of reparations that empowers Latinx families born and bred in the Barrio, as well as more recent Latinx immigrants. These imaginative renderings correspond with historical experiences of displacement and gentrification, which in turn encourages readers to envision an alternative future. I argue that the protagonist and narrator of the novel, Chino, develops a decolonial love that helps him reimagine Spanish Harlem beyond the dualistic paradigms that circumscribe his existence at the beginning of the novel. Though they are initially on opposing sides, Bodega's grand vision eventually helps Chino find beauty in his neighborhood, love for his community, and respect for their language.

Arlene Dávila's study *Barrio Dreams: Puerto Ricans, Latinos, and the Neoliberal City* (2004) delves into the sociopolitical, cultural, spatial, and economic politics of neoliberalism as they manifest in El Barrio. Dávila shows how neoliberalism—"the rubric of economic and urban development policies that favor state deregulations, that is, a decrease in state involvement accompanied by privatization and free market approaches, all in the guise of fostering more efficient technologies of government"—has rapidly transformed Spanish Harlem through gentrification, consumption, and marketing in ethnic enclaves.[34] Spanish Harlem, like many other urban centers, faces rapid commercialization, the rampant corruption of real estate corporations, and the lobbing of racist "culture of poverty" discourses as a way to bolster the idea of "progress" as development and eventual displacement associated with gentrification.

What Dávila uncovers is that 93.6 percent of the population of East Harlem are renters, most of whom are Latinx and Black. Her study shows how the ongoing neoliberal policies in New York City would serve to displace the majority of this largely working class community.[35] Furthermore, *Barrio Dreams* highlights that Puerto Rican residents of Spanish Harlem are cast as "a passing group . . . [that is] just a backdrop to current housing development rather than being a possible target of affordable housing."[36] The constant threat of displacement, the erasure of rent-controlled apartments, and real estate developers and district representatives' incessant double-talk are the backdrop of Quiñonez's *Bodega Dreams*, a novel that takes place in the same spatial location and temporal scope as Dávila's anthropological study.

Readers are introduced to Willie Bodega and his grand vision of liberating Nuyoricans in New York City.[37] Ylce Irizarry argues: "Quiñonez's portrayal of Bodega explicitly represents Nuyoricans' cultural pride as a weapon against neoliberalism's flattening of ethnic difference and façade of neighborhood revitalization."[38] Bodega's vision of a Great Society and grand-scale welfare state echo the sociopolitical activism of the Young Lords Party in the 1960s and 1970s. Bodega was a member of the Young Lords Party, and this sets the pace for his ideations. His dream of reparations includes providing for the basic needs of Spanish Harlem community members, nurturing a middle class of mainland Puerto Ricans, and eventually using these empowered elites to wield political power. Much of the literature and films on the movement documents the failures that resulted in the Young Lords' move from the diaspora to Puerto Rico.[39] In the novel, Bodega holds on to the core of these liberation ideas but relies on drug money to fund and propel his reparations project. The drug money is laundered, via his best friend and lawyer Nazario, and used to purchase and restore real estate in Spanish Harlem. These spaces are then returned to Puerto Rican and Latinx community members. Bodega also uses these funds for medical, educational, and other related needs that arise in the community. Willie Bodega is a notorious, shadowy figure who is known to support the needs of his immediate community but who requires Nazario, and later Chino, as front men for his operation. Nazario however, seems to have even larger goals, as he openly discusses how their efforts in Spanish Harlem can be used as political clout to liberate Puerto Rico from U.S. colonial possession. Nazario's hopes reflect some of the loftier goals of the Young Lords Party, which sought to extend its community and political programming to the island, and worked towards organizing independence efforts.[40]

Bodega's imagined reparations work within, while attempting to subvert, the capitalist system that sees Puerto Ricans as disposable subjects. Audre Lorde's words loom over Bodega's plan: "The master's tools will never dismantle the master's house," she argues. "[They] may allow us temporarily to beat him at his own game, but they will never enable us to bring about genuine change."[41] And perhaps this is where Bodega's dream fails. His radical imagining, to use the words of Anthony Bogues, is not *heretical*.[42] For Bogues, heretical thinking first engages and then critiques Western epistemes, while the redemptive prophetic stream incites people to organize through a retelling of history and circumstance. What makes this particular heretical discourse fitting for a critique of Willie Bodega is precisely his failure to think outside of the capitalistic model of accumulation and distribution. He believes that reparations for his Spanish Harlem community will be achieved by mimicking New York City's corrupt Anglo political and economic patterns on the one hand, and the U.S. national politic on the other.

Bodega is reliant on Nazario, who maintains a façade of legality which soothes Bodega into complacency. Bodega's own double consciousness rears its head in his awareness that he can never be the "face" of his own empire, because he is hyper-aware of how the New York City political establishment views his lack of cultural capital, education, and upper-middle-class finesse. Irizarry argues that Bodega and Nazario represent "the foil of the other in racial, national, and class contexts" from the moment they met, when "Bodega had left the Young Lords, [and] Nazario was finishing Brooklyn Law School."[43] Bodega lacks Nazario's political clout. Instead of imagining a subversion of neoliberal politics, Bodega plays into them by providing the resources for a community of Latinx middle-class elites to emerge through the legality that Nazario provides. All the while, Chino is being groomed to take part in this arrangement, while Bodega remains unknown and unrecognized as the propelling agent of the neighborhood's economic and social uplift. Despite this invisibility, Bodega believes that if he were ever to be arrested or killed, the neighborhood would rally and rise up against the police and the city. This illusion of himself as a figurehead and leader in the community serves his need for recognition and respect, which, as Irizarry argues, "fractures the notion [that] activists are primarily concerned with community empowerment. Unfortunately for East Harlem, Bodega's desire for respect can *only* come with an individual mobility that undermines communal uplift."[44]

Bodega's approach to community-wide liberation and political self-determination is single-minded. While it may at first be interpreted as an instance of decolonial love, his ideations are more selfish than selfless. Bodega emulates the elite power structures that he critiques, and attempts to mimic them at the barrio level. His attempt to use the same capitalist methods that made the Rockefellers rich and the Kennedys a political powerhouse inhibits the possibility of radical politics—perhaps even limiting his profound envisioning of the Nuyorican future of El Barrio. Bodega tells Chino:

> Yo, *ese tipo era un raquetero.* Joe Kennedy was no different from me. He already had enough money in the twenties but he still became a rumrunner. Alcohol is a drug, right? Kennedy sold enough booze to kill a herd of rhinos. Made enough money from that to land other, legal schemes. Years later he bought his kids the White House. Yeah, he broke the law like I'm breaking the law, but I get no recognition because I am no Joe Kennedy. (25–26)

Bodega explains that the name "Kennedy" allowed criminality without indictment, and through that corruption Kennedy brought political clout and even prestige to his family. But Bodega's position as a racially and linguistically colonized Other prevents the New York political elite from recognizing him as an equal. Thus, he realizes that although he can mimic Kennedy's path of corruption to political power, he cannot achieve the same results.

For Bodega, Chino represents his hope that the next generation can attain the respectability he desires. His imagined Great Society, which begins with social, economic, and residential reparations in his local Nuyorican community in Spanish Harlem, would eventually extend to exert international influence. The neologism "Nuyorican" is key here, as Bodega's immediate concern is with the Puerto Rican diaspora in general and Nuyoricans in particular. His preoccupation with the futures of diasporic Boricuas, colonial subjects thrust onto settled lands across North America, becomes an important marker that often goes unnoticed. Diasporic Boricuas' ties to community and community-building create a lifeline in the treacherous landscapes of U.S. domination. Thus, by paying close attention to Nuyoricans' approaches to the vaíven and the ontology of "ni de aquí ni de allá," we see emerge a distinctly different approach to reparations that can subvert the logics of coloniality that often undermine liberation struggles.[45]

Furthermore, Bodega's notion of community reparations involves only a limited scope for love and responsibility; instead, he relies on tropes of respectability for transformative projects. For example, Bodega does not recognize that the junkies to whom he sells drugs are part and parcel of the "community" he is trying to create in his new society. When Chino questions him on this point, he replies, "Any Puerto Rican or any of my Latin brothers who are stupid enough to buy that shit don't belong in my Great Society" (31). Bodega mimics the existing power structures, thereby bolstering coloniality and circumventing the logic that centers his drug-pushing within neighborhood and familial crises.[46] Bodega's nationalist visions rely on (re)inscriptions of structural patterns of power, which in turn, engender heteropatriarchal nationalism.

Women of color writers, activists, and artists have long eschewed these kinds of sexist and cis heteronormative ideologies. The *Combahee River Collective Statement*, published in 1977, critiques nationalist movements that relegate women to subservient and reproductive roles by virtue of their sex. "Feminism," the collective argues, "is, nevertheless, very threatening to the majority of Black people because it calls into question some of the most basic assumptions about our existence, i.e., that sex should be a determinant of power relationships."[47] Of particular interest is the history of the Young Lords Party and how that organization dealt with heteropatriarchy and machismo. In "Bridging Homeland and Barrio Politics: The Young Lords in Philadelphia," Carmen Theresa Whalen argues that "the Young Lords' ideology, while based on ethnic pride, was not narrowly Nationalist and instead opened the doors to discussions of gender and the possibility of political coalitions."[48] She explains that nationalist and paramilitary movements often struggled with creating equal and open spaces for women to participate. These groups have been critiqued for frequently reinscribing patriarchal norms and colluding against women in leadership roles. The literature on the Black Panther Party, the American Indian Movement, and the Chicano Movement shows that issues of gender, sex, reproductive labor, and leadership had to be addressed forthrightly by women and queer folks within those organizations. Attending to sex and gender within these paramilitary organizations became an essential part of imagining a revolutionary nationalism and deterring internal factionalism.[49]

Many branches of the Young Lords Party excluded women from leadership roles. It was not until 1971, when the Women's Caucus formed in New York and Philadelphia, that the organization's leadership shifted their attitude from one that "based their definition of Puerto Rican culture on a reassertion of traditional gender roles for women" to one that allowed for the equal participation and leadership of women in the movement.[50] Whalen documents that "they changed their platform from a demand that '*machismo* must be revolutionary *machismo*' to 'We want equality for women. Down with male chauvinism.' "[51] The Young Lords demonstrated this shift in their party platform and by restructuring the organization. But we see the remnants of this earlier omission of women in the movement and its narrow view of nationalist politics reflected in Willie Bodega's imagined reparations.

While Bodega's revolutionary imaginary does not include women, the core of his philosophy hinges on his unrequited love for Veronica. His pining for Veronica, his teenage sweetheart, is revealed to be one of the reasons why he brought Chino into the fold of his empire. This is because Veronica's niece is Blanca, Chino's wife. When finally disentangled, Bodega's plans reveal that what drives him is not a singular love for the barrio, but rather unrequited love and class aspirations that refuse to bear witness to what they leave in their wake. This conflation of his political commitments with his aspirational love is what ultimately leads to his death at the hands of his business partner Nazario and his lover—Veronica.

While these love entanglements can be reductive, they underscore some of the dualities at play throughout the novel. These dichotomies are most obvious when women are centered in the narrative, and their characterizations reflect a deeper racial and sexual inquietude. One such example is the treatment of Chino's hyper-Christian wife, Blanca, and her sister, Negra, who are depicted as representatives of different and radically unequal value systems. Of Blanca, Chino says:

> Her face could envelop you, almost convert you. She had light tan skin, hazel eyes, and a beautiful mane of semibrown semiblonde hair. Nancy exuded a purity rarely found among the church girls. She was genuine as a statue of a saint you want to light candles to, steal flowers for, or pray in front of. When she'd say "Gloria a Dios!" she meant it. She was intelligent, polite, and friendly, and since she never cursed everyone called her Blanca. (9)

Blanca is framed as a studious and devout Pentecostal who encourages Chino to succeed at City College in order to move away from El Barrio. Blanca, though pregnant, is depicted as virginal, idealistic, and suspicious of Chino's dealings with Bodega and his close friendship with Sapo, another of Bodega's associates.

Negra, on the other hand, is depicted as a dark and troubled character. The reader first meets her in a scene in which she has stabbed her adulterous lover for lying about his whereabouts. Negra is characterized as volatile, untrustworthy, and cunning. She is often seen blackmailing Chino for information and trying to profit from the misfortunes of others. Blanca and Negra represent conflicting sides, and mirror Chino's relationship with Bodega. These women are not part of Bodega's rebuilding of the community and national imaginings, and are simple extensions of the male characters. Irizarry argues:

> The nicknaming of Blanca (Nancy) and her sister, Negra (Debra), reflects the simplistic, racist binaries. . . . To be a "Blanca" is to be culturally "White" and enjoy social mobility by abandoning your cultural roots. To be a "Negra" is to be culturally "Black" and to be tied to Harlem without hope of mobility. Neither choice reflects the complexity of Puerto Rican racial, cultural, or class realities. Quiñonez reinscribes a problematic gender system . . . and is not successful in scripting a more realistic puertorriqueñidad for Puerto Rican women.[52]

While the female characters are underdeveloped figures overall, Blanca and Negra, along with Vera (née Veronica, Bodega's love interest), are the most prominent ones in the novel. They represent a light and dark side, opposing each other but also pulling Chino in divergent directions.[53] Chino's dualistic mentality is what drives him to initially reject Bodega's offer to work in his growing empire. As the novel develops, Chino attempts to go beyond this fixed binary. While he is at first skeptical and even indifferent to Willie Bodega's plan for economic reparations on his own terms, he ultimately begins to believe in Bodega's intentions.

These racializing dualities can also be seen in other characters in the novel. Although the novel does not directly reveal that its characters are Afro-Latinx, it is situated within a predominantly Afro-Latinx community. Furthermore, Quiñonez's characters, such as Sapo and Bodega, are depicted as having stereotypical African or Black features and phenotypes.[54] Of Sapo, Quiñonez says, "He was strong, squatty, with a huge mouth framed by fat lips, freaking bembas that would almost swallow you" (1). Sapo is Chino's best friend, a fighter and a drug-dealing high school dropout, constrained by his loyalty and his penchant for violence. Quiñonez's description of Sapo opens parts 1 and 2 of the novel: "Sapo was different. Sapo was always Sapo, and no one messed with him because he had a reputation for biting. 'When I'm in a fight,' Sapo would spit, 'whass close to my mouth is mine by right and my teeth ain't no fucken pawn-shop'" (85). Sapo has a fixed subjectivity, his violence is inherent, and while Chino often goes along with him and helps him store and transport drugs, Sapo's actions are often juxtaposed with Chino's seemingly "respectable" choices. Here, Quiñonez underscores the tensions of how complex subjects in peripheralized spaces are often reduced to binaries that cast them as valuable, or inherently devalued, members of a larger society.

Of Willie Bodega, the novel tells us: "[He] was a man in his forties with a goatee and the droopy eyes of an ex-heroin addict. His hair was curly and he was about five feet ten" (23). The dichotomies that emerge with Bodega are both linguistic and spiritual. In Chino's conversations with Bodega, we see a shift in language. For example, when Chino exhibits shame at attending a small public college, Bodega answers, "Yo, college is college and thass all that maras" (24). Throughout the text, Sapo and Bodega are the only two characters who repeatedly speak in this way. Quiñonez portrays Afro-Latinx characters who inhabit and represent Spanish Harlem, and while Chino is born and bred there, his own speech patterns never fall into this kind of accented language. These characters are a fixed part of Chino's world, while he remains nimble across spatial locales (the barrio, the church, the college). Chino triumphs in being street smart, but he can remove himself from the pull of criminality, poverty, and linguistic markers. These nuances of depiction allow us to glimpse vectors of race, sex, and power that mark racialized Others as backdrops to the unfolding story.

Chino is the novel's most visibly raced character. Chino, whose given name is Julio, explains that he wanted to get a name that means something: "Getting a name meant I had to fight. . . . So I decided that I no longer wanted to be called by the name my parents had given me, Julio. I wanted a name like Sapo and so I looked for fights" (4). Chino describes how he achieved his goal and got his nickname: "During my three years at Julia de Burgos, I had more fights than Sapo. And since I was born with high, flat cheekbones, almond-shaped eyes, and straight black hair (courtesy of my father's Ecuadorian side of the family), and because kung fu movies were very popular at the time, when I was in the eighth grade, I was tagged Chino" (7–8). His nickname, Chino, is undoubtedly a middleman minority reference, and he operates in this role to a degree.[55] He serves Bodega as a middleman, one who carries a kind of social capital, not attained through material wealth but through achievements such as graduating from high school and attending college. Chino as protagonist sets up the story for the reader, and both translates and vacillates between these two worlds: Bodega's corrupt scheme for reparations, and the future Chino has planned with Blanca.

Another example of deploying Afro-Latinidad as a racial marker can be seen in the chapter titled "Que Viva Changó." In it, Sapo and Chino bring a goose to Doña Ramonita's "botánica," or spiritual marketplace. She is described as "a heavy woman with strong African roots from Puerto Rico's Loíza Aldea. With her hair pulled back in a pink bandana and her hands on her hips, she looked like Aunt Jemima from the pancake boxes" (51). Doña Ramonita is depicted as a mammy, a Black woman from a renowned (but hardly the only) Afro-descended community in Puerto Rico. These simplistic descriptions of Doña Ramonita rest on stereotypical descriptors of phenotype, making her a caricature that represents a racialized ritual practice. The novel thus brings Afro-diasporic symbolism to the heart of Spanish Harlem. As Solimar Otero argues, the novel includes descriptions of

> diasporas twice or three times removed, as they are located in a particular isla remembrance of the Afro-Puerto Rican in mentioning places like Loíza Aldea, or describe santeros as distinctly having what are coded in North American culture as physically "black" features. In this manner, and not in an unproblematic fashion, Nuyorican authors locate the spirituality of the African Diaspora in their communities by writing the botánica onto the streets of their urban imaginary. The botánica brings the African part of the isla into the 'hood, it brings el monte, or the forest, into the city in ways that are specifically coded.[56]

Doña Ramonita is of course from Loíza Aldea, a community in northern Puerto Rico considered one of the epicenters of Blackness on the island. The region is also heavily associated with Afro-syncretic practices, which has given rise to heavy-handed stereotyping on the island and in the diaspora.[57] Doña Ramonita functions as a mystic keeper of Afro-Caribbean rituals through her labor in the botánica, and this function continues as she remerges in the scene dressed in white with beads and rosaries (51–52). Her role in the novel is to act as a spiritual go-between for Willie Bodega to access Changó—the most feared orisha—and her spiritual intervention will help summon Vera back to New York from Miami. Doña Ramonita thus signifies Bodega's beliefs in Afro-syncretic religiosity. Furthermore, her spiritual practices, including the beheading and spilling of the goose's blood, are a striking juxtaposition to Blanca's pure white Pentecostalism. Race, then, in this narrative about reparations and love, is a vital component of the storyline, even as Blackness is portrayed as scaffolding rather than structure.

By the end of the novel, however, Chino realizes that his goal to leave Bodega and the streets behind, amass capital, and build a middle-class life with Blanca is no longer viable. As Hubert Blalock's theory of the middleman minority points out, often the middleman is isolated or alienated from both the homeland (in Chino's case, the barrio) and the host society (middle-class upward mobility).[58] For Chino, Bodega's illusions of a grand-scale welfare state gradually become much more complex (and perhaps even achievable). For a time, he ceases to vacillate between these contrasting ethics: his individualistic approach to achievement, and Bodega's community welfare state. He begins to appreciate El Barrio's history and art by visiting its museums, enjoying its vibrant murals, and seeing the community as pulsating, not vanishing.

Chino develops a decolonial love that goes beyond the good/bad, black/white paradigm that has defined him throughout most of the novel. Unlike Bodega and Sapo, Chino initially cannot see the beauty in the brokenness of El Barrio. At one point, he tells a story of flying a kite over Spanish Harlem, a passage that shows the deep difference between his vision(s) and how Bodega and Sapo see their community: "'You know Sapo,' I said to him one day as we were preparing to fly kites on the roof of a project, 'if we could ride on the tip of these things we could get out of here. You know?' 'Why would you want to fucken leave this place?' he said with his Sapo smile, showing all his teeth as he glues some razors to his kite. 'This neighborhood is beautiful, bro' " (10–11). For Chino, this is a revolutionary perspective because his own views of El Barrio are imbued with negativity, despair, misogyny, and disgust:

> It was easy to be big and bad when you hated your life and felt meaningless. You lived in projects with pissed-up elevators, junkies on the stairs, posters of the rapist of the month, and whores you never knew were whores until you saw men go in and out of their apartments like through revolving doors. You lived in a place where vacant lots grew like wild grass does in Kansas. . . . All you knew was that one day a block would have people, the next day it would be erased by a fire. (5)

Chino's childhood in a blighted neighborhood, seeing little that was good and witnessing how arbitrarily it could be "erased," fomented his indifference for El Barrio.

Throughout the novel, he only sees an end to El Barrio, not a new beginning and definitely not a reparative possibility. At the end, this belief is radically transformed. A moment of decolonial love is revealed when Chino makes room in the cramped apartment he shares with his pregnant wife for a grandfather and grandson who arrive in search of Willie Bodega's patronage (210–11). Chino's acceptance of the grandfather and grandson, although a small gesture, could only occur in light of Bodega's utopian imaginings. However, unlike Bodega, Chino wants nothing in return for his hospitality. This decolonial love is a possibility that Bodega cannot even imagine: "He was grateful. Told me his name was Geran and his grandson was Hipolito, and then he made me all sorts of promises that I knew to be true. He had come to work and start a new life and would get out of my hair as soon as possible. I told him there was no rush" (211). Though Bodega's radical dreams of a powerful mainland middle class and grand-scale welfare state in the barrio are dashed, they have transformed Chino. He transforms a reparation built on drug economies and accumulation into a reparation that is contingent on complex coalition-building and a "relation carved out of and in spite of difference."[59] That Geran's sincere promises quell Chino's distrust reflects a deep and foundational shift from early in the novel, when Chino was not only skeptical of Bodega's "Great Society" spiel, but also dismissive of his dreams of transformation as "bullshit" (39–41).

The novel ends with Chino dreaming of Willie Bodega as a young man in his Young Lords beret and with an issue of their newspaper *P'alante* tucked under his arm. In this dream, Bodega asks Chino to take another look at El Barrio through the fire escape window. Chino sees a mother talking to her son in Spanglish,[60] and Bodega asks him to reimagine the imperfect reparative possibilities in their community:

> "You know what is happening here, don't you? Don't you? What we just heard is a poem, Chino. It's a beautiful new language. Don't you see what's happening? A new language means a new race. Spanglish is the future. It's a new language being born out of the ashes of two cultures clashing with each other. You will use a new language. Words they might not teach you in that college. Words that aren't English or Spanish. But at the same time are both. Now that's where it's at. Our people are evolving into something completely new. . . . Just like what I was trying to do. This new language is not completely correct; but then few things are." (212)

Chino awakes from his dream to find a bustling, beautiful day in Spanish Harlem. Music, dancing, yelling, and laughing set the stage for this final musing: "The neighborhood might have been down, but it was far from out. Its people far from defeat. They had been bounced all over the place but they were still jamming. It seemed like a good place to start" (213). The "not completely correct" language also cues Bodega's imperfect reparations project and makes Spanglish into an art form that represents the creative capacities of Nuyorican survival. Beyond the poetic aesthetics of Spanglish, this living language is likewise a radical political project that enables people to speak their lived experiences of "ni de aquí, ni de allá" into existence. The anthropolitical linguist Ana Celia Zentalla argues that Spanglish, as exemplified by Nuyorican poets, "made it clear to me that the poets were in the avant-garde of adopting the name Nuyorican and the word Spanglish and performing a semantic inversion on them. In other words, they transformed them into something that they owned and that they were proud of."[61] Quiñonez's emphasis on Spanglish at the end of the novel offers readers an opportunity to consider the critical and reparative force of the languages being honed in diasporas. Chino's vision of the barrio is transformed not only by seeing it through Sapo's eyes or by imagining it beyond the limited scripts of neoliberalism, but by the embodied practices of language and the carving out of new subjectivities in spite of the tribulations of diaspora and displacement. Language becomes a reparative force, and Chino is left with the language and possibilities of a people "far from defeat." Murals throughout the neighborhood are left to commemorate Bodega and the "light" of possibilities his dreams offered. The "new language" that Chino hears, the affected Nuyorican speech that he does not take on throughout the novel, he now understands as the fuel for his own continued struggle.

By exploring the idea of reparations as political and social power, and later, through acts of decolonial love, Quiñonez's text reimagines sites of power within the neoliberal city, and socioeconomic politics within the lower-class populations in New York City's neighborhoods. Decolonial love, in Quiñonez's rendering of Spanish Harlem, consists of acts of "building a world in which genuine ethical relations become the norm and not the exception."[62] Even in Bodega's failure there exist possibilities for reparative futurities, as Chino begins to build ethical relationships within his extended community.

Imagining a Stronger Loving World

If decolonial reparations begin with understanding and subverting long histories, then Junot Díaz's *The Brief Wondrous Life of Oscar Wao* (2007) can be considered a groundbreaking text in this regard. While I analyzed this novel in my chapter on witnessing, here I reprise my meditation on this book in order to offer a brief reading in the context of reparations. Indeed, the novel can lend itself to multiple readings, as the scholarship of Monica Hanna, Elena Machado Sáez, Anne Garland Mahler, and Ashley Kunsa demonstrate, traversing topics of historiography, genre, dictatorship, colonial curses, and the role of hair and phenotype as racializing tropes.[63] Their work represents just a fraction of the scholarly criticism on the novel, a richly layered piece of fiction that utilizes multiple genres, narrators, and time-play to portray the intergenerational histories of a diasporic Dominican family and their battles with the foundational colonial curse, the fukú.

The Brief Wondrous Life of Oscar Wao imagines reparations and futurities as intimately tied to the colonial and postcolonial moment. It is a text in which the protagonist incessantly imagines fantastic "futures" in his "never-to-be-completed opus" (333). The novel centers on a Dominican-American antihero, Oscar de León, who shuffles back and forth between New Jersey's urban centers and the post-dictatorial Dominican Republic. Through an analysis of Oscar's family history, Díaz critiques the volatile and often violent nature of postcolonial governments and their effects on national subjects on the island and in diaspora. Díaz interrogates the coloniality of power and gender that perpetuates sexual and political violence as a normalized factor in the lives of Dominicans on the island and in diaspora. The novel further tracks how the everyday nature of these forms of violence affects each generation of the Cabral and de León families. Yunior, the novel's primary narrator, is also caught in this matrix of coloniality. However, despite this long legacy of violence, the characters continually hope for the possibility of a different future.

The traveling curse, the fukú, frames the novel and is associated with Columbus, the "discovery of the Americas," and the subsequent slave trade. The fukú is later linked to processes of diaspora, characterized as "Trujillo's payback to the pueblo that betrayed him" (5). By depicting diaspora as the final curse of a heinous dictator, Díaz highlights how the fukú travels from the cries of the enslaved, to the islands of the Caribbean, and beyond. *Oscar Wao* begins with the pillaging violence of the "New World"—the release of the fukú—and ends with Oscar's last written words: "The beauty! The beauty," a phrase strikingly resonant with Kurtz's horrified cries, "The horror! The horror!" in Joseph Conrad's *Heart of Darkness* (335). Scenes of imperial violence and domination in which Kurtz acts as perpetrator are thus turned upside-down as Díaz's Yunior takes on the role of faithful witness. The deficit lens is transformed as subjects on the underside of a cracked imperialism find beauty and possibility in its incompleteness. Oscar attributes these final words, penned to Yunior while on a hideaway with his love interest Ybón, to his achievement of both love and intimacy. After pining for sex and loving relationships throughout the novel, Oscar finally has sex with Ybón, but he tells Yunior, "what really got him was . . . the little intimacies that he'd never in his whole life anticipated" (334). Achieving this kind of intimacy, though it is fleeting and ultimately deadly, enables Oscar to lay claim to the possibilities of love. Here, Oscar's writing is the point of departure for this analysis of reparations of a beautiful future which centers decolonial love.

As a sign of Oscar's utopian imaginings, Yunior notes that Oscar—who had never before defaced a piece of literature—circles the words "a stronger loving world" three times in his beloved copy of the comic *Watchmen* (331).

Oscar is a non-normative character for both his family and for the reader, and dwells outside the norms of his community: "He had none of the Higher Powers of your typical Dominican male . . . Had no knack for music or business or dance, no hustle, no rap, no G. And most damning of all: no looks" (19–20). This lack of prowess makes Oscar an outsider both at home, where his often-intoxicated uncle serves as a model of hypermasculinity, and in his personal and social life, where he can never embody the trappings of manhood as defined by both U.S. and Dominican standards.[64]

Oscar's only escape is imagining an unknown future, first through sci-fi escapism and later through writing his own narratives, a form of "zafa," or counter-spell, that he hopes will alleviate the family curse and transform the future. Oscar dedicates hours of labor to his craft, writing books that Yunior reads closely, including a final manuscript that is lost in the ether of the "Dominican Express" (333). Through his writings, Oscar conjures a future in which he finds beauty in the possibilities of love. Díaz portrays Oscar as a hopeless romantic, one who keeps the idea of love alive through writing and fantasy, and later through his relationship with Ybón. Oscar believes in love so deeply that he is even willing to face death by firing squad.

The final pages of the novel are intently focused on Oscar's writings and the possibilities therein. Yunior lovingly stores all of Oscar's manuscripts in a refrigerator, "the best proof against fire, against earthquake, against almost anything" (330). The reader discovers that Oscar has completed a science fiction "opus" which he believes will be the "cure to what ails us, the cosmos D.N.A." (333). This cosmos D.N.A. is the answer, the final zafa to the fukú that betrays the Cabral and de León families, the curse that enables violence beyond measure. The cosmos D.N.A. is decolonial love. In an interview with Paula Moya, Díaz explains that the text was meant to unravel a complex and decolonial understanding of love: "The kind of love that I was interested in, that my characters long for intuitively, is the only kind of love that could liberate them from that horrible legacy of colonial violence. I am speaking about decolonial love."[65] Only decolonial love can hope to liberate them from the inheritance of perpetual violence, the kind of violence that the narrators all face in small and large ways.

The inability to confront sexual, gender, and structural violence stifles Yunior's relationship with his girlfriend, Oscar's sister, Lola. Yunior laments that if he could have loved himself enough, he could have confided his deepest secret and built with Lola an affinity across difference: "I'd finally try to say the words that could have saved us. ____ ____ ____" (327). These words, which are unknown to the reader, Díaz later reveals are "I too have been molested." For Díaz, this means that "[Yunior] couldn't bear witness to his own sexual abuse. He couldn't tell the story that would have tied him in a human way to Lola, that indeed could have saved him."[66] In the novel, Yunior bears witness to the prevalence of the sexual violence and patriarchal rape culture in the Dominican Republic and in the United States, yet he shies away from intimacy and participates in patterns of hypersexual masculinity in his own relationships, constantly cheating on Lola and his other girlfriends.[67] The love that Oscar achieves with Ybón at the end of the novel is a kind of love that Yunior could not access.[68] Admitting to sexual violence, to the brokenness and dehumanization engendered by the coloniality-of-power, would have undermined his performative hypermasculinity, which in turn would have undercut the only kind of privilege available to him as an Afro-Dominican immigrant subject.

Building a loving and ethical relationship, one that would have tied him in a "human way" to Lola, would have allowed Yunior to connect with her experience of sexual violence. The reader learns early in the novel about Lola's sexual assault at the age of eight, and her mother's determination to negate it: "When that thing happened to me when I was eight and I finally told her what he had done, she told me to shut my mouth and stop crying, and I did exactly that, I shut my mouth and clenched my legs, and my mind, and within a year I could not have told you what that neighbor looked like, or even his name" (57). Lola's silence-turned-denial feeds intergenerational reticence and resentment. Her tumultuous relationship with her mother Belicia is circumscribed by the suppression of violence and fear. A rebellious and indignant Lola can only envision showing the depths of her anger: "If I could have I would have broken the entire length of my life across her face" (55). It is years later when Lola learns about her own mother's experience with physical and sexual violence, and it is only in this knowledge and recognition of Belicia's past that Lola can "begin" to unravel her own experiences (75).

Díaz tells Moya in their interview that the central question of the novel is about the possibilities of decolonial love: "Is it possible to overcome the horrible legacy of slavery and find decolonial love? Is it possible to love one's broken-by-the-coloniality-of-power self in another broken-by-the-coloniality-of-power person?"[69] And in *Oscar Wao*, we see the legacies of slavery and violence in multiple instances. We first encounter the voices of the enslaved during the Middle Passage, slaves who bring the cries of the fukú with them. We then see Trujillo's repressive postcolonial regime, since he "treated the country like it was a plantation and he was the master" (2), and later we see the post-dictatorial island, replete with intimate violence wielded by the state and its agents. Belicia's early years of servitude as a criada leave her with a massive scar, "as vast and inconsolable as a sea" (51). As Jennifer Harford Vargas incisively reads, this mark is akin to the violence endured by the enslaved and on the Middle Passage.[70] Lola and Oscar cannot escape the perpetual violence of coloniality, as they are conscripted into the diasporic-induced self-hatred that "short-circuited their minds" (160). Furthermore, Yunior and Oscar's dependence on notions of sex, gender conformity, and masculinity only serve to uproot and destroy them from the inside out.

The legacy of slavery and the brokenness engendered by colonialism and the coloniality-of-power are at the very heart of the matter. Díaz poses a question of love and repair in his novel: is it possible to traverse this perpetual violence and domination through a reparation of the broken self and the broken other? Yunior tells the reader that during one of their last nights as "novios," Lola cried, "Ten million Trujillo's is all we are," meaning that it is not only Trujillo's looming presence that is to blame, but also those Dominicans who have internalized this violence and perpetuate it among each other across time and space, diaspora and destierro (324).[71] The future is seemingly left uncertain by Oscar's death in the cane fields, echoing Belicia's vicious beating years earlier at the hands of Trujillo's henchmen.

Though colonization and slavery ended, their structures remain deeply embedded in the spaces they once occupied and in the psyches of the people they dominated. The legacy of slavery, rape, co-optation, violence, and oppression is what creates the broad strokes of brokenness. Through the story of Oscar and his family, Díaz attempts to unpack the self-hatred and inferiority complexes introduced by the colonial difference and bred by inequality and the repetition of violent patterns. That the novel deals with gender and sex as central issues is of major importance. Both coloniality, or the "order of things that put people of color under the murderous and rapist sight of a vigilant ego," and the coloniality-of-gender are essential parts of Oscar's narrative, and of the history of the Dominican Republic and Dominicans in the diaspora.[72]

It is clear through the telling and (re)telling of these familial, national, and Dominican diasporic histories that Oscar inherits oppression, violence, pain, rape, degradation, and the curse of the fukú. His own status as a child of Dominican immigrants in the United States marks him doubly as a racial and linguistic Other, and he is triply negated by his inability to be accepted as a "real" Dominican man. Though Oscar is continuously and obsessively writing his opus throughout the text, the content of his writing remains unknown to the reader. We do not have access to its plots, characters, or narrative arcs. However, by the end, we know that Oscar's death leaves his intellectual legacy mostly unknown. His final chapter is lost and never recovered. The text ends with Yunior anticipating that Oscar's niece Isis will hold the key to unraveling the fukú through her own readings of Oscar's papers and his incomplete opus.

In this way, Oscar's imaginings are saved for the next generation. His idea of reparation is immaterial, or never materializes. Yet somehow it is transformative for his contemporaries and holds promise for future generations. Oscar's hope for a "stronger loving world" is an impetus for other characters to imagine another way of living and being. This is reflected in the ways in which Yunior, a decade after Oscar's death, makes incredible changes in his life: "Finally I woke up next to somebody I didn't give two shits about, my upper lip covered in coke-snot and coke-blood and I said, OK, Wao, OK. You win" (325). Yunior begins to write "from can't see in the morning to can't see at night" (326). Through reading and writing about Oscar's incomplete manuscript and his unyielding belief in love and the cosmos D.N.A., Yunior is fueled to (re)imagine the possibilities of a life outside of patriarchal masculinity and violence, and the ability to transform himself into a new man: "Learned that from Oscar. I'm a new man, you see, a new man, a new man" (326). I contend that Díaz's novel proposes a future in which being a man does not involve sexual or structural violence against the bodies of women, girls, and femmes, where love and intimacy are beautiful achievements, and where decolonial love is finding the human in the dehumanized subject. This future also hinges on Isis, Lola's young daughter, "dark and blindingly fast," who wears on a string around her neck "three azabaches" to protect her from any kind of fukú (329). For Yunior, Isis is not only the daughter he never could have had with Lola, but also the key to ending the cycle of the fukú—someone who will read, add to, and complete Oscar's manuscript. Reparation of the imagination is imperative for both this generation and future generations. In *The Brief Wondrous Life of Oscar Wao* as in *Bodega Dreams*, reparations are conceptual, political, and intimate projects that are deeply embedded in resistance to colonial imaginaries of being. They are likewise matters of futurities and future generations—a preoccupation which is also seen in the Equatoguinean novel *Matinga, sangre en la selva*.

Reparations as Generations

Joaquín Mbomío Bacheng's *Matinga, sangre en la selva* (2013; *Matinga, Blood in the Jungle*) demonstrates a (re)articulation of reparations and futurities in the context of Equatoguinean struggles for liberation. The novel ties together power, gender, and bodies in a narrative that radically critiques colonial, postcolonial, and dictatorial power structures through a retelling of Benga mythologies imbued with history. *Matinga, sangre en la selva* tells the story of a young girl from Bolondo named Matinga who is a nymph, a siren, and a savior to the peoples of Equatorial Guinea. The novel centers the mythologies of the Benga or Ndowe/Playero culture of Río Muni (the Equatoguinean continental mainland) and the island of Corisco, which represents a turn toward the narratives of minoritized ethnic groups in Equatoguinean literature.[73] Matinga is a girl-made-nymph, sent forth from the world of the dead to save her people with her blood. Mbomío Bacheng's narrative is a radical retelling of Spanish Guinean history, within and beyond colonial borders, and a radical reimagining of reparations as pronatalism and familial reconciliation. Rather than self-sacrifice, this story is about the ways in which Matinga's menstrual blood, imbued with the power of the ancestors, is seen as a reparative force through which to heal and rebuild a nation in the midst of anticolonial and anti-dictatorial revolutions. Marvin Lewis's ecocritical and sociopolitical reading of *Matinga, sangre en la selva* argues that in the novel "colonialism and the fight for independence serve as a backdrop for the examination of how characters perceived the transition and its impact upon traditional modes of existence."[74] Furthermore, he argues that the novel is "imbued with an African cosmology revealing the interconnectedness between the living and the dead, between humans and nature. In the novel's worldview, this relationship will endure and supersedes the violence and brutality committed in the name of greed and power."[75] In *Matinga, sangre en la selva*, reparations are first envisioned as anti-genocidal movements and are later reconceived as Matinga's search for a kind of collective and communal love that she has never known. In what follows, I problematize the ways in which the power and bodies of women are diminished by ideologies of compulsory pronatalism. I argue that the novel first situates Matinga as a vessel of reparations for the future of Equatorial Guinea, and then juxtaposes this narrative by highlighting Matinga's agency, well beyond her initial blood offerings. Matinga's rearticulation of the relationship between her body and her community is a form of decolonial love that creates possibilities for a reparation of the imagination.

Matinga, Mbomío Bacheng tells us, "nació donde mueren las olas, en una angosta playa guineana del universo tropical, donde termina el oceano y empieza la selva. Entre tierra y mar" (9; "was born where the waves die, on a narrow Guinean beach of the tropical universe, where the ocean ends and the jungle begins"). This immediate depiction of life and death, "born where the waves die," foreshadows the perilous nature of Matinga's life. *Matinga, sangre en la selva* paints the reader a juxtapositional portrait: jungle and fluvial natures living in the same historical present as the civil and political unrest of the (post)colony.[76] At the center of this story, we see an isolated Matinga who, once she reaches post-pubescence, travels every month to the coastlines of new communities in order to offer her menstrual blood as a token of fertility to Equatoguinean women. The bloodstained sand left in her wake is then given to the men of that community as additional tokens of fertility. Matinga's blood is life-giving, though she is unaware of the reasons why this is so, and she is unable to control both the fecundity of her blood and the movement of her body from island to island. Lewis argues, "Matinga is special, it seems, because she carries in her very genetic makeup a chemistry that embraces the animal, plant, and mineral universes. She is a product of the syncretism of three ancestral religions."[77] The novel juxtaposes Matinga's blood offering by the ocean waters with the bloodshed of the jungle where Equatoguineans are fighting for liberation, first from the Franco regime and later from their president-turned-dictator, Francisco Macías Nguema. Matinga's blood, then, is an integral part of building and replenishing a nation that is undergoing internal and external tumult. "Matinga's sacred, regenerative blood," contends Lewis, "assures the prosperity of her people and the universe."[78]

This imagining of menstrual blood as a fertile reparative force, or as a reparation of the homeland, speaks to the role of women as builders of the nation. In "Affirmations of an Indigenous Feminist" (2010), Kim Anderson considers pronatalism within Indigenous communities, arguing that "because we are survivors of smallpox, massacres, eugenics, enforced sterilization, residential schools, and child welfare interventions, it is not surprising that there has been some pro-natalist (i.e., encouraging women to bear children) sentiment in our communities."[79] As Anderson notes, nationalist and revolutionary groups, such as the American Indian Movement, have in the past supported and encouraged these ideologies of women as bearers of the nation.[80] Mbomío Bacheng is writing between and across two distinct continents (Africa and Europe), and walks us through this challenge as imagined from the perspective of an Iberian-influenced African nation.

Matinga inhabits the role of an involuntary fertility symbol for an emerging state in the midst of a liberation struggle against colonial Spanish rule and political repression. Anderson, who is critical of this pronatalist role for Indigenous women, suggests that feminist literature offers insightful critiques that turn the gaze away from women's wombs and towards the confining dictates of patriarchy: "Feminist literature exposes how pro-natalist movements and ideologies related to the mothers of the nation have been common in countries worldwide during war or postwar periods and within liberation movements. Feminist history has shown just how disempowering these movements have been for the women involved, because they typically confine women to motherhood roles within the patriarchal family."[81] Reading this novel in relation to Indigenous feminism from North America/Turtle Island generates multiple interpretations. For example, Matinga's role as a fluvial token of fecundity could be read as disempowering because she has no corporeal control over where she journeys. Furthermore, the novel reveals that she is isolated from her kin and is unaware of her origin story. There are certain arcs in the novel in which the story of a nation caught between anticolonial struggles and dictatorial repression makes Matinga a secondary character to the male political actors, rather than the center of the narrative. However, if we read this text with a different consciousness, one which takes seriously the practices, cosmologies, and mythologies of Central and Hispanophone African Benga populations, we can come to a different reading. Within African feminist contexts, the narrative of Matinga can be understood as a complex oral tradition woven into fictional narrative that can hold and tell many stories simultaneously. We can see the African feminist concept of motherism, or "the entrusting of rural women with the task of nurturing society," as an empowering and central role within the novel.[82] As such, the character of Matinga can be seen as a powerful figure who is "equated with the life force itself" and is central to reparations and bringing forth future generations.[83]

In the penultimate pages of the novel, we see Matinga pregnant and widowed after a brief affair with Mbele, the love of her life, who is also a mythical water nymph. While avenging the death of his brother and several fishermen, Mbele loses his life in slaying a sea beast—a shark-whale from what seems like another epoch (94). Lewis argues that this sea creature is "paradoxically a symbol of Spanish colonialism and its end within the context of Ndowe culture."[84] Matinga's relationship with Mbele represents a step toward fulfilling her own desires and rejecting the involuntary movements of her body. As she comes to consciousness through the fulfillment of her own corporeal desires, we see her self-determination. Her emotional ties to Mbele in spite of her body's overbearing directives mark the beginning of her willingness to exercise erotic and corporeal sovereignty. Matinga, now pregnant, travels to Bolondo to visit a "curandero," or medicine man, in order to understand the source of her blood's power. There, under a trance, she learns that her father was a man named Mecheba who was an "amante de la justicia y de la libertad" (125; "a lover of justice and of liberty"). He is revealed to be a colonial-era revolutionary who, in dying, bartered his newborn daughter's body in order to allow his spirit to see his child for a first and final time.

Mecheba had to "aceptar que los ancestros utilizaran el cuerpo de su criatura para repoblar el espacio playero, para palír las bajas causadas por el periodo colonial y prever también el derramamiento de sangre que tendría lugar despúes de la independencia" (126; "allow the ancestors to use the body of his child to repopulate the spatial beaches, to alleviate the depressions caused by the colonial period, and to forestall the bloodshed that would occur after independence"). The ancestors transformed Matinga's blood into a reparative force that could offer life-giving sacraments to replenish the decimated nation. Matinga is told that she was sent by "los ancestros, para repoblar este país que va a perder a muchos de sus hijos en los años sangrientos que se avecinan, como precio por su independencia" ("the ancestors, to repopulate this country which will lose many of its sons in the bloody years that are to come as price for their independence"); and that her nymph blood has "germinado el suelo de nuestra tierra. Por tu labor, nuevas generaciones han nacido para apagar mañana la hoguera encendida por el drama que hoy se gesta en nuestra patria guineana" (124; "germinated the soil of our lands. As a result of your labor, new generations have been born to extinguish the fires of tomorrow that are gestating today in our Guinean nation"). The news that her blood is a reparation which helps to produce generations is transformative for Matinga, particularly because this knowledge liberates her from uncertainty.

In Matinga's newfound understanding of her familial past and the nature of her powers, she is relieved of her blood's reparative acts. The curandero tells her, "Hoy te liberan los espíritus para que puedas volver a la isla junto a tu madre en Corisco" (125; "Today the spirits liberate you so you may return to the island of Corisco and join your mother"). Matinga reclaims her body as her own, free from ancestral control, and takes on a life beyond the reparations her blood offers. While the revelation of her origin story provided her comfort, in the novel Matinga suffered through the inability to control her body, struggled with her complete isolation from her kin, and lamented the early foreclosure of a life spent within a family and community. Mecheba's decision to barter her body for his own solace as he lay dying underscores a patriarchy reinforced by sentimental nationalism, similar to the heteropatriarchal trope found in Willie Bodega's scheme for reparations. With regard to this limiting position, Anderson laments, "Sadly, dominance and control of women have been the classic response to nations struggling with liberation movements, war, or postwar recovery."[85]

Matinga's pregnancy, however, is also presented as the next possibility, a continuation of the struggle for liberation and reparations, evoking Olivares's call for "having babies" as a practice of hope for future generations. However, if this is so, Matinga's impending motherhood can be read as a perpetuation of the novel's pronatalist sentiments, yet Matinga's agency as well as Benga practices of fertility reverberate in the text.[86] Women of color feminisms offer ways to think about the roles of motherhood and the maternal body that counter Western feminist cynicism towards their perceived injustice. Anderson offers community and collectivity as approaches to think outside of the fixed subjectivities that Western liberalism offers. "If we want to embrace essential elements of womanhood that have been problematic for Western feminists (such as motherhood and the maternal body)," she says, "then we have to ensure that these concepts don't get stuck in literal or patriarchal interpretations."[87] Thus, engaging Indigenous feminisms emerging from North America/Turtle Island alongside Indigenous African feminisms can offer us critical points of relation. For example, the anthropologist Virginia Fons observes that within Benga practices concerning conception and birth, the concept of being "llena de sangre," or full of blood, is critical. This speaks to the centrality of Matinga's blood as a reparative force within the novel. Furthermore, for postpartum women it is imperative that they are cared for by their kin: "la madre es atendida por su madre u otra parienta de confianza con experiencia procreativa, que pretende crear las condiciones óptimas para que cuide de su hijo y recupere su salud y, si es primípara, transmitirle sus propios conocimientos" ("The mother is taken care of by her mother or another trusted relative with procreative experience, who intends to create the optimal conditions to take care of her child and recover her health and, if she is primiparous (a first-time mother), to transmit her own knowledge").[88] In the novel, Matinga leaves Bolondo and travels to her mother and her kin on the island of Corisco in order to raise her child among her relations. Benga ritual practices around conception and birth as well as postpartum care underpin the narrative. Matinga comes to a confrontation with her history and her obligation to offer her blood and comes to understand this role beyond a dispossession of her own body. Her role as mother, daughter, and community member is not constrained by nationalist ideologies, colonization, or even by the ancestors. The reparation of her blood as a fertile force results in the reformulation of kinship and community relationships beyond her immediate family. The novel then offers the possibility of decolonial love as a response beyond the carnage of the colony, just as Matinga's life force offers the possibility of a reparation of human life.

Matinga, sangre en la selva is a novel inspired by mythology and ritual practice and is likewise imbued with the long and lingering histories of colonial, postcolonial/dictatorial, and decolonial imaginings. The narrative bears fruit much like Matinga's blood: radical reimaginings of the future are made possible through acts of love, but also through a belief in the power of future generations. It is in literary (re)imaginings that the difficult process of conceiving of decolonial reparations and a reparation of the imagination can take flight.

Futures of Blood and Bricks

While *Bodega Dreams*, *The Brief Wondrous Life of Oscar Wao*, and *Matinga, sangre en la selva* have different approaches to the notion of reparations, they are useful for thinking about the array of possibilities for achieving a reparation of the imagination. Quiñonez, Díaz, and Mbomío Bacheng's narratives feature protagonists living in nations under postcolonial and (post)dictatorial rule. In *Bodega Dreams*, reparation as self-determination within capitalist constructs ruptures and gives way to a decolonial love and a reparation of the imagination that sees liberatory possibilities in relations across difference, diasporic cultural language, and cultural productions. In the case of *The Brief Wondrous Life of Oscar Wao*, coloniality, represented by Trujillo's postcolonial dictatorial rule and the 500-year-old curse of the fukú, sets the stage for gendered violence and co-optation that affect multiple generations of Oscar's family. *Matinga, sangre en la selva* portrays the struggle against colonial and postcolonial dictatorships in Equatorial Guinea, and imagines the reparation of the nation as intimately tied to the bodies of women. Thus, reparations are also seen as acts of agency and as the continuation of sacred and necessary ritual practices concerning fertility and birth. In making the mythology of Matinga part of larger histories of anticolonial struggle, the author's depiction of reparation as part of a decolonial imagination shows how the perpetuation of ritual and kinship practices is critical for the future.

All three of these texts feature characters who have hope in future generations' abilities to continue the struggle for reparations in the face of colonization, coloniality, and ongoing forms of colonialism, dispossession, and oppression. In *Bodega Dreams*, Chino hears the vibrant language of El Barrio and sees the beauty in Nuyorican culture as signs of a reparative future beyond capitalist accumulation. In *The Brief Wondrous Life of Oscar Wao*, Yunior believes that Isis will eventually unlock the written imaginings of her uncle Oscar, and with her own knowledge, provide the zafa to the family's fukú. In *Matinga, sangre en la selva*, the ancestors believe that Matinga's unborn child will become a leader in struggles for justice and liberation, while Matinga returns to her family to reestablish kinship ties and to raise her child among the community in keeping with a long-established tradition of her people.

Although these novels imagine reparations through future generations, they also imagine reparations as decolonial love in the present. Chino takes in an unknown grandfather and grandson and takes Bodega's place while fundamentally transforming Bodega's reparations. Matinga's choice to unite with her family and radically redefine the terms of her body is a form of decolonial love that restores her relationship to herself, the ancestors, and her extended community. In *The Brief Wondrous Life of Oscar Wao*, Yunior's recognition of being "broken by the coloniality-of-power" is the first step in atrophying the inherent violence of colonization and moving toward a practice of decolonial love.[89] In his attempts to move beyond heteropatriarchal masculinity, which prevents him from achieving intimacy and building an ethical relationship with Lola, Yunior works toward the "stronger loving world" that Oscar had envisioned.

These literary interventions are tied to a long-standing commitment among marginalized and disenfranchised peoples to work toward decolonial reparations in the modern/colonial world. The texts speak to this longing to continually (re)imagine reparations in ways that address the injustices of the past, and the current social and political inequalities that stem from those injustices. Quiñonez, Díaz, and Mbomio Bacheng, along with Olivares's creative visioning, craft different ideas of what a more loving and repaired world could be. These imagined future worlds emphasize the need for reparations as a project beyond positivistic attitudes that translate historical and contemporary harms into quantifiable variables. These texts are but three contemporary examples of literary poetics that engage in a reparation of the imagination. They move beyond the scope of the material and toward a praxis of decolonial love as an ethics of relationality that can transform their worlds and futurities. While these authors look toward decolonial reparations and a reparation of the imagination, in the next chapter I track how diasporic Afro-Atlantic Hispanophone writers and artists imagine futurities as worlds imagined otherwise by engaging in the Sacred and by conjuring apocalypsos.

Chapter 5

Apocalypso

> When the Other appears to be the One. Apocalypso.
>
> —Michelle Cliff, "In My Heart a Darkness"

In the last chapter I argued that a decolonial reparation must sustain a reparation of the imagination. Such a process would necessarily entail an ethical demand for decolonial love re/produced through technologies of relations across difference, and the labor of imagining other ways of being human in the modern/colonial and settler colonial world. This chapter examines the futurities that emerge from the Afro-Atlantic Hispanophone diaspora, and traces forms of decolonial love and resistance conjured through Afro-Atlantic imagined futures. The preoccupation with futurities and imagining possibilities beyond coloniality is central to decolonial poetics, practices, and politics. This is because the science of transforming the human is not only about historicizing how Man has come to overrepresent himself as the human, but also about mapping and imagining new ways of being human in the present and future.[1] Thus, I trace some of the ways in which these Afro-Atlantic authors and artists trouble tropes of racialized Blackness, conjure apocalyptic worlds, and center Lucumí and other Afro-Atlantic systems of religious syncretism as acts of decolonial love. Rather than imagine utopian liberation or dystopian futures, the writers that I study in this chapter imagine how apocalypsos and what I call "worlds/otherwise" take root in the ruptures between modernity and coloniality, and are forged by the collision of domination and resistance. Their temporal scope is both the present and the near future.

Ruptures

In this chapter, I examine some of the tropes that emerge when Afro-Latinx and Afro-Hispanic cosmologies and ontologies collide against past and ongoing colonial forms of domination. The Afro-Latinx and Equatoguinean poetics I engage with throughout this book offer other ways of understanding physical and metaphysical borderlands, including thinking through islands, archipelagoes, and transatlantic migrations and diasporas. They also reimagine temporal, spatial, and affective boundaries through their troubling of colonial logics and their centering of being human as praxis.[2] Gloria Anzaldúa's conception of *la frontera* as a space where the "Third World grates against the first and bleeds" is an apt scaffolding for ways to think through how Black ontologies and forms of domination endemic to coloniality can be imagined and experienced as two worlds cutting against each other.[3] For Anzaldúa, these worlds grate against one another, creating ruptures or borderlands where languages, peoples, and land and spiritual practices survive, adapt, and resist domination. Building on Anzaldúa's metaphor, I contend that ichorous or sanguinary ruptures across modernity and coloniality contain the makings of new worldviews, or worlds/otherwise, which have the potential to reimagine the human and humanity.

The imaginative potential that arises from within these ruptures articulates new possibilities. In examining these ruptures and resistances, we bear witness to the fantastic, the spectacular, and the unnerving. These moments verge on the supernatural and let us glimpse what I am calling worlds/otherwise, or the Afro-Atlantic imagination, which center practices, knowledges, and histories that span centuries. Worlds/otherwise fashions new possibilities for Black life and ways of being in the world for both the present moment and the future. Imagining worlds/otherwise entails engaging the apocalyptic, the ends of worlds birthed by the non-ethics of modernity, coloniality, and settler colonialism.[4] These worlds/otherwise turn the known trajectory of the present on its head, and center Black women and femmes as the linchpins for salvation in the apogee of anti-Black and heteropatriarchal modernity. These worlds/otherwise are part and parcel of a reparation of the imagination, and offer perspectives from the peripheries of the Afro-Atlantic world.

Tracing worlds/otherwise means engaging in the future work of thinking, writing, and acting that humanize peoples condemned by coloniality and ongoing forms of colonialism. Worlds/otherwise understands how people's lives matter in the present and how they are essential to the future.[5] Future work, as I employ it here, brings the *damnés* into the present and imagines them in the future as fully human subjects. I see this as a practice in relation to Christina Sharpe's articulation of what she calls "wake work," or "new ways to live in the wake of slavery, in slavery's afterlives, to survive (and more) the afterlife of property." Wake work is "a mode of inhabiting *and* rupturing this episteme with our known lived and un/imaginable lives."[6] Imagining worlds/otherwise is a form of future work that acts as both a refusal and an indictment: it is a refusal to succumb to the necropolitics of modernity and an indictment of the interlocking systems of oppression which demand and produce destierro and advance the continued destruction of the global environment. Future work is also an embodied—corporeal and affective—rejection of that which requires the death of the Sacred. In this way, future work makes space for worlds/otherwise or other ways of practicing humanity in the present, in the past, in futures, and across diasporic spaces and imaginations.

While Afrofuturism engages across similar politics, modalities, themes, and sciences, I posit that Afrofuturism and imagining worlds/otherwise are not simply synonymous or reducible to one another. For example, many of the works that engage in imagining worlds/otherwise may not self-select or fit neatly within the bounds of the genre of Afrofuturism. In my analyses of these works, I make every attempt to respect the authors and their contexts. Thus, I am careful not to label them as Afrofuturist solely because they may be legible within the genre. Rather, I attempt to see how their works fit both within and outside of the parameters of Afrofuturism, and represent a form of future work produced by Afro-Atlantic writers, thinkers, and artists. One such work that falls both within and outside of the genre is Juan Tomás Ávila Laurel's *Panga Rilene*.[7] When this book was published in 2016, he was asked at a public round table in Barcelona if he had used the genre of Afrofuturism as inspiration for the novel. He noted that he had not heard of the genre or knew of the work, but he showed interest in how the category could expose him to a wider readership.[8]

In the 2002 special issue on Afrofuturism in *Social Text*, Alondra Nelson defines Afrofuturism as "sci-fi imagery, futurist themes, and technological innovation in the African diaspora."[9] The special issue marked one of Afrofuturism's most visible forays into digital and academic modalities. Since then, Afrofuturism as a field has grown to include work across myriad forms, genres, and centuries. Currently, work on Latinx-futurism is found primarily in Chicano studies, but Latinx Caribbean writers and artists, on the islands and in the diaspora, have taken up the genre in written works and digital media.[10] Online communities have also been essential to the collective envisioning of Latinx-Caribbean-futurism.[11] The dominance of Anglophone Afrofuturist work also requires structural analysis. We must contend with how racist and sexist publishing markets and venues (which are more readily accessible in the global North and in Anglophone-dominant spaces) shape what works are circulated, and where, when, and how. As a result of these factors, the Internet becomes the next best place to create and imagine Afrofuturist work. Within these contexts, Afro-Latinx and Afro-Hispanic futurities remain underexamined.

In developing the concept of worlds/otherwise, I engage the study of Afrofuturism and Afro-Latinx futurities as related genres. My meditation focuses on the tropes and practices that emerge in the future-oriented work of Afro-Latinx and Afro-Hispanic artists. In Equatoguinean literature, the genre play that often marks the interest and investment in futurities has only recently made it to publication. *Panga Rilene* (2016), for example, centers on an African femme (in an unknown future time) who continually attempts to piece together the histories that provoked her community's dystopic existence. In Ávila Laurel's imagination, Africans in general, and African women and femmes in particular, survive in a catastrophic future engineered by the heteropatriarchal, anti-Black, and anti-Indigenous exploits of modernity. Yet these characters are understood to be fully human subjects who enact self-determination. His work illuminates the slivers of liberatory possibilities that exist even within a dismal global outlook. Junot Díaz's short story "Monstro" has a similar apocalyptic plot that demonstrates a related interest in what happens at the nexus of late capitalism and environmental exploitation.[12] Both texts imagine worlds/otherwise as an apocalypse in the immediate future.

In another framing of worlds/otherwise, I examine the visual/sonic work of the Afro-Cuban French musical duo Ibeyi and the Cuban-American writer Daniel José Older's young adult novel, *Shadowshaper*.[13] I argue that Ibeyi and Older take up Lucumí, Santería, and related ritual practices as central to imagining worlds/otherwise. Their work is representative of a break from the fixed temporality of secular modernity, and demands that we contend with the spatial, spiritual, and temporal divides of the here and now. Imagining and calling forth worlds/otherwise requires a centering of other ways of knowing. The prophetic (foretelling near-future apocalypses) and syncretic (ritual practice) future works that I examine in this chapter are not utopian by any stretch of the imagination. They are shaped and fashioned by the crossings made during the transatlantic slave trade, and the myriad known and unknown lives sacrificed to the sea, to plantations, to the compound, to the whims of masters, mistresses, overseers, and hunters. They center the afterlives of slavery, colonialism, dictatorship, and destierro. They offer practices to bring ancestors to the present and bring generations into the future. These imaginaries and practices are culled from flesh, and as such carry with them the weight of over five centuries.

Sacred

In her chapter "Pedagogies of the Sacred," M. Jacqui Alexander engages memory as "a Sacred dimension of the self." Alexander examines how Sacred knowledge "comes to be inscribed in the daily lives of women through an examination of work—spiritual work—which like crossing is never undertaken once and for all." Thinking through the Sacred is of critical importance because "the majority of people in the world—that is, the majority of women in the world—cannot make sense of themselves without it."[14] Thus, our liberation practices must think through and with the potentiality of the Sacred, which is inextricable from the lives and histories of women of color. These pedagogies of the Sacred can be seen across Ibeyi's 2015 eponymous album, which features the delicate vocal and artistic mastery of sisters Lisa-Kaindé Díaz and Naomi Díaz. The Díaz twins are Afro-Cuban French artists who, with their 2015 album, track the connection between the spirit world and the sonic using Afro-Cuban ritual practices, or Santería, to trouble temporality.

In his book *¡Santo! Varieties of Latino/a Spirituality*, Edwin David Aponte explains that Santería is an African-based belief system:

> *Orishas* (Spanish: *Orichas*; Portuguese: *Orixas*) also traveled across the Atlantic with the captured enslaved Africans to the Americas. In the context of the horror, persecution, and death that defined colonial slavery throughout the Americas, transported African-based belief systems interacted with the Christianity presented to the slaves, as well as with indigenous beliefs and practices. These enslaved societies of the African diaspora in the Americas formed and fashioned new ways of knowing and being connected to the past that have contextual relevance to the present time. The translated African traditions developed in many ways in the Americas. One way this blended and contextualized sense of the holy developed was in the tradition that developed in Cuba, commonly known as Santería, "the way of the saints," but also by the name Lucumí (also spelled "Lukumi"), La Regla de Ocha (the way of the Ocha), or as Ifa/Orisha worship.[15]

"Ibeyi" is the Yoruba word for "twins," and within the cosmology of Santería, Ibeyi are the children of Changó, the orisha of fire, thunder, and justice, and of Oyá, guardian of the cemetery and the orisha of tempests and storms.[16] Some practitioners believe that Ibeyi are actually the children of Oshún, the orisha of sensuality and the river, and many others understand that Ibeyi are raised by Yemayá, the orisha of the sea. It is important to note, then, that the *Ibeyi* album includes songs dedicated to both of these orishas. According to Miguel A. De La Torre, "there are seven paths to Ibeyi, each with different gender combinations and names."[17] Lisa-Kaindé and Naomi are female twins, and the orishas Ibeyi are represented as "sacred twins" who are "treasured" by all the orishas.[18] I contend that Ibeyi's move to bring Santería into their public and mainstream musical practice is part of a radical tradition of salsa, rumba, jazz, and other musical forms that have brought Afro-syncretic practices to public audiences. This is particularly important because, as Aisha Beliso-De Jesús has argued, Santería has been "publicly demonized" and "used as justification for racial dominance in the transition from Spanish colonial governance to a republican nation in the early twentieth century."[19] In focusing on Ibeyi, this chapter expands the cartographies of the Hispanophone Caribbean diaspora linguistically, temporally, and spatially to include France as a place of diaspora/exile, and as an integral node of the African diaspora and the Caribbean. It also adds a different vector to the Cuban diaspora, and makes a connection to France as part of the La Regla de Ocha or Santería diaspora.

The *Ibeyi* album includes several "cantos," or songs, and intonations dedicated to the orishas in Lucumí, which is a practice of Afro-Cuban Santería. Ibeyi's lyrics, music, and video images serve as palimpsests; overlaid texts, images, and sounds that are elegies to Eleggua, Oyá, Ochún, Changó, Yemayá, and other orishas. These cantos to the orishas include chants in Yoruba, French, English, and Spanish and are reflections on mourning, ecology, and love. These languages and modalities are likewise markers of the impact and reach of past and present colonial empires, and mark forms of embodied resistance—a central aspect of ritual practices in the "New World." Here I examine a series of Ibeyi's songs and accompanying videos, stills, and visuals in order to track how they trouble temporality, charge the listener/viewer to conjure worlds/otherwise, and create audio and visual palimpsests that fashion spaces to imagine Afro-Cuban and Afro-diasporic syncretic and cultural practices as part of the future.

In Lucumí, all ceremonies open with a tribute to Eleggua, the first orisha to be greeted, as he is the guardian of the crossroads.[20] Ibeyi begin their album with a chant for Eleggua as the necessary link to the ancestral worlds, and follow with a song to Oyá, the orisha of the marketplace, guardian of the cemetery gates, and wielder of hurricanes, lightning, and an army of the dead. In "Oya," Ibeyi describe everyday moments of joy followed by a problematic schema. These lyrics are accompanied by their digitized voices, which create the sound of an organ and baroque chords. When the beat drops, the rapid and deep sounds of the batá drum emerge in full force. Ibeyi follow a call-and-response pattern with one another. Throughout "Oya" they pose the possibility of small delights—"even if I feel the sun on my skin," "even if I see the most beautiful thing up in the sky," "even if my hand's skin catches the wind"—juxtaposed against the challenge, ("if I don't feel you"). After each verse, Ibeyi cry "Take me Oya," four times in chorus.[21]

Ibeyi position spirits and ancestors as necessary if they are to take pleasure in living. Having gained access to the ancestors from Eleggua, they plead with Oyá to take them past the gates of the cemetery so that they may merge their living world with the ancestral world. The video for "Oya" (figure 6) is a black-and-white matrix that takes the viewer from a black hole into a cypher of bare trees and dense forests. Continuously entering new forest landscapes is disorienting, haunting, and dizzying. The viewer is simultaneously made to focus on the inextricable link between ritual practice and the landscape. In fact, throughout the video the twins become a visual representation of a human and ecological palimpsest. Here Ibeyi clues us in to their practice of futurities by enticing the viewer to fall into their digital and visual/sonic scape, beckoning towards worlds/otherwise.

In their music and their video images, Ibeyi make future work into a dialectical practice. Following George Ciccariello-Maher's meditation, decolonizing dialectics marks the emergence of "new struggles" and "new ruptures throwing forth new renewed identities that deepen contradictions and press toward different possible futures."[22] While Ciccariello-Maher takes up political theory and Venezuelan radical politics, his discussion of the role of dialectics in ushering in futurities through struggle is critical, particularly

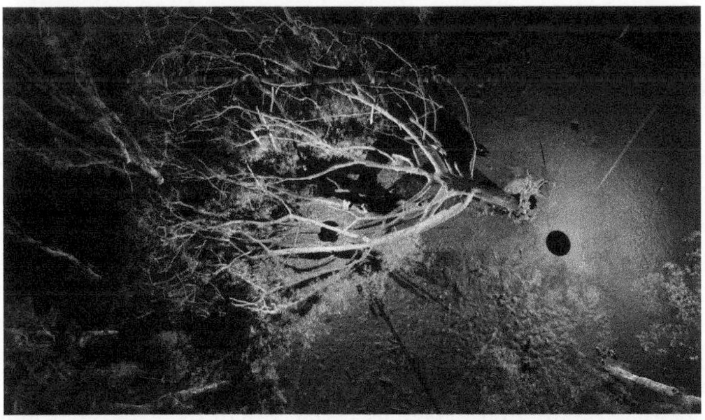

Fig. 6. Stills from Ibeyi's video for "Oya"—a haunting nightscape of trees and the specters of Ibeyi as a palimpsestic image; aerial view of tree cypher in a nightscape; an overlay of images showing Ibeyi sitting on the branches of a felled tree.

for those operating in peripheralized positions or condemned to the underside of modernity. Ibeyi thus engage in a dialectical play that moves towards worlds/otherwise, highlighting practices, knowledges, and histories towards new possible futurities that center relationships with the ancestors and ritual practice. For example, through their sonic and visual works, Ibeyi take the ancestors with them into their future work, as they simultaneously demand to be taken by the ancestors to a known and unknowable past. This struggle, represented by dueling demands within the practice, continues to play out as they link their music to the practice of Osha throughout the album.

By making this musical offering to the ancestors, Ibeyi follow a ceremonial pattern in their music. It is significant that they follow "Oya" with "Ghosts," as Lucumí practitioners often say "Egun first," meaning "ancestors first." In "Ghosts," their second full-length song, Ibeyi welcome the listener and describe a scape of destruction: "Welcome to my earth / It's a crying shame / We have built a foolish world / Busy fighting, full of lying and denying." In these lines we glimpse a possible present, but certainly an imagined dystopian future world. The sisters then hail worlds/otherwise by singing, "My ghosts are not gone / They dance in the shade / And kiss the black core of my heart / Making words making sounds making songs."[23] Their ghosts, the ancestors and the generations to come, are not gone but rather right there alongside them, dancing "in the shade." Ibeyi have crushed modern colonial logics that imagine time as linear and ghosts as implausible beings. They do away with the hard-and-fast divides of the living and the dead by singing that these ghosts "kiss the black core" of their hearts and make words, sounds, and songs. The core of their hearts are black, or Black, and as they beckon the ancestors, their Black hearts are kissed, blessed, taken care of by the ancestors. Here, they signify that Blackness is the core of their ontological being, a generative life force that is affirmed and loved by those who matter the most: Egun, first. Ibeyi thus conjure Blackness in diametrical opposition to the deficit signifiers that Blackness has been assigned in the modern/colonial and settler colonial world. As we listen to Ibeyi, we can imagine that these songs are the very ones the ancestors are singing over the beat that Ibeyi provide.

Moreover, the lyrics in Ibeyi's "Ghosts" depict a shameful and foolish world where a lack of love among humans has left little goodness or love in the world. The ghosts are a haunting and we are the haunted. The video for "Ghosts" uses a double exposure to create a palimpsest of the twins' images (figure 7). The effect creates a scene where the viewer cannot see where one twin ends and the other begins. The palimpsestic form is important to note because it highlights another palimpsest: that of the sonic soundscape which the twins deploy (using ritual practice rhythms and instruments, electronica, and multiple languages) and which presents Yoruba ritual as an Afro-syncretic practice (overlapping African ritual practice, Indigenous/New World practices, and Roman Catholic syncretism).

Fig. 7. Still from Ibeyi's video for "Ghosts"—a palimpsest close-up of the twins' faces.

These palimpsests exemplify what Ngũgĩ wa Thiong'o calls "something torn and new."[24] Ngũgĩ follows Edward Kamau Brathwaite's poetic trilogy *The Arrivants*, in which he envisions Black people in the Caribbean as "those among whom the god walks," and celebrates their words, sounds, and spirituality as moments in which they are "now waking/making/with their/ rhythms some-/thing torn/and new."[25] Ngũgĩ calls on creative writers and arts practitioners to conjure ties to African ancestors before and after 1492, writing: "Memory is the link between the past and the present, between space and time, and it is the base of our dreams. Writers and intellectuals in these movement are aware that without a reconnection with African memory, there is no wholeness."[26] While I am skeptical of the "wholeness" that Ngũgĩ exalts as a possibility through the act of memory, I am committed to the vision that re-membering and rememory are acts that make fully human lives in the past-future-present possible for Black- and Indigenous-descended peoples. Ngũgĩ argues that "creative imagination is one of the greatest re-membering practices," and cites the prayer-poetry of Léopold Senghor as an example of the importance of ancestral memories: "Let the children in bed talk about their ancestors like their parents" and "breathe the smell of our dead" and "contemplate and repeat their living voice."[27] Ibeyi's album is engaged in this creative imagination that invokes the dead and makes of them living memories. Pablo López Oro argues that "ancestral memory is sacred. Ancestral memory is political. Ancestral memory is an embodied archive passed on transgenerationally to and through the flesh vis-à-vis oral traditions," and Ibeyi's poetic forms, the music and visual arts, highlight the delicate interplay between the ancestors and the human world, underscoring the thin veil between what is past and future (165).[28]

Ibeyi are not the first to create elegies in the form of songs. In fact, "Ghosts" hails an older form of sonic remembrance. The song "Llora Timbero" is a moving requiem in guanguancó form for José Rosario Oviedo. Born in 1885 to an enslaved mother, Funciana Oviedo, his birth preceded the abolition of slavery in Cuba by one year. However, he was afforded free status due to the Moret Law, passed fifteen years earlier in 1870. The Moret Law, known as the "ley de vientre libre," or free womb law, broke with the legal doctrine of *partus sequitur ventrem* in Cuba and Puerto Rico, and ushered in a pre-abolition window in which the mother's enslaved status would not be passed on to children in the womb.[29] Oviedo was best known by his nickname "Malanga" and was a famed rumbero player, dancer, and singer, as well as a Santero from Unión de Reyes Matanzas, Cuba.[30] After his mysterious death in 1927, his close friend and cajón player, Faustino Drake, penned the song "Malanga Murió" to honor his memory.

The song, which became as popular as Malanga himself, took on a life of its own and was later recorded as "Llora Timbero." Ritual practitioners and myriad rumba and salsa artists have covered the song throughout the twentieth century. The lyrics mourn Malanga's passing and declare that his hometown weeps because of his death. A famous version of the song, Tito Rodriguez's "Llora Timbero" (1968), begins with a call and response that centers the singer's feeling upon hearing the news of Malanga's death, and the chorus subsequently responding: "Siento una voz que me dice / (coro): Are niye-e, o / Siento una voz que me llama / (coro): Malanga murió" ("I feel a voice that says to me / (chorus): Are niye-e, o / I feel a voice that calls to me / (chorus): Malanga has died").[31] The singer then breaks out into the oft-repeated chorus "Unión de Reyes llora / a ese timbero mayor / que viene regando flores / desde Matanzas a Morón" ("Unión de Reyes cries / for the great timbero / who comes watering flowers / from Matanzas to Morón").[32] Music makes of Malanga a living memory, but more so documents the mourning felt with his departure.

While the emotional aspect is primary in this song, the lyrics are also of interest in thinking about geography and spatiality. The grieving singer has memories of Malanga "regando flores" from Matanzas to Morón, a distance of almost two hundred miles (figure 8). The song's lyrics trace Malanga's movement across the northern side of Cuba and bear witness to his famed rumba, the public's demand to see him perform, and the joy he brought as he "watered flowers" across the island. Within these contexts we come to a different understanding of Afro-Atlantic geographies, informed by an Afro-Atlantic cosmology, and are able to track movements across Afro-Atlantic Hispanophone diasporic locations through the medium of music.

A Cuban documentary on Malanga, titled *Al compás de Cuba* (ca. 1960), takes place in Unión de Reyes about fifty years after his death. None of the

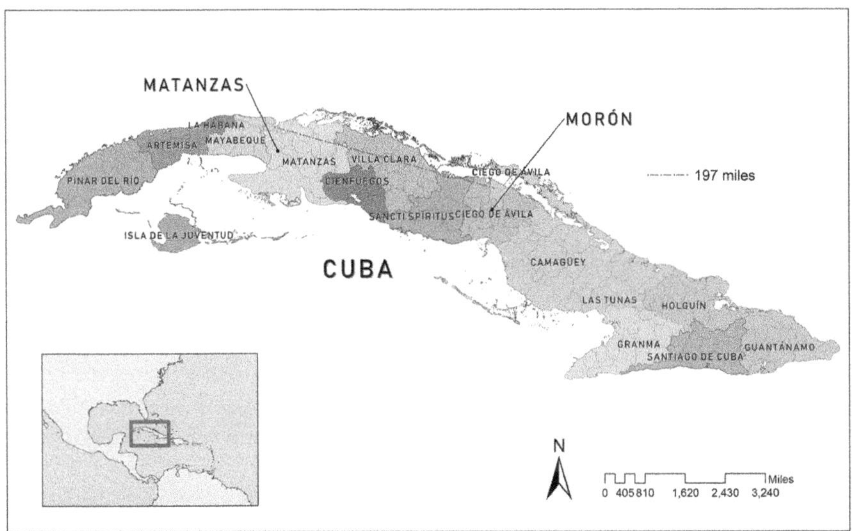

Fig. 8. Map of Cuba with Matanzas and Morón marked. These are the cities that are referenced in the sonic elegy dedicated to Malanga.

people interviewed there could remember where he lived or what he did for a living (he was an agricultural worker), but they all knew the song and knew that he was an important person from their town and was famous throughout the island. The narrator tells the viewer that although no one had tangible details about his life, they all knew him: "Efectivamente nadie pudo darnos detalles concretos de la vida de Malanga. Pero todos conocían a Malanga. Malanga no existía en un lugar específico de Cuba, pero estaba en toda Cuba. Malanga se convertía en un símbolo. No estaba en ninguna parte y estaba en todas, como la rumba" ("Indeed, nobody could give us concrete details of the life of Malanga. But everyone knew Malanga. Malanga did not exist in a specific place in Cuba, but was in all of Cuba. Malanga became a symbol. He was not anywhere and was everywhere, just like the rumba").[33] Of importance is Malanga's role as a symbol for Cuba and as a stand-in for the music and art of rumba. Likewise, the lack of any photographs or images of Malanga is also significant. Some accounts note that he was self-conscious about being photographed due to his short stature and features: "Era bajito, prieto, gordo, barrigón, de ojos saltones y expresivos, nariz afilada, con marcas en la cara como de viruela: hombre de muchas mujeres, fiestero, simpático, ocurrente, además persona bien llevada y querida por todo el pueblo" ("He was short, black, fat, potbellied, with bulging and expressive eyes, sharp nose, with marks on his face like from smallpox: a man of many women, partying, nice, witty, a person well taken and loved by all the people").[34] Whatever the reason, Malanga refused to be photographed, and so the only record of his craft and his impact come from documented firsthand accounts and Faustino Drake's 1927 song.

If we juxtapose the absence of visual images of Malanga with Ibeyi's relative photographic and visual overrepresentation, we beget yet another way of mapping the geographies of Afro-Atlantic syncretic practices. Ibeyi's work overwhelms the viewer and listener with possibilities of seeing, hearing, and feeling the collision of the spiritual and material worlds. They make Egun's presence and ancestral memories known through the embodied practices of music-making, dance, and image curation. On the other hand, "Llora Timbero" is a sonic remembrance with no visual counterpart beyond the embodied memory of those who cover the song in ritual practice and popular culture. When we overlay the re-membering work of Ibeyi and the elegy dedicated to Malanga, a vibrant palimpsest of future work practices emerges. Through stories, songs, images, and blank spaces, these works hold space for us to continually bring forth ancestral futures in the present.

Another such elegy is Mongo Santamaría's song "Chano Pozo," dedicated to the late Afro-Cuban jazz musician Luciano Pozo González. Chano Pozo, as he was best known, was also a Santero (dedicated to the orisha Changó/ Santa Barbara) and was recognized as one of the greatest Cuban percussionists on the island and in the United States.[35] His murder in New York City in 1948 rocked the jazz world and inspired the masterful rumbero Mongo Santamaría to write the requiem "Chano Pozo." The song mourns his passing but declares that his memory lives on as long as drums sound: "Este güiro es para Chano aunque en la gloria él está / Después de haberlo perdido lo temenos que mentar / Mientras suenan los tambores / Nadie te podrá olvidar / A ti, Chano Pozo / A ti, Chano Pozo / Mi amigo Manteca adiós, mi amigo adiós / Adiós mi amigo del alma, adiós" ("This güiro is for Chano / Although in the Glory he be / After having lost him / We have to tell him / While the drums sound / Nobody will be able to forget you / You, Chano Pozo / You, Chano Pozo / My friend Goodbye / goodbye, my friend / goodbye / Chorus: Goodbye my soul friend, goodbye").

In highlighting these two examples of musical elegies in my discussion of Ibeyi's future work practice, I aim to underscore that the act of remembering through ceremonies and music is a long-standing practice within Santería. What Ibeyi offer as Afro-Cuban Santería singers and artists in the twenty-first century is a critically related practice. Instead of mourning their dead, Ibeyi imagine the dead as behind them, holding them, and most importantly, continuing alongside the living.[36] This is not to qualify songs of homage and grief as being less prescient, but rather to show how Ibeyi's poetic forms, the music and visual arts, highlight the delicate interplay between the spirit and human worlds, and underscore the thin veil between what is past and the future. That their songs on the *Ibeyi* album are dedicated to both their father and their sister is also important to note, for it interrupts the masculinist movidas made within some forms of Santería that often hold space to laud

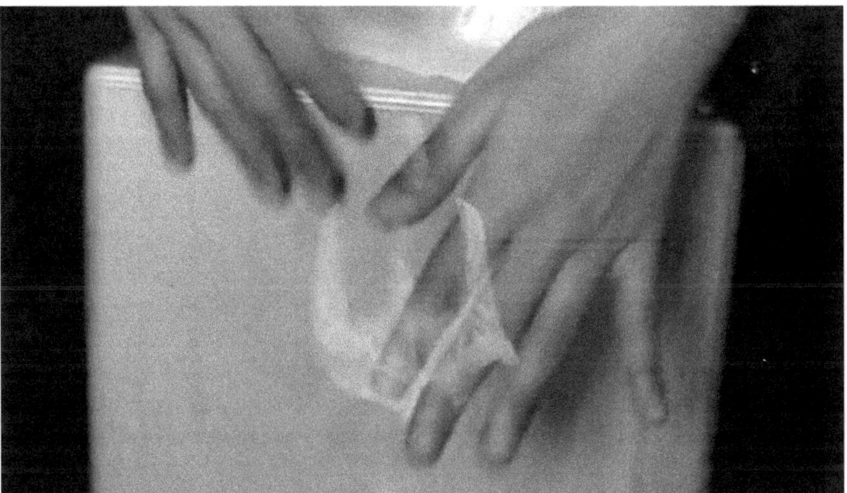

Fig. 9. Still from Ibeyi's video for "Ghosts"—palimpsest of hands playing the cajón and Naomi playing the cajón.

the greatness of male practitioners. Ibeyi's sisterhood, kinship, and spiritual and feminist practice create a critical space within this genre of music that is linked to syncretic remembering practices that bear witness to intergenerational and ancestral influences.

The images in the video for "Ghosts" underscore the witnessing of the ghosts in the song—they are "not gone." Instead, Ibeyi visualize a haunting. This haunting is a mirror that reflects the twins back to one another, reveals them to us (the viewer), and exposes them to their ancestors. The video shows multiple images of the twins overlaid and in the midst of movement. In figure 7 they emerge from within each other, while in figure 9 we see the image of the cajón being played up close. The video then shows the image from further away, zooming out to see the player. The image of hands playing a cajón is important here, as Naomi learned to play the cajón and the batá drum in memory of their father, the famed percussionist Anga Díaz.[37]

The viewer sees Ibeyi as ghostly figures always accompanied by another version of themselves or the other. As Ibeyi trouble sight, they trouble worlds. As each twin appears as the other and then as one, I follow Michelle Cliff's speculation, "When the Other appears to be the One. Apocalypso."[38] Cliff makes this statement as an observation on passing for white as a Jamaican woman and confronting anti-Black racism within a presumed white space. The revelation of Cliff as Black is the "Other" appearing as the "One." In the retelling of this encounter, Cliff posits that the colonizer's perspective cannot understand her fair skin as being related to Blackness, Jamaica, or the Caribbean. The wonder, the anxiety that it provokes, creates what she calls an "apocalypso," a cataclysmic failure. Part of this is that Cliff is the living proof of foundational violence, and the other is that the colonizer does not expect to see this person—one who does not fit into the boxes they have made for the colonized—looking back at them, looking *like* them. "When the Other appears to be the One" is likewise useful for thinking about the relationship between generations of Afro-descendants.

Ibeyi act as both the apparitions of the ancestors and the generations to come. This worldview destabilizes dominant logics and dismantles colonial worlds. In other words: Apocalypso. Ibeyi emerge as the apparitions of the ancestors, as reflections of each other, and as a specter of the generations to come. The ghosts are the Other and the One. They bring forth an apocalypso of colonial logics that seek to sever or deny the roots of ritual practice and the power of memory. Katherine McKittrick contends that "the site of memory begins to re-imagine a different worldview, wherein black lives are validated through black intellectual histories and the physical landscape" (32).[39] I build here on both Sylvia Wynter's meditations on the catastrophe of 1492 and Nishitani Osamu's argument that the colonial logics of "Man1" turned colonial cartographic or spatial movement across the Atlantic into a temporal movement that cast Indigenous peoples, and later Africans, as ahistorical nonhumans and exploitable subjects.[40] Ibeyi subvert the founding colonial logic of Man1 and atheistic Man2, and in turn offer the possibility of the Other appearing as the One.

In figure 10 we see Lisa-Kaindé emerge as a ghostly spirit from within her own prostrated body. Her body may be asleep but the spirit is awake or awakening, perhaps being beckoned by worlds/otherwise. The first lines of "Ghosts" point to the ecological and human destruction brought on by the living: "Welcome to my earth / It's a crying shame / We have built a foolish world / Full of lying, full of crying and denying." This beginning can be juxtaposed with their hook: "We ain't nothing without love."[41] Thus, even a world destroyed by human limits can be, to some extent, remedied by love. This is not just any love, but a decolonial love, an ancestral love, a black femme love, a kinship love, and a sisterhood love. It is a sustaining love that underscores the limits of the living while pointing to the abundant possibilities of finding fulfillment in ritual practice.

Ibeyi's next song, "River," beckons Ochún, the orisha of love, sweet water, and fertility. They sing, "I will come to your river / Wash my soul again / Carry away my dead leaves / Let me baptize my soul with the help of your waters / Sink my pains and complaints / Let the river take them, river drown them."[42] In this video we see the sisters lying side by side, submerged underwater (figure 11). They are being held down, fists on their chests, and pulled under by disembodied arms below them. They take turns surfacing, singing their portion of the song to Ochún, and then are submerged again. During different parts of the video, the sisters open their eyes under the water, proof of its sweetness, for they would not open their eyes under salt waters. They

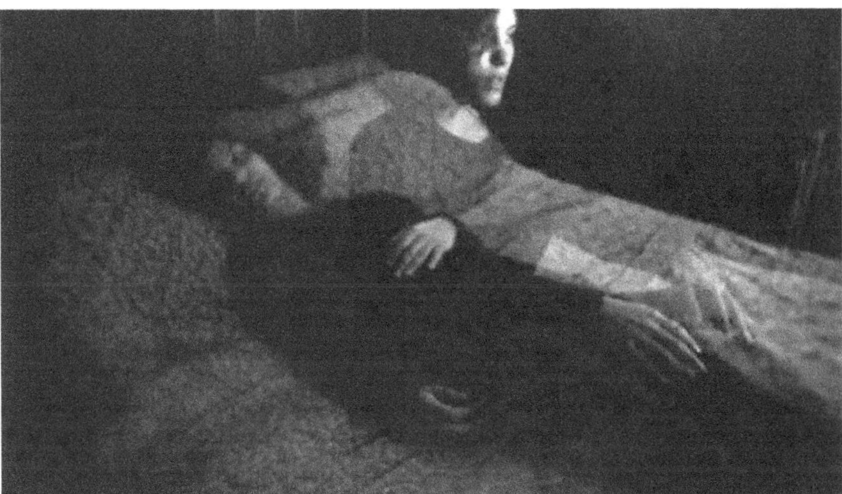

Fig. 10. Still from Ibeyi's video for "Ghosts"—an afterimage of Lisa-Kaindé lying down and sitting up from within her own body.

remain in this underwater world, a womb, throughout the song, sacrificing breath for communion with Ochún. The song ends with a slow chant to Ochún in Yoruba. This is one of many times that ritual songs are chanted in the album, marking another level of their musicality and another traversing of worlds—communing with other practitioners of Lucumí.

Finally, the song "Think of You" opens and ends with a sample of the artists' father, Anga Díaz, playing a beat on what may be the batá. He instructs them, "Usted va jugando siempre con los sonidos. Pueden hacerlo, por ejemplo" ("You go playing always with the sounds. You can do it, for example"). He then begins to give an example that is never heard or unheard because Ibeyi's own music comes in.[43] Ibeyi immediately begin with the "moyuba," an ancestral roll call or invocation, which "can be understood as a structuring ritual" that "generates a hierarchy linking living priests, the dead, and oricha."[44] Thus, Ibeyi sing to acknowledge the ancestors and orishas. M. Jacqui Alexander explains the moyuba as "an expansive memory refusing to be housed in any single place, bound by the limits of time, enclosed within the outlines of a map, encased in the physicality of the body, or imprisoned as exhibit in a museum." This refusal, she adds, "takes its inheritance from the Crossing, which earlier prophets had been forced to undertake from the overcrowded passageways in a place called Gorée, the door of no return, still packed centuries later with the scent of jostled grief so thick that no passage of human time could absorb it."[45] Ibeyi chant the moyuba with all its complex and attended grief, accompanied by bare drums and intermittent synthesized clapping. They sing, "We hear laughter and we think of you," "If

Fig. 11. Stills from Ibeyi's video for "River"—Naomi and Lisa-Kaindé submerged under water dressed in white; in one image Lisa-Kaindé opens her eyes under water, in the other image Naomi emerges to sing lyrics.

we sing they may come guiding all of our steps," "You live through us, Papa, we're singing for you," and "We walk on rhythm and we think of you." The palimpsest that Ibeyi design in "Think of You" includes the sonic and vocals, the drums, and the voice of their late father, which opens and closes the song. They conjure images of laughter and of walking on rhythm. In effect, this masterful song is a rupture in the veil of modernity, a crack where worlds/otherwise are being created.

Ibeyi's future work makes space for us to faithfully witness and remember the past, to strengthen us for present struggles, and to bring forth different futures. By playing with the sonic, they also play with temporality, taking us deep into the rhythmic and spiritual world of Lucumí epistemologies and describing the hauntings and futurities embedded in this Afro-syncretic practice. This is powerful for a number of reasons, primarily because of how ritual practice and the Sacred have been evacuated from the secular logics of modernity. Alexander writes, "It is not only that (post)modernity's secularism renders the Sacred as tradition, but it is also that tradition, understood as an extreme alterity, is always made to reside elsewhere and denied entry into the modern."[46] Through their use of the sonic/visual, Ibeyi emphasize that knowledge of ritual practice and Afro-diasporic cosmologies is key to subverting narratives that evacuate ancestral ties and cast syncretic practices as unimportant or illegitimate forms of epistemology.[47] Ibeyi's album and its accompanying videos are likewise maps of colonial modernity, as Santería is being practiced and reimagined by Afro-Cuban French femme twins in France. In doing so, Ibeyi represent other and more recent forms of transatlantic crossings, including the surge of Latinx Caribbean migration to European metropoles. Ibeyi are part of a long line of practitioners who have used the Sacred in their artistic practices and who break away from dehumanizing logics as they bring worlds/otherwise into being.

Spirit Work

Daniel José Older's young adult novel *Shadowshaper* (2015) is the first novel in the "*Shadowshaper* Cypher," and takes up many of the same themes seen and heard in the *Ibeyi* album. Older, a fantasy and young adult writer of Cuban and Jewish ancestry, is, like Ibeyi, a practitioner of Lucumí or Santería.[48] For Older, Lucumí is a faith that he carries "in the blood" and it represents "a very beautiful, very deep, very philosophical religion with lots of complex spirituality and community."[49] Writing from his adopted home of Brooklyn, New York, Older's work is part of a growing number of critical novels for young adults written by Latinx authors.[50] *Shadowshaper*'s protagonist is Sierra Santiago, a talented Afro-Puerto Rican muralist who lives in Brooklyn with her mother, father, and grandfather and is mourning the recent loss of her grandmother, Mama Carmen. Once Sierra notices the supernatural events happening around her and her role within them, she joins her friends Bennie and Tee, her brother Juan, her love interest Robbie, and a Columbia University librarian named Nydia Ochoa in a race against time to decipher why the murals in her neighborhood seem to be fading, crying tears, and changing shape before her eyes. Sierra suspects that this has to do with the disappearance and sudden apparition of community elders as zombie-like "corpuscles." She soon realizes that there are battling ancestral spirits, anthropological co-optation, and familial secrets involved.

Set in contemporary Brooklyn, the novel conjures worlds/otherwise wherein the spirits of the dead are clamoring to speak to the living through an innate spiritual and corporeal practice called "shadowshaping." Shadowshapers must be initiated, similar to ritual practice, and must be taught how to become available vessels and wielders of the spirits that surround them. As the story progresses, Older reveals that shadowshaping is a practice that creates space for ancestral spirits to become embodied through artistic and creative expression—painting, drawing, dancing, storytelling, body art such as tattoos, and so on. Shadowshaping has its roots across different Caribbean Afro-syncretic belief systems, including Santería, Lucumí, Voudoun, Candomblé, and Lwa; and water, the sea, and ancestral veneration are central to the operative system.

Furthermore, shadowshaping is a practice forged in kinship and community relations. Shadowshapers are initiated by other shadowshapers across racial, ethnic, and national backgrounds. Thus, the practitioners are pan-Caribbean and intergenerational, and as a result, heterogeneous art forms and creative practices lure the spirits to the shadowshapers. The spirits lure the shadowshapers, as well, by moving through paintings, drawings, sketches, and music. When Sierra begins shadowshaping, she is visited in her dreams by "[a] hundred million souls," who, with centuries-long stretches, "reached their long shadowy fingers up from the depths of the sea" (148). For Sierra, these dreams beget feelings that are at once "calming, uplifting, terrifying, sorrowful," and movements that are "gentle and deadly like the tide" (148). The souls that visit Sierra in her sleep are bounded within and outside of the sea, hailing crossings of the Middle Passage, migration voyages, and other diasporic movements. Shadowshaping in conscious and unconscious states allows Sierra to drift "somewhere in the middle of all those souls—a flash of living flesh amidst so much death" (148). She is able to listen to these centuries-old spirits as they "whispered songs about their lives and deaths, a swirl of loves lost and remembrances, hymns and murder ballads" (148). Through her dreams, Sierra realizes that to be a shadowshaper is not only "the power to transfer spirit into form" but to be a conduit for history itself—one antithetical to the patriarchal production of knowledge (225). As Xhercis Méndez notes, in the ritual practice of Ocha, "the materiality of the 'human body' functions as both a sacred vessel for the Orisha and a channel for communal well-being."[51]

Shadowshaper engages in future work by creating worlds/otherwise in at least three ways. First, like Ibeyi, Older's novel ruptures colonial temporal and spatial logics, incorporating ancestors and spirits within the narrative as active participants in the lives of the living. This construct centers and values Afro-Caribbean cosmologies, which have been historically devalued and "subordinated to the European cosmos," and not "expected to accord any significance to modernity's itinerary."[52] Second, in challenging Western conceptions of the body (and particularly the white supremacist and cis heterosexist biometrics of race and gender), the narrative documents the destructive implications of those structural logics within familial, interpersonal, and spiritual relations. The protagonist, Sierra, is a teenage Afro-Latina who, despite her age, race, and gender, is not only initiated as a shadowshaper but also becomes the most powerful wielder of spirits in the city. Finally, the act of shadowshaping, or becoming a vessel for ancestral spirits through the creative arts, is an action that defies coloniality. Older creates worlds/otherwise by making shadowshaping the ability to reconfigure the body as a conduit for the spirit worlds. This destabilizes temporal, spatial, and spiritual logics that would cast such spirits as inherently evil.[53] Méndez contends that "practices such as ritual possession rematerialize 'human bodies' as open, porous, and ultimately permeable to divine forces."[54] I argue that by casting the spirits as divine, powerful, and in communion with the living, Older offers a generous and complex (and perhaps more familiar) schema for understanding relations with the dead—particularly for Afro-Diasporic and Latinx readers of young adult literature. Finally, in *Shadowshaper*, apocalypso appears within the very structures of shadowshaping. For example, Sierra learns more about her skills as she deciphers the poetic riddle, "The one lures the other who in turn lures the one" (188). As she unravels the clues that lead to the culprit behind the death of the elders and the restless stirring of the spirits, Sierra realizes that she must become the other by taking in the spirits and fighting against the colonizing forces that want to bring about the shadowshapers' end. Sierra is both the other and the one, shattering colonial logics, traversing planes between the spirit and material worlds, and accepting her inheritance as the most powerful shadowshaper.[55]

In crafting this novel, Older marks Brooklyn as a critical site for the Puerto Rican diaspora. He traces the intimate syncretic and cultural ties of Afro-Puerto Ricans to Africa and the Antilles. It is critical to emphasize that the protagonist is Afro-Puerto Rican, a political move that centers Blackness in Puerto Rico despite the ways in which it is often evacuated or minimized in the histories told about the island. Puerto Rico, as noted by Kelvin Santiago-Valles and Petra Rivera-Rideau, has been marked erroneously as the whitest nation of the Hispanophone Caribbean.[56] Rather than an empty marker or catchall trope for Afro-syncretic practices, Blackness or African descent scaffolds the structure, choices, and contentions that Sierra faces within the spirit world while she is grappling with her own personal identity, transition to adulthood, and familial relationships. Older's young adult novel is likewise a kind of spiritual bildungsroman, with the protagonist coming to consciousness about her place within her family, community, and ancestral lineage.

While the novel's setting showcases a rapidly gentrifying city with accompanying dispossession and racism, Older also puts significant emphasis on challenging these structures as well as subverting the insidiousness of anti-Blackness in Puerto Rican families. The "off-hand bigotry" that Sierra faces from her aunt, Tía Rosa, becomes an important part of how we understand her resilience; we witness her identity formation in the face of Tía Rosa's racist remarks and her own internalized self-doubt (78, 151). For example, while Sierra positively describes her hair as a "fro stretched magnificently around her [like a] halo," Tía Rosa derisively describes it as "all wild and nappy" (10, 78). Although neither "wild" nor "nappy" can be construed as inherently negative, for Tía Rosa these comments signal her disapproval of Sierra's disregard for the unspoken yet understood project of Latinx mestizaje, which telegraphs the desirability of whiteness and its aesthetic and sociocultural trappings. Carlos Pozzi argues, for example, that the racial colonial project has had lasting effects on Latinxs, visible in the "implicit statements" and dichos that attribute "value to 'being white,'" despite their denial of racist attitudes.[57] In one scene, Tía Rosa scowls at Robbie's Haitian roots, and warns Sierra that if a potential partner is "darker than the bottom of your foot, he's no good for you!" (77). Sierra faces an unspoken hierarchy in her family since, as Ylce Irizarry notes, "[one's] skin color is not a problem in and of itself; rather, one's skin shade—the level of its lightness or darkness—is the determining factor of one's place in social and familial hierarchies" (158).[58] At one point, Sierra realizes that although she has "shrugged off" her aunt's insidious anti-Blackness, it has stayed inside her like a "tentacle," and reemerges as self-doubt "from somewhere deep inside her" (77, 80). In one of the most intimate moments of the book, Sierra reflects on her own utterances of being "not enough" and confidently declares in front of her mirror that she is "more than enough" (80). Older underscores that self-acceptance and self-love are not instantaneous movidas for Sierra, but rather ones that come with time and with the realization of her identity as a descendant of the most powerful lineage of shadowshapers.[59]

Shadowshaper reveals that migration and diaspora to urban centers like New York City require the formation of complex community relations and "interdependence" in order to sustain syncretic belief systems.[60] While shadowshaping and its accompanying knowledges are difficult to protect, the novel shows that practices and histories which are passed down can thrive in ever-changing spatial locales. Older writes that even as the "details change from generation to generation, across time and place," the "deeper secret remains the same" (219). New York City, which is teeming with a palimpsest of spirits, becomes a fertile ground for shadowshapers and the myriad souls who wish to commune with and communicate through the living.[61] Sierra and her friends are living through a wrenching transition in Brooklyn, and the shifts in the ways that the spirits must be protected mirrors the struggle of gentrification in the neighborhood. Older underscores how developing strong ties with the ancestors and spirit world leads to collaborative and communal practices—in Sierra's case, access to a pan-Caribbean collective of shadowshapers. These practices serve the needs of both the living and the dead.

Furthermore, the novel indicts those who undermine the work of women in the spirit world, and condemns colonizing researchers who, in the quest to accumulate power, come to see themselves as deserving of all Sacred knowledges. Sierra's grandmother, Mama Carmen, was Lucera, the most powerful shadowshaper, but Grandpa Lázaro's machismo and male ego slowly infiltrated the practice. He attempted to excise Mama Carmen and refused to initiate Sierra as a rightful heir of Lucera's powers because he had convinced himself that "shadowshaping was for men" (218). In "Transcending Dimorphism," Méndez counters scholarship on Santería that attempts to circumscribe its practices through modern/colonial gender arrangements. Rather than center dimorphic human bodies and "read" gender within ritual practice, Méndez argues that certain aspects of ritual practice can and should be read as non-gendered. Specifically, she contends that ritual possession makes it possible for different bodies (race, gender, sex, ability, age, and class notwithstanding) to embody an orisha and thus be reconstituted as Sacred. While in the novel the spirits of ancestors and of the dead are not necessarily orishas, there are similar logics at play. The shadows are able to take multiple shapes, forms, and movements from shadowshapers of all different bodies. Thus, Méndez argues, "to only foreground the Orishas as dimorphically sexed or racially gendered is to obscure the extent to which Orishas are themselves fluid and can be understood to manifest in and flow between multiple forms and materialities."[62]

While Grandpa Lázaro's stubbornness weakens the shadowshapers, the novel's antagonist is Dr. Jonathan Wick, a Columbia University professor who encounters the shadowshapers in his research on "urban spirituality systems" (40–41). He attempts to extract and consume all the Sacred knowledge he can co-opt, even that to which he is not entitled. Wick tries to manipulate the spirits rather than be a vessel through which they act and move in the world of the living (275). By colluding with a trio of dark spirits called The Sorrows and through the use of "binding magic," Wick tracks down and kills shadowshapers as he attempts to find and steal power from the mightiest shadowshaper, Lucera (129). Wick is representative of those who inherit a legacy only to control and destroy it. His desire to "wipe out the 'shapers and keep the power to himself" ignores the fact that "without Lucera there's no shadowshaping, but without shadowshaping there is no Lucera" (220). As "entwined" forces, Lucera "drew power from the spirits and the spirits workers" and "returned it to them tenfold" (220). Thus, Wick's radical individualism is antithetical to the spiritual kinship and community linkages that are the crux of shadowshaping.

Sierra grows to know more about herself as she learns how shadowshaping links her to her ancestors, and specifically to her grandmother Mama Carmen, whose position as the centrifugal force of shadowshapers had been felled by her husband's machismo. Her husband turned the shadowshapers into a "boys' club," thereby facilitating Dr. Wick's patriarchal and colonizing research. As Sierra inherits Lucera's matrilineal powers through Mama Carmen, she feels that "light, invincible, unstoppable, infinite light flooded through her veins, filled each of her organs, poured out of her mouth, covered her skin" (224). Of these spirits Sierra says, "they were so full of life it was easy to forget they were dead. They pulsated with the love of all things alive, a powerful yearning that Sierra could taste" (148–49). The novel also serves as a critique of academics who attempt to co-opt spiritual practices, knowledge, and power. Older thereby indicts the forms and functions by which white supremacy enables unethical researchers to act as definitive, all-knowing vessels.

Luminous/Dystopias

If Ibeyi and Older beckon us to their worlds/otherwise and challenge us to see beyond our immediate realms to the spirit world around us, then the works of Junot Díaz and Juan Tomás Ávila Laurel problematize the role of Blackness in our past and futures. The second half of this chapter engages Díaz's short story "Monstro" (2012) and Ávila Laurel's novel *Panga Rilene* (2016). I examine the role that Afro-Atlantic subjects play in reckoning with Blackening diseases at the end of the world(s). In a stark contrast to the ruptures and luminous possibilities across Ibeyi's sonic/visual work and Older's young adult novel, both "Monstro" and *Panga Rilene* point to ruptures that beget dystopias in an unknown near-future. In these dystopian worlds, forty-foot-tall cannibal monsters and square-faced women isolated atop beam-like structures live apocalyptic realities produced by technologies of oppression and violence.

Díaz tells us that the word "apocalypse comes to us from the Greek *apocalypsis*, meaning to uncover and unveil."[63] Here, apocalypso takes on another form, a form in which the schema of Man, who has overrepresented himself as the human, brings on its own catastrophic demise. Hailing Cliff's provocation, "When the Other appears to be the One. Apocalypso," I contend that the apocalypso of colonialism for the Other becomes the Apocalypso for the One.[64] These texts bring Aimé Césaire's "boomerang effect" into the imaginary by conjuring decolonial futurities wherein the colonial world of Man is destroyed by its own in/action.[65] These worlds/otherwise emerge from within nations and peoples wracked by legacies of colonial, neocolonial, and capitalist logics and exist in a time of extensive environmental destruction, geopolitical instability, and racial, economic, and social inequality.

Race, gender, and sex become central to the narratives; racialized Blackness becomes a deadly and incurable epidemic that changes the course of history.

In "Monstro" and *Panga Rilene*, Black girls and femmes are the key to the future. While in Ibeyi's sonic/visual work and Older's *Shadowshaper* Black women and girls are vital conduits to spiritual worlds, Black girls and femmes are central to world-saving, or at least truth-seeking, in "Monstro" and *Panga Rilene*. Thus, the futurities emerging out of these peripheralized Latinx and Hispanic Afro-Atlantic worlds are fiercely femme, feminist, and Black. In *Panga Rilene*, sexual and reproductive labor is transformed through a man-made ecological catastrophe, while in "Monstro" sex and desire propel the protagonist towards an apocalyptic epidemic. As Díaz notes in an interview with Paula Moya, "The whole reason I started writing this book is because of this image I have of this fourteen-year-old girl, a poor, black, Dominican girl, half-Haitian—one of the Island's *damnés*—saving the world." For Díaz, the narrative is also about a Black girl finding love in an anti-Black world: "It's a book about this girl's search for—yes—love in a world that has made it its solemn duty to guarantee that poor raced 'conventionally unattractive' girls like her are never loved."[66] In *Panga Rilene*, the young femme protagonist, Panga, is in search of both her mother's history and the history of how their dystopian reality came to be. In her quest for knowledge about the world around her, she begins to piece together the histories of environmental and human exploitation. Her community's past takes place, arguably, in our contemporary reality, and Panga is not only mapping the lives of the women in her community, but also offering readers a glimpse into potentially apocalyptic futures.

Apex

Junot Díaz's short story "Monstro" (2012) imagines the end of worlds brought on by a rapidly spreading and mysterious Blackening disease.[67] The reader encounters a nameless narrator contending with an apocalyptic epidemic: an unknown virus which has taken root in the Caribbean. The island of Hispaniola, specifically Haiti, is ground zero for this virulent disaster. Thus Hispaniola, the touchstone for New World modernity, the space through which modern colonialism, empire, dispossession, and slavery spread, is now the place where a disease to end humanity will incubate. Díaz offers a narrative of a cataclysmic disaster as a decimating terror that will cause a pandemic attacking a civilization which is incapable and uncommitted to solving the catastrophes it has called into being. Here, Césaire's indictment is prescient: "A civilization that proves incapable of solving the problems it creates is a decadent civilization. A civilization that chooses to close its eyes to its most crucial problems is a stricken civilization. A civilization that uses its principles for trickery and deceit is a dying civilization."[68] Following the destructive and deadly path of colonialism, the disease in "Monstro" is a global threat. Césaire's articulation of the boomerang effect is prophetic for the uncontrollable Blackening disease that spreads as virulently as imperialism and colonialism.

"Monstro" takes place during an exacerbated environmental and humanitarian crisis: an overheated planet, a dying ocean, and egregious inequalities of race, wealth, and health that allow the affluent to live safeguarded from the dying Earth through technologies ("bafflers") that literally shield them from the elements. This near future also features radical geopolitical shifts, including the revelation of Chinese and Indian currency as the global standard (renminbi/lakhs) and a change in geopolitical roles between nations and superpowers (highlighting Crimea's attack on the Russian hinterlands). The story is narrated by an unnamed protagonist, but one who reads as similar in character to Yunior in *The Brief Wondrous Life of Oscar Wao*, a working-class diasporic Dominican who is attempting to tarry with the island's elite during a summer vacation. Like Yunior, the protagonist is a "time witness" who recounts the epidemic that transpired during his summer visit to the Dominican Republic (2).

Under the guise of accompanying his ill mother to the island to oversee her treatment and recovery, the "shallow" nineteen-year-old narrator quickly finds himself in a matrix of misadventures alongside his wealthy college schoolmate and his elite circles (3). Díaz deftly loads us with race, class, and gender dynamics as the protagonist outlines a scene in which his sick mother is tended by tía Livia, a nurse and "the muchacha who cooked and cleaned," and whom we can infer is a criada conscripted to labor in the family home. In doing so, Díaz underscores how late "hyper-capitalism" and collapsing ecosystems demand racialized femme and underclass child labor (3, 4).[69] By chronicling and critiquing structural and everyday forms of anti-Blackness and anti-Haitianismo, Díaz makes palpable the racial politics undergirding "Monstro." These forms of racialization include intense economic and social stratification, which in turn are aggravated by the rapidly spreading disease called "la Negrura," or "the Blackening" (2).

As the protagonist moves between his lower-middle-class familial and elite Dominican circles, we bear witness to what Lorgia Garcia-Peña calls the "prevalence of anti-Haitianismo in the Archive of Dominicanidad."[70] The looming shadow of the U.S. Empire is also present as the protagonist struggles with his desire to belong to the privileged circles of his university classmate, a playboy and aspiring photographer named Alex. The protagonist understands Alex's privileges as part of a set of resources and opportunities that have been foreclosed to him as a working-class Afro-Dominican diasporic subject.[71] While his mother and family were "stuck in Darkness, with mosquitoes fifty to a finger and the heat like the inside of a tailpipe," he was with Alex and his wealthy friends, "privando en rico inside the Dome, where the bafflers held the scorch to a breezy 82 degrees F. and one mosquito a night was considered an invasion" (4). Yet while the narrator accompanies those living in luxurious homes overlooking the "Drowned Sectors" of Zona Colonial, his phenotype and "Dark Accent" mark him as Other, an outsider to their world (4). He thus inhabits multiple levels of what Josefina Báez calls "el Níe," the phenomenon of being neither from here, nor there (ni de aquí ni de allá).[72] In her analysis of Báez, Garcia Peña underscores el Níe's queerness, pointing out that the word is a Dominican colloquialism for the "taint," or perineum.[73] Thus, the dimensions of race, class, and sexual desire reflected in the secondary arc of the story—the narrator's erotic desire for the beautiful Mysty and her suggestive relationship with Alex (who is bisexual)—demarcate the protagonist's own sexual desires and limits. Similar to Yunior's foils in *Oscar Wao* and in Díaz's short-story collection *This Is How You Lose Her*, the protagonist of "Monstro" declares that "culo," or ass, was the "end" of him; or rather, "when the world came to an end, [he] was chasing a girl" (1).[74]

The virus begins with a small boy in a relocation camp during one of the harshest heat waves on record: "Shit a hundred straight days over 105 degrees F. in our region alone, the planet cooking like a chimi and down to its last five trees" (2). At first the outbreak doesn't cause alarm because there are "all sorts of bizarre outbreaks already in play: diseases no one had names for, zoonotics by the pound," and those who seem to succumb to the disease are the most vulnerable members of the island's population (2). This disease, la Negrura, starts with the skin, the epidermis, and then "work[s] its way up and in." The infected rarely die but rather become comatose and zombie-like. The symptoms, described as a "black mold-fungus-blast that come on like a splotch and then gradually started taking over you, tunneling right through you," are likewise metaphors for the growth of empire (1). "Coral reefs might have been adios on the ocean floor," the narrator notes, "but they were alive and well on the arms and back and heads of the infected. Black rotting rugose masses fruiting out of bodies," therein linking the flesh-infecting disease to the effects of global climate change (2).

La Negrura is quickly misidentified as a local Haitian disease and thus loses the attention of international medical teams. As the disease progresses, those afflicted begin to fuse together. The narrator describes a "glypt" (a form of visual technology) of the first victims: "a pair of naked trembling Haitian brothers sharing a single stained cot, knotted together by horrible mold, their heads slurred into one" (2). The disease became comic fodder: "Negroes thought it funny. A disease that could make a Haitian blacker?" (1). This story, like much of Díaz's work, reveals the racism, misogyny, and anti-Haitianismo in everyday conversations. While the protagonist's mother and aunt feel empathy for their neighbors, one of his tíos dismissively opines, "Someone needs to drop a bomb on those people" (2, 4).[75] The general resignation in the face of a catastrophic ecological and health epidemic uncovers a deep-rooted refusal to bear witness to the humanity of the infected Haitians. The prospect of blowing up Haiti during a crisis is something that even the protagonist considers a mercy, illuminating a pitiful anti-Haitianismo spreading like la Negrura within himself (4).

As la Negrura develops and spreads without a known pattern, relocation camps are established for the infected. There, the latter began to congregate and demonstrate strange behavior, demanding to be in close quarters with other infected, or "ingathering" (3). Seemingly healthy people also suddenly began to migrate involuntarily to the quarantine zones (3). Soon, the "viktims" stop speaking, with the exception of collective bloodcurdling shrieks called "the Chorus" (4). The fear of these victims being zombie-like undead creatures emerges when one of the only remaining researchers, a Haitian epidemiologist named Noni DeGraff, learns that thermal images of the infected and those exposed to the camp "radiated blue" like the dead, rather than the red of a living person (9). The disease peaks when the "Possessed" begin a chaotic massacre described as "an outbreak of homicidal violence" and a "berserk murderous blood rage." Afterwards, the borders between the Dominican Republic and Haiti are sealed, even as hundreds of thousands of non-infected Haitians flee the zone for safety (10).

When a bomb is dropped on Haiti shortly thereafter, its effects permeate the Caribbean, causing "8.3 tremors felt as far away as Havana, San Juan, and Key West" (12). These cities represent some of the earliest Spanish territories in the Americas, mirroring the spread of colonization throughout the Caribbean and the Americas, and the *longue durée* of its effects. "The Detonation Event" deadens every electronic apparatus "within a six-hundred-mile radius," destroying the bomber that dropped the bomb, causing thirty-two commercial planes to "plummet" from the sky, drowning hundreds of ships and seacraft, causing fires, crumbling sea walls and the heat-protective domes (12). In other words, it causes apocalyptic ramifications, with a telecommunication dead zone that impedes all communication across the Caribbean. Hence, those on the island of Hispaniola are the only witnesses to the "forty-foot-tall cannibal motherfuckers running loose on the island" (12). Documentation in the form of "soon-to-be-iconic Polaroids" (photos) confirm the existence of a giant zombie-like cannibal, "what later came to be called a Class 2, in the process of putting a slender broken girl in its mouth" (12). These Polaroids include captions with biblical verses: "Numbers 11:18. *Who shall give us flesh to eat?*" (12).[76] Since, according to Alex, "a photograph can change todo," the story ends with Alex, Mysty, and the protagonist setting out to document the fall of humanity with a Polaroid camera. The reader can deduce that this is the very same camera that captures the infamous Polaroid photo of the "slender broken girl" in the mouth of the cannibal (12).

Díaz's dystopian scenario imagines the end of the modern colonial world through a precise and humiliating formula. The spatial and temporal locus of colonial horror, the place where millions of humans are subjected to "thingification," is likewise the place where cannibals who eat the Man who has subjugated them are bred.[77] La Negrura, as the precursor to the colossal cannibals in the Caribbean, requires contending with meditations on the figure of Caliban in *The Tempest*. The colonial, linguistic, and racial subjugation in the play, alongside Caliban's constant resistance, have made *The Tempest* and the character critical tropes for writers across the postcolonial Caribbean and its diasporas.[78] "Monstro" forces us to engage with the *longue durée* of the cannibal trope: the "cannibal" of 1492, the Shakespearean anagram of cannibal and Caliban as signifier in 1611, and the diseased-transformed cannibals that Díaz conjures at the end of the world in the Caribbean.

In his famous treatise on Caliban, the Cuban critic Roberto Fernández Retamar cites Columbus's *Diario de navegación* in order to locate the earliest accounts of said encountered cannibals. Fernández Retamar cites this entry, dated November 23, 1492: "[The island of Haiti], which they said was very large and that on it lived people who had only one eye and others called cannibals, of whom they seemed very afraid" (6).[79] In this colonial record, Haiti is the initial locus of modernity's cannibals. For Díaz, Haiti is the place from which modernity may find its end at the hands of cannibals created by the disaster of ecological corruption caused by modernity.

Díaz's "Monstro" is thus a form of future work that foretells of another boomerang effect. Bearing this mark of an inhuman Other, the Carib, Fernández Retamar continues, "will become a *cannibal*—an anthropophagus, a bestial man situated on the margins of civilization."[80] Following Armando García's reading of racialized and sexed Caliban figures in Migdalia Cruz's play *Fur*, I argue that Díaz's dystopian worlds/otherwise imagines the end of the modern colonial world through a precise and humiliating formula.[81] García juxtaposes *The Tempest* with Aimé Césaire's *A Tempest*, and posits a conceivable sociality against colonialism that can, in effect, emancipate a dehumanized subject. Cruz's play—about a Latina named Citrona who is enslaved by Michael, an older white man, and his servant, Nena, who is also his psychological captive—ends with Citrona killing and cannibalizing both Michael and Nena. "Citrona," García argues, "turns to cannibalism as the only expression of freedom available to her."[82] While both Shakespeare and Césaire's plays end with Caliban still enslaved, García argues that when Cruz's cannibal "eats her oppressors, she challenges the idea that freedom from colonial terror is dependent primarily on the oppressed being able to speak."[83] The protagonist truly frees herself through the act of eating those who have enslaved her, and in the act of killing and "cannibalizing her master," Citrona "desires to end the time of the colony and also move toward a different world" (351). Likewise, "Monstro" complicates Cliff's assertion, for in this story the Other appears to *eat* the One. Apocalypso. Díaz, then, offers us a complex Afro-Latinx futurist narrative that centers class, race, sex, and gender relations at the apex of worlds/otherwise.

TODO

Juan Tomás Ávila Laurel's novel *Panga Rilene* (2016) is also set in an apocalyptic future where ecological destruction remaps the lives of the protagonist and her nation, which is known only by the coordinates 08°28'00"E-26°29'00"N (often shortened to "NE"). This novel marks a turn to a new genre for this seasoned author, who has primarily written about the colonial and contemporary dictatorial period in Equatorial Guinea, and it is in fact the first Equatoguinean novel to extend into the genre of science fiction and Afrofuturism.[84] Ávila Laurel's work has long borne witness to lived experiences that often remain unseen and unheard, particularly for Africans living on Atlantic islands under dictatorial regimes. In *Panga Rilene*, he moves into some unknown time in the future in which the nation has emerged following an occurrence that changed "TODO" (15; "EVERYTHING"). The novel is a retrospective account wherein the protagonist, Panga Rilene, learns about her mysterious mother, for whom she is named, and by extension, about the histories that created life in NE. Early in the narrative Panga inherits an apparatus, a "bumping machine," and later a small tablet, which allow her to search and document her experiences. These technologies, which function only by bodily touch or blood sample, are essential for Panga to come to consciousness about the dystopian existence of her nation (73, 97).

Panga begins by offering geographical overviews and temporal references for NE (15). The novel takes place in an unknown future beyond A.D., where "kriptón" is the epoch reference (34). In this era after "TODO" has happened, Panga's nation is reclusive and comprised only of women—all with square faces, "tan rectas como las paredes de una caja" ("as straight as the walls of a box")—children of all ages, and a singular elderly man named Netig (27). The nation of 08°28'00"E-26°29'00"N consists of communities of square homes suspended in the air on a single beam covered with a material akin to coconut fiber. From each beam hang four to seven square houses, creating the effect of leaves on a tree. A common terrace atop each of these beams acts as the only communal space available to the women and children. Each beam features an unused staircase and an aerial pulley system, which allows the watchman, Netig, to access any of the homes. The women reach their houses by climbing up and down the fiber-covered beams, often with children clinging to their backs (29).

It is revealed that the women, so isolated, are called to engage in a ritual procreation practice in which they sit on penetrating apparatuses and recite loyalties to the state: "Ninguna de nosotras se atrevería a lanzar su desafío al estado de cosas tal como se presenta ahora" (174–76; "None of us would dare to launch a challenge to the state of affairs as it is presently"). While the female children stay in the community, all the male children mysteriously vanish after a few years, thus sustaining a women-only society: "Todos los niños que abrían los ojos en nuestro sitio llevaban en una parte desconocida de su pequeño ser la llamada de otro sitio que no conocíamos, una llamada tan fuerte que propiciaba su abandono de nuestro país tan pronto como ganaban aptitudes con los dos pies" (70; "All of the boys who opened their eyes on our site carried in an unknown part of their little being the call from another place that we did not know, a call so strong that it propitiated their abandonment of our country as soon as they gained skills with both feet").

This reclusive existence is further impacted by environmental disasters. Panga details the barren valleys that surround 08°28'00"E-26°29'00"N, and notes how even the rains "transportaban un número tan elevado de sustancias químicas que los que tuvieran algún tipo de patología, o aquejados de alguna debilidad especial, podían morir ante la mera exposición a los mismos" (38; "transported such a high level of chemical substances that those who had any illness or were somehow in a weakened state could die from the mere exposure to it"). This chemical-laced rain akin to toxic gravel is far from the only danger the women face, since they are randomly accosted and searched by soldiers: "No tardaban en aparecer los soldados del fierro, ataviados con llamativas botas y acompañados de perros furiosos" (41; "The soldiers of the iron, dressed in flashy boots and accompanied by furious dogs, soon appeared"). The community subsists on a single food source, *smigg*, "un combinado de granos y crustáceos que decían que era un alimento equilibrado" ("a combination of grains and crustaceans that was said to be a balanced food") around which they develop a digestion ritual called "la danza del puf" ("the puff dance"), which consists of dancing and passing gas on the communal terrace (44, 67). Panga's narrative seeks to understand the precarious nature of their lives, a "supervivencia" that "pendía de un hilo" (42; "survival that hung by a thread").

In Ávila Laurel's narrative, the future is also predicated on exploitative practices and maintaining silence around oppression. In fact, dictatorship is remembered as instrumental in the creation of 08°28'00"E-26°29'00"N. The narrative follows the series of events that led to Panga's catastrophic reality, which indicts contemporary forms of power and domination, and likewise engages in a foreboding meditation on the human impact on the environment and nonhuman animals.[85] Panga's ancestors are said to be people "gently rocked by the sea," or people living on islands. The processes leading up to "TODO" left those living on islands and in littoral spaces in destierro, torn from their lands. She learns that in the hyper-capitalist world that preceded "TODO," the sea was privatized and emptied of all life. The privatization of the sea was later accompanied by control over access to the sea; wealthy world leaders, dictators, and other powerful men would prohibit access in order to prevent witnesses to the ecological catastrophe. The ensuing exploitative and toxic agricultural practices turned lands barren and produced mass starvation in NE (144–46).

Here, Junot Díaz's meditation on the forces that wield natural disasters into postcolonial apocalypses becomes a prophetic lens through which to read Ávila Laurel's narrative. "The very forces that place us in harm's way," Díaz argues, "often take advantage of the confusion brought by apocalyptic events to extend their power and in the process increase [our] vulnerability."[86] In Panga's epoch, the sea itself is utilized as a site of terror and control. In one telling scene, Panga recognizes that a ritual pilgrimage to look upon the sea is in fact part of a set of scare tactics that agents use to ensure that women cooperate with the reproductive politics of their nation. The ritual pilgrimage culminates when the women are brought to the sea. But rather than an expansive ocean, the group gazes upon the corpse of woman with an unexpelled umbilical cord, floating in a clear bucket of water (88). There, Panga comes to understand that this pilgrimage is an implicit threat, a warning to not impede their male children from leaving, to not obstruct the new order of things, for fear of becoming like the corpse of the woman floating in the "sea."

As the novel examines the sociopolitical and economic processes that generated "TODO," the reader becomes aware that Ávila Laurel's pre-apocalyptic time is eerily similar to contemporary geopolitical occurrences. This is acutely revelatory if we are to conceive of apocalypse across different worldviews. For example, the Potawatomi philosopher Kyle Whyte argues that for many Indigenous communities, the catastrophe of current and impending climate change is not a coming apocalypse but rather *the* apocalypse, here and now. [87] Whyte argues that this is because Indigenous ancestors would not recognize the kinds of capital-driven, ecologically splintered practices that we understand to be commonplace within contemporary Western epistemes. Thus, if apocalypses arrive to "uncover and unveil," we can understand *Panga Rilene* as future work that exposes our current apocalypse and its heinous, desolate, and exploitative aftermath.

Panga Rilene is not only a foreboding notice against the death sentence of late capitalism, mass consumption, and environmental destruction; it is also a warning that centers colonialism, racialized Blackness, and the practices of faceless corporations, greed-driven dictators, and First World consumers that upend the lives of poor and dispossessed classes. At the crux of the narrative is Ávila Laurel's critique of how wealthy and powerful people dispossess the poor of their lives: "En aquellos tiempos en que los poderosos podían disponer de las vidas ajenas y comerciar con ellas como si se tratara de cualquier mercancía" (106; "In those times in which the powerful could dispose of the lives of others and trade them as if they were any merchandise"). We learn that the mining of a powerful mineral by the company SA Manto or Manto SA (which we can read as an anagram for the agricultural corporation Monsanto) has accelerated "TODO." This company "se dedicaba a la extraccíon de un mineral que en la lengua local recibía el nombre de malañang, que era una sustancia no solamente llamativa por su exótico nombre, que lo era en aquellos tiempos, sino por el asepecto desagradable del mismo, asimilable a los despojos desechables de algunos animales" (106–7; "[it] was dedicated to the extraction of a mineral that in the local language was called malañang, which was not only a noteworthy substance because of its exotic name, which it was in those times, but because of the unpleasant aspect of it, similar to the feces of some animals"). The repulsive and fetid mineral "tenía muchas aplicaciones en la industria, pues tanto podía usarse como combustible, y como aislante de primer nivel" ("had many applications in industry, since it could be used as fuel, and as a first-class insulation"), but its power likewise led the miners to a "desplome espiritual" (107; "spiritual crash").

Similar to Díaz's inexplicable "Negrura," Panga learns that the malañang mining advanced into a Blackening disease, or "Negruzco," which blackened and rotted the miners' skin and also caused spiritual devastation for those in contact with it (107–9). The Negruzco and the "desplome," or ontological desolation, spread widely due to the overseer's cruel treatment of the miners, as he toyed with their lives and safety by limiting their access to gloves and other basic protective equipment (107). The trial that attempted to confront these atrocities ended with the miners being disappeared, all except for one. Netig, a senior engineer, was ordered to establish NE's community of women, potentially the widows of the miners. Thus, rather than an all-powerful watchman, Netig is actually a man in service to others, and his rotting-flesh condition—which Ávila Laurel alludes to in scenes where he painfully urinates pus—correlates to his history as a miner.

Netig's powerlessness within the matrix of the apocalyptic system is perhaps what leads him to offer Panga the forbidden objects: the bumping machine and the tablet. It is Panga, however, who learns how to use these machines with her body and blood, and in so doing asks the questions that lead her to imperfectly trace the histories that have created the conditions for her very existence. Her quest to learn about her mother and about the types of kinship formed in her community means that she is one of the very few people in NE to understand their histories before and after "TODO." Thus, she develops a sense of duty to the liberation of her kin and community.[88] Furthermore, Panga's blood and flesh are needed for the technology to function, creating a corporeal connection to the machines that troubles facile notions that divide human and analog, and digital and cyborg. In fact, Panga's questioning, her epistemic concerns, and her ontological experiences during the catastrophic kryptón era suggest a fundamental shift in the world that she inhabits. And while Panga can and should be read as a femme hero, Panga herself resists gender dimorphism, questioning if she is in an anatomically female or male body. This becomes a critical challenge to the terror-driven reproductive world she inhabits. Her intimate, personal, and public resistance underscores many forms of coming-to-consciousness within community.[89]

Panga Rilene showcases a future that mirrors both Junot Díaz's "Monstro" and his essays on the disastrous effects of the 2010 earthquake on Haiti. Díaz forecasts a collective global future of "stricken, forlorn desolation, a future out of a sci-fi fever dream where the super-rich [will] live in walled-up plantations of impossible privilege and the rest of us [will] wallow in unimaginable extremity." Those who remain on the underside of such a system are left "staggering around the waste and being picked off by the hundreds of thousands by 'natural disasters'—by 'acts of god.' "[90] However, I argue that Ávila Laurel's narrative is not solely reducible to a dystopia orchestrated by greed, racism, and disregard for human and nonhuman life. Instead, a glimpse of worlds/otherwise emerges at the moment of Panga's coming-to-consciousness, thus mirroring Fanon's turn in *Black Skin, White Mask* where he asks his readers to feel "the open dimension of every consciousness."[91] In Panga, we have a character who embodies and complicates the last line of Fanon's text: "O my body, always make me a [femme] who questions!"[92] *Panga Rilene* takes place in a community of Black femmes and indicts structures—eerily comparable to our present-day structures and practices—that require Black and Indigenous death. The novel offers us a glimpse into an apocalyptic worlds/otherwise similar to Diaz's "Monstro," where a Blackening disease represents the inception of the end of the world. Both narratives have apocalypse at their center, albeit in different ways. But unlike Diaz's narrative in which the afflicted Haitians become zombie-like cannibals who threaten to consume the One, *Panga Rilene* has no triumphant rise. Instead, it reveals a slow coming-to-consciousness, resolute but without a known resolution.

Reveal

In examining four distinct works and genres (sonic/visual, young adult literature, short story, and novel), this chapter engages distinct yet related aspects of future work. I first examined how Afro-syncretic cosmologies, or the Sacred, are conjured to produce apocalypsos. They thus fracture colonial, temporal, and spatial boundaries, and usher in worlds/otherwise. The music and videos of Ibeyi and Daniel José Older's young adult novel *Shadowshaper* center practices of Santería and trouble notions of fixed temporalities and futurities. In doing so, they invoke worlds/otherwise or present futures in which ancestors live alongside and guide modes and practices of being in the world. In the second half of the chapter, I analyzed how dystopian worlds and contagious viruses become part of Afro-Atlantic apocalypsos wherein only Black women and femmes can bring hope to these worlds/otherwise. Junot Díaz's short story "Monstro" and Juan Tomás Ávila Laurel's novel *Panga Rilene* each center a disease of Blackness—Negrura and Negruzco, respectively—at the end, or arguably the beginning, of worlds. In these two texts, a mysteriously incurable disease and the mining of a black mineral act as the backdrop to social/political struggles and challenges to the oppressive order of knowledge and being. Blackness is thus deployed as both a curse and a salve in these worlds/otherwise. However, in each of these four works, Black women, girls, and femmes are the epicenter of possible futures: they are the ones who have the power to conjure ancestors into the present/future, and they are the ones who can either detonate the end of worlds, or save them.

These narratives, emerging from a distinct yet related set of histories, languages, and realities thrust through the ruptures of coloniality, represent an/other appendage of Afro-Atlantic futurisms. Thus, it is in those ruptures that Ibeyi (*Ibeyi*), Older (*Shadowshaper*), Díaz ("Monstro"), and Ávila Laurel (*Panga Rilene*) break apart fixed spatial and temporal planes by troubling Blackness and racialization, and insisting that Afro-syncretic practices, including Lucumí and Santería, are key lenses through which to imagine other ways of being human, and being human as practice within a *longue durée* of ancestral memory. The futurities depicted across these texts are made possible by engaging practices that lead readers and the protagonists in a seemingly backward motion. They take us past the "future" and into a realm where, if we are to see liberation, we must take our ancestors and our histories along with us. This, then, is representative of a practice of decolonial love, a recuperative project that is both futuristic and liberatory.[93]

Decolonial love as future work envisaged through our pasts is necessarily a technology for social transformation, and is a method through which we can reimagine human ontogeny and sociogeny.[94] Decolonial love in worlds/otherwise manifests as attention to 1492: the past before it, the past since, the subterranean roots created by it, and the dead beneath the sea.[95] It can be imagined as looking into the "vast and inconsolable" sea to make visible what was disappeared, and make futurities beyond coloniality perceptible.[96] Worlds/otherwise is invoked and revealed through ritual practice and human and ancestral communion, even as widespread diseases, desolate quarantine camps, and the clash of spirit worlds threaten to collapse the earth.

Coda

✦

Sea

> And the literary texts turn to ocean waters themselves as an archive, an ever-present, ever-reformulating record of the unimaginable.
>
> —Omise'eke Natasha Tinsley, "Black Atlantic, Queer Atlantic: Queer Imaginings of the Middle Passage"

Decolonizing Diasporas has attended to some of the longer as well as more recent histories of Latinx Caribbean and Equatoguinean diasporas, examining literary, cultural, and thematic preoccupations that emerge in the work of African and Afro-descended writers, artists, and thinkers. The concepts in each chapter build to the next and open discursive spaces through which to imagine and reimagine possibilities beyond dispossession, coloniality, and domination. In doing so, *Decolonizing Diasporas* maps archives of indictment and insurgency in some of the most peripheralized Afro-Atlantic diasporas. Following Angelique V. Nixon's statement that "to love blackness is then to resist and struggle against systems of oppression designed to make us hate ourselves," I argue that the writers and artists examined throughout this book make loving gestures toward Blackness and relationality that are anchored in praxes of humanity (362).[1]

In engaging relationality as a site of possibility that refuses reducibility, I necessarily engage women of color feminist, decolonial, and Caribbean thought. My aim has been to trace relations that are often understudied or peripheralized across the Afro-Atlantic. In doing so, my intent has been to demonstrate that the relations between Afro-Latinx Caribbean and Equatoguinean diasporas are not exceptions, to paraphrase Glissant, but rather are matters of Blackness, matters of histories, and matters of futurities. These meditations are made possible only through the works and thought of women of color feminists and decolonial feminist activists, scholars, and artists, for through their struggles, they have defined and shaped a method that allows us to read generously and deeply. In illuminating what these works reveal, we take up part of the labor of decolonization and liberation.

The book opened with an overview of some of the historical, material, and affective relations between Equatorial Guinea, Cuba, Puerto Rico, the

Dominican Republic, and their diasporas in the United States and Spain. I showed the archipelagic connection between these nations and nation-states through a geographical and historical analysis of Atlantic world crossings and contemporary migrations that are propelled by similar processes of political repression, economic instability, and other voluntary and involuntary phenomena. Thinking from the space of islands and their respective diasporas offers the possibility of tracking points on the matrix of the Afro-Atlantic. While none of these movements are new (movements seldom are), I was inspired by Aurora Levins Morales's understanding of doing the work of curandera medicinal historical practices. In *Medicine Stories*, she argues that "centering women changes the landscape," and she contends that "making truly medicinal history requires that we do more than just add women (or any other 'disappeared' group of people) to the existing framework." Morales urges us to consider how the questions change when we assume that women are the "most important people in the story." [2] In her article "Radical Love: Black Philosophy as Deliberate Acts of Inheritance" (2013), Kristie Dotson argues: "One of the roles of black philosophy is to demonstrate radical love for black people by performing acts of inheritance of theoretical production created and maintained by black peoples."[3] Dotson asserts that the labor of centering the lives and work of Black women "requires that one is committed to valuing the theoretical production of black people, in general, and black women, in particular."[4] This is an act of radical love because "it results in a steadfast commitment, unwavering trust, and, in some contexts, a daring that defies current dominant reason."[5] Likewise, decolonial love requires a commitment to creating philosophical, material, and theoretical works that stem from the lived experiences of Black, Indigenous, and women of color, culled from their literary and cultural productions.

Such a project offers scholars invested in decolonial love the tools through which to build an ethical analytic that undermines agendas of anti-Blackness. Taking this impetus and scholarly position seriously, *Decolonizing Diasporas* centers the critical and creative works of Black, Indigenous, and women of color feminist and decolonial thinkers, and creates theoretical frameworks and analytics of their labor. Their work is the organizing framework for my practice of reading literary works as decolonizing texts that bear witness to colonial oppressions and resistance. Rather than reading the literary and cultural productions of Afro-Atlantic Latinx and Equatoguinean writers through the lens of dominant or Eurocentric literary theory, *Decolonizing Diasporas* examines the works themselves to see how they radically remap diasporas and decolonial politics—in the past, in the present, and for the future. Each chapter traces a concept that has emerged from the works of Afro-Atlantic writers and artists, and underscores their contributions to decolonizing projects and politics.

Paying attention to the ways in which race, gender, and racialization are subjective experiences, I propose the concept of critical cartographies of racialization, which allows me to hold space for the ever-shifting attitudes and behaviors associated with racial projects in homelands, diasporic locales, and points in between. Aaron Pinnix argues that we must attend to "gaps in knowledge and interconnection" and "vagaries of fluid currents and the ways that such connections entail loss, as well as exchange."[6] Critical cartographies of racialization enable me to account for the ethnic solidarities and conflicts within contemporary Equatorial Guinea, while also showing how these heterogeneous groups are racialized as a monolith in diasporic locales in Spain. Similarly, the concept allows me to approach the complex racial and ethnonational identities and beliefs that challenge Latinx Caribbean and diasporic racial ideologies. As Antonio Benítez-Rojo says, "The peoples of the sea, or better, the People of the Sea proliferate incessantly while differentiating themselves from one another, trailing together toward the infinite."[7] Within this context, the shift between Latin American and Anglo-American conceptions of race explored in the works—mestizaje or mulataje and hypodescent—offers a discursive space through which to trouble and resist anti-Black and anti-Indigenous racial logics. While we understand race as socially and politically constructed, making space to trace how and where racialization occurs, and the impacts of racialization and heteropatriarchy, allows for fuller and more strategic forms of resistance.

Chapter 1 examined the intimacies of coloniality to reveal the phenomenological and ontological experiences that are so richly woven into the Afro-Atlantic Hispanophone literary corpus. Meditating on the intimacies of occupation, dictatorship, and coloniality offered the opportunity to track Black femme freedom practices and the emergence of corporeal consciousness, or what Chela Sandoval calls a differential consciousness that is anchored in the body. I traced how marronage, queer kinship, and corporeal freedom in the novels offer ways to bear witness to resistance practices in the face of political and structural impossibilities. I argued that Nelly Rosario's *Song of the Water Saints*, Juan Tomás Ávila Laurel's *By Night the Mountain Burns*, and Trifonia Melibea Obono's *La bastarda* demand faithful witnessing. This ethical and radical feminist practice was the topic of chapter 2. In that chapter, I engaged in close readings of Donato Ndongo's *Shadows of Your Black Memory* and Junot Díaz's *The Brief Wondrous Life of Oscar Wao*. I centered faithful witnessing as a decolonial feminist philosophical concept that builds on women of color methodologies, and urges insurgent and complex coalition-building and aligning oneself with those who are most imperiled by systems of domination and coloniality.

In chapter 3, I argued that faithful witnessing allows us to bear witness to resistance, while also complicating our relationship to land and dispossession. I examined Loida Maritza Pérez's *Geographies of Home* and Juan Tomás Ávila Laurel's *El dictador de Corisco*, and argued that overlapping histories of dispossession are fundamental to understanding contemporary conditions under coloniality and settler colonialism. I developed the decolonial feminist concept of destierro, the ongoing event and legacy of being torn away from land, and examined how it emerges in Afro-Dominican and Equatoguinean literatures. This meditation on dispossession led to chapter 4, which focused on reparations in the wake of centuries of theft, loss, and genocide. In that chapter, I considered Ernesto Quiñonez's *Bodega Dreams* and Joaquín Mbomío Bacheng's *Matinga, sangre en la selva* and briefly discussed Junot Díaz's *The Brief Wondrous Life of Oscar Wao* to track the potential for reparations as a transformation beyond positivist calculations and towards a practice of decolonial love. I demonstrated that conceptions of reparations and decolonial love, as both individual and community projects, have always existed in the literatures of the Afro-Atlantic diaspora. Through a discussion of Christina Olivares's "Letter," I argued that these writers propose and practice a reparation of the imagination, wherein they must engage the ethical imagination to conjure what a more just, liberatory, and transformative future could look like. A keen eye towards relationality and the practice of faithful witnessing allows us to see the decolonial possibilities of reparations as "a process of undoing coloniality and its multiple hierarchies of power as a whole."[8] This, in turn, is part of an intimate and communal practice of decolonial love, and a reparation of the imagination.

This consideration of futurities and decolonial love led to chapter 5, where my close reading of four works in various genres—the musical artists Ibeyi's sonic/visual works, Daniel José Older's young adult novel *Shadowshaper*, Junot Díaz's short story "Monstro," and Juan Tomás Ávila Laurel's novel *Panga Rilene*—examined how Afro-Atlantic authors and artists imagine futurities or worlds/otherwise. These distinct works call forth Afro-syncretic practices and conjure apocalyptic futures. I argued that the Afro-Atlantic imagination challenges practices of decolonization, and offers the potential to invoke futurities that emphasize relations with ancestors, spiritual practices that trouble colonial temporal and spatial orders, and indict the structural domination and forms of coloniality that threaten to destroy ecology, economies, and possibilities for human life. In doing so, these works labor to humanize generations present, past, and those to come while also calling forth an apocalypso for the colonial order.

Relating the work and imaginations of Ibeyi, Older, Díaz, and Ávila Laurel surfaced a common theme: the sea. In each of these works, the image of the water recurs as a site of possibility, a reminder of the past, and the linchpin to the future. In fact, the sea or water, as material and as metaphor, emerges in almost every text I have examined in this book, underscoring its salience and the present past of what separates and connects the Afro-Atlantic. In her examination of diasporic Dominican women writers, Rebeca Hey-Colón argues that the use of the sea in their works "serves not only to expand the burgeoning conversation surrounding the role of the sea in the Caribbean, but also [provides] evidence that, even when removed from the Caribbean island scenario, the sea overflows into the pages of its writers. Furthermore, the sea's persistence challenges and enriches the overwhelmingly urban picture that comes to mind when visualizing Latino/a literature."[9] Likewise, the poetry of the Equatoguinean poet Raquel Ilombe del Pozo Epita (1931–1992) is replete with elegies to the sea as well as to the land. In the most complete collection of her work, *Ceiba II* (2014), we are able to see all at once how important the islands and seas of Equatorial Guinea are to her imaginary as a situated, diasporic, and migrant subject.[10]

Born on the island of Corisco, Ilombe was the daughter of a Spanish father and a Ndowe mother and lived in both Madrid and Bata, Equatorial Guinea, at different times throughout her life.[11] Reading Ilombe's poetry offers readers an opportunity to understand the experiences of destierro, belonging, and love, as well as reflections on nature that are not often seen through the perspective of Equatoguinean women writers. In the preamble to the edited collection, Benita Sampedro Vizcaya argues that

> leer la poesía de Raquel Ilombe a travês de la dimensiones espistemológicas del afecto y las emociones, de los sistemas de conocimiento de la intimidad, de la economía emocional de la pertenencia, de la exposición del afecto, y de la relación con el entorno natural (de la ceiba, el mar, la playa, la isla, . . .) o con la familia, así como las implicaciones físicas y políticas de esta manifestaciones, es en sí mismo un modo de descolonización critica y espistémica.[12]

> reading the poetry of Raquel Ilombe through epistemological dimensions of affect and emotions, the knowledge systems of intimacy, the emotional economy of belonging, the exposure of affection, and the relationship with the natural environment (of the ceiba, the sea, the beach, the island, . . .) or with the family, as well as the physical and political implications of these manifestations, is in itself a way of critical and systemic decolonization.

The longing for Corisco and the sea, the land, trees, and for belonging to these places and spaces is central to some of the most powerful and moving poems in Ilombe's oeuvre. For example, in the poem "Mar y olas" Ilombe states: "Otra vez mar, / otra vez olas, / sonido que no puedo olvidar" ("Again sea, / again waves, / sounds I cannot forget"), while in the poem "Tierra y agua" she writes, "Tierra y agua nunca olvidan, / por ser / dos elementos que no mueren" ("Earth and water never forget, / for being / two elements that do not die").[13] In these two poems Ilombe conjures the sea as a welcome haunting, an unforgettable phenomenon, and she depicts the land and the sea as elements that have eternal memory because they are bodies that never die. Several poems are dedicated to the island of Corisco and its primary place in her body, soul, and memory. The poem "Mi isla" ("My Island") opens with the lines "Se rasgó mi alma / al sentirme cerca" ("My soul was torn / when

I felt close") and later reads "Unos brazos negros / ante mí se abrieron, / me sentí una barca / en un gran océano" ("Black arms / opened before me / I felt like a ship / in a great ocean").[14] This poem reveals a longing even as she reaches her homeland, and her arrival at its shores ushers in a feeling of oneness with the island and the sea, as she imagines herself as a ship afloat on an immense ocean. In the poem "Mi mar" ("My Sea") Ilombe writes with a deep desire to be remembered by the sea, "Gracias, mar, mar amigo. / Espérame, que algún día volveré" ("Thank you, sea, sea friend. / Wait for me, I'll be back one day") and vows to return in the hope of being always within and alongside the sea.[15] The diasporic longing for and intimate relation to the sea are consecrated in these works, and reading these poems as both an ontological and phenomenological practice illuminates some of the ways in which the natural world, and especially the force and hold of the sea, is central to Equatoguinean poetics. It is precisely here, in thinking about the sea as practice, that I want to open this final meditation.

Constellations: The Sea and the Celestial

Aracelis Girmay's 2016 collection of poetry, *The Black Maria*, does a particular kind of radical diasporic labor.[16] In the tradition of many Afro-Atlantic artists, intellectuals, and poets (for example, Derek Walcott, Romare Bearden, M. NourbeSe Philip, and Dionne Brand, to name a few),[17] Girmay, a Puerto Rican, African American, and Eritrean writer, links the histories of the transatlantic slave trade, histories before it, and histories beyond it to contemporary phenomena and tragedies across

> the Mediterranean Sea
> the Red Sea
> the Caribbean Sea
> the Atlantic Ocean
> the Afterworld Sea/Sea of Death
> any Sea (13)

The Black Maria, a title based on seventeenth-century astronomy's misrecognition of the moon's craters and basins as seas, is a poetic rendering of grief and possibilities within the murky and unknowable depths of earthly waters. By linking the sea to the stars and cosmos, Girmay connects Black histories to the celestial plane. The first cycle of poems in the book is focused on Eritrean history and the more than 20,000 lives lost in the sea migration from North Africa to Europe in the two decades before 2016. The collection is a dedication to the "history of people searching for polity and opportunity," which is "much larger than Eritrean history alone" (10). The second cycle of poems links the vast histories of life and death at sea to the mortal violence against

Black people in the United States, and to the living thought of Black and Indigenous writers who have influenced her work. In doing so, Girmay creates a constellation of love, grief, and resistance through her poetic practice.

The Black Maria is a demanding collection of poetry. In her opening "Elegy," Girmay tells us that throughout the collection the word "sea" is "also a 'you,' talkless 'witness,' body of water, body of bodies" (11). The collection asks us to bear witness to the sea, to find ways to survive and live with and beyond the infinity of grief, to link ourselves to ongoing forms of exile, diaspora, and dispossession that drive Africans and Black people to the sea, and to see the ways that anti-Blackness is imbued in the most intimate parts of modern life. In linking the Middle Passage to contemporary Eritrean migration, survival, and death across the straits of Gibraltar, and to the kinds of violence that Black people face in the Americas, Girmay urges us, like Glissant, Alexander, and so many others, to consider the living legacies of colonialism, slavery, and coloniality. Girmay opens the collection by demanding that readers trouble temporality and cartography, linking the fifteenth century to the present, linking New York City to Umbertide, Italy and to Asmara/Asmera, Eritrea. These poetics are forms of seeing, a poetry of witness, and are an act of faithful witnessing to that which we cannot see but which we intimately know.[18]

The Black Maria offers powerful evocations of each of the central themes and concepts examined in *Decolonizing Diasporas*. The intimacies of coloniality can be seen in the poem "Inside the sea, there is more," wherein Girmay posits that the sea's "flat blue line" hides intimate pieces of history both material and intangible, including "rockets," "amphora," "debris," "shoes in pairs," "the photographs," and "gold earrings" (40). "The dead," Girmay tells us, "move mammalian through / its buried light, / & a graveyard is built / out of history & time" (40). The sea appears as a vast chamber that has swallowed and taken technologies, ephemera, human bodies, and their wares. Girmay names the extraordinary and the everyday, offering readers the possibility of seeing the impact of colonization of the past and of coloniality in the present. We again see an intimacy with the sea in the series of seven poems titled "to the sea." In one poem, Girmay beckons the sea to take "our messages & theirs"—that is, the messages of the living and the dead—to those who are in its depths. She begs the sea, "what would it cost you?" and ends the poem with a response to that rhetorical question: "nothing" (64).

The collection's first poem, "prayer & letter to the dead," is written in couplets and extends across twelve pages, each spilling grief and hope to those who have ventured across the sea and lost their lives searching for futures and possibilities beyond the Mediterranean, as well as to the myriad seas across which people have been carried. Girmay documents the love of homelands made impossible and is a faithful witness to voyages on "the old & broken boat" (16). The poem/letter weeps at the thought of the sea as a grave, "& you are filling the sea (Courages). / & the fishermen drop their veils / into your grave" (16). The poem continues, "I am marked by the dead, your sea-letters / of salt & weeping. / Now I am ready to lay myself down / on the earth, to listen to the instructions / for how to talk of love & land, to sing / of home in the horrible years, & to fill / my language, like the stars do, / with the light, anyway, of a future tense" (25). Destierro, the experience of being torn from the earth, emerges here as resignation and resistance to the experience of overlapping and intergenerational dispossession. Girmay rails against the visible and invisibilized political and socioeconomic structures that propel forced and voluntary migration.

We see the demand for reparation in the second "to the sea (any)" poem, where the sea is interrogated and asked to return and carry back the dead; "you carry what is human / without being human," the poem reads, "at the shorelines when we ask, / *Where are our dead, have you carried them/back to us?* / You repeat only, / *Who, who?*" (30). In the first of two poems titled "The Black Maria," Girmay tracks the Black lives taken by state-sanctioned and extralegal forms of anti-Blackness in relation to celestial formations—to the misnamed black maria. The reparation of the imagination sees beyond the ways these lives go unwitnessed: "If this is a poem about misseeing—Renisha McBride, Trayvon Martin, / Rekia Boyd / then these are also three of the names of the black maria," and later, "If this is a poem about estrangement & waters made dark with millions / of names & bodies—the Atlantic / Ocean, the Mediterranean & Caribbean Seas, the Mississippi, then these / are also the names of the black maria" (74). The moon in this poem also bears witness, it is also grieving, "always wearing a veil of the black / maria"; the celestial clings to the terrestrial (74). The poem is a radical act of naming, calling forth the dead, and refusing to see the deaths of Black people as anything less than catastrophic events that demand a reparation of the imagination, a remapping of the value of these lives on Earth and in celestial spaces.

The poems "strange earth, strange" and "to the sea" bring forth themes of futurity and relationality. In "strange earth, strange," Girmay talks of the earth "that we will die into" as "this bright, blue oblivion," whose nights are also made "(beautiful)" by the sound of crickets who creak "with desire & the dusk" (61). The six-stanza couplet ends with the lines, "we will call these sounds / 'the future continuous,' us" (61). While human mortality is hailed in the opening line, futurity is called forth through a recognition of nonhuman animals' ongoing cycle of life. However, in Girmay's poem, Black people are central to the "future continuous," and this is a futurity that cannot be taken for granted in light of the material histories of anti-Blackness. This futurity is predicated on the ability to take up remembering practices, and the act of relating histories of Black life and the sea. The connection between the fluvial cycle of the sea and the sky and its relation to human life in the sixth "to the sea" poem also marks futurity. Here, the sea is a body that "cannot hear" and "cannot know" what Girmay calls "the terrible intricacies of our species, / our minds, / the extent to which we have done / what we have done, & yet the depth to which / we have loved, what we have / loved—" (62). She asks the sea, "How dare I move into the dark space of your body / carrying my dreams, without an invitation," and yet she asks again, "Sea, my oblivious afterworld, / grant us entry, please, when we knock" (62). In asking this of the sea, Girmay is also demanding that the sea bring "our flowers & himbasha bread" to the dead (62). She ends the poem by asking the waters to yield futures: "Please, you, / being water too, / find a way into the air & then / the river & the spring / so that your waters can wash the elders / with the medicine of the trying of / their children / cold & clean" (63). The sea here is not only a bottomless grave, but also medicine for the elderly and their children. Girmay holds the sea accountable to humanity and holds humanity accountable to the sea. This connection to the waters is a relationship beyond mourning; it is a link to possible futures.

Importantly, relationality is the overarching context for this collection of poetry. In the second poem titled "The Black Maria," Girmay recounts the way that she moves from a space of fractured identity to a relational consciousness: "Somewhere I got the idea / to keep them separate: / this story from that one, / these stars from those, / the history of that sea from / the history of that sea" (97). She goes on to critique the ways that colonial divisions of the terrestrial into territories are incommensurable with the ways that the sky is "marked by light" and constellations (97). These constellations, however, are also circumscribed by colonial knowledge, or "someone else's myth" (97). These myths belong to other cosmologies, other astrological formations, and do not connect to her own ways of seeing the sea or the celestial. Rather than charting borders and boundaries of colonial modernity onto the sky, the poem offers a different charting, in which the moon and stars and sea "abide by different sight" (97). Instead of seeing celestial constellations "as bears or sisters," Girmay sees them as "a route dense with fires, / dark time adorned by / the messages of mirrors," which remind her that she is connected to histories of life and death and the sea. The poem ends with the sky's message: "saying: you are made with every where" (97). Rather than "everywhere," the poem talks of "every where," which connotes an ontological connection to all wheres, all places, all histories, rather than belonging to any or every history. The collection itself underscores what it means to come from a place, from every where, and to see this as calling to the sea and to the sky, to the (ongoing) Black histories of the Atlantic, the Mediterranean, the Caribbean Sea, to any sea. *The Black Maria* speaks of entangled human lives, and offers a radical remapping of the Atlantic that understands contemporary migrations across the sea as a palimpsest.

After/Images

If indeed "the sea is history," as Derek Walcott's poem announces, then in *Decolonizing Diasporas* the sea is a raging, mourning, bountiful, and

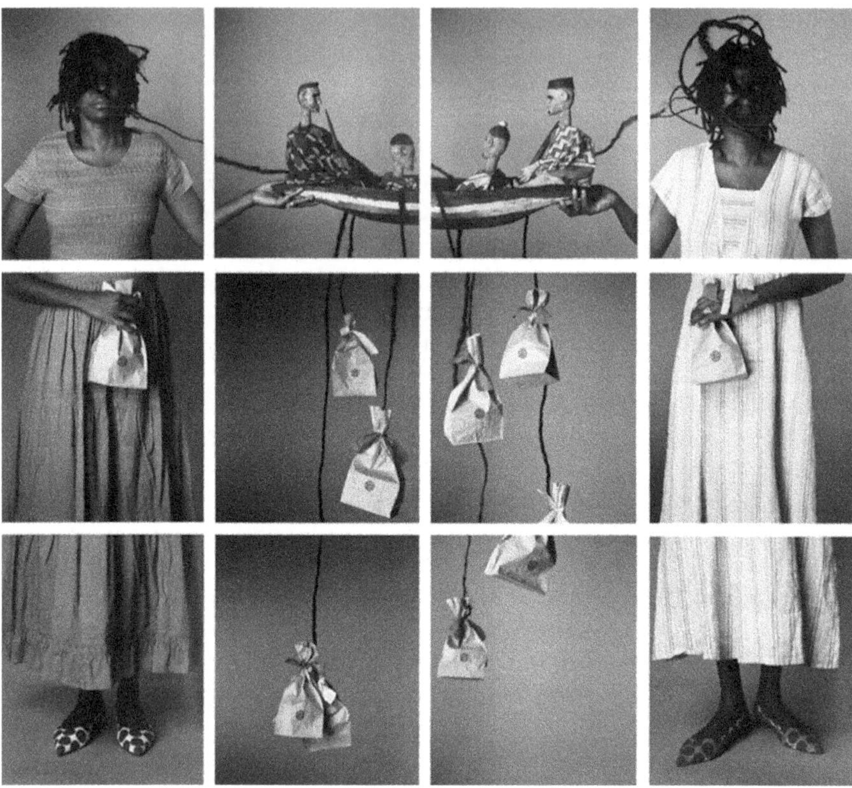

Fig. 12. María Magdalena Campos-Pons, *De las dos aguas* (2007).

sometimes muted backdrop to all of the works examined in this book.[19] The sea is central to each of these works geographically (island, archipelagic), cosmologically (Afro-syncretism, witchcraft), and historically (crossings, diasporas, exile). Relation allows us to glimpse similarities while also accounting for the incommensurable differences between populations living along the coast of Africa and migrating to Europe, and populations living on Caribbean islands and migrating to the United States and Europe. We can imagine these migrations crossing once and again from shared experiences under the colonial heel of Spain to the effects of postcolonial dictatorship, occupation, coloniality, and U.S. political and corporate interventions. We can also picture the diasporic and exilic migrations across bluescapes of sea, displacement overlaid by dispossession, movements that miss or touch, knowing and unknowing, creating new layers on the palimpsest of the Afro-Atlantic.

The opening of this book considered the plaque in Equatorial Guinea dedicated to Cuban emancipados, exiled on a sub-Saharan African island after attaining their freedom. That plaque represents just part of a constellation of possible relations. The work of the contemporary Afro-Cuban visual artist María Magdalena Campos-Pons (b. 1959) offers another set of relational constellations. Campos-Pons's work conjures relation and memory as an archive of the Afro-Atlantic.

Campos-Pons's plate installation *De las dos aguas* (2007; figure 12), for example, is comprised of twelve 20 × 24-inch Polaroid photo prints showing the dissected image of two women—one dressed in blue, another in white—holding a canoe with four figures inside of it. The women's clothes evoke the orisha of the sea, Yemayá, in her preferred color, blue; and the orisha of the skies, Obatalá, in his preferred white. The image is thus overlaid by Afro-Atlantic syncretism and, like Girmay's work, links the sea to the sky and to the survival of these African cosmologies in the diaspora. In the image, extensions of braided or locked hair reach from both of the women's heads toward the ships, linking or locking into the body of the canoe. The hair trickles down below, and affixed to the strands are seven brown paper bags tied with blue ribbons, bearing the words "THIS IS NOT ART" within blue ink circles. In their hands, the two women also hold replicas of these marked brown bags, and their faces, covered by braided hair, are almost completely concealed from the viewer. What are we to gather from this image? Perhaps the connection among those at sea? Witnessing those on either side of the sea? The hair and hands and sinew of sameness? Femme figures holding up the canoe, holding up history? Unknown and forever unknowable faces and relations? The ferrying of gods, orishas, or men? The bags like anchors, warning us that what lies beneath the sea is not art? A humbling practice of recognizing one's past?

Campos-Pons's work offers us more questions than answers, and the prescience of her visual, installation, and performance art has attracted critical analysis, exhibitions, and awards. In her essay accompanying Campos-Pons's exhibition catalog, Okuwi Enwezor says that "Campos-Pons is heir to the fraught history of the Middle Passage; she has submitted the weight of its historical and theoretical possibilities to some of the most trenchant, poetic, and radically introspective artistic reflection on the displaced agency of Africans in the Americas."[20] Enwezor pushes the viewer to see Campos-Pons's work as a constellation that is generated in relation to other artistic works, traditions, and histories:

> While the coordinates of the diasporic often invoke race and ethnicity, they also connect with language and culture. The diasporic imagination not only operates within the boundary of multiplicity but also locates itself in the historical vector that acknowledges that creative ideas are never self-enclosed, and that traditions of artistic practice are generated through creative dialogue and interaction with other traditions. More important, the diasporic imagination recognizes that when subjectivities are displaced—when cultural traditions

> become discontinuous, dislocated, and transformed by the exigencies of historical and temporal processes—the context of production is often burdened by the memory of the past and the actuality of the present.[21]

Campos-Pons's diasporic imagination offers sites of memory as possibility and evidence of relation. The diasporic imagination adds a new dimension to the *studia humanitatis* that Sylvia Wynter argues is the umbrella system under which we define and create new ways of being human in a world that thrives on processes of stripping people of their humanity.

Reader, sit with Campos-Pons's image (figure 12) and consider intimacies, witnessing, destierro, reparations, and futurities. In her work, all of these vectors (and more) are made visible through a meditation on the sea. The sea opens a space to consider the how and why of relating across the Afro-Atlantic.

Nadie sabe lo que hay en el fondo del mar.

Relations Again

I think we both felt it. On a rainy morning in October, I was driving up to El Yunque, Puerto Rico's rainforest, with Remei Sipi Mayo, a beloved writer from Equatorial Guinea who lives in diaspora in Barcelona, and her partner. We had just wrapped up all of the readings, presentations, and festivities for the 2016 Festival de la Palabra in Ponce and San Juan.[22] The entire visit was exciting because two years earlier I had visited Remei's village of Rebola on the island of Bioko in Equatorial Guinea, and she was now a guest in my homeland, my island.[23] It was her first time in Puerto Rico, and I, a diasporic subject, was delighted to be her guide. We drove up the steep inclines that lead to the mountains of El Yunque and as we hugged the winding roads, our conversation centered on the similarities between El Yunque and the forests of Bioko that she knew so intimately. She said that the rainforest reminded her of her own Atlantic Ocean island, and whispered that it looked like home. As we jumped in and out of the car at various points to look at the lush vegetation, crawling creeks, and gushing waterfalls, a dizzying feeling coursed through me. Not the kind of vertigo that is par for the course when trudging up mountains, but a revelation, a fleeting feeling of a lifting veil. For a brief moment, I felt myself as an extension of something greater, a present past, a relation to things known and unknown.

NOTES

Preface

1. Germán de Granda, "Negros emancipados cubanos en Fernando Poo," *Revista de Indias* 44 (1984): 174.

2. Benita Sampedro Vizcaya, "Rethinking the Archive and the Colonial Library: Equatorial Guinea," *Journal of Spanish Cultural Studies* 9, no. 3 (November 2008): 341–63, https://doi.org/10.1080/14636200802563600.

3. Adam Lifshey, "'No podemos soñar': A Hispanophone African Literary Displacement of the Spanish-American War of 1898," *Hispanic Journal* 27, no. 1 (Spring 2006): 119–34.

4. Land Acknowledgement by Dylan Miner and the American Indian and Indigenous Studies program, Michigan State University, East Lansing, Mich., http://aisp.msu.edu/.

5. Wenona T. Singel and Matthew L. Fletcher, "Power, Authority, and Tribal Property," *Tulsa Law Review* 41, no. 1 (2005): 21–24.

6. Alicia Campos, "The Decolonization of Equatorial Guinea: The Relevance of the International Factor," *Journal of African History* 44, no. 1 (2003): 95–116.

7. Achille Mbembe, *On the Postcolony*, Studies on the History of Society and Culture, vol. 41 (Berkeley: University of California Press, 2001).

8. Benita Sampedro Vizcaya, "African Poetry in Spanish Exile: Seeking Refuge in the Metropolis," *Bulletin of Hispanic Studies* 81, no. 2 (2004): 201–14.

9. Sampedro Vizcaya, "African Poetry in Spanish Exile," 204.

10. Alicia Campos Serrano, *Petróleo y estado postcolonial: Transformaciones de la economía política en Guinea Ecuatorial, 1995–2010: Implicaciones para la coherencia de políticas españolas* (Madrid: CeALCI-Fundación Carolina, 2011).

11. Enrique Beldarraín Chaple, "La salud pública en Cuba y su experiencia internacional (1959–2005)," *História, Ciências, Saúde-Manguinhos* 13, no. 3 (2006): 709–16.

12. Some of these migrations are forced, some are voluntary, and some writers take on the challenge of circular migrations between the homeland and Spain.

13. Marvin Lewis, *An Introduction to the Literature of Equatorial Guinea: Between Colonialism and Dictatorship* (Columbia: University of Missouri Press, 2007).

14. Marvin Lewis, *Equatorial Guinean Literature in Its National and Transnational Contexts* (Columbia: University of Missouri Press, 2017), 5.

15. Juan González, *Harvest of Empire: A History of Latinos in America* (New York: Penguin, 2000).

16. Miriam Jiménez Román and Juan Flores, eds., *The Afro-Latin@ Reader: History and Culture in the United States* (Durham, N.C.: Duke University Press, 2010).

17. Ramón Grosfoguel, *Colonial Subjects: Puerto Ricans in a Global Perspective* (Berkeley: University of California Press, 2003).

18. Nelson Denis, "Due to Crisis, More Puerto Ricans Now Live in the U.S. Than on the Island," The *Atlantic*, July 6, 2015, https://www.theatlantic.com/politics/archive/2015/07/due-to-crisis-more-puerto-ricans-now-live-in-the-us-than-on-the-island/432246/.

19. Laird Bergad, "Have Dominicans Surpassed Puerto Ricans to Become New York City's Largest Latino Nationality? An Analysis of Latino Population Data from the 2013 American Community Survey for New York City and the Metropolitan Area," Center for Latin American, Caribbean, and Latino Studies, CUNY Graduate Center, 2014, http://clacls.gc.cuny.edu/files/2014/11/AreDominicansLargestLatinoNationality.pdf.

20. "In the nineteenth century, the island of Bioko (then Fernando Po) was a penal colony and the Spanish shipped Cuban rebels (some of them white planters) and Filipino insurrectionists to the African coast to suffer the torments of malaria and torrential rain." Ibrahim K. Sundiata, "The Diaspora and a Very Small Place in Africa," *Transition*, no. 119 (2016): 143–44; Benita Sampedro Vizcaya, "Engaging the Atlantic: New Routes, New Responsibilities," *Bulletin of Hispanic Studies* 89, no. 8 (2012): 905–22; Elisa Rizo, "Equatorial Guinean Literature in a Context of State-Promoted Amnesia," *World Literature Today* 86, no. 5 (September/October 2012): 32–36; Joanna Boampong, ed., *In and Out of Africa: Exploring Afro-Hispanic, Luso-Brazilian, and Latin-American Connections* (Newcastle upon Tyne, Eng.: Cambridge Scholars, 2012).

21. John Lipski, "The Spanish Language of Equatorial Guinea," *Arizona Journal of Hispanic Cultural Studies* 8, no. 1 (2004): 115–30; Susana Castillo-Rodriguez, "African Diaspora and the Circulation of Language: Cuba and Afro-Cuban Loanwords in Equatorial Guinea," *International Journal of the Sociology of Language* 2016, no. 239 (May 2016): 157–92, https://doi.org/10.1515/ijsl-2016-0008.

22. Katherine McKittrick, *Demonic Grounds: Black Women and the Cartographies of Struggle* (Minneapolis: University of Minnesota Press, 2016), xix.

23. For more on Negrismo, see Yolanda Martínez-San Miguel, *Coloniality of Diasporas: Rethinking Intra-Colonial Migrations in a Pan-Caribbean Context* (New York: Palgrave Macmillan, 2014); and Lesley Feracho, "The Legacy of Negrismo/Negritud: Inter-American Dialogues," *Langston Hughes Review* 16, no. 1/2 (Fall/Spring 1999–2001): 1–7. We also see the preoccupations with the legacy of slavery and the relationship with Black peoples in the Americas; see Martin Repinecz, "Raza or Race? Remembering Slavery in Equatorial Guinean Literature," *Hispanic Studies Review,* vol. 4 (2019): 121–35.

24. Carlos Nsue Otong, "Salud: A Nicholás Guillén," *El Patio: La Revista de la Cultural Hispano-Guineana*, no. 25 (June 1993): 6.

Introduction

1. Paul Gilroy, *The Black Atlantic: Modernity and Double Consciousness* (Cambridge, Mass.: Harvard University Press, 1995), 3–4.

2. Gilroy, *Black Atlantic*, 15.

3. Adolfo Campoy-Cubillo and Benita Sampedro Vizcaya, "Entering the Global Hispanophone: An Introduction," *Journal of Spanish Cultural Studies* 20, nos. 1–2 (2019): 12.

4. M. Jacqui Alexander, *Pedagogies of Crossing: Meditations on Feminism, Sexual Politics, Memory, and the Sacred* (Durham, N.C.: Duke University Press, 2005), 6.

5. Édouard Glissant, *Poetics of Relation*, trans. Betsy Wing (Ann Arbor: University of Michigan Press, 1997), 4–7.

6. Agustín Laó-Montes, "Afro-Latinidades and the Diasporic Imaginary," *Iberoamericana* 5, no. 17 (2005): 120–21.

7. Joseba Gabilondo, "The Hispanic Atlantic," *Arizona Journal of Hispanic Cultural Studies* 5, no. 89 (2001): 92, 100.

8. For more on research that discusses African islands, see Benita Sampedro Vizcaya, "Inscribing Islands: From Cuba to Fernando Poo and Back," in *Transatlantic Studies: Latin America, Iberia, and Africa*, ed. Cecilia Enjuto-Rangel, Sebastiaan Faber, Pedro García-Caro, and Robert P. Newcomb (Liverpool, Eng.: Liverpool University Press, 2019); and Beatriz Celaya Carrillo, "Atlántico negro y africano: Travesías de Inongo-Vi-Makomè, Maximiliano Nkogo Esono, y César A. Mba Abogo," *TRANSMODERNITY: Journal of Peripheral Cultural Production of the Luso-Hispanic World* 7, no. 2 (Spring 2017): 139–64.

9. While I use the term "diaspora" throughout this book, I am aware that some of these writers and artists are indeed living in exile. Rather than repeatedly using both terms, I have chosen to use "diaspora" in order to underscore the ways that the status of migration changes for individuals and across generations. Marvin Lewis writes: "In the diasporic and transnational realities of artists, some migrations are 'voluntary' while others are 'forced' due to the political, social, and economic situations in Equatorial Guinea. Their transnational experiences are often determined by national forces such as dictatorship and repression over which they have no control. Creative writers interpret their realities within the contexts of exile, post-colonialism, place and displacement, as well as other causes for trans-border activities." Lewis, *Equatorial Guinean Literature*, 7.

10. Laó-Montes, "Afro-Latinidades," 125. For more on diaspora studies, see Jacqueline Nassy Brown, "Black Liverpool, Black America, and the Gendering of Diasporic Space," *Cultural Anthropology* 13, no. 3 (August 1998): 291–325; Tina Campt, "The Crowded Space of Diaspora: Intercultural Address and the Tensions of Diasporic Relation," *Radical History Review* 83, no. 1 (2002): 94–113; Brent Hayes Edwards, "The Uses of Diaspora," *Social Text* 19, no. 1 (Spring 2001): 45–73; and Brent Hayes Edwards, *The Practice of Diaspora: Literature, Translation, and the Rise of Black Internationalism* (Cambridge, Mass.: Harvard University Press, 2009).

11. Lewis, *Equatorial Guinean Literature*, 5.

12. Kim D. Butler, "Defining Diaspora, Refining a Discourse," *Diaspora: A Journal of Transnational Studies* 10, no. 2 (Fall 2001): 212.

13. Yolanda Martínez-San Miguel, *Caribe Two Ways: Cultura de la migración en el Caribe insular hispánico* (San Juan, P.R.: Ediciones Callejón, 2003).

14. Marisel C. Moreno, *Family Matters: Puerto Rican Women Authors on the Island and the Mainland* (Charlottesville: University of Virginia Press, 2012), 11.

15. Samantha Pinto, *Difficult Diasporas: The Transnational Feminist Aesthetic of the Black Atlantic* (New York: NYU Press, 2013). For Pinto, difficult diasporas are "the aesthetic and critical terrains that imagine the feminist potential for occupying diaspora's very form itself, the transgressive and often unexpected

loops of circulation that cannot easily be traced to fixed points of origin and return" (3–4).

16. Antonio Benítez-Rojo, *The Repeating Island: The Caribbean and the Postmodern Perspective* (Durham, N.C.: Duke University Press, 1996), 215.

17. Silvia Torres-Saillant, *Caribbean Poetics: Toward an Aesthetic of West Indian Literature*, 2nd ed. (Leeds, Eng.: Peepal Tree, 2013); Silvio Torres-Saillant and Ramona Hernández, *The Dominican Americans (The New Americans)* (Westport, Conn.: Greenwood, 1998). Peripheral is an important concept that emerges in the Latino studies context with Torres-Saillant and Hernández's work, which aptly notes that Dominicans represent the periphery of the margins; that is, if Latinos are marginal, then the vastly understudied Dominicans and Dominican-Yorks are on the periphery of that margin.

18. Sampedro Vizcaya, "Engaging the Atlantic," 907–8.

19. Petra R. Rivera-Rideau, "'If I Were You': Tego Calderón's Diasporic Interventions," *Small Axe: A Caribbean Journal of Criticism* 22, no. 1 (55) (March 2018): 56, https://doi.org/10.1215/07990537-4378924.

20. Rafael Pérez-Torres, *Movements in Chicano Poetry: Against Myths, Against Margins* (New York: Cambridge University Press, 1995), 3, 12.

21. For more on "la gran familia" and its limits, see Moreno, *Family Matters*.

22. See Lorgia García-Peña, "Translating 'Blackness': Dominicans Negotiating Race and Belonging across the Atlantic," in "Dominican Black Studies," special issue, *The Black Scholar* 45, no. 2 (Summer 2015): 10–20, https://doi.org/10.1080/00064246.2015.1012993; Omaris Z. Zamora, "Refashioning Blackness, Refashioning Our Histories," *Portal*, no. 8 (2013): 24–25; Dixa Ramírez, *Colonial Phantoms: Belonging and Refusal in the Dominican Americas, from the 19th Century to the Present* (New York: NYU Press, 2018); and Paul Joseph López Oro, "'Ni de aquí, ni de allá': Garífuna Subjectivities and the Politics of Diasporic Belonging," in *Afro-Latin@s in Movement: Critical Approaches to Blackness and Transnationalism in the Americas*, ed. Petra R. Rivera-Rideau, Jennifer A. Jones, and Tianna Paschel (New York: Palgrave Macmillan, 2016), 61–83.

23. For a few examples, see Ginetta E. B. Candelario, *Black Behind the Ears: Dominican Racial Identity from Museums to Beauty Shops* (Durham, N.C.: Duke University Press, 2007); Miriam Jiménez Román and Juan Flores, eds., *The Afro-Latin@ Reader: History and Culture in the United States* (Durham, N.C.: Duke University Press, 2010); Frank Graziano, *Undocumented Dominican Migration* (Austin: University of Texas Press, 2013); Petra Rivera-Rideau, *Remixing Reggaetón: The Cultural Politics of Race in Puerto Rico* (Durham, N.C.: Duke University Press, 2015); and Tianna S. Paschel, *Becoming Black Political Subjects: Movements and Ethno-Racial Rights in Colombia and Brazil* (Princeton, N.J.: Princeton University Press, 2016).

24. Miriam DeCosta-Willis, ed., *Daughters of the Diaspora: Afra-Hispanic Writers* (Kingston, Jamaica: Ian Randle, 2003); María Mercedes Jaramillo and Lucía Ortiz, *Hijas del muntu: Biografías críticas de mujeres afrodescendientes de América Latina* (Bogota, Colombia: Panamericana Editorial, 2011); José L. Torres-Padilla and Carmen Haydee Rivera, eds., *Writing Off the Hyphen: New Perspectives on the Literature of the Puerto Rican Diaspora* (Seattle: University of Washington Press, 2008); Marion Rohrleitner and Sarah E. Ryan, eds., *Dialogues across Diasporas: Women Writers, Scholars, and Activists of Africana*

and Latina Descent in Conversation (Lanham, Md.: Rowman and Littlefield, 2013).

25. Laó-Montes, "Afro-Latinidades," 120. Laó-Montes also contends that "in so far as Afro-Latinidades are marginalized from hegemonic narratives of African-ness, Blackness, Latinidad, and Hispanicity, and therefore from their corresponding world-regional (Black Atlantic, Latin America, African-America, Afro-Caribbean) and national ideologies of identity (racial, ethnic), Afro-Latina/o, as a subalternized diasporic form of difference, should be transformed into a critical category to deconstruct and redefine all of the above cartographies of self, culture, and power" (119).

26. See the work of Joanna Boampong and Dorothy Odartey-Wellington for some of these works, in the special issue on "Global Hispanophone" of the *Journal of Spanish Cultural Studies* 20, no. 1–2 (May 2019).

27. See Juan Flores, *From Bomba to Hip-Hop: Puerto Rican Culture and Latino Identity* (New York: Columbia University Press, 2000); Raquel Rivera, *New York Ricans from the Hip Hop Zone* (New York: Palgrave Macmillan, 2003); Jorge Duany, *The Puerto Rican Nation on the Move: Identities on the Island and in the United States* (Chapel Hill: University of North Carolina Press, 2003); and Arlene Dávila, *Barrio Dreams: Puerto Ricans, Latinos, and the Neoliberal City* (Berkeley: University of California Press, 2004).

28. See SA Smythe, "Smythe, The Black Mediterranean, and the Politics of Imagination," *Middle East Report: Suffering and the Limits of Relief* 286 (Spring 2018): 3–9, https://essaysmythe.files.wordpress.com/2018/06/smythe-the-black-mediterranean-and-the-politics-of-imagination.pdf; and García-Peña, "Translating 'Blackness.'"

29. Alexander Weheliye, *Habeas Viscus: Racializing Assemblages, Biopolitics, and Black Feminist Theories of the Human* (Durham, N.C.: Duke University Press), 13. For more on relationality in contexts of race, sex, gender, sexuality, coloniality, settler colonialism, and positionality, see Sabrina L. Hom, "Between Races and Generations: Materializing Race and Kinship in Moraga and Irigaray," *Hypatia* 28, no. 3 (Summer 2013): 419–35, https://doi.org/10.1111/j.1527-2001.2012.01271.x; Evelyn Nakano Glenn, "Settler Colonialism as Structure: A Framework for Comparative Studies of U.S. Race and Gender Formation," *Sociology of Race and Ethnicity* 1, no. 1 (January 2015): 52–72, https://doi.org/10.1177/2332649214560440; Alice Liao, "Contra Queer: The Metaphoric Incommensurability between Queer Politics and Coming Out," *Journal of Information Ethics* 19, no. 2 (fall 2010): 17–32; and Audrey Thompson, "Listening at an Angle," *Philosophy of Education* (2010): 1–10, https://ojs.education.illinois.edu/index.php/pes/article/view/2990/1071.

30. Keith P. Feldman, "On Relationality, on Blackness: A Listening Post," *Comparative Literature* 68, no. 2 (June 2016): 108, https://doi.org/10.1215/00104124-3507892.

31. Nelson Maldonado-Torres, "On the Coloniality of Being: Contributions to the Development of a Concept," in "Globalization and the De-Colonial Options," special issue, *Cultural Studies* 21, no. 2–3 (March/May 2007): 243, https://doi.org/10.1080/09502380601162548.

32. Lisa Lowe, *The Intimacies of Four Continents* (Durham, N.C.: Duke University Press, 2015), 16.

33. Jodi A. Byrd, "'Variations under Domestication': Indigeneity and the Subject of Dispossession," *Social Text* 36, no. 2 (135) (June 2018): 128, https://doi.org/10.1215/01642472-4362397.

34. Nelson Maldonado-Torres, "The Decolonial Turn," trans. Robert Cavooris, in *New Approaches to Latin American Studies: Culture and Power*, ed. Juan Poblete (New York: Routledge, 2017), 112.

35. Barbara Christian, "The Race for Theory," *Cultural Critique* 6 (Spring 1987): 76.

36. Isar P. Godreau, *Scripts of Blackness: Race, Cultural Nationalism, and US Colonialism in Puerto Rico* (Champaign: University of Illinois Press, 2015).

37. Christina Sharpe, *In the Wake: On Blackness and Being* (Durham, N.C.: Duke University Press, 2016), 21.

38. Katherine McKittrick, *Demonic Grounds: Black Women and the Cartographies of Struggle* (Minneapolis: University of Minnesota Press, 2016), ix.

39. Frantz Fanon, *Black Skin, White Masks* (New York: Grove, 1952), 89.

40. Chandra Talpade Mohanty, *Feminism without Borders: Decolonizing Theory, Practicing Solidarity* (Durham, N.C.: Duke University Press, 2003); McKittrick, *Demonic Grounds.*

41. See Agustín Palacios, "Multicultural Vasconcelos: The Optimistic, and at Times Willful, Misreading of *La Raza Cósmica*," *Latino Studies* 15, no. 4 (2017): 416–38; and Daphne V. Taylor-García, *The Existence of the Mixed Race Damnés: Decolonialism, Class, Gender, Race* (Lanham, Md.: Rowman and Littlefield, 2018).

42. Robert J. Priest and Alvaro L. Nieves, eds., *This Side of Heaven: Race, Ethnicity, and Christian Faith* (New York: Oxford University Press, 2007); Eduardo Bonilla-Silva, *Racism without Racists: Color-Blind Racism and the Persistence of Racial Inequality in America* (Lanham, Md.: Rowman and Littlefield, 2017).

43. Milagros Denis-Rosario, "Following Their Footsteps: Tracing Puerto Ricans' Sociopolitical Activism in New York City from an Afro-Centric Perspective," *Journal of Pan African Studies* 5, no. 4 (June 2012): 116.

44. See Silvio Torres-Saillant, "The Tribulations of Blackness: Stages in Dominican Racial Identity," *Latin American Perspectives* 25, no. 3 (May 1998): 126–46.

45. One recent example is the organizing work of Colectivo Ilé around the 2020 census in Puerto Rico and their consciousness raising work to encourage folks to self-identify as "Afroboricua" or "Afrodescendiente."

46. Angela Jorge, "The Black Puerto Rican Woman in Contemporary Society," in *The Puerto Rican Woman: Perspectives on Culture, History, and Society*, ed. Edna Acosta-Belén (New York: Praeger, 1986), 180–87.

47. Jorge, "Black Puerto Rican Woman." Jorge argues that the choice one makes as a Black Puerto Rican woman in American society means that both her own and her children's ability to be Puerto Rican, in a sociocultural sense, can be imperiled by partnering with an African American or Anglophone Black man. See also Barbara Smith and CenCen, "The Blood—Yes, the Blood: A Conversation," in *Home Girls: A Black Feminist Anthology*, ed. Barbara Smith (New Brunswick, N.J.: Rutgers University Press, 2000), 31.

48. Remei Sipi Mayo, *Inmigración y género: El caso de Guinea Ecuatorial* (Donostia-San Sebastián, Spain: Gakoa Liburuak, 2002).

49. Sipi Mayo, *Inmigración y género,* 22.

50. Michael Ugarte, *Africans in Europe: The Culture of Exile and Emigration from Equatorial Guinea to Spain* (Champaign: University of Illinois Press, 2010), 25.

51. Sylvia Wynter, "Unsettling the Coloniality of Being/Power/Truth/Freedom: Towards the Human, after Man, Its Overrepresentation—An Argument," *CR: The New Centennial Review* 3, no. 3 (fall 2003): 257–337, https://doi.org/10/1353/ncr.2004.0015.

52. Lewis, *Equatorial Guinean Literature*, 8.

53. Lewis, *Equatorial Guinean Literature*, 12.

54. Lewis, *Equatorial Guinean Literature*, 8. While these perspectives vary within Equatorial Guinea, it is important to note how colonial impositions aided in fracturing peoples across difference. We see here a fundamental violence and indifference in the ways that colonial empires carved out colonies in African territories with no knowledge or interest in existing kinship ties, community territories or needs, clan links and practices, or Indigenous spatiality.

55. Donato Ndongo-Bidyogo, interview with the author, Madrid, Spain, July 2016.

56. Combahee River Collective, *The Combahee River Collective Statement: Black Feminist Organizing in the Seventies and Eighties* (Latham, N.Y.: Kitchen Table/Women of Color, 1986).

57. Audre Lorde, "Age, Race, Class, and Sex: Women Redefining Difference," in *Sister Outsider: Essays and Speeches* (Berkeley, Calif.: Crossing, 2012), 114–23.

58. Mohanty, *Feminism without Borders*, 46.

59. Aurora Levins Morales, *Medicine Stories: History, Culture, and the Politics of Integrity* (Boston: South End, 1998), 125.

60. Angelique V. Nixon, "'Relating across Difference': Caribbean Feminism, bell hooks, and Michelle Cliff's Radical Black Subjectivity," in The *Caribbean Woman Writer as Scholar: Creating, Imagining, Theorizing*, ed. Keshia N. Abraham (Coral Springs, Fla.: Caribbean Studies, 2009), 366.

61. Lorde, "Age, Race, Class, and Sex," 118.

62. Ngũgĩ wa Thiong'o, *Decolonising the Mind: The Politics of Language in African Literature* (Portsmouth, N.H.: Heinemann, 2011), 3.

63. Laura E. Pérez, "Enrique Dussel's *Etica de la liberación*, U.S. Women of Color Decolonizing Practices, and Coalitionary Politics amidst Difference," *Qui Parle: Critical Humanities and Social Sciences* 18, no. 2 (Spring/Summer 2010): 123, https://doi.org/10.5250/quiparle.18.2.121.

64. When I am talking about relations beyond the human, I am referring to our ethical interdependence with nonhuman animals, ecology, and the environment—cosmologies that include the presence of ancestors, and other forms of relations that are beyond the scope of colonial logics. For more on the colonial difference, see Walter D. Mignolo, *Local Histories/Global Designs: Coloniality, Subaltern Knowledges, and Border Thinking* (Princeton, N.J.: Princeton University Press, 2012).

65. María Lugones, "Toward a Decolonial Feminism," in "Feminist Legacies/Feminist Futures: The 25th Anniversary Issue," special issue, *Hypatia* 25, no. 4 (fall 2010): 742–59; Xhercis Méndez, "Notes toward a Decolonial Feminist Methodology: Revisiting the Race/Gender Matrix," *Trans-Scripts* 5 (2015): 41–56.

66. Maldonado-Torres, "The Decolonial Turn," 120.

67. Nelson Maldonado-Torres, "Epistemology, Ethics, and the Time/Space of Decolonization: Perspectives from the Caribbean and the Latina/o Americas," in *Decolonizing Epistemologies: Latina/o Theology and Philosophy*, ed. Ada María Isasi-Díaz and Eduardo Mendieta (New York: Fordham University Press, 2012), 200. See also Pérez, "Enrique Dussel's *Etica de la liberación*."

68. Maldonado-Torres, "The Decolonial Turn," 112.

69. Nelson Maldonado-Torres, "Reconciliation as a Contested Future: Decolonization as Project or Beyond the Paradigm of War," in *Reconciliation, Nations and Churches in Latin America*, ed. Iain S. Maclean (Brookfield, Vt.: Ashgate, 2006), 225–45.

70. Flores, *From Bomba to Hip-Hop*, 42.

71. Some of these authors are Kelvin Santiago, Ramón Grosfoguel, Agustín Laó-Montes, Nelson Maldonado-Torres, Sabelo J. Ndlovu-Gatsheni, Ngũgĩ wa Thiong'o, and Yuderkys Espinosa Miñoso. See Sabelo J. Ndlovu-Gatsheni, *Coloniality of Power in Postcolonial Africa: Myths of Decolonization* (Codesria, Senegal: African Books Collective, 2013); Yuderkys Espinosa Miñoso, Diana Gómez Correal, and Karina Ochoa Muñoz, eds., *Tejiendo de otro modo: Feminismo, epistemología y apuestas descoloniales en Abya Yala* (Popayán, Colombia: Editorial Universidad del Cauca, 2014); and Kelvin A. Santiago-Valles, "'Race,' Labor, 'Women's Proper Place,' and the Birth of Nations: Notes on Historicizing the Coloniality of Power," *CR: The New Centennial Review* 3, no. 3 (fall 2003): 47–69.

72. Xhercis Méndez and Yomaira Figueroa, "Not Your Papa's Wynter: Women of Color Contributions toward Decolonial Futures," in *Beyond the Doctrine of Man: Decolonial Visions of the Human*, ed. Joseph Drexler-Dreis and Kristien Justaert (New York: Fordham University Press, 2020), 60–88.

73. Sylvia Wynter, "The Ceremony Must Be Found: After Humanism," *Boundary* 2, no. 12/13 (1984): 45.

74. Sampedro Vizcaya, "Engaging the Atlantic," 909. See also Rod Edmond and Vanessa Smith, eds., *Islands in History and Representation* (New York: Routledge, 2003); and Tobias Green, "Fear and Atlantic History: Some Observations Derived from the Cape Verde Islands and the African Atlantic," *Atlantic Studies* 3, no. 1 (2006): 25–42, https://doi.org/10.1080/14788810500525424.

75. Epeli Hau'ofa, "Our Sea of Islands," in *A New Oceania: Rediscovering Our Sea of Islands*, ed. Epeli Hau'ofa, Vijay Naidu, and Eric Waddell (Suva, Fiji: University of the South Pacific, 1993), 2–16.

76. For more on the United States as an extension of the Caribbean, see Yolanda Martínez-San Miguel, *Coloniality of Diasporas: Rethinking Intra-Colonial Migrations in a Pan-Caribbean Context* (New York: Palgrave Macmillan, 2014).

77. Rebeca Hey-Colón, "Transformative Currents: An Exploration of the Sea and Identity in the Works of Angie Cruz and Nelly Rosario," in *Negotiating Latinidades, Understanding Identities within Space*, ed. Kathryn Quinn-Sánchez (Newcastle upon Tyne, Eng.: Cambridge Scholars, 2015), 9.

78. Hey-Colón, "Transformative Currents," 10.

79. Rebecca Solnit and Joshua Jelly-Schapiro, *Nonstop Metropolis: A New York City Atlas* (Berkeley: University of California Press, 2016), 84.

80. McKittrick, *Demonic Grounds*, xiii.

81. Rutgers Center for Cultural Analysis, "Archipelagos," Rutgers University, New Brunswick, N.J., 2015–16, http://cca.rutgers.edu/annual-seminar/past-seminars/308-archipelagoes.

82. Paul Lyons and Ty P. Kawika, eds., "Pacific Currents," special issue, *American Quarterly* 67, no. 3 (September 2015); Brian Russell Roberts and Michelle Ann Stephens, eds., *Archipelagic American Studies* (Durham, N.C.: Duke University Press, 2017). .

83. Hau'ofa, "Our Sea of Islands"; Craig Santos Perez, "Transterritorial Currents and the Imperial Terripelago," in "Pacific Currents," special issue, *American Quarterly* 67, no. 3 (September 2015): 619–24.

84. Vanessa Pérez-Rosario, "On the Hispanophone Caribbean Question," *Small Axe: A Caribbean Journal of Criticism* 20, no. 3 (51) (November 2016): 29.

85. Hey-Colón, "Transformative Currents," 10.

86. Michael Ugarte, "Where Do We Fit? The Place of Afro-Hispanic and Afro-Iberian Studies in US University Curricula," in *In and Out of Africa: Exploring Afro-Hispanic, Luso-Brazilian, and Latin-American Connections*, ed. Joanna Boampong (Newcastle upon Tyne, Eng.: Cambridge Scholars, 2012), 10–17; Global Hispanophone Forum, *MLA Commons*, https://mla.hcommons.org/groups/global-hispanophone/.

87. Sampedro Vizcaya, "Engaging the Atlantic," 910.

88. Feldman, "On Relationality, on Blackness," 112.

89. Ruth Wilson Gilmore, *Golden Gulag: Prisons, Surplus, Crisis, and Opposition in Globalizing California* (Berkeley: University of California Press, 2007), 28.

90. Here I am referencing Ann Laura Stoler, "Tense and Tender Ties: The Politics of Comparison in North American History and (Post) Colonial Studies," *Journal of American History* 88, no. 3 (December 2001): 829–65, https://doi.org/10.2307/2700385.

91. Eve Tuck and K. Wayne Yang, "Decolonization Is Not a Metaphor," *Decolonization: Indigeneity, Education, and Society* 1, no. 1 (2012): 7.

92. Maldonado-Torres, "Reconciliation as a Contested Future."

93. Christian, "Race for Theory," 68–69.

94. Christian, "Race for Theory," 69, 78.

95. Nancy Morejón, "Toward a Poetics of the Caribbean," *World Literature Today* 76, no. 3/4 (Summer/Autumn 2002): 52–53.

96. Gloria Anzaldúa, *Borderlands/La Frontera: The New Mestiza* (San Francisco: Aunt Lute Books, 1987), 3.

97. Sampedro Vizcaya, "Engaging the Atlantic," 910.

98. Christian, "Race for Theory," 78.

99. Wynter, "Unsettling the Coloniality."

Chapter 1

Epigraph: Audre Lorde, *Sister Outsider: Essays and Speeches* (Berkeley, Calif.: Crossing, 2012), 57.

1. Interview with the dramaturge, January 2014, Malabo, Bioko, Equatorial Guinea.

2. Ann Laura Stoler, "Intimidations of Empire: Predicaments of the Tactile and Unseen," in *Haunted by Empire: Geographies of Intimacy in North American History*, ed. Laura Ann Stoler (Durham, N.C.: Duke University Press, 2006), 4.

3. Christina Sharpe, *Monstrous Intimacies: Making Post-Slavery Subjects* (Durham, N.C.: Duke University Press, 2009), 3.

4. B. B. Buchanan, "Women and Femmes Unite: A Structural and Political Analysis of Femininity," Wear Your Voice, March 21, 2018, https://wearyourvoicemag.com/lgbtq-identities/women-and-femmes-femininity. I am grateful to Jessica Marie Johnson for this source and for our dialogues on these and other critical issues related to Black and Afro-femmes of the Atlantic world.

5. Macarena Gómez-Barris, *The Extractive Zone: Social Ecologies and Decolonial Perspectives* (Durham, N.C.: Duke University Press, 2017), 9.

6. Jafari S. Allen, *¡Venceremos? The Erotics of Black Self-Making in Cuba* (Durham, N.C.: Duke University Press, 2011), 97.

7. Régine Michelle Jean-Charles, *Conflict Bodies: The Politics of Rape Representation in the Francophone Imaginary* (Columbus: Ohio State University Press, 2014), 10.

8. These works subvert silencing power structures in myriad ways. In some cases, they do so by creating satires that reveal the absurdities of corruption. An excellent example is Ramón Esono Ebalé's *La pesadilla de Obi*, a graphic novel that satirizes the dictatorship under the premise that Obiang's greatest nightmare is to be an everyday Guinean. Ebono was imprisoned for this comic from 2017 to 2018. Ramón Esono Ebalé, *La pesadilla de Obi* (Washington, D.C.: EG Justice, 2015).

9. Donette Francis, *Fictions of Feminine Citizenship: Sexuality and the Nation in Contemporary Caribbean Literature* (New York: Palgrave Macmillan, 2010), 52.

10. Nadia Celis Salgado, *La rebelión de las niñas: El Caribe y la "conciencia corporal"* (Madrid: Iberoamericana, 2015). She says, "Mi conceptualización de la 'conciencia corporal' se adhiere al esfuerzo . . . por crear un corpus de conceptos propios para refuter la arraigada cultural machista y legitimar los sabers feminism en la region" (29; "My conceptualization of the 'corporeal consciousness' adheres to the effort . . . to create a corpus of own concepts to refute the deeply rooted macho culture and legitimize the feminist knowledge in the region"). Jessica Marie Johnson, *Wicked Flesh: Black Women, Intimacy, and Freedom in the Atlantic World* (Philadelphia: University of Pennsylvania Press, 2020). Johnson writes: "Using black femme in the context of women of African descent's practicies of freedom in the eighteenth century surfaces foundational strains of this resistive femininity and intimacy between women. In a setting where assault and rape, brandings and burnings, and broken limbs and dismemberment awaited black women who refused to submit to their owners or defied the men around them, daring to form intimate bonds with women a strategy for survivial. In the eighteenth-century context, black femme freedom articulates the audacity of a freedom that dared to reach past masculinity and empire for satisfaction. It infuses black women's choosing of each other with carnal and erotic stickiness" (174–75).

11. Celis Salgado, *Rebelión de las niñas*, 21.

12. Celis Salgado, *Rebelión de las niñas*, 40.

13. I must credit Katsi Rodríguez Velázquez for the discussion of how the term "flesh" in Anglo academic writing does not translate or travel in the same way in Spanish. Flesh, in fact, becomes its closest synonym, "carne," or meat, and the slippages leave space for loss and enunciation.

14. Celis Salgado, *Rebelión de las niñas*, 25.
15. Celis Salgado, *Rebelión de las niñas*, 25.
16. Johnson, *Wicked Flesh*, pg. 172–73. Johnson also writes: "Invoking black femme instead of (black) women or womanhood remembers the slipperiness of the category of woman in a multilingual world of slaves" (173).
17. Some excellent examples of literary criticism on the dictator novel include Jennifer Harford Vargas, "Dictating a Zafa: The Power of Narrative Form in Junot Díaz's *The Brief Wondrous Life of Oscar Wao*," *MELUS* 39, no. 3 (2014): 8–30; Elena Machado Sáez, "Dictating Desire, Dictating Diaspora: Junot Díaz's *The Brief Wondrous Life of Oscar Wao* as Foundational Romance," *Contemporary Literature* 52, no. 3 (2011): 522–55; Michael Ugarte, "Spain's Heart of Darkness: Equatorial Guinea in the Narrative of Donato Ndongo," *Journal of Spanish Cultural Studies* 7, no. 3 (2006): 271–87, https://doi.org/10.1080/14636200601084071; and Robert Spencer, "Ngũgĩ wa Thiong'o and the African Dictator Novel," *Journal of Commonwealth Literature* 47, no. 2 (2012): 145–58, https://doi.org/10.1177/0021989412447490.
18. The Fang are Equatorial Guinea's most numerous (and politically powerful) ethnic group.
19. Religiosity, in the form of Catholicism and African and Afro-syncretic belief systems, is included among these power structures, although it is not the center of my analysis in this chapter. For more on religiosity and syncretism in *By Night the Mountain Burns* and *Song of the Water Saints*, see Ineke Phaf-Rheinberger, "Migration versus Stagnation in Equatorial Guinea: The Sea as the Promise of Modernity," *Research in African Literatures* 48, no. 3 (fall 2017): 55–71; and Rebeca Hey-Colón, "Transformative Currents: An Exploration of the Sea and Identity in the Works of Angie Cruz and Nelly Rosario," in *Negotiating Latinidades, Understanding Identities within Space*, ed. Kathryn Quinn-Sánchez (Newcastle upon Tyne, Eng.: Cambridge Scholars, 2015), 9.
20. This contention with the dark is also central in Ávila Laurel's novel *Awala cu sangui*, in which the darkness propels fear, and folklore acts as a salve against the dark.
21. Thenesoya Vidina Martín de la Nuez, "(Re)escribiendo la historia desde la agencia africana: La reconstrucción narrativa de la realidad en la obra de Ávila Laurel," *Afro-Hispanic Review* 28, no. 2 (2009): 222.
22. The Treaty of El Pardo also recognized the Portuguese territories in Brazil and its more western occupations in South America (established by the 1494 Treaty of Tordesillas). This treaty thus launched the beginnings of the Spanish Guinea territories in the nineteenth century.
23. For a history of sacristans and Annobonese resistance to colonial imposition, see Arlindo Manuel Caldeira, "Organizing Freedom: De Facto Independence on the Island of Ano Bom (Annobón) during the Eighteenth and Nineteenth Centuries," *Afro-Hispanic Review* 28, no. 2 (2009): 293–310. Also, significant to considering Annobón are the distinct practices that show fundamental differences in what are supposed (or at least imagined) to be "homogenous" Equatoguinean islands under the banner or myth of "Bantu unity." This is similar to narratives of *mestizaje*, *multajae*, or *la gran familia*, which sought to obfuscate the heteropatriarchal and racial projects in the Americas, particularly in the Hispanophone world.

24. See Samuel Decalo, *Psychoses of Power: African Personal Dictatorships* (Gainesville: Florida Academic Press, 1998). See also Geoffrey Wood, "Business and Politics in a Criminal State: The Case of Equatorial Guinea," *African Affairs* 103, no. 413 (2004): 547–67.

25. "U.S. Department of State Country Report on Human Rights Practices 1993–Equatorial Guinea," United Nations High Commissioner for Refugees, January 30, 1994, https://www.refworld.org/docid/3ae6aa4c14.html.

26. See Geoffrey Wood, "Business and Politics in a Criminal State: The Case of Equatorial Guinea," http://www.jstor.org.proxy2.cl.msu.edu/stable/3518490; James Brooke, "Waste Dumpers Turning to West Africa," New York Times, July 17, 1988, https://www.nytimes.com/1988/07/17/world/waste-dumpers-turning-to-west-africa.html; Francisco Zamora Loboch, *La república fantástica de annobón (Madrid: Sial* Casa de Africa, 2018); Baffour Ankomah, "African Wasteland," *Index on Censorship* 18, no. 6–7 (1989): 34–37; and Dominic A. Akpan and Bassey Inyang, "Economic Diplomacy, Global Waste Trade: The African Perspective since the 20th Century," *African Journal of History and Archaeology* 2 (2016): 1–10. Ávila Laurel's 2013 novel *El dictador de Corisco* (which I take up in chapter 3) examines some of these themes, as a family is left landless after the government plans to build a new airport over the lake on another remote Equatoguinean island, Corisco. The subsequent ecological destruction devastates the family's livelihood. Here, we have a tangible example of the realities of coloniality, and within this context, the remnants of the colonial project—ideologies, power, valuations of bodies, knowledge, and accumulation—are deeply imbedded in "postcolonial" structures. Juan Tomás Ávila Laurel, *El dictador de Corisco* (Malabo, Equatorial Guinea: Ediciones Pángola, 2014).

27. Phaf-Rheinberger, "Migration versus Stagnation," 62.

28. Tamara T. Butler, "What Do We Owe the Dead? Making Space for Humanizing Pedagogies" (lecture, Responsibility of Teachers in the Wake of Racial Violence Teach-In, Michigan State University, East Lansing, Mich., August 29, 2015).

29. Juan Tomás Ávila Laurel, *La carga* (Valencia, Spain: Palmart, 1999).

30. Tina Campt, *Listening to Images* (Durham, N.C.: Duke University Press, 2017), 72.

31. Juan Tomás Ávila Laurel, personal conversation with the author, March 19, 2019.

32. Here, I use the word "spill" in reference to Alexis Pauline Gumbs, *Spill: Scenes of Black Feminist Fugitivity* (Durham, N.C.: Duke University Press, 2016).

33. I am building here on a now almost defunct Puerto Rican mourning ritual in which funeral guests greet families with the phrase "Te acompaño en tus sentimientos" (I accompany you in your feelings [of mourning or grief]). This sentiment is also found in the novel. The English translation reads, "No one would accompany them in their grief" (150), and the original reads, "Y no habría nadie que las acompañara" (130).

34. Tamara T. Butler, "#Say[ing] Her Name as Critical Demand: English Education in the Age of Erasure," *English Education* 49, no. 2 (2017): 153.

35. There is a connection here to folklorized Puerto Rican practices around women and witchcraft. In the song "Doña Chana," made popular by Cortijo y Su Combo and Ismael Rivera (recorded in 1959), we hear about the bruja doña Chana who has dogs released on her.

36. Lewis, *Introduction to the Literature of Equatorial Guinea*, 189.
37. Phaf-Rheinberger, "Migration versus Stagnation," 64.
38. Stoler, "Intimidations of Empire," 13.
39. Mayra Santos-Febres, *Sobre piel y papel*, 2nd ed. (San Juan, P.R.: Ediciones Callejon, 2005), 13.
40. Francis, *Fictions of Feminine Citizenship*, 10.
41. Mónica G. Ayuso, "'How Lucky for You That Your Tongue Can Taste the 'r' in 'Parsley': Trauma Theory and the Literature of Hispaniola," *Afro-Hispanic Review* 30, no. 1 (Spring 2011): 53.
42. Lorgia García-Peña, *The Borders of Dominicanidad: Race, Nation, and Archives of Contradiction* (Durham, N.C.: Duke University Press, 2016), 84–85.
43. Hey-Colón, "Transformative Currents," 16; Mimi Sheller, *Citizenship from Below: Erotic Agency and Caribbean Freedom* (Durham, N.C.: Duke University Press, 2012), 22.
44. Dixa Ramírez, *Colonial Phantoms: Belonging and Refusal in the Dominican Americas, from the 19th Century to the Present* (New York: NYU Press, 2018), 88.
45. Victoria A. Chevalier, "Alternative Visions and the Souvenir Collectible in Nelly Rosario's *Song of the Water Saints*," in *Contemporary U.S. Latino/a Literary Criticism*, ed. Lyn Di Iorio Sandín and Richard Perez (New York: Palgrave Macmillan, 2007), 44. Chevalier argues that as a literary device, ekphrasis "vexes the difference between text and image; in describing a visual object it figures forth that object a presence." (36).
46. Chevalier, "Alternative Visions," 41.
47. Omaris Z. Zamora, "(Trance)forming AfroLatina Embodied Knowledges in Nelly Rosario's *Song of the Water Saints*," special issue, "Black and Latin@: Conceptualizing Afro-Latinidad in Afro-Latina/o Literature and Performance," ed. Michele Shaul and Kathryn Quinn-Sánchez, *Label Me Latina/o* 7 (Summer 2017): 7, http://labelmelatin.com/wp-content/uploads/2017/07/Omaris-Z.-Zamora-Tranceforming-AfroLatina-Embodied-Knowledges-in-Nelly-Rosarios-Song-of-the-Water-Saints-final.pdf.
48. Lorde, *Sister Outsider*, 56.
49. Francis, *Fictions of Feminine Citizenship*, 56.
50. Campt, *Listening to Images*, 4.
51. Ann Laura Stoler, *Duress: Imperial Durabilities in Our Times* (Durham, N.C.: Duke University Press, 2016), 16.
52. Francis, *Fictions of Feminine Citizenship*, 56.
53. García-Peña, *Borders of Dominicanidad*, 89.
54. Zamora, "(Trance)forming," 8.
55. Ginetta E. B. Candelario, "Voices from Hispaniola: A Meridians Roundtable with Edwidge Danticat, Loida Maritza Pérez, Myriam Chancy, and Nelly Rosario," *Meridians: Feminism, Race, Transnationalism* 5, no. 1 (January 2004): 73.
56. Neil Roberts, *Freedom as Marronage* (Chicago: University of Chicago Press, 2015), 11. Petit marronage is but one form of fugitivity. Grand marronage, Roberts argues, is the "creation of communities of freedom outside the parameters of a (plantation) society" (11).
57. Chevalier, "Alternative Visions," 48.

58. Lorde, *Sister Outsider*, 54.

59. Frances R. Aparicio, "On Subversive Signifiers: US Latina/o Writers Tropicalize English," *American Literature* 66, no. 4 (December 1994): 795–801.

60. Zamora, "(Trance)forming," 7.

61. Eliana Castro, "From the Entrails of the Monster" (unpublished paper submitted to Yomaira Figueroa, Chicano/Latino Studies 811, Michigan State University, East Lansing, Mich., October 4, 2018), 2.

62. Key here is that the photo was whitened in order to ensure that the husband's darker skin appeared lighter or whiter. Mercedes comes to believe that this man, a stranger, was in fact her father Silvio, whom she has never met.

63. Megan Adams, "'A Border Is a Veil Not Many People Can Wear': Testimonial Fiction and Transnational Healing in Edwidge Danticat's *The Farming of Bones* and Nelly Rosario's *Song of the Water Saints*" (master's thesis, University of South Florida, 2010).

64. Ayuso, "'How Lucky for You,'" 48.

65. Hey-Colón, "Transformative Currents," 19.

66. Chevalier, "Alternative Visions," 50.

67. Omise'eke Natasha Tinsley, "Black Atlantic, Queer Atlantic: Queer Imaginings of the Middle Passage," *GLQ: A Journal of Lesbian and Gay Studies* 14, no. 2–3 (June 2008): 196, https://doi.org/10.1215/10642684-2007-030.

68. Lorde, *Sister Outsider*, 55.

69. Xhercis Méndez, "Decolonial Feminist Methodologies" (paper presented at the annual meeting of the Caribbean Philosophical Association, Dakar, Senegal, June 2018).

70. Obono argues that *la dote*, or "dowry," has slowly transformed into a capitalist rather than a communal structure. This means that marriages or partnerships are not only ordered by the logics of first or second wives, or eldest to youngest children, but also by status as concubine (rather than wife) and the amount of la dote that was paid. In recent years, demands for larger and more lavish dotes have also been a point of contention within the Fang and Ndowe ethnic groups. III Seminario Internacional sobre Guinea Ecuatorial, Universidad Nacional de Educación a Distancia, Madrid, Spain, July 6, 2016.

71. Luis Melgar Valero is also the author of the novel *Los blancos estais locos* (2017), which discusses the LGBTQ experience in Equatorial Guinea from the perspective of a Spanish diplomat stationed there.

72. Parker Brookie, "In Review: *La Bastarda* by Trifonia Melibea Obono," *Asymptote* (blog), May 21, 2018, https://www.asymptotejournal.com/blog/2018/05/21/in-review-la-bastarda-by-trifonia-melibea-obono/.

73. Tinsley, "Black Atlantic, Queer Atlantic," 193.

74. Johnson, *Wicked Flesh*, 175.

75. Roberts, *Freedom as Marronage*, 5. Hubert Edzodzomo Ondo also sees the trope of "cimarronaje" within *La bastarda*. Hubert Edzodzomo Ondo, "Reconocimiento, negación, y exclusión de las identidades en *Le Pacte d'Afia* (2009) y *La Bastarda* (2016)," in *XVI Congreso Nacional Educación Comparada Tenerife* (La Laguna, Spain: Universidad de La Laguna, 2018), 304.

76. Lorde, *Sister Outsider*, 57.

77. Edzodzomo Ondo, "Reconocimiento," 303.

78. Roberts, *Freedom as Marronage*, 11.

79. Roberts, *Freedom as Marronage*, 11.
80. Johnson, *Wicked Flesh*, 173.

Chapter 2

Parts of chapter 2 were previously published in an earlier version as "Faithful Witnessing in Decolonial Readings of *Shadows of Your Black Memory* and *The Brief Wondrous Life of Oscar Wao*," *Hypatia: A Journal of Feminist Philosophy* 30, no. 4 (2015): 641–56.

1. lê thi diem thúy, *The Gangster We Are All Looking For* (New York: Knopf, 2003), 90.

2. Piri Thomas, *Down These Mean Streets* (Los Angeles: Graymalkin Media, 2016; originally published New York: Knopf, 1967).

3. See Nicholas De Genova and Ana Yolanda Ramos-Zayas, *Latino Crossings: Mexicans, Puerto Ricans, and the Politics of Race and Citizenship* (New York: Routledge, 2004); Raquel Rivera, *New York Ricans from the Hip Hop Zone* (New York: Palgrave Macmillan, 2003); Juan Flores, *The Diaspora Strikes Back: Caribeño Tales Of Learning and Turning* (New York: Routledge, 2010); Lisa Sánchez-González, *Boricua Literature: A Literary History of the Puerto Rican Diaspora* (New York: NYU Press, 2001); Raphael Dalleo and Elena Machado Sáez, *The Latino/a Canon and the Emergence of Post-Sixties Literature* (New York: Palgrave Macmillan, 2007); Irene López, "'But You Don't Look Puerto Rican': The Moderating Effect of Ethnic Identity on the Relation between Skin Color and Self-Esteem among Puerto Rican Women," *Cultural Diversity and Ethnic Minority Psychology* 14, no. 2 (2008): 102, http://dx.doi.org/10.1037/1099-9809.14.2.102; and Marta E. Sánchez, "La Malinche at the Intersection: Race and Gender in *Down These Mean Streets*," *PMLA* 113, no. 1 (January 1998): 117–28.

4. See Edna Acosta-Belén and Carlos E. Santiago, *Puerto Ricans in the United States: A Contemporary Portrait* (Boulder, Colo.: Lynne Rienner, 2006); Lillian Comas-Diaz, "LatiNegra: Mental Health Issues of African Latinas," *Journal of Feminist Family Therapy* 5, no. 3–4 (October 1994): 35–74; Arnaldo Cruz-Malavé, "What a Tangled Web! Masculinity, Abjection, and the Foundations of Puerto Rican Literature in the United States," *differences: A Journal of Feminist Cultural Studies* 8, no. 1 (1996): 132–52; and Marta E. Sánchez, *"Shakin' Up" Race and Gender: Intercultural Connections in Puerto Rican, African American, and Chicano Narratives and Culture (1965–1995)* (Austin: University of Texas Press, 2005).

5. See Dell Hymes, "Ways of Speaking," in *Explorations in the Ethnography of Speaking*, ed. Richard Bauman and Joel Sherzer (Cambridge: Cambridge University Press, 1974), 433–51; Ana Celia Zentella, *Growing Up Bilingual: Puerto Rican Children in New York* (Malden, Mass.: Blackwell, 1997); Lyn Di Iorio Sandín, *Killing Spanish: Literary Essays on Ambivalent US Latino/a Identity* (New York: Palgrave Macmillan, 2004); Arlene Dávila, *Barrio Dreams: Puerto Ricans, Latinos, and the Neoliberal City* (Berkeley: University of California Press, 2004); and Laura Callahan, *Spanish/English Codeswitching in a Written Corpus* (Amsterdam: John Benjamins, 2004).

6. Gordon Parks, *The World of Piri Thomas* (New York: National Educational Television and Radio Center, 1968).

7. The term "gutter language" appears in Daniel Stern's review of *Down These Mean Streets*. Daniel Stern, "One Who Got Away," *New York Times*, May 21, 1967.

8. For a primary example of "culture of poverty" theory as it relates to Puerto Rican families, see Oscar Lewis, *La Vida: A Puerto Rican Family in the Culture of Poverty—San Juan and New York* (New York: Random House, 1966).

9. Sánchez González coins the term "coming-to-consciousness literature" in *Boricua Literature*.

10. Junot Díaz, *The Brief Wondrous Life of Oscar Wao* (New York: Riverhead Books, 2007); Donato Ndongo-Bidyogo, *Shadows of Your Black Memory*, trans. Michael Ugarte (Chicago: Swan Isle, 2007).

11. Carolyn Forché, ed., *Against Forgetting: Twentieth-Century Poetry of Witness* (New York: W. W. Norton, 1993), 30.

12. With "economy" here, I am thinking of Audre Lorde's foundational poem "Poetry Is Not a Luxury," in *Sister Outsider: Essays and Speeches* (Berkeley, Calif.: Crossing, 2012), 36–39.

13. Forché, *Against Forgetting*, 31.

14. Aimé Césaire, *Discourse on Colonialism* (New York: Monthly Review, 2000), 41.

15. Audre Lorde, *Our Dead Behind Us: Poems* (New York: W. W. Norton, 1986), 4.

16. María Lugones, *Pilgrimages/Peregrinajes: Theorizing Coalition against Multiple Oppressions* (Lanham, Md.: Rowman and Littlefield, 2003), introduction.

17. Kelly Oliver, *Witnessing Beyond Recognition* (Minneapolis: University of Minnesota Press, 2001), 80. Oliver is not without critics, however. Michael Monahan's "Recognition beyond Struggle: On a Liberatory Account of Hegelian Recognition" argues that there is another path through which to understand Hegelian concepts of recognition, one that is not the eternally agonistic "master-slave dialectic"—that is, the concept of pure recognition. Nevertheless, Monahan's elucidation of pure recognition, as he notes, does not invalidate the myriad critiques of Hegelian agonistic recognition. Michael J. Monahan, "Recognition beyond Struggle: On a Liberatory Account of Hegelian Recognition," *Social Theory and Practice* 32, no. 3 (July 2006): 389–414.

18. Oliver, *Witnessing Beyond Recognition*, 79.

19. Nelson Maldonado-Torres, *Against War: Views from the Underside of Modernity* (Durham, N.C.: Duke University Press, 2008), 151–53.

20. Linda Tuhiwai Smith, *Decolonizing Methodologies: Research and Indigenous Peoples*, 2nd ed. (London: Zed Books, 2012), 144–45. Here Smith also notes that *testimonio* is a familiar project in Latin America, one that "has become one of a number of literary methods for making sense of histories, of voices and representation, and of the political narrative of oppression" (145).

21. Smith, *Decolonizing Methodologies,* 145.

22. Donna McCormack reads fictional narratives at the intersections of queer and postcolonial studies through a framework of witnessing in *Queer Postcolonial Narratives and the Ethics of Witnessing*. Although McCormack does not engage the concept of *faithful* witnessing, she does use witnessing, recognition, and the importance of seeing these as critical concepts in fictional narratives. Donna McCormack, *Queer Postcolonial Narratives and the Ethics of Witnessing* (New York: Bloomsbury Academic, 2014).

23. Lugones, *Pilgrimages/Peregrinajes*, 4.

24. María Lugones, "Heterosexualism and the Colonial/Modern Gender System," in "Writing Against Heterosexism," special issue, *Hypatia* 22, no. 1 (Winter 2007): 191.

25. Lugones, *Pilgrimages/Peregrinajes*, 7.

26. Lugones, *Pilgrimages/Peregrinajes*, 11.

27. Lugones, *Pilgrimages/Peregrinajes*, 7.

28. Oliver, *Witnessing Beyond Recognition*, 81.

29. Oliver, *Witnessing Beyond Recognition*, 83.

30. Chela Sandoval, *Methodology of the Oppressed* (Minneapolis: University of Minnesota Press, 2000), 6.

31. Ramón Grosfoguel, "Decolonizing Post-Colonial Studies and Paradigms of Political-Economy: Transmodernity, Decolonial Thinking, and Global Coloniality," *TRANSMODERNITY: Journal of Peripheral Cultural Production of the Luso-Hispanic World* 1, no. 1 (January 2011): 3, https://escholarship.org/uc/item/21k6t3fq.

32. Lugones, *Pilgrimages/Peregrinajes*, 5.

33. One example that Cruz offers is of a queer black man who is ignored in the predominantly middle-class gay community of gentrifiers. In a moment of crisis and attempted suicide, this young man chooses composure when confronted with police involvement. Cruz reads this moment as an act of resistance, highlighting the young man's "stoicism" as a survival strategy in the face of looming police violence. She argues that "recognition of the resistance in these tight spaces belies a history of often hostile negotiations and struggle waged by LGBTQ youth everyday." Cindy Cruz, "LGBTQ Street Youth Talk Back: A Meditation on Resistance and Witnessing," *International Journal of Qualitative Studies in Education* 24, no. 5 (2011): 553.

34. Cruz, "LGBTQ Street Youth," 550, emphasis added.

35. Ian Baucom, *Specters of the Atlantic: Finance Capital, Slavery, and the Philosophy of History* (Durham, N.C.: Duke University Press, 2005), 77.

36. Baucom, *Specters of the Atlantic,* 72.

37. Baucom, *Specters of the Atlantic,* 332.

38. The concept of the decolonial attitude is part of a philosophical intervention related to Husserl's conception of the phenomenological attitude, Heidegger and Sartre's work on authenticity, and Habermas's philosophical meditation on the post-conventional attitude. The term "decolonial attitude," coined by Maldonado-Torres, refers to a subjective disposition toward knowledge. For more on the decolonial attitude, see Maldonado-Torres, "Reconciliation as a Contested Future," 225–45; and Maldonado-Torres, *Against War*.

39. Maldonado-Torres, "Reconciliation as a Contested Future," 242.

40. Ugarte, *Africans in Europe*, 25.

41. Esther Sánchez-Pardo, "Adrift on the Black Mediterranean Diaspora: African Migrant Writing in Spain," *Social Identities* 17, no. 1 (January 2011): 113.

42. Susan Martin-Márquez, *Disorientations: Spanish Colonialism in Africa and the Performance of Identity* (New Haven, Conn.: Yale University Press, 2008), 294.

43. Ngũgĩ, *Decolonising the Mind*, 3.

44. Martin-Márquez, *Disorientations*, 294.

45. This can also be read in relation to José Esteban Muñoz's theories of "disidentification" wherein "for some, disidentification is a survival strategy that works within and outside the dominant public sphere simultaneously." José Esteban Muñoz, *Disidentifications: Queers of Color and the Performance of Politics* (Minneapolis: University of Minnesota Press, 1999), 5.

46. Ngugi, *Decolonising the Mind*, 3.

47. Ngũgĩ, *Decolonising the Mind*, 2.

48. Sánchez-Pardo, "Adrift on the Black Mediterranean Diaspora," 118.

49. This moment of contact in 1492 is what many scholars point to as the birth of modernity. See C. L. R. James, *The Black Jacobins: Toussaint L'Ouverture and the San Domingo Revolution* (New York: Random House, 1963; originally published London: Secker and Warburg, 1938); Eric Williams, *Capitalism and Slavery* (Chapel Hill: University of North Carolina Press, 1994; originally published 1944); Sidney Mintz, "The Caribbean Region," *Daedalus* 102, no. 2 (1974): 45–71; Hilary Beckles, "Capitalism, Slavery and Caribbean Modernity," *Callaloo* 20, no. 4 (fall 1997): 777–89; Sylvia Wynter, "1492: A New World View," in *Race, Discourse, and the Origin of the Americas: A New World View*, ed. Vera Lawrence Hyatt and Rex Nettleford (Washington, D.C.: Smithsonian Institution, 1996), 5–57. While this temporal and spatial framework remains central to contemporary studies of the Caribbean and modernity, the field of critical colonial studies has made critical contributions to traversing Eurocentric chronologies that elide the histories of Indigenous agency, social and political organization, and practices before 1492.

50. On private indirect government, see Achille Mbembe, *On the Postcolony* (Berkeley: University of California Press, 2001).

51. For reviews that critique Díaz's writing as misogynistic, see Abigail Nussbaum, "*The Brief Wondrous Life of Oscar Wao* by Junot Díaz," *Asking the Wrong Questions* (blog), July 19, 2008, http://wrongquestions.blogspot.com/2008/07/brief-wondrous-life-of-oscar-wao-by.html; Maestra Coffey, "Internalized Misogyny," *Critical Literacy* (blog), December 22, 2011, https://coffeyenglish.blogspot.com/2011/12/internalized-misogyny.html; and Andreana Clay, "This Is How You Lose Her (And by Her, I Mean Me)," *Queer Black Feminist* (blog), November 12, 2012, http://queerblackfeminist.blogspot.com/2012/11/this-is-how-you-lose-her-and-by-her-i.html.

52. Junot Díaz, "The Silence: The Legacy of Childhood Trauma," *New Yorker*, April 9, 2018, https://www.newyorker.com/magazine/2018/04/16/the-silence-the-legacy-of-childhood-trauma.

53. Aya de Leon, "Reconciling Rage and Compassion: The Unfolding #MeToo Moment for Junot Díaz," *Aya de Leon* (blog), May 5, 2018, https://ayadeleon.wordpress.com/2018/05/05/reconciling-rage-and-compassion-the-unfolding-metoo-moment-for-junot-diaz/.

54. Achille Mbembe argues that "commandment" is part of the imaginary of the power state sovereignty. Commandment features three sorts of violence: founding violence, legitimation of violence, and finally "war," which refers not only to our contemporary articulations of war, but also to the violence that maintains, spreads, and ensures permanence. Mbembe, *On the Postcolony*.

55. Taryne Jade Taylor, "A Singular Dislocation: An Interview with Junot Díaz," *Paradoxa* 26 (2014): 107. For more, see Yomaira C. Figueroa, "Junot

Díaz's Diasporic Discontents: Race, Sex, Violence and the Promise of Decolonial Love," in *Oxford Encyclopedia of Latino/a Literature* (2020).

56. Dixa Ramírez, *Colonial Phantoms: Belonging and Refusal in the Dominican Americas, from the 19th Century to the Present* (New York: NYU Press, 2018), 125.

57. On futurities beyond the material, see Yomaira C. Figueroa, "Reparation as Transformation: Radical Literary (Re)imaginings of Futurities through Decolonial Love," *Decolonization: Indigeneity, Education and Society* 4, no. 1 (2015): 41–58.

58. Monica Hanna, "'Reassembling the Fragments': Battling Historiographies, Caribbean Discourse, and Nerd Genres in Junot Díaz's *The Brief Wondrous Life of Oscar Wao*," *Callaloo* 33, no. 2 (March 2010): 498.

59. Jennifer Harford Vargas, "Dictating a Zafa: The Power of Narrative Form in Junot Díaz's *The Brief Wondrous Life of Oscar Wao*," *MELUS* 39, no. 3 (July 2014): 12.

60. One notable example is Elena Machado Sáez, "Dictating Desire, Dictating Diaspora: Junot Díaz's *The Brief Wondrous Life of Oscar Wao* as Foundational Romance," *Contemporary Literature* 52, no. 3 (fall 2011): 522–55.

61. Elena Machado Sáez, "Dictating Desire, Dictating Diaspora: Junot Díaz's 'The Brief Wondrous Life of Oscar Wao' as Foundational Romance." *Contemporary Literature* 52, no. 3 (2011): 524.

62. Aishih Wehbe-Herrera, "Transnational Legacies and Masculinity Politics in *The Brief Wondrous Life of Oscar Wao*," in *Masculinities and Literary Studies: Intersections and New Directions*, ed. Joseph M. Armengol et al. (New York: Routledge, 2017), 59.

63. Díaz writes: "Poor Oscar. Without even realizing it he'd fallen into one of those Let's Be Friends Vortexes, the bane of nerdboys everywhere. These relationships were love's version of a stay in the stocks, in you go, plenty of misery guaranteed and what you got out of it besides bitterness and heartbreak nobody knows. Perhaps some knowledge of self and women" (Díaz, Oscar W ao, 41).

64. Edwidge Danticat, *Create Dangerously: The Immigrant Artist at Work* (New York: Vintage, 2011), 63.

65. We see Ana and Maritza's (Oscar's love interests) tragic romantic relationships in New Jersey, as well as Lola's verbally abusive relationship with her first boyfriend.

66. Hortense J. Spillers, "Mama's Baby, Papa's Maybe: An American Grammar Book," *Diacritics* 17, no. 2 (1987): 67.

67. Stuart Jeffries, "Angela Davis: 'There Is an Unbroken Line of Police Violence in the US That Takes Us All the Way Back to the Days of Slavery,'" *Guardian*, December 14, 2014, https://www.theguardian.com/global/2014/dec/14/angela-davis-there-is-an-unbroken-line-of-police-violence-in-the-us-that-takes-us-all-the-way-back-to-the-days-of-slavery.

68. Spillers, "Mama's Baby, Papa's Maybe," 68–69.

69. Vargas, "Dictating a Zafa," 18.

70. Antonio Benítez-Rojo. *The Repeating Island: The Caribbean and the Postmodern Perspective* (Durham, N.C.: Duke University Press, 1996).

71. Wehbe-Herrera, "Transnational Legacies," 60.

72. Maja Horn, *Masculinity after Trujillo: The Politics of Gender in Dominican Literature* (Gainesville: University Press of Florida, 2017), 129.

73. Juan Tomás Ávila Laurel, interview with the author, January 2014, Barcelona, Spain.

Chapter 3

1. Achy Obejas, *Days of Awe* (New York: Ballantine, 2001), 309. "Destierro" is sometimes used to denote the condition or sentence of "exile" in Spanish (the more common term is "exilio"). However, "destierro" is considered one of the untranslatable terms for exile because it is a condition that denotes action: "1. m. Acción y efecto de desterrar o desterrarse. 2. m. Pena que consiste en expulsar a alguien de un lugar o de un territoriodeterminado, para que temporal o perpetuamente resida fuera de él. 3. m. Tiempo durante el cual se cumple un destierro (pena). 4. m. Pueblo o lugar en que vive el desterrado. 5. m. Lugar alejado, remoto o de difícil acceso." Real Academia Española, *Diccionario de la lengua española: Edición del tricentenario*, 23rd ed., s.v. "destierro," https://dle.rae.es/?id=DTh9AQi. Throughout this chapter, however, I expand and depart from this definition of "destierro" in order to show its significance to decolonization projects (political and cultural) and to Afro- and Indigenous-descended peoples in the modern world outside of penal or bourgeois connotations.

2. For more on practices of diaspora and Black internationalism, see Brent Hayes Edwards, *The Practice of Diaspora: Literature, Translation, and the Rise of Black Internationalism* (Cambridge, Mass.: Harvard University Press, 2009); and Minkah Makalani, *In the Cause of Freedom: Radical Black Internationalism from Harlem to London, 1917–1939* (Chapel Hill: University of North Carolina Press, 2011).

3. Loida Maritza Pérez, *Geographies of Home* (New York: Penguin, 1999); Juan Tomás Ávila Laurel, *El dictador de Corisco* (Malabo, Equatorial Guinea: Ediciones Pángola, 2014).

4. When talking about destierro in this chapter and beyond, I wish to wrestle the term away from its associations with elitism and bourgeois political exiles. In doing so, I want to make space to think about dispossession that centers those who are most directly affected by domination and colonialism.

5. To be clear, I am not thinking of African-descended peoples and Indigenous peoples as mutually exclusive groups, for African peoples are indeed Indigenous. Colonialism, slavery, and forms of resistance to these oppressions brought forth Afro-Indigenous-descended peoples. Bearing witness to Black Indigeneity in the Americas is critical if we are to think about destierro, justice, and reparations. Within the context of this chapter, I am thinking about Indigenous peoples on Abya Yala and Turtle Island as well as Indigenous Africans and Afro-Indigenous peoples.

6. Yolanda Martínez-San Miguel, *Coloniality of Diasporas: Rethinking Intra-Colonial Migrations in a Pan-Caribbean Context* (New York: Palgrave Macmillan, 2014), 3.

7. In fact, the first iteration of this chapter was rooted in postcolonial discourse. In revising this research over the last five years, I have come to this concept of destierro, a mere footnote in previous drafts, and decided to "put teeth on it," so to speak, and offer decolonial thought a way to address how physical and

metaphysical diasporic lived experiences are constitutive of the sociopolitical economy that is so richly theorized in literary works.

8. Edward W. Said, *Reflections on Exile and Other Literary and Cultural Essays* (London: Granta, 2001), 11.

9. Jorge Duany, "Nation on the Move: The Construction of Cultural Identities in Puerto Rico and the Diaspora," *American Ethnologist* 27, no. 1 (February 2000): 8, https://doi.org/10.1525/ae.2000.27.1.5.

10. When I use the term "dislocation" within this context, I am building on the work of Brinda Mehta, whose scholarship on the Atlantic (*kala pani*) crossing of Indian women created waves of diasporic dislocations. She argues, "The *kala pani* discourse stresses that, rather than there being a single 'Indian' experience, there has been a series of displacements or dislocations which can be identified historically and culturally—and which can be used to develop a critical methodology for reading the fiction of Indo-Caribbean women." Brinda J. Mehta, *Diasporic (Dis)locations: Indo-Caribbean Women Writers Negotiate the Kala Pani* (Jamaica: University of the West Indies Press, 2004), 10.

11. Remei Sipi Mayo, "Crónica de un viaje a Guinea Ecuatorial: Entrando y saliendo de la modernidad (entre corrupción, turismo y tradición)," *Afro-Hispanic Review* 28, no. 2 (2009): 171. For more on Obono's experiences, see Beatriz Celaya Carrillo, "Atlántico negro y africano: Travesías de Inongo-Vi-Makomè, Maximiliano Nkogo Esono, y César A. Mba Abogo," *TRANSMODERNITY: Journal of Peripheral Cultural Production of the Luso-Hispanic World* 7, no. 2 (2017): 158.

12. Said, *Reflections on Exile,* chapter 17. See also Mahmoud Darwish, "Edward Said: A Contrapuntal Reading," trans. Mona Anis, special issue, "Edward Said and After: Toward a New Humanism," *Cultural Critique* no. 67 (Autumn 2007): 175–82.

13. Paul Tiyambe Zeleza, "The Politics and Poetics of Exile: Edward Said in Africa," special issue, "Edward Said, Africa, and Cultural Criticism," *Research in African Literatures* 36, no. 3 (Autumn 2005): 10.

14. Said says, "Nationalisms are about groups, but in a very acute sense exile is a solitude experienced outside the group: the deprivations felt at not being with others in the communal habitation." Said's concern is the exiled subject's lack of access to communal sharing and a sense of belonging to a larger group: the nation. Said, *Reflections on Exile*, 140.

15. Said, *Reflections on Exile,* 140.

16. Zeleza, "Politics and Poetics of Exile," 9.

17. Zeleza, "Politics and Poetics of Exile," 11.

18. Azade Seyhan, *Writing Outside the Nation* (Princeton, N.J.: Princeton University Press, 2000), 5.

19. Seyhan, *Writing Outside the Nation,* 4.

20. I follow Seyhan's point in *Writing Outside the Nation*: "Descriptions such as exilic, ethnic, migrant, or diasporic cannot do justice to the nuances of writing between histories, geographies, and cultural practices. Although as critics we do not have the language commensurate with our task, we have the responsibility to reflect, problematize, and preface the terms we employ. In this study, I do not use the terms exilic, diasporic, or ethnic writing in a strictly technical sense, but as signifiers of texts conceived in and operative between two or more languages and cultural heritages" (9).

21. Zeleza, "Politics and Poetics of Exile," 9. According to Emilio del Valle Escalante, "the term Abya Yala, the concept emerged toward the end of the 1970s in *Dulenega*, or what, for others, is today San Blas, Panama, a Kuna Tule territory. Abya Yala in the Kuna language means 'land in its full maturity.' Akir Mamani, the Bolivian Aymara leader, and Tupaj Katari, one of the founders of the indigenous rights movement in Bolivia, suggested that Indigenous peoples and indigenous organizations use the term Abya Yala in their official declarations to refer to the American continent." Emilio del Valle Escalante, "Self-Determination: A Perspective from Abya Yala," *E-International Relations,* May 20, 2014, https://www.e-ir.info/2014/05/20/self-determination-a-perspective-from-abya-yala/.

22. Jodi A. Byrd, "'Variations under Domestication': Indigeneity and the Subject of Dispossession." *Social Text* 36, no. 2 (135) (2018): 129–30.

23. Leanne Betasamosake Simpson, "Land as Pedagogy: Nishnaabeg Intelligence and Rebellious Transformation," *Decolonization: Indigeneity, Education & Society* 3, no. 3 (2014): 8.

24. Simpson, "Land as Pedagogy," 12.

25. See Cherríe Moraga and Gloria Anzaldúa, eds., *This Bridge Called My Back: Writings by Radical Women of Color*, 4th ed. (Albany: State University of New York Press, 2015); Audre Lorde, *Our Dead Behind Us: Poems* (New York: W. W. Norton, 1986); Wendy Rose, *Going to War with All My Relations: New and Selected Poems* (Flagstaff, Ariz.: Northland, 1993); and Aurora Levins Morales, *Medicine Stories: History, Culture, and the Politics of Integrity* (Boston: South End, 1998).

26. Alexander, *Pedagogies of Crossing,* 274.

27. Alexander, *Pedagogies of Crossing,* 274.

28. Alexander, *Pedagogies of Crossing,* 274

29. Alexander, *Pedagogies of Crossing,* 274.

30. For more on ruination in Jamaica, see Michelle Cliff, *No Telephone to Heaven* (New York: Plume, 1996); and Michelle Cliff, "Caliban's Daughter," *Journal of Caribbean Literatures* 3, no. 3 (2003): 157–60.

31. Alexander, *Pedagogies of Crossing*, 274.

32. For more on neocolonialism and ongoing forms of settler colonialism, see Byrd, "'Variations under Domestication,'" 123–41, https://doi.org/10.1215/01642472-4362397; Joanne Barker, "Territory as Analytic: The Dispossession of Lenapehoking and the Subprime Crisis," *Social Text* 36, no. 2 (135) (June 2018): 19–39, https://doi.org/10.1215/01642472-4362337; Nakano Glenn, "Settler Colonialism as Structure," 52–72, https://doi.org/10.1177/2332649214560440; and Kwame Nkrumah, *Neo-Colonialism: The Last Stage of Imperialism* (New York: International, 1965).

33. Patrick Wolfe, *Settler Colonialism and the Transformation of Anthropology: The Politics and Poetics of an Ethnographic Event* (London: Cassell, 1999).

34. Although an ecocritical reading of this novel, and perhaps many of Ávila Laurel's works, would be illuminating, it is beyond the scope of this project.

35. Vanessa K. Valdés, *Oshun's Daughters: The Search for Womanhood in the Americas* (Albany: State University of New York Press, 2014), 69.

36. Valdés, *Oshun's Daughters*, 63. See also María Cristina Rodríguez, *What Women Lose: Exile and the Construction of Imaginary Homelands in Novels by Caribbean Writers* (New York: Peter Lang, 2005).

37. Valdés, *Oshun's Daughters*, 70.

38. My use of identity reclamation is influenced by the Nuyorican Poets Movement of the 1970s and 1980s, in which diasporic Puerto Rican youth learned to reconstitute their identities as part of anti-imperial and antiracist radical politics. Furthermore, within the context of women of color feminist politics, my use of reclaiming identity is deeply indebted to the work of Michelle Cliff and in particular her essay "Claiming an Identity They Taught Me to Despise." See Michelle Cliff, *The Land of Look Behind: Prose and Poetry* (Ithaca, N.Y.: Firebrand, 1985).

39. Valdés, *Oshun's Daughters*, 59.

40. Lyn Di Iorio Sandín, *Killing Spanish: Literary Essays on Ambivalent US Latino/a Identity* (New York: Palgrave Macmillan, 2004), 66.

41. Jill Toliver Richardson, "Gendered Migrations: The Migratory Experience in Loida Maritza Pérez's *Geographies of Home*," *Label Me Latina/o* 1 (2011): 1. Susan C. Méndez also examines this novel in the context of violence and agency within spiritual practices in "Afro-Caribbean Spiritual Practices, Race, Gender, and Violence in Loida Maritza Pérez's *Geographies of Home*," *Afro-Hispanic Review* 31, no. 1 (Spring 2012): 105–18.

42. Valdés argues that Pérez "underscores the importance of sensuality in the development of one's identity" (*Oshun's Daughters*, 76).

43. Kenneth F. Kiple, *The Caribbean Slave: A Biological History* (New York: Cambridge University Press, 1984); Michelle Gadpaille, "Eating Dirt, Being Dirt: Backgrounds to the Story of Slavery," *AAA: Arbeiten aus Anglistik und Amerikanistik* 39, no. 1 (2014): 3–20; Sera L. Young, *Craving Earth: Understanding Pica; The Urge to Eat Clay, Starch, Ice, and Chalk* (New York: Columbia University Press, 2011). For more on the practice of rural U.S. Black women craving and eating dirt, see Donald E. Vermeer and Dennis A. Frate, "Geophagy in a Mississippi County," *Annals of the Association of American Geographers* 65, no. 3 (September 1975): 414–24; William E. Schmidt, "Southern Practice of Eating Dirt Shows Signs of Waning," *New York Times*, February 13, 1984, https://www.nytimes.com/1984/02/13/us/southern-practice-of-eating-dirt-shows-signs-of-waning.html; and Linda Chen, "The Old and Mysterious Practice of Eating Dirt, Revealed," *NPR*, April 2, 2014, https://www.npr.org/sections/thesalt/2014/04/02/297881388/the-old-and-mysterious-practice-of-eating-dirt-revealed.

44. Simpson, "Land as Pedagogy," 20.

45. Lorde, *Sister Outsider*, 53.

46. Myriam J. A. Chancy, "Subversive Sexualities: Revolutionizing Gendered Identities," *Frontiers: A Journal of Women Studies* 29, no. 1 (2008): 52.

47. For more on marriage and racial mixing, see Angela Jorge, "The Black Puerto Rican Woman in Contemporary Society," in *The Puerto Rican Woman: Perspectives on Culture, History, and Society*, ed. Edna Acosta-Belén (New York: Praeger, 1986), 180–87; and Carlos Pozzi, "Race, Ethnicity, and Color Among Latinos in the United States," in *This Side of Heaven: Race, Ethnicity, and Christian Faith*, ed. Robert J. Priest and Alvaro L. Nieves (New York: Oxford University Press, 2007), 47–62.

48. M. Jacqui Alexander, "Remembering This Bridge, Remembering Ourselves: Yearning, Memory, and Desire," in *This Bridge We Call Home: Radical Visions for Transformation*, ed. Gloria E. Anzaldúa and AnaLouise Keating (New York: Routledge, 2013), 96.

49. Chancy, "Subversive Sexualities," 66.

50. Valdés, *Oshun's Daughters*, 63.

51. C. Christina Lam, "Trauma and Testimony: Embodied Memory in Loida Maritza Pérez's *Geographies of Home*," *Rocky Mountain Review of Language and Literature* 69, no. 1 (Spring 2015): 43.

52. Benita Sampedro Vizcaya, "Routes to Ruin," *Lengua y Literatura* 7, no. 2 (November 2012), https://lljournal.commons.gc.cuny.edu/2012–2-sampedro-texto/. "The event goes like this . . . On a late afternoon in the month of April, some time during the 1940s—they recall—a fire of unprecedented magnitude burned to the ground the grandiose buildings of the Claretian Mission, church, and house on the island of Corisco. It was a day of absolute horror in the island, flames falling from the sky; the fire could not be contained, although all the children at the boarding school were safely rescued. They recall, too, the man held responsible for the fire: his name was Father Andrés Bravo."

53. Sampedro Vizcaya, "Routes to Ruin."

54. The Ndowe are an ethnic minority group predominantly living on the littoral coast of Equatorial Guinea, the island of Corisco, and in other African nations as well.

55. Sampedro Vizcaya, "Routes to Ruin."

56. Ruth Wilson Gilmore, *Golden Gulag: Prisons, Surplus, Crisis, and Opposition in Globalizing California* (Berkeley: University of California Press, 2007), 28.

57. See Ugarte, *Africans in Europe*.

58. Sampedro Vizcaya, "Routes to Ruin."

59. Reflections on the experiences of Equatoguinean women during and after colonial era rule can also been seen in the poetry of Raquel Ilombe del Pozo Epita. See Raquel Ilombe del Pozo Epita, *Ceiba II*, ed. Benita Sampedro Vizcaya and Baltasar Fra Molinero (Madrid: Editorial Verbum, 2014). See also Gustau Nerín, *Guinea Ecuatorial, historia en blanco y negro: Hombres blancos y mujeres negras en Guinea Ecuatorial (1843–1968)* (Ediciones Península, 1998).

60. Sampedro Vizcaya, "Routes to Ruin."

61. In a personal correspondence with Juan Tomás Ávila Laurel, he explained that *motodu*, an Ndowe word for *jefe* or chief, is one that reflects a position of power that is not coated ("revestido") in dignity. Later in this chapter we will see the word *ekambi* used to signal another kind of jefe. According to Ávila Laurel, ekambi is a powerful position of jefe that is coated in high dignity. When speaking about motodu Don Francisco and motodu Obiang, Ávila Laurel is referring to Francisco Macías Nguema and his nephew Teodoro Obiang Mbasogo, who took dictatorial power in Equatorial Guinea after independence—in 1968 and 1979, respectively. Teodoro Obiang Mbasogo remains the current dictator of Equatorial Guinea.

62. Nakano Glenn, "Settler Colonialism as Structure"; Tuck and Yang, "Decolonization Is Not a Metaphor," 1–40.

63. Sampedro Vizcaya, "Routes to Ruin."

64. Ávila Laurel provided this information in our personal correspondence. Furthermore, according to Benita Sampedro Vizcaya, the airport's status is tenuous at best: "As we look to the future, a brand new airport that traverses the island of Corisco has just been inaugurated on 12 October 2011, its landing

strips running from north to south, from coast to coast, with the linear precision of a ruler. But it would be ingenuous to believe that the current generation of Corisco citizens will benefit from it" (Sampedro Vizcaya, "Routes to Ruin").

65. Francisco Zamora Loboch, *Desde el viyil y otras crónicas* (Madrid: Sial Casa de África, 2008), 27.

66. For more on colonial-era resistance, see Arlindo Manuel Caldeira, "Organizing Freedom: De Facto Independence on the Island of Ano Bom (Annobón) during the Eighteenth and Nineteenth Centuries," *Afro-Hispanic Review* 28, no. 2 (2009): 293–310.

67. This insight is based on personal correspondence between Ávila Laurel and the author, June 2014.

68. Primero is carrying on a sexual affair with the tourist Anika. This son, who is quiet and very close to his mother, confides in Malela that Anika has one breast, that she is difficult to satisfy sexually, and that she desires anal sex. Malela counters that this sexual practice is unheard of on their island, and worries that she will become the grandmother of a feces-covered baby: "Yo Malela, sería la primera mujer del pueblo que iría a la playa a lavar al niño porque nació con caca en todo el cuerpo" (54).

69. Coloniality of land and of power means that people are continually stripped of the right to their own land, the land on which they may have been born. They must buy it outright within a system that is meant to disenfranchise them at every turn. This multiplies the meaning of Alexander's question, "What does it mean to be an exile on the land on which you are born?" These Equatoguinean experiences align with Puerto Rican and First Nations and Indigenous concerns and political mobilization around land. Jodi Byrd reminds us that settler colonialism is a "grasping network of relational and precarious dispossessions that enable dispossession to continue in perpetuity. Indigenous studies might be able to contend with how the vexed histories of slavery and colonization continue to inflect our understandings of the past and present and help us imagine decolonial futures for all those who find themselves now here in our lands" (Byrd, "Variations under Domestication," 138–39).

70. Some of these themes are also found in Trifonia Melibea Obono's work (which was discussed in chapter 1). In her first novel, *La herencia de bindendee*, Obono tracks the ontological realities of being a Fang woman in Equatorial Guinea. The novel's title translates roughly as "the inheritance of the prostitute," and as in her second novel, *La bastarda,* she examines the conflation of traditional knowledge practices with heteropatriarchy to show how contemporary Fang kinship and social structures have made it nearly impossible for women in Equatorial Guinea to participate in public life without the support of a brother or husband. Furthermore, this has made it difficult for women to leave abusive marital arrangements—within monogamous or polygamous relationships—without facing backlash and other forms of destierro. The inheritance of the *bindedee* reflects a recent phenomenon. Obono has noted that the more formal education a woman gets, the more structured job and higher salary her prospective partner must have. If she fails to partner in this way, her marital arrangement may not be accepted by her family. If she persists with an unacceptable arrangement, and in lieu of an acceptable dote or bride price, both she and her partner will have to financially support her extended family—a responsibility that normally falls

solely on the male partner within the kinship structure. However, because this is not desirable, women feel compelled to partner with the "highest bidder"—therein lies the "herencia de bindendee." To go to the highest bidder, one must potentially be close to power, and thus be aligned with the very forms of coloniality that one attempts to subvert in everyday life. In this way, Fang women, although part of the ruling ethnic group within Equatorial Guinea, face the effects of the coloniality of gender and destierro.

71. For more on the concept of corporeal consciousness, see chapter 1, "Intimacies," and Nadia Celis Salgado, *La rebelión de las niñas: El Caribe y la "conciencia corporal"* (Madrid: Iberoamericana, 2015).

Chapter 4

Parts of chapter 4 were previously published in an earlier version as "Reparation as Transformation: Radical Literary (Re)imaginings of Futurities through Decolonial Love," in the *Journal of Decolonization: Indigeneity, Education & Society* 4, no. 1 (2015): 41–58.

1. CARICOM member states include Antigua and Barbuda, The Bahamas, Barbados, Belize, Dominica, Grenada, Guyana, Haiti, Jamaica, Montserrat, Saint Lucia, St. Kitts and Nevis, St. Vincent and the Grenadines, Suriname, and Trinidad and Tobago. CARICOM Secretariat, "CARICOM Reparations Commission Press Statement Delivered by Professor Sir Hilary Beckles (Chairman) on Behalf of the CARICOM Reparations Commission Press Conference Regional Headquarters," press release no. 285/2013, December 10, 2013, https://caricom.org/media-center/communications/press-releases/caricom-reparations-commission-press-statement-delivered-by-professor-sir-h.

2. The CARICOM lawsuit also implicates other European slave-owning nations, including Spain, Portugal, Norway, Sweden, and Denmark.

3. Here I am referring to the genealogy of decoloniality for the modern/colonial world, which begins in the fifteenth century. I agree with Ramón Grosfoguel's definition of coloniality as "the continuity of colonial forms of domination after the end of colonial administrations." Ramón Grosfoguel, "Colonial Difference, Geopolitics of Knowledge, and Global Coloniality in the Modern/Colonial Capitalist World-System," *Review (Fernand Braudel Center)* 25, no. 3 (2002): 205. The coloniality-of-power also "brings together race and capital" to form new relations of power. Maldonado-Torres, "Reconciliation as a Contested Future," 233. See also Anzaldúa, *Borderlands/La Frontera*; Aníbal Quijano, "Coloniality of Power and Eurocentrism in Latin America," *International Sociology* 15, no. 2 (June 2000): 215–32, https://doi.org/10.1177/0268580900015002005; Walter D. Mignolo, "The Geopolitics of Knowledge and the Colonial Difference," *South Atlantic Quarterly* 101, no. 1 (Winter 2002): 57–96; Maldonado-Torres, *Against War*; Nelson Maldonado-Torres, "Decoloniality at Large: Towards a Trans-Americas and Global Transmodern Paradigm," in "Thinking through the Decolonial Turn," special issue, *TRANSMODERNITY: Journal of Peripheral Cultural Production of the Luso-Hispanic World* 1, no. 3 (2012): 1–10; and Xhercis Méndez, "Transcending Dimorphism: Afro-Cuban Ritual Praxis and the Rematerialization of the Body," *Journal for Cultural and Religious Theory* 13, no. 1 (Winter 2014): 101–21. This temporal scope is not representative of all decolonial or anticolonial thought.

4. Quijano, "Coloniality of Power and Eurocentrism in Latin America."

5. Fanon, *Black Skin, White Masks*, xiv.

6. Though Fanon is speaking of anticolonial realities of the mid-twentieth century, his relevance further manifests after the failed political decolonization projects of the 1950s and 1960s. Advancing Fanonian thought in the context of theories of decoloniality crystallizes its significance outside of his temporal moment.

7. See Linda Tuhiwai Smith, *Decolonizing Methodologies: Research and Indigenous Peoples*, 2nd ed. (London: Zed Books, 2012); Bernard Boxill, "Black Reparations," in *The Stanford Encyclopedia of Philosophy*, ed. Edward N. Zalta (Stanford, Calif.: Stanford University, 2011), http://plato.stanford.edu/archives/spr2011/entries/black-reparations/; and Staceyann Chin, "Should Caribbean Nations Be Compensated for the Legacy of Slavery?" interview by John Hockenberry, *The Takeaway*, Public Radio International, October 29, 2013, https://www.pri.org/stories/2013-10-29/should-caribbean-nations-be-compensated-legacy-slavery.

8. Ernesto Quiñonez, *Bodega Dreams* (New York: Vintage, 2000); Joaquín Mbomío Bacheng, *Matinga, sangre en la selva* (Barcelona: Editoriales Mey, 2013); Junot Díaz, *The Brief Wondrous Life of Oscar Wao* (New York: Riverhead Books, 2007).

9. This is the title of the issue in which "Letter" was published. Christina Olivares, "Letter," *About Place Journal* 3, no. 4 (October 2015), https://aboutplacejournal.org/issues/future-imagined/section-5/christina-olivares.

10. Sandoval, *Methodology of the Oppressed*, 4.

11. Sandoval, *Methodology of the Oppressed*, 187. Walter D. Mignolo argues that the colonial difference is the colonial classification of the world in the modern/colonial imaginary. This system of classification "converted differences," for example race, "into values." To transform or traverse these differences/values requires a fundamental shift in human relations. One way to transform these human relations is through decolonial love, which requires a decolonial attitude or a subjective disposition that turns away from dominant hierarchies and is instead aligned with those who are most oppressed and silenced. Walter D. Mignolo, "The Geopolitics of Knowledge and the Colonial Difference," *South Atlantic Quarterly* 101, no. 1 (Winter 2002): 71.

12. Sandoval, *Methodology of the Oppressed*, 414.

13. Audre Lorde, "Scratching the Surface: Some Notes on Barriers to Women and Loving," *Black Scholar* 9, no. 7 (April 1978): 31, https://doi.org/10.1080/00064246.1978.11414006.

14. Lorde, *Sister Outsider*, 123.

15. Maldonado-Torres, *Against War*, 244.

16. Maldonado-Torres, *Against War*, 244.

17. Maldonado-Torres, *Against War*, 187.

18. Maldonado-Torres, *Against War*, 187.

19. Maldonado-Torres, *Against War*, 244.

20. See also Mignolo, "Geopolitics of Knowledge," 74–80.

21. Ciann Wilson et al., "Relationships as Resistance: Dismantling Anti-Black Racism and Settler Colonialism," closing plenary session at the annual Critical Ethnic Studies Conference, Toronto, Canada, May 3, 2015.

22. Barker, "Territory as Analytic," 19–39.

23. Tuck and Yang, "Decolonization Is Not a Metaphor," 31.

24. Ta-Nehisi Coates, "The Case for Reparations," *Atlantic* 313, no. 5 (June 2014): 54–71, https://www.theatlantic.com/magazine/archive/2014/06/the-case-for-reparations/361631/.

25. Online Etymology Dictionary, s.v. "Reparation," http://www.etymonline.com/index.php?term=reparation.

26. Oxford English Dictionary, s.v. "Reparation," http://www.oed.com/view/Entry/162653?redirectedFrom=reparation#eid.

27. Consider a few historical examples of reparations: the United States' reparations to Japanese Americans interned during World War II; the Canadian apology for the Chinese Head Tax; multiple apologies to Aboriginal and Indigenous populations (including Australia, Canada, and the United States); the German Holocaust reparations; and the recent lawsuit brought forth by CARICOM.

28. Robin D. G. Kelley, *Freedom Dreams: The Black Radical Imagination* (New York: Beacon, 2003), 110.

29. Chin, "Should Caribbean Nations Be Compensated for the Legacy of Slavery?"

30. For a critique of state reparations, see Mitch Miyagawa's essay and documentary, both entitled "A Sorry State," in which he examines his familial history and the multiple apologies they have received from the Canadian government. Mitch Miyagawa, "A Sorry State," *Walrus*, December 12, 2009, updated May 1, 2017, https://thewalrus.ca/a-sorry-state/; Mitch Miyagawa, *A Sorry State* (Whitehorse, Canada: Up and Away Productions, 2012). For an example of reparations as reconciliation at the intersection of Asian Canadian and First Nations Studies in the Pacific Northwest, see Janey M. Lew, "In Place/Of Solidarity: Acknowledgement and Reciprocity with/in Indigenous and Asian Canadian Writing" (Ph.D. diss., University of California, Berkeley, 2018).

31. As Ylce Irizarry notes, the protagonist is also Puerto Rican and Ecuadorian, and he "prioritizes his *puertorriqueñidad* even though he is also Ecuadorian." Ylce Irizarry, "Because Place Still Matters: Mapping Puertorriquenidad in *Bodega Dreams*," *Centro Journal* 27, no. 1 (Spring 2015): 156.

32. See Antonia Domínguez Miguela, "Literary Tropicalizations of the Barrio: Ernesto Quiñonez's *Bodega Dreams* and Ed Vega's *Mendoza's Dreams*," in *Writing Off the Hyphen: New Perspectives on the Literature of the Puerto Rican Diaspora*, ed. José L. Torres-Padilla and Carmen Haydee Rivera (Seattle: University of Washington Press, 2008), 165–83; June Dwyer, "When Willie Met Gatsby: The Critical Implications of Ernesto Quiñonez's *Bodega Dreams*," *Lit: Literature Interpretation Theory* 14, no. 2 (2003): 165–78, https://doi.org/10.1080/10436920306616; Elena Machado Sáez, *Market Aesthetics: The Purchase of the Past in Caribbean Diasporic Fiction* (Charlottesville: University of Virginia Press, 2015); and Raphael Dalleo and Elena Machado Sáez, *The Latino/a Canon and the Emergence of Post-Sixties Literature* (New York: Palgrave Macmillan, 2007).

33. Arlene Dávila, "Dreams of Place: Housing, Gentrification, and the Marketing of Space in El Barrio," *Centro Journal* 15, no. 1 (March 2003): 114.

34. Arlene Dávila, *Barrio Dreams: Puerto Ricans, Latinos, and the Neoliberal City* (Berkeley: University of California Press, 2004), 9.

35. This statistic was accurate in 2004 when *Barrio Dreams* was published. Futhermore, Dávila notes that while there were no official statistics detailing the number of Puerto Ricans displaced by "urban renewal" the numbers were, "likely to be great, as indicated by the estimates from 1959–1961, when Puerto Ricans accounted for up to 76 percent of the people displaced from various urban renewal sites in the city" (31).

36. Dávila, *Barrio Dreams*, 58.

37. "*Nuyorican*" is a neologism for New York Rican or New York Puerto Rican. First pejoratively used to describe the generations of diasporic Puerto Ricans coming of age on the mainland (specifically New York City), it was then reclaimed by young poets, artists, and activists in the 1970s, who saw value in the kinds of diasporic life and culture being created by working-class and working-poor Puerto Rican communities. For more on the term, see Juan Flores, *From Bomba to Hip-Hop: Puerto Rican Culture and Latino Identity* (New York: Columbia University Press, 2000); Yolanda Martínez-San Miguel, "Coloniality of Diasporas: Racialization of Negropolitans and Nuyoricans in Paris and New York," in *Hispanic Caribbean Literature of Migration: Narratives of Displacement*, ed. Vanessa Pérez Rosario (New York: Palgrave Macmillan, 2010), 189–206; and Miriam Jiménez Román, "Boricuas vs. Nuyoricans—Indeed! A Look at Afro-Latinos," *ReVista: Harvard Review of Latin America* (Spring 2008): 8–11.

38. Irizarry, "Because Place Still Matters," 160.

39. Iris Morales, dir., *¡Pa'lante, Siempre Pa'lante! The Young Lords* (New York: Third World Newsreel, 1996).

40. Carmen Theresa Whalen, "Bridging Homeland and Barrio Politics: The Young Lords in Philadelphia," in *The Puerto Rican Movement: Voices from the Diaspora*, ed. Andrés Torres and José Velázquez (Philadelphia: Temple University Press, 1998), 107–23; Darrel Enck-Wanzer, ed., *The Young Lords: A Reader* (New York: NYU Press, 2010).

41. Lorde, *Sister Outsider*, 112.

42. Anthony Bogues, *Black Heretics, Black Prophets: Radical Political Intellectuals* (New York: Routledge, 2003).

43. Irizarry, "Because Place Still Matters," 169.

44. Irizarry, "Because Place Still Matters," 165.

45. See chapter 3 for more on these terms.

46. I use the term "community" tentatively, since Bodega's conception of community is tied both to the locality of Spanish Harlem and to the Puerto Rican diaspora. These two imagined communities—to borrow from Benedict Anderson—are points of pride for Bodega, and yet he remains unknown to them; the residents of Spanish Harlem do not know who "Bodega" actually is. Benedict Anderson, *Imagined Communities: Reflections on the Origin and Spread of Nationalism*, rev. ed. (London: Verso, 2016).

47. Combahee River Collective, *The Combahee River Collective Statement: Black Feminist Organizing in the Seventies and Eighties* (Latham, N.Y.: Kitchen Table/Women of Color, 1986).

48. Whalen, "Bridging Homeland and Barrio Politics," 120.

49. For more on the American Indian Movement and organizing within Native social and political movements, see Kim Anderson, "Affirmations of an Indigenous Feminist," in *Indigenous Women and Feminism: Politics, Activism,*

Culture, ed. Cheryl Suzack et al. (Vancouver, Canada: UBC Press, 2010), 81–91. For scholarship on the Chican@ Movement's struggles with gender, feminism, and leadership, see Maylei Blackwell, *¡Chicana Power! Contested Histories of Feminism in the Chicano Movement* (Austin: University of Texas Press, 2016).

50. Whalen, "Bridging Homeland and Barrio Politics," 120.

51. Whalen, "Bridging Homeland and Barrio Politics," 120.

52. Irizarry, "Because Place Still Matters," 162.

53. Vera/Veronica is perhaps the more elusive character, as she shapeshifts from an affectionate to a faithless lover. She has attained wealth through marriage, and holds onto the trappings of whiteness (for example, she changes her name from Vera to Veronica to escape her Puerto Rican/Nuyorican roots). She eventually colludes with Nazario to murder Bodega, and attempts to abscond with his properties and fortune.

54. I presented an early version of this chapter at the 2011 American Studies Association Conference in Baltimore, Maryland. In the audience was Juan Flores, one of the foremost scholars of Puerto Rican studies. During the Q&A and later in our post-panel discussion, Flores urged me to theorize the "Afro" in Afro-Latinx (at that point Afro-Latin@), and to be clear about which authors I characterize as Afro-Latino, versus having created Afro-Latino characters. Flores shared that in his own conversations with Quiñonez, the author allegedly denied having Afro-Latinx characters; in other words, he denied the novel as an Afro-Latinx cultural production. I agree with Ylce Irizarry, however, that Quiñonez uses racializing features for the characters in his novel.

55. Many thanks to Jason Chang for this insight. See Edna Bonacich, "A Theory of Middleman Minorities," *American Sociological Review* 38, no. 3 (October 1973): 583–94; Joe R. Feagin and Clairece Booher Feagin, *Racial and Ethnic Relations*, 7th ed. (Upper Saddle River, N.J.: Prentice Hall, 2003); and Alejandro Portes and Ruben Rumbaut, *Immigrant America: A Portrait* (Berkeley: University of California Press, 1990).

56. Solimar Otero, "Barrio, Bodega, and Botánica Aesthetics: The Layered Traditions of the Latino Imaginary," *Atlantic Studies* 4, no. 2 (2007): 188.

57. See Samiri Hernández Hiraldo, *Black Puerto Rican Identity and Religious Experience* (Gainesville: University Press of Florida, 2006).

58. Hubert M. Blalock, *Toward a Theory of Minority-Group Relations* (New York: Wiley, 1967).

59. Sandoval, *Methodology of the Oppressed*, 187.

60. "*Mira*, Junito, go buy *un mapo, un conten de leche*, and tell *el bodeguero yo le pago* next Friday. And I don't want to see you in *el rufo.*" Ernesto Quiñonez, Bodega Dreams (New York: Vintage, 2000), 212.

61. Yomaira C. Figueroa, "The Life Work of Ana Celia Zentella: Anthropolitical Linguistics, Bilingualism, and Linguistic Communities at a Crossroads," *CENTRO Journal* 28, no. 1 (Spring 2016): 152–71.

62. Maldonado-Torres, *Against War*, 244.

63. Monica Hanna, "'Reassembling the Fragments': Battling Historiographies, Caribbean Discourse, and Nerd Genres in Junot Díaz's *The Brief Wondrous Life of Oscar Wao*," *Callaloo* 33, no. 2 (March 2010): 498–520; Elena Machado Sáez, "Dictating Desire, Dictating Diaspora: Junot Díaz's *The Brief Wondrous Life of Oscar Wao* as Foundational Romance," *Contemporary Literature* 52, no. 3 (fall

2011): 522–55; Anne Garland Mahler, "The Writer as Superhero: Fighting the Colonial Curse in Junot Díaz's *The Brief Wondrous Life of Oscar Wao*," *Journal of Latin American Cultural Studies* 19, no. 2 (August 2010): 119–40, https://doi.org/10.1080/13569325.2010.494928; Ashley Kunsa, "History, Hair, and Reimagining Racial Categories in Junot Díaz's *The Brief Wondrous Life of Oscar Wao*," *Critique: Studies in Contemporary Fiction* 54, no. 2 (April 2013): 211–24, https://doi.org/10.1080/00111619.2011.574747.

64. Machado Sáez's reading of masculine queerness in *Oscar Wao* indicts the narrator, Yunior, as the orchestrator of Oscar's inability to belong to Dominican masculinity or the diasporic conception of maleness. It is Oscar's "sentimentality, virginity, and tears" that enable the reader to conceive him as queer, but it is also Yunior's hypermasculinity and his hyperawareness of its tenuous claims that compel him to narrate Oscar in such hopeless ways. Machado Sáez, "Dictating Desire, Dictating Diaspora," 534–35.

65. Moya, "The Search for Decolonial Love."

66. Moya, "The Search for Decolonial Love."

67. Taryne Jade Taylor, "A Singular Dislocation: An Interview with Junot Díaz," *Paradoxa* 26 (2014): 107.

68. Though *Oscar Wao* does not indicate Yunior's sexual abuse, in Díaz's first novel, *Drown* (1996), we read that seven-year-old Yunior is the victim of a sexual assault on a bus. This may or may not be the violence that Díaz attests to in his interview with Moya, but nevertheless, I believe the narrative arc of Yunior's own history of sexual abuse. Junot Díaz, *Drown* (New York: Riverhead, 1996).

69. Moya, "The Search for Decolonial Love."

70. Jennifer Harford Vargas, "Dictating a Zafa: The Power of Narrative Form in Junot Díaz's *The Brief Wondrous Life of Oscar Wao*," *MELUS* 39, no. 3 (July 2014): 16.

71. Harford Vargas makes a similar claim in "Dictating a Zafa."

72. Maldonado-Torres, "On the Coloniality of Being," 247.

73. Marvin Lewis writes that "Annobón and Malabo, as island populations, have been at the center of Equatorial Guinean island literary discourse for some time, but this is the first contemporary extended tribute to Corisco. While this assertion can be disputed, it bears to mention that the author of *Matinga, sangre en la selva* is not of Benga or Ndowé origin. This means that while this story emerges from within Benga cosmology, many Benga or Ndowé peoples may see this story as an ingenuine use of the myths and origin stories. The narrator speaks of its indigenous past, origins of its populations, cultural traditions, as well as the impact of colonialism. Although most of *Matinga, Blood in the Jungle* is devoted to the Río Muni mainland context of coastal 'playero' culture, the reader receives a good idea of the importance of Corisco to the national ethos." Lewis, *Equatorial Guinean Literature*, 128.

74. Lewis, *Equatorial Guinean Literature*, 111.

75. Lewis, *Equatorial Guinean Literature*, 138.

76. The novel's temporal and spatial location is at the very heart of the renewed interest of the Spanish in their sub-Saharan African colony. Spain lost its colonies in the Americas after its 1898 defeat in the Spanish-American War, which required a reassessment of its remaining colonies in northern and sub-Saharan Africa. The renewed focus on Equatorial Guinea meant that political decolonization for that

nation would not come until 1968; this was followed by Spain's transition from fascism to democracy in 1975. See Ugarte, *Africans in Europe*.

77. Lewis, *Equatorial Guinean Literature*, 127.

78. Lewis, *Equatorial Guinean Literature*, 128.

79. Anderson, "Affirmations of an Indigenous Feminist," 87.

80. This is also true of Black Nationalist movements. See Lauri Umansky, "The Sister Reply: Black Nationalist Pronatalism, Black Feminism, and the Quest for a Multiracial Women's Movement, 1965–1974," *Critical Matrix* 8 (December 1994): 19–50.

81. Anderson, "Affirmations of an Indigenous Feminist," 87.

82. Naomi Nkealah, "(West) African Feminisms and Their Challenges," *Journal of Literary Studies* 32, no. 2 (2016): 62.

83. Filomena Steady, "African Feminism: A Worldwide Perspective," in *Women in Africa and the African Diaspora*, ed. R. TerborgPenn, S. Harley, and R. Benton Rushing (Washington, D.C.: Howard University Press, 1987).

84. Lewis, *Equatorial Guinean Literature*, 133.

85. Anderson, "Affirmations of an Indigenous Feminist," 87.

86. See also the interpretation of this novel within the Mami-Wata myths which Marvin Lewis does in chapter 4 of *Equatorial Guinean Literature in Its National and Transnational Contexts*.

87. Anderson, "Affirmations of an Indigenous Feminist," 88.

88. Virginia Fons. "Algunas consideraciones teóricas a propósito de la concepción de la salud procreativa de las mujeres ndowe de Guinea Ecuatorial," *Revista Epàta-Ekulàko: Comuniad Global Ndowe de Guinea Ecuatorial,* Numero Especial (October 2012): 24. See also Sarah Lázare and Virginia Fons. "Los procesos procreativos desde la antropología: El caso de las madres de Barcelona por un parto respetado," *Quaderns-e de l'Institut Català d'Antropologia* 21, no. 2 (2016): 21–37.

89. Moya, "The Search for Decolonial Love."

Chapter 5

1. Wynter, "Unsettling the Coloniality," 257–337, https://doi.org/10/1353/ncr.2004.0015.

2. Katherine McKittrick, ed., *Sylvia Wynter: On Being Human as Praxis* (Durham, N.C.: Duke University Press, 2014).

3. Anzaldúa, *Borderlands/La Frontera*, 3; Frances Negrón-Muntaner, "Bridging Islands: Gloria Anzaldúa and the Caribbean," *PMLA* 121, no. 1 (January 2006): 272–78, https://doi.org/10.1632/003081206X129792.

4. See Nelson Maldonado-Torres's analysis of the non-ethics of modernity as creating a state of perpetual war in *Against War: Views from the Underside of Modernity*.

5. With this formulation, I also hail the politics and possibilities of the #BlackLivesMatter movement.

6. Christina Sharpe, *In the Wake: On Blackness and Being* (Durham, N.C.: Duke University Press, 2016), 18.

7. Juan Tomás Ávila Laurel, *Panga Rilene* (Madrid: Calambur, 2016).

8. Roundtable discussion, III Seminario Internacional sobre Guinea Ecuatorial, Universidad Nacional de Educación a Distancia, Madrid, Spain, July 6, 2016;

Interview with the author, July 7, 2016. Ávila Laurel later asked for fiction, criticism, and scholarly readings about Afrofuturism.

9. Alondra Nelson, "Introduction: Future Texts," in special issue, "Afrofuturism," ed. Alondra Nelson, *Social Text* 20, no. 2 (71) (Summer 2002): 9.

10. Catherine S. Ramírez was one of the first scholars to write about Chicanafuturism in her 2008 piece "Afrofuturism/Chicanafuturism: Fictive Kin," *Aztlán: A Journal of Chicano Studies* 33, no. 1 (Spring 2008): 185–94. She has been followed by more recent scholarship, including the work of Lysa Rivera and Catheryn Josefina Merla-Watson. See Cathryn Josefina Merla-Watson and B. V. Olguín, "Introduction: ¡Latin@futurism Ahora! Recovering, Remapping, and Recentering the Chican@ and Latin@ Speculative Arts," *Aztlán: A Journal of Chicano Studies* 40, no. 2 (fall 2015): 135–46.

11. Using digital platforms and blogging in Trinidad and Tobago as a case study, Tonya Haynes finds that "online Caribbean feminisms are extremely diverse, heterogeneous, and polyvocal. Networks may be simultaneously regional, national, and global, or transnational and diasporic." Through digital media practices, Caribbean feminists "knit together online communities that are often linked to on-the-ground organizing and action." Tonya Haynes, "Mapping Caribbean Cyberfeminisms," *sx archipelagos* no. 1 (May 2016).

12. Junot Díaz, "Monstro," *The New Yorker*, June 4, 2012, https://www.newyorker.com/magazine/2012/06/04/monstro.

13. Ibeyi, *Ibeyi* (London: XL Recordings, 2015); Daniel José Older, *Shadowshaper (The Shadowshaper Cypher Series #1)* (New York: Scholastic, 2015).

14. Alexander, *Pedagogies of Crossing*, 14–15.

15. Edwin David Aponte, *¡Santo! Varieties of Latino/a Spirituality* (Maryknoll, N.Y.: Orbis Books, 2012), 28.

16. Migene González-Wippler, *Santería: The Religion, Faith, Rites, Magic* (Woodbury, Minn.: Llewellyn Worldwide, 1994), 40–44.

17. Miguel A. De La Torre, *Santería: The Beliefs and Rituals of a Growing Religion in America* (Grand Rapids, Mich.: Eerdmans, 2004), 84. He explains, "As male twins they are Taewo and Kainde, Ibbo and Iwe, or Alawa Akuario and Eddeu. As female twins, they are Olori and Oroina, or Ayaba and Alba. As male and female twins, they are Araba and Ainá, or Adden and Alabba" (84).

18. González-Wippler, *Santería*, 142; De La Torre, *Santería*, 84.

19. Aisha M. Beliso-De Jesús, *Electric Santería: Racial and Sexual Assemblages of Transnational Religion* (New York: Columbia University Press, 2015), 5. See also Robert Farris Thompson, *Flash of the Spirit: African and Afro-American Art and Philosophy* (New York: Vintage Books, 1983).

20. González-Wippler, *Santería*, 28–33.

21. Ibeyi, "Oya," *Ibeyi* (London: XL Recordings, 2015).

22. George Ciccariello-Maher, *Decolonizing Dialectics* (Durham, N.C.: Duke University Press, 2017), 2.

23. Ibeyi, "Ghosts," *Ibeyi* (London: XL Recordings, 2015).

24. Ngũgĩ wa Thiong'o, *Something Torn and New: An African Renaissance* (New York: Basic Books, 2009).

25. Edward Kamau Brathwaite quoted in Ngũgĩ, *Something Torn and New,* 49.

26. Ngũgĩ, *Something Torn and New,* 39.

27. Ngũgĩ, *Something Torn and New,* 39.

28. Paul Joesph López Oro, "Digitizing Ancestral Memory: Garifuna Settlement Day in the Americas and in Cyberspace," in *Indigenous Interfaces: Spaces, Technology, and Social Networks in Mexico and Central America*, ed. Arturo Arias (University of Arizona Press, 2019).

29. Jennifer L. Morgan, "*Partus sequitur ventrem*: Law, Race, and Reproduction in Colonial Slavery," *Small Axe: A Caribbean Journal of Criticism* 22, no. 1 (55) (March 2018): 1–17, https://doi.org/10.1215/07990537-4378888; Rebecca J. Scott, "Gradual Abolition and the Dynamics of Slave Emancipation in Cuba, 1868–1886," *Hispanic American Historical Review* 63, no. 3 (August 1983): 449–77.

30. Mario Gallo, dir., *Al compás de Cuba* (Havana: Instituto Cubano del Arte e Industria Cinematográficos, 1960), https://www.youtube.com/watch?v=QuI_aiDacRo.

31. Tito Rodríguez, vocalist, "Llora Timbero," *El Doctor de la Salsa* (Un Latino, 1968).

32. The translation of these lyrics is my own, sourced from Tito Rodríguez's 1968 cover of the song from his album *El Doctor de la Salsa*. This was the version of the song that I grew up listening to and that I began listening to again when writing this section on Ibeyi. Rodríguez's version of "Llora Timbero" uses the present-tense verb "viene" whereas earlier versions, for example, the circa 1934 recording of "Malanga murió" by the Orquesta Cheo Belen Puig, use the past tense "vino." There are other versions of this song with freestyle verses, a single singer, and/or with choral unison throughout.

33. Gallo, *Al compás de Cuba*.

34. EcuRed, "José Rosario Oviedo," https://www.ecured.cu/José_Rosario_Oviedo.

35. Diego Del Pozo, "Heterotopías insulares: Identidad y resistencia en el teatro de Alberto Pedro" (Ph.D. diss., University of Georgia, 2008).

36. See "Sisters in Arms" in Audre Lorde, *Our Dead Behind Us: Poems* (New York: W. W. Norton, 1986).

37. Liz Tracy, "Ibeyi Mixes Music and Santería to Make Something Truly Original," *Miami New Times*, February 21, 2017.

38. Michelle Cliff, *If I Could Write This in Fire* (Minneapolis: University of Minnesota Press, 2008), 87.

39. Katherine McKittrick, *Demonic Grounds: Black Women and the Cartographies of Struggle* (Minneapolis: University of Minnesota Press, 2016), 32.

40. Wynter, "1492: A New World View," 5–57; Nishitani Osamu, "Anthropos and Humanitas: Two Western Concepts of 'Human Being,'" in *Translation, Biopolitics, Colonial Difference*, ed. Naoki Sakai and Jon Solomon (Aberdeen, Hong Kong: Hong Kong University Press, 2006), 259–74.

41. Ibeyi, "Ghosts."

42. Ibeyi, "River," *Ibeyi* (London: XL Recordings, 2015).

43. Ibeyi, "Thinking of You," *Ibeyi* (London: XL Recordings, 2015).

44. Beliso-De Jesús, *Electric Santería*, 82.

45. Alexander, *Pedagogies of Crossing*, 288.

46. Alexander, *Pedagogies of Crossing*, 296.

47. "If Africa functions largely as an epistemic gap," says Alexander, "then its cosmological systems cannot be made to figure legitimately in (post)modernity's

consciousness . . . And yet some of its most formative categories—migration, gender, and sexuality, experience, home, history, and memory—can be made intelligible within these very systems" (*Pedagogies of Crossing*, 297).

48. The second novel in the *Shadowhouse Fall* trilogy was published in 2017: Daniel José Older, *Shadowhouse Fall (The Shadowshaper Cypher Series #2)* (New York: Scholastic, 2017).

49. Mensah Demary, "A Conversation with Daniel José Older," *Specter*, April 21, 2014, http://www.spectermagazine.com/interviews/older/; Matt Staggs, "Author Daniel José Older Talks Santeria, Cockroach Men, and Changing Minds through Fiction," *Unbound Worlds*, November 2, 2016, https://www.unboundworlds.com/2015/10/author-daniel-jose-older-talks-santeria-cockroach-men-and-changing-minds-through-fiction/.

50. Recent publications include Erika L. Sánchez, *I Am Not Your Perfect Mexican Daughter* (New York: Alfred A. Knopf, 2017); Lilliam Rivera, *The Education of Margot Sanchez* (New York: Simon and Schuster, 2017); and Elizabeth Acevedo, *The Poet X* (New York: HarperCollins, 2018).

51. Xhercis Méndez, "Transcending Dimorphism: Afro-Cuban Ritual Praxis and the Rematerialization of the Body," *Journal for Cultural and Religious Theory* 13, no. 1 (Winter 2014): 115. She further explains, "For instance, Orishas as ashé are capable of inhabiting everything from stones to the variated 'bodies' of their initiates. The capacity to manifest in various material forms, then, suggests that the Orishas are not only fluid, but also capable of shape-shifting" (108).

52. Alexander, *Pedagogies of Crossing*, 296.

53. Lulu García-Navarro, "Brooklyn Is Magical in 'Shadowhouse Fall,' " NPR, September 17, 2017, https://www.npr.org/2017/09/17/551604574/brooklyn-is-magical-in-shadowhouse-fall.

54. Méndez, "Transcending Dimorphism," 115. Méndez argues that "this openness to invisible forces calls practitioners to conceive of their 'bodies' as protean, as a shape-shifter of sorts. . . . This often entails both metaphysical and physical transformations in those being inhabited" (116).

55. Older does away with the logics of seniority, heteropatriarchy, and white supremacy in order to create a world in which Sierra, a novice, is to inherit the role of the most powerful shadowshaper. Her race, gender, age, and sex do not inhibit her from taking up these responsibilities, and her community of expert and apprentice shadowshapers supports her efforts.

56. Kelvin Santiago-Valles, "Policing the Crisis in the Whitest of All the Antilles," *CENTRO: Journal of the Center for Puerto Rican Studies* 8, no. 1–2 (1996): 43–55; Petra R. Rivera-Rideau, " 'If I Were You': Tego Calderón's Diasporic Interventions," *Small Axe: A Caribbean Journal of Criticism* 22, no. 1 (55) (March 2018): 55–69, https://doi.org/10.1215/07990537-4378924.

57. Carlos Pozzi, "Race, Ethnicity, and Color among Latinos in the United States," in *This Side of Heaven: Race, Ethnicity, and Christian Faith*, ed. Robert J. Priest and Alvaro L. Nieves (New York: Oxford University Press, 2007), 52. See also Suzanne Oboler and Anani Dzidzienyo, *Neither Enemies nor Friends: Latinos, Blacks, Afro-Latinos* (New York: Palgrave Macmillan, 2005).

58. Ylce Irizarry, "Because Place Still Matters: Mapping Puertorriqueñidad in *Bodega Dreams*," *Centro Journal* 27, no. 1 (2015): 152–85.

59. Sandoval, *Methodology of the Oppressed*, 182.

60. Alexander, *Pedagogies of Crossing*, 220.

61. In *Pedagogies of Crossing*, Alexander frames the difficulties of practicing the Mojuba in spaces that are teeming with overlapping and contested histories as "living an ancient memory in a city overcrowded with errant spirits, teeming with yearnings not easily satisfied in towering buildings or in slabs of concrete" (287).

62. Méndez, "Transcending Dimorphism," 108.

63. Junot Díaz, "Apocalypse: What Disasters Reveal," *Boston Review*, May 1, 2011, 46, http://bostonreview.net/junot-diaz-apocalypse-haiti-earthquake.

64. Cliff, *If I Could Write This in Fire*, 87.

65. Aimé Césaire, *Discourse on Colonialism* (New York: NYU Press, 2001), 36.

66. Paula M. L. Moya, "The Search for Decolonial Love: An Interview with Junot Díaz," *Boston Review*, June 26, 2012, http://bostonreview.net/books-ideas/paula-ml-moya-decolonial-love-interview-junot-d%C3%ADaz.

67. The 2012 short story appeared as a teaser for his now-abandoned sci-fi novel.

68. Césaire, *Discourse on Colonialism*, 31.

69. The protagonist learns that Alex's friend (and the protagonist's unrequited love interest) Mysty had been raped by her father until the age of twelve. The dimension of sexual exploitation in "Monstro" becomes part of understanding the coloniality of gender—"In the D.R. incest was like the other national pastime."

70. García-Peña, *Borders of Dominicanidad*, 10.

71. Alex joins the ranks of what Díaz calls the "Sovereign kids," generally independent and wealthy offspring of the Dominican elite who go to the Dominican Republic to enjoy luxurious summers and then return to U.S. universities to earn their elite degrees.

72. Josefina Báez, *Levente no: Yolayorkdominicanyork* (New York: Ay Ombe Theatre, 2011). See also chapter 3 of this book for a discussion of "*ni de aquí ni de allá*."

73. García-Peña, *Borders of Dominicanidad*, 4–6.

74. Mysty is a transnational Dominican who grew up in Montreal and is back in the Dominican Republic against her will. Her Francophile ways are documented by her impeccable French, her French novels, and her ultimate goal of working for the United Nations in France. For these elites, the cultural capital of wealth and family connections coupled with the cultural nationalism that Alex exhibits (a pride of country) are allegiances too small to combat the inferiority complex of being Dominican. What sets this story in motion is that the protagonist decides to stay in the Dominican Republic to win her over.

75. This is also the way that *Drown*, Díaz's first book of short stories, begins. The protagonist's older brother, Rafa, is making fun of Yunior, telling him that he was picked up at the Haitian/Dominican border. Junot Díaz, *Drown* (New York: Riverhead, 1996).

76. The biblical verse cited on the photo caption concludes, "Therefore the LORD will give you flesh, and ye shall eat."

77. Césaire, *Discourse on Colonialism*, 42.

78. George Lamming, *The Pleasures of Exile* (Ann Arbor: University of Michigan Press, 1992); Sylvia Wynter, "Afterword: Beyond Miranda's Meanings: Un/

silencing the 'Demonic Ground' of Caliban's 'Woman,'" in *Out of the Kumbla: Caribbean Women and Literature*, ed. Carol Boyce Davies and Elaine Savory Fido (Trenton, N.J.: Africa World, 1990), 355–72; Edward Kamau Brathwaite, *History of the Voice: The Development of Nation Language in Anglophone Caribbean Poetry* (London: New Beacon, 1984).

79. Roberto Fernández Retamar, "Calibán: Notes toward a Discussion of Culture in Our Americas," *Massachusetts Review* 15, no. 1/2 (Winter/Spring, 1974): 6.

80. Fernández Retamar, "Calibán," 7. Fernández Retamar's "Calibán" offers a literary historiography of Caliban and *The Tempest* across the Caribbean, Latin America, and Europe. Similarly, in *The Pleasures of Exile,* George Lamming posits that "Caliban *is* Man and *other* than Man. Caliban is his [Próspero's] convert, colonized by language, and excluded by language" (15). Furthermore, Prospero requires Caliban for his own survival. Caliban is a laboring body, and he is the figure through which Prospero gets to define himself as Man and as monarch. Lamming contends that "Prospero dare not dynamite Caliban. . . . To murder Caliban would be an act of pure suicide" (99). In "Monstro," the "dynamiting" of the Other is an act with both immediate and unknowable consequences that creates the conditions for apocalypse. As colonialism dehumanizes the colonizer, so too does Caliban haunt Prospero—"in a way that is almost too deep and too intimate to communicate" (Lamming, *Pleasures of Exile*, 99).

81. Armando García, "Freedom as Praxis: Migdalia Cruz's *Fur* and the Emancipation of Caliban's Woman," *Modern Drama* 59, no. 3 (Fall 2016): 343–62, https://doi.org/10.3138/md.0705R. See also Silvia Federici, *Caliban and the Witch* (Brooklyn, N.Y.: Autonomedia, 2004).

82. García, "Freedom as Praxis," 345.

83. García, "Freedom as Praxis," 346.

84. Ávila Laurel has said that *Panga Rilene* is just a story that came to him while traveling in Southeast Asia. When asked about the possibility of the work being Afrofuturistic, he replied that he had never heard of the genre, but was interested to know more about what it was and what it meant.

85. An ecocritical reading of Equatoguinean literature and of Juan Tomás Ávila Laurel's work in particular is beyond the scope of this project, but would be a worthwhile endeavor.

86. Díaz, "Apocalypse."

87. Kyle Powys Whyte, "Living in Our Ancestors' Dystopia: Indigenous Research Confronts Climate Change," NPM Media Centre, November 18, 2016, http://mediacentre.maramatanga.ac.nz/content/professor-kyle-powys-whyte-potawatomi. See also Kyle P. Whyte, "Indigenous Science (Fiction) for the Anthropocene: Ancestral Dystopias and Fantasies of Climate Change Crises," *Environment and Planning E: Nature and Space* 1, no. 1–2 (May 2018): 224–42, https://doi.org/10.1177/2514848618777621.

88. Confusion abounds when a dozen white men, and later a dozen Black men, arrive in uniforms. They are thought to be the disappeared brothers of the children in NE. They demand an audience with the women in the beam structure. In response to this perceived threat, Panga's mother bares her breast and the men, struck with fear, flee. Panga believes they are suffering from trypophobia, a fear of holes, which foretells her mother's own illness. The story ends with Panga's mother leaving NE, and Panga finds out that her mother is not from NE at all but

rather from that gluttonous place where the rich and powerful dominate others. Her mother left "that place" to come to NE, and in the end, returns to that other place.

89. There are many passages in the novel wherein Panga questions if she is in an anatomically female or male body, and there is an entire subplot in which she dresses like a man and visits bordellos in Singapore, Manila, and other Asian Pacific and Southeast Asian locales. There is a sense that global geographies and cores/peripheries have shifted as well, but this is beyond the scope of this chapter, even as it mirrors some of the geopolitical shifts in Díaz's "Monstro."

90. Díaz, "Apocalypse," 46.

91. Fanon, *Black Skin, White Masks*, 206.

92. Fanon, *Black Skin, White Masks*, 206.

93. See chapter 4 of this book for more on decolonial love as a practice and as a form of reparation.

94. Sandoval, *Methodology of the Oppressed*, 4 and chapter 6; Fanon, *Black Skin, White Masks.*

95. Derek Walcott, "The Sea Is History," in *Collected Poems: 1948–1984* (New York: Farrar, Straus and Giroux, 1986), 364–67; Édouard Glissant, *Caribbean Discourse: Selected Essays*, trans, J. Michael Dash (Charlottesville: University of Virginia Press, 1989).

96. Díaz, *Oscar Wao*, 51.

Coda

1. Angelique V. Nixon, "'Relating across Difference': Caribbean Feminism, bell hooks, and Michelle Cliff's Radical Black Subjectivity," in The *Caribbean Woman Writer as Scholar: Creating, Imagining, Theorizing*, ed. Keshia N. Abraham (Coral Springs, Fla.: Caribbean Studies, 2009), 331–73.

2. Aurora Levins Morales, *Medicine Stories: History, Culture, and the Politics of Integrity* (Boston: South End, 1998), 26.

3. Kristie Dotson, "Radical Love: Black Philosophy as Deliberate Acts of Inheritance," *Black Scholar* 43, no. 4 (Winter 2013): 38.

4. Dotson, "Radical Love," 39.

5. Dotson, "Radical Love," 38.

6. Aaron Pinnix, "Sargassum in the Black Atlantic: Entanglement and the Abyss in Bearden, Walcott, and Philip," *Atlantic Studies* (2018): 4, https://doi.org/10.1080/14788810.2018.1510700.

7. Antonio Benítez-Rojo, *The Repeating Island: The Caribbean and the Postmodern Perspective* (Durham, N.C.: Duke University Press, 1996), 16.

8. Nelson Maldonado-Torres, "The Decolonial Turn," trans. Robert Cavooris, in *New Approaches to Latin American Studies: Culture and Power*, ed. Juan Poblete (New York: Routledge, 2017), 120.

9. Rebeca Hey-Colón, "Transformative Currents: An Exploration of the Sea and Identity in the Works of Angie Cruz and Nelly Rosario," in *Negotiating Latinidades, Understanding Identities within Space*, ed. Kathryn Quinn-Sánchez (Newcastle upon Tyne, Eng.: Cambridge Scholars, 2015), 9.

10. Ilombe, *Ceiba II*.

11. Her book *Ceiba* was first published in 1978. See Raquel Ilombe del Pozo Epita, *Ceiba* (Madrid: Editorial Madrid, 1978).

12. Benita Sampedro Vizcaya, "Preamble," in Ilombe, *Ceiba II*, 19–20.
13. Ilombe, Ceiba II, 148–49.
14. Ilombe, Ceiba II, 202–3.
15. Ilombe, Ceiba II, 252.
16. Aracelis Girmay, *The Black Maria* (Rochester, N.Y.: BOA Editions, 2016).
17. Walcott, "The Sea Is History," 364–67; M. NourbeSe Philip and Setaey Adamu Boateng, *Zong!* (Middletown, Conn.: Wesleyan University Press, 2008); Sally Price and Richard Price, *Romare Bearden: The Caribbean Dimension* (Philadelphia: University of Pennsylvania Press, 2006); Dionne Brand, *A Map to the Door of No Return: Notes to Belonging* (Toronto: Vintage Canada, 2001).
18. Forché, ed., *Against Forgetting*.
19. Walcott, "The Sea Is History."
20. María Magdalena Campos-Pons and Okwui Enwezor, *María Magdalena Campos-Pons: Everything Is Separated by Water* (New Haven, Conn.: Yale University Press, 2007), 72.
21. Campos-Pons and Enwezor, *María Magdalena Campos-Pons*, 70.
22. Salon Literario's Festival de la Palabra is created by the Afro-Puerto Rican writer and professor Mayra Santos Febres.
23. The fact that Remei Sipi Mayo and another writer, Edjanga Jones Ndjoli, were participants in the Festival de la Palabra that year felt like my book project in practice: relations across Afro-Atlantic Hispanophone islands.

BIBLIOGRAPHY

Acevedo, Elizabeth. *The Poet X*. New York: HarperCollins, 2018.

Acosta-Belén, Edna, and Carlos E. Santiago. *Puerto Ricans in the United States: A Contemporary Portrait*. Boulder, Colo.: Lynne Rienner, 2006.

Adams, Megan. "'A Border Is a Veil Not Many People Can Wear': Testimonial Fiction and Transnational Healing in Edwidge Danticat's *The Farming of Bones* and Nelly Rosario's *Song of the Water Saints*." Master's thesis, University of South Florida, 2010.

Akpan, Dominic A., and Bassey Inyang. "Economic Diplomacy, Global Waste Trade: The African Perspective since the 20th Century." *African Journal of History and Archeology* 2 (2016): 1–10.

Alexander, M. Jacqui. *Pedagogies of Crossing: Meditations on Feminism, Sexual Politics, Memory, and the Sacred*. Durham, N.C.: Duke University Press, 2005.

———. "Remembering This Bridge, Remembering Ourselves: Yearning, Memory, and Desire." In *This Bridge We Call Home: Radical Visions for Transformation*, edited by Gloria E. Anzaldúa and AnaLouise Keating, 81–103. New York: Routledge, 2013.

Allen, Jafari S. *¡Venceremos? The Erotics of Black Self-Making in Cuba*. Durham, N.C.: Duke University Press, 2011.

Anderson, Benedict. *Imagined Communities: Reflections on the Origin and Spread of Nationalism*. Revised edition. London: Verso, 2016.

Anderson, Kim. "Affirmations of an Indigenous Feminist." In *Indigenous Women and Feminism: Politics, Activism, Culture*, edited by Cheryl Suzack, Shari M. Huhndorg, Jeanne Perreault, and Jean Barman, 81–91. Vancouver, Can.: UBC, 2010.

Ankomah, Baffour. "African Wasteland." *Index on Censorship* 18, no. 6–7 (1989): 34–37.

Anzaldúa, Gloria. *Borderlands/La Frontera: The New Mestiza*. San Francisco: Aunt Lute Books, 1987.

Aparicio, Frances R. "On Subversive Signifiers: US Latina/o Writers Tropicalize English." *American Literature* 66, no. 4 (December 1994): 795–801.

Aponte, Edwin David. *¡Santo! Varieties of Latino/a Spirituality*. Maryknoll, N.Y.: Orbis Books, 2012.

Ávila Laurel, Juan Tomás. *Arde el monte de noche*. Valencia, Spain: Calambur Editorial, 2009.

———. *Awala cu sangui*. Malabo, Equatorial Guinea: Ediciones Pángola, 2000.

———. *By Night the Mountain Burns*. Translated by Jethro Soutar. New York: And Other Stories, 2014.

———. *El dictador de Corisco*. Malabo, Equatorial Guinea: Ediciones Pángola, 2014.

———. *La carga*. Valencia, Spain: Palmart, 1999.

———. *Panga Rilene*. Barcelona: Calambur, 2016.

Ayuso, Mónica G. "'How Lucky for You That Your Tongue Can Taste the 'r' in 'Parsley': Trauma Theory and the Literature of Hispaniola." *Afro-Hispanic Review* 30, no. 1 (Spring 2011): 47–62.

Báez, Josefina. *Levente no: Yolayorkdominicanyork*. New York: Ay Ombe Theatre, 2011.

Barker, Joanne. "Territory as Analytic: The Dispossession of Lenapehoking and the Subprime Crisis." *Social Text* 36, no. 2 (135) (June 2018): 19–39. https://doi.org/10.1215/01642472-4362337.

Baucom, Ian. *Specters of the Atlantic: Finance Capital, Slavery, and the Philosophy of History*. Durham, N.C.: Duke University Press, 2005.

Beckles, Hilary. "Capitalism, Slavery, and Caribbean Modernity." *Callaloo* 20, no. 4 (Fall 1997): 777–89.

Beldarraín Chaple, Enrique. "La salud pública en Cuba y su experiencia internacional (1959–2005)." *História, Ciências, Saúde-Manguinhos* 13, no. 3 (2006): 709–16.

Beliso-De Jesús, Aisha M. *Electric Santería: Racial and Sexual Assemblages of Transnational Religion*. New York: Columbia University Press, 2015.

Benítez-Rojo, Antonio. *The Repeating Island: The Caribbean and the Postmodern Perspective*. Durham, N.C.: Duke University Press, 1996.

Bergad, Laird. "Have Dominicans Surpassed Puerto Ricans to Become New York City's Largest Latino Nationality? An Analysis of Latino Population Data from the 2013 American Community Survey for New York City and the Metropolitan Area." Center for Latin American, Caribbean, and Latino Studies at the CUNY Graduate Center, 2014. http://clacls.gc.cuny.edu/ files/2014/11/AreDominicansLargestLatinoNationality.pdf.

Blackwell, Maylei. *¡Chicana Power! Contested Histories of Feminism in the Chicano Movement*. Austin: University of Texas Press, 2016.

Blalock, Hubert M. *Toward a Theory of Minority-Group Relations*. New York: Wiley, 1967.

Boampong, Joanna, ed. *In and Out of Africa: Exploring Afro-Hispanic, Luso-Brazilian, and Latin-American Connections*. Newcastle upon Tyne, Eng.: Cambridge Scholars, 2012.

Bogues, Anthony. *Black Heretics, Black Prophets: Radical Political Intellectuals*. New York: Routledge, 2003.

Bonacich, Edna. "A Theory of Middleman Minorities." *American Sociological Review* 38, no. 3 (October 1973): 583–94.

Bonilla-Silva, Eduardo. *Racism without Racists: Color-Blind Racism and the Persistence of Racial Inequality in America*. Lanham, Md.: Rowman and Littlefield, 2017.

Boxill, Bernard. "Black Reparations." In *The Stanford Encyclopedia of Philosophy*, edited by Edward N. Zalta. Stanford, Calif.: Stanford University, 2011. http://plato.stanford.edu/archives/spr2011/entries/black-reparations/.

Brand, Dionne. *A Map to the Door of No Return: Notes to Belonging*. Toronto: Vintage Canada, 2001.

Brathwaite, Edward Kamau. *The Arrivants: A New World Trilogy—Rights of Passage Island Masks*. New York: Oxford University Press, 1988.

———. *History of the Voice: The Development of Nation Language in Anglophone Caribbean Poetry*. London: New Beacon, 1984.

Brooke, James. "Waste Dumpers Turning to West Africa." *New York Times*, July 17, 1988. https://www.nytimes.com/1988/07/17/world/waste-dumpers-turning-to-west-africa.html.

Brookie, Parker. "In Review: *La Bastarda* by Trifonia Melibea Obono." *Asymptote* (blog), May 21, 2018. https://www.asymptotejournal.com/blog/2018/05/21/in-review-la-bastarda-by-trifonia-melibea-obono/.

Brown, Jacqueline Nassy. "Black Liverpool, Black America, and the Gendering of Diasporic Space." *Cultural Anthropology* 13, no. 3 (August 1998): 291–325.

Buchanan, B. B. "Women and Femmes Unite: A Structural and Political Analysis of Femininity." Wear Your Voice. March 21, 2018. https://wearyourvoicemag.com/lgbtq-identities/women-and-femmes-femininity.

Butler, Kim D. "Defining Diaspora, Refining a Discourse." *Diaspora: A Journal of Transnational Studies* 10, no. 2 (Fall 2001): 189–219.

Butler, Tamara T. "#Say[ing] Her Name as Critical Demand: English Education in the Age of Erasure." *English Education* 49, no. 2 (2017): 153–78.

———. "What Do We Owe the Dead? Making Space for Humanizing Pedagogies." Lecture presented at the Responsibility of Teachers in the Wake of Racial Violence Teach-In, Michigan State University, East Lansing, Mich., August 29, 2015.

Byrd, Jodi A. "'Variations under Domestication': Indigeneity and the Subject of Dispossession." *Social Text* 36, no. 2 (135) (June 2018): 123–41. https://doi.org/10.1215/01642472-4362397.

Caldeira, Arlindo Manuel. "Organizing Freedom: De Facto Independence on the Island of Ano Bom (Annobón) during the Eighteenth and Nineteenth Centuries." *Afro-Hispanic Review* 28, no. 2 (2009): 293–310.

Callahan, Laura. *Spanish/English Codeswitching in a Written Corpus*. Amsterdam: John Benjamins, 2004.

Caminero-Santangelo, Marta. "'Puerto Rican Negro': Defining Race in Piri Thomas's *Down These Mean Streets*." *MELUS* 29, no. 2 (2004): 205–26.

Campos, Alicia. "The Decolonization of Equatorial Guinea: The Relevance of the International Factor." *Journal of African History* 44, no. 1 (2003): 95–116.

Campos-Pons, María Magdalena, and Okwui Enwezor. *María Magdalena Campos-Pons: Everything Is Separated by Water*. New Haven, Conn.: Yale University Press, 2007.

Campos Serrano, Alicia. *Petróleo y estado postcolonial: Transformaciones de la economía política en Guinea Ecuatorial, 1995–2010; Implicaciones para la coherencia de políticas españolas*. Madrid: CeALCI-Fundación Carolina, 2011.

Campoy-Cubillo, Adolfo, and Benita Sampedro Vizcaya. "Entering the Global Hispanophone: An Introduction." *Journal of Spanish Cultural Studies* 20, nos. 1–2 (2019): 1–16.

Campt, Tina. "The Crowded Space of Diaspora: Intercultural Address and the Tensions of Diasporic Relation." *Radical History Review* 83, no. 1 (2002): 94–113.

———. *Listening to Images*. Durham, N.C.: Duke University Press, 2017.

Candelario, Ginetta E. B. *Black behind the Ears: Dominican Racial Identity from Museums to Beauty Shops*. Durham, N.C.: Duke University Press, 2007.

———. "Voices from Hispaniola: A Meridians Roundtable with Edwidge Danticat, Loida Maritza Pérez, Myriam J. A. Chancy, and Nelly Rosario." *Meridians: Feminism, Race, Transnationalism* 5, no. 1 (January 2004): 69–91.

CARICOM Secretariat. "CARICOM Reparations Commission Press Statement Delivered by Professor Sir Hilary Beckles (Chairman) on behalf of the CARICOM Reparations Commission Press Conference Regional Headquarters." Press release no. 285/2013. December 10, 2013. https://caricom.org/media-center/communications/press-releases/caricom-reparations-commission-press-statement-delivered-by-professor-sir-h.

Castillo-Rodriguez, Susana. "African Diaspora and the Circulation of Language: Cuba and Afro-Cuban Loanwords in Equatorial Guinea." *International Journal of the Sociology of Language* 2016, no. 239 (May 2016): 157–92.

Castro, Eliana. "From the Entrails of the Monster." Unpublished paper submitted to Yomaira Figueroa, Chicano/Latino Studies 811, Michigan State University, East Lansing, Mich., October 4, 2018.

Celaya Carrillo, Beatriz. "Atlántico negro y africano: Travesías de Inongo-Vi-Makomè, Maximiliano Nkogo Esono y César A. Mba Abogo." *TRANSMODERNITY: Journal of Peripheral Cultural Production of the Luso-Hispanic World* 7, no. 2 (Spring 2017): 139–64.

Celis Salgado, Nadia. *La rebelión de las niñas: El Caribe y la "conciencia corporal."* Madrid: Iberoamericana, 2015.

Césaire, Aimé. *Discourse on Colonialism*. New York: NYU Press, 2001.

Chancy, Myriam J. A. "Subversive Sexualities: Revolutionizing Gendered Identities." *Frontiers: A Journal of Women Studies* 29, no. 1 (2008): 51–75.

Chen, Linda. "The Old and Mysterious Practice of Eating Dirt, Revealed." *NPR*, April 2, 2014. https://www.npr.org/sections/thesalt/2014/04/02/297881388/the-old-and-mysterious-practice-of-eating-dirt-revealed.

Chevalier, Victoria A. "Alternative Visions and the Souvenir Collectible in Nelly Rosario's *Song of the Water Saints*." In *Contemporary U.S. Latino/a Literary Criticism*, edited by Lyn Di Iorio Sandín and Richard Perez, 35–59. New York: Palgrave Macmillan, 2007.

Chin, Staceyann. "Should Caribbean Nations Be Compensated for the Legacy of Slavery?" Interview by John Hockenberry. *The Takeaway*, Public Radio International, October 29, 2013. https://www.pri.org/stories/2013-10-29/should-caribbean-nations-be-compensated-legacy-slavery.

Christian, Barbara. "The Race for Theory." *Cultural Critique* 6 (Spring 1987): 51–63.

Ciccariello-Maher, George. *Decolonizing Dialectics*. Durham, N.C.: Duke University Press, 2017.

Clay, Andreana. "This Is How You Lose Her (And by Her, I Mean Me)." *Queer Black Feminist* (blog), November 12, 2012. http://queerblackfeminist.blogspot.com/2012/11/this-is-how-you-lose-her-and-by-her-i.html.

CLCS Global Hispanophone Forum. MLA Commons. https://mla.hcommons.org/groups/global-hispanophone/.

Cliff, Michelle. "Caliban's Daughter." *Journal of Caribbean Literatures* 3, no. 3 (2003): 157–60.

———. *If I Could Write This in Fire*. Minneapolis: University of Minnesota Press, 2008.

———. *The Land of Look Behind: Prose and Poetry*. Ithaca, N.Y.: Firebrand, 1985.

———. *No Telephone to Heaven*. New York: Plume, 1996.

Coates, Ta-Nehisi. "The Case for Reparations." *The Atlantic* 313, no. 5 (June 2014): 54–71. https://www.theatlantic.com/magazine/archive/2014/06/the-case-for-reparations/361631/.

Coffey, Maestra. "Internalized Misogyny." *Critical Literacy* (blog), December 22, 2011. https://coffeyenglish.blogspot.com/2011/12/internalized-misogyny.html.

Comas-Diaz, Lillian. "LatiNegra: Mental Health Issues of African Latinas." *Journal of Feminist Family Therapy* 5, no. 3–4 (October 1994): 35–74. https://doi.org/10.1300/J086v05n03_03.

Combahee River Collective. *The Combahee River Collective Statement: Black Feminist Organizing in the Seventies and Eighties*. Latham, N.Y.: Kitchen Table/Women of Color, 1986.

Cruz, Angie, and Nelly Rosario. "Angie Cruz in Conversation with Nelly Rosario." *Callaloo* 30, no. 3 (2007): 743–53.

Cruz, Cindy. "LGBTQ Street Youth Talk Back: A Meditation on Resistance and Witnessing." *International Journal of Qualitative Studies in Education* 24, no. 5 (2011): 547–58.

Cruz-Malavé, Arnaldo. "What a Tangled Web! Masculinity, Abjection, and the Foundations of Puerto Rican Literature in the United States." *differences: A Journal of Feminist Cultural Studies* 8, no. 1 (1996): 132–52.

Cusack, Igor. "Hispanic and Bantu Inheritance, Trauma, Dispersal and Return: Some Contributions to a Sense of National Identity in Equatorial Guinea." *Nations and Nationalism* 5, no. 2 (1999): 207–36.

Dalleo, Raphael, and Elena Machado Sáez. *The Latino/a Canon and the Emergence of Post-Sixties Literature*. New York: Palgrave Macmillan, 2007.

Danticat, Edwidge. *Create Dangerously: The Immigrant Artist at Work*. New York: Vintage, 2011.

Darwish, Mahmoud. "Edward Said: A Contrapuntal Reading." Translated by Mona Anis. Special issue, "Edward Said and After: Toward a New Humanism," *Cultural Critique* no. 67 (Autumn 2007): 175–82.

Dávila, Arlene. *Barrio Dreams: Puerto Ricans, Latinos, and the Neoliberal City*. Berkeley: University of California Press, 2004.

———. "Dreams of Place: Housing, Gentrification, and the Marketing of Space in El Barrio." *Centro Journal* 15, no. 1 (March 2003): 112–38.

Decalo, Samuel. *Psychoses of Power: African Personal Dictatorships*. Gainesville: Florida Academic Press, 1998.

DeCosta-Willis, Miriam, ed. *Daughters of the Diaspora: Afra-Hispanic Writers*. Kingston, Jamaica: Ian Randle, 2003.

De Genova, Nicholas, and Ana Yolanda Ramos-Zayas. *Latino Crossings: Mexicans, Puerto Ricans, and the Politics of Race and Citizenship*. New York: Routledge, 2004.

de Granada, Germán. "Un caso de transferencia léxica intercolonial: Cuba-Fernando Poo (Bioko)." *Anuario de Letras: Lingüística y Filología* 23 (1985): 131–59.

———. "Negros emancipados cubanos en Fernando Poo." *Revista de Indias* 44 (1984): 174.

de la Nuez, Thenesoya Vidina Martín. "(Re)escribiendo la historia desde la agencia africana: La reconstrucción narrativa de la realidad en la obra de Ávila Laurel." *Afro-Hispanic Review* 28, no. 2 (Fall 2009): 219–30.

De La Torre, Miguel A. *Santería: The Beliefs and Rituals of a Growing Religion in America*. Grand Rapids, Mich.: Eerdmans, 2004.

de Leon, Aya. "Reconciling Rage and Compassion: The Unfolding #MeToo Moment for Junot Díaz." *Aya de Leon* (blog), May 5, 2018. https://ayadeleon.wordpress.com/2018/05/05/reconciling-rage-and-compassion-the-unfolding-metoo-moment-for-junot-diaz/.

del Pozo, Diego. "Heterotopías insulares: Identidad y resistencia en el teatro de Alberto Pedro." Ph.D. dissertation, University of Georgia, 2008.

del Valle Escalante, Emilio. "Self-Determination: A Perspective from Abya Yala." E-International Relations, May 20, 2014. https://www.e-ir.info/2014/05/20/self-determination-a-perspective-from-abya-yala/.

Demary, Mensah. "A Conversation with Daniel José Older." *Specter*, April 21, 2014. http://www.spectermagazine.com/interviews/older/.

Denis, Nelson. "Due to Crisis, More Puerto Ricans Now Live in the U.S. Than on the Island." *The Atlantic*, July 6, 2015. https://www.theatlantic.com/politics/archive/2015/07/due-to-crisis-more-puerto-ricans-now-live-in-the-us-than-on-the-island/432246/.

Denis-Rosario, Milagros. "Following Their Footsteps: Tracing Puerto Ricans' Sociopolitical Activism in New York City from an Afro-Centric Perspective." *Journal of Pan African Studies* 5, no. 4 (June 2012): 112–30.

Díaz, Junot. "Apocalypse: What Disasters Reveal." *Boston Review*, May 1, 2011. http://bostonreview.net/junot-diaz-apocalypse-haiti-earthquake.

———. *The Brief Wondrous Life of Oscar Wao*. New York: Riverhead Books, 2007.

———. *Drown*. New York: Riverhead Books, 1996.

———. "Monstro." *New Yorker*, June 4, 2012. https://www.newyorker.com/magazine/2012/06/04/monstro.

———. "The Silence: The Legacy of Childhood Trauma." *New Yorker*, April 9, 2018. https://www.newyorker.com/magazine/2018/04/16/the-silence-the-legacy-of-childhood-trauma.

Domínguez Miguela, Antonia. "Literary Tropicalizations of the Barrio: Ernesto Quiñonez's *Bodega Dreams* and Ed Vega's *Mendoza's Dreams*." In *Writing Off the Hyphen: New Perspectives on the Literature of the Puerto Rican Diaspora*, edited by José L. Torres-Padilla and Carmen Haydee Rivera, 165–83. Seattle: University of Washington Press, 2008.

Dotson, Kristie. "Radical Love: Black Philosophy as Deliberate Acts of Inheritance." *The Black Scholar* 43, no. 4 (Winter 2013): 38–45. https://doi.org/10.5816/blackscholar.43.4.0038.

Duany, Jorge. "Nation on the Move: The Construction of Cultural Identities in Puerto Rico and the Diaspora." *American Ethnologist* 27, no. 1 (February 2000): 5–30. https://doi.org/10.1525/ae.2000.27.1.5.

———. *The Puerto Rican Nation on the Move: Identities on the Island and in the United States*. Chapel Hill: University of North Carolina Press, 2003.

Dwyer, June. "When Willie Met Gatsby: The Critical Implications of Ernesto Quiñonez's *Bodega Dreams*." *Lit: Literature Interpretation Theory* 14, no. 2 (2003): 165–78. https://doi.org/10.1080/10436920306616.

EcuRed. "José Rosario Oviedo." https://www.ecured.cu/José_Rosario_Oviedo.

———. "Juan Gualberto Gómez." https://www.ecured.cu/Juan_Gualberto_Gómez.

Edmond, Rod, and Vanessa Smith, eds. *Islands in History and Representation*. New York: Routledge, 2003.

Edwards, Brent Hayes. *The Practice of Diaspora: Literature, Translation, and the Rise of Black Internationalism*. Cambridge, Mass.: Harvard University Press, 2009.

———. "The Uses of Diaspora." *Social Text* 19, no. 1 (Spring 2001): 45–73.

Edzodzomo Ondo, Hubert. "Reconocimiento, negación y exclusión de las identidades en *Le Pacte d'Afia* (2009) y *La Bastarda* (2016)." In *XVI Congreso Nacional Educación Comparada Tenerife*, 299–306. La Laguna, Spain: Universidad de La Laguna, 2018.

Enck-Wanzer, Darrel, ed. *The Young Lords: A Reader*. New York: NYU Press, 2010.

Esono Ebalé, Ramón, Chino, and Tenso Tenso. *La pesadilla de Obi*. Washington, D.C.: EG Justice, 2015.

Espinosa-Miñoso, Yuderkys. "Una crítica descolonial a la epistemología feminista crítica." *El Cotidiano* 29, no. 184 (2014): 7–12. https://www.redalyc.org/html/325/32530724004/.

Fanon, Frantz. *Black Skin, White Masks*. New York: Grove, 1952.

Feagin, Joe R., and Clairece Booher Feagin. *Racial and Ethnic Relations*. 7th edition. Upper Saddle River, N.J.: Prentice Hall, 2003.

Federici, Silvia. *Caliban and the Witch*. Autonomedia, 2004.

Feldman, Keith P. "On Relationality, on Blackness: A Listening Post." *Comparative Literature* 68, no. 2 (June 2016): 107–15. https://doi.org/10.1215/00104124-3507892.

Feracho, Lesley. "The Legacy of Negrismo/Negritud: Inter-American Dialogues." *Langston Hughes Review* 16, no. 1/2 (Fall/Spring 1999–2001): 1–7.

Fernández Retamar, Roberto. "Caliban: Notes toward a Discussion of Culture in Our Americas." *Massachusetts Review* 15, no. 1/2 (Winter/Spring 1974): 7–72.

Figueroa, Yomaira C. "Junot Díaz's Diasporic Discontents: Race, Sex, Belonging and the Promise of Decolonial Love." In *Oxford Encyclopedia of Latino/a Literature* (March 2020), https://oxfordre.com/literature/view/10.1093/acrefore/9780190201098.001.0001/acrefore-9780190201098-e-403?rskey=NGpMa7&result=4.

———. "The Life Work of Ana Celia Zentella: Anthropolitical Linguistics, Bilingualism, and Linguistic Communities at a Crossroads," *CENTRO Journal* 28, no. 1 (Spring 2016): 152–71.

———. "Reparation as Transformation: Radical Literary (Re)imaginings of Futurities through Decolonial Love." *Decolonization: Indigeneity, Education and Society* 4, no. 1 (2015): 41–58.

Flores, Juan. *The Diaspora Strikes Back: Caribeño Tales of Learning and Turning*. New York: Routledge, 2010.

———. *From Bomba to Hip-Hop: Puerto Rican Culture and Latino Identity*. New York: Columbia University Press, 2000.

Fons, Virginia. "Algunas consideraciones teóricas a propósito de la concepción de la salud procreativa de las mujeres ndowe de Guinea Ecuatorial." *Revista Epàta-Ekulàko: Comuniad Global Ndowe de Guinea Ecuatorial,* Numero Especial (October 2012): 1–31.

Forché, Carolyn, ed. *Against Forgetting: Twentieth-Century Poetry of Witness.* New York: W. W. Norton, 1993.

Fra-Molinero, Baltasar. "La educación sentimental de un exilado africano: Las tinieblas de tu memoria negra, de Donato Ndongo-Bidyogo." *Afro-Hispanic Review* 19, no. 1 (Spring 2000): 49–57.

Francis, Donette. *Fictions of Feminine Citizenship: Sexuality and the Nation in Contemporary Caribbean Literature.* New York: Palgrave Macmillan, 2010.

Gabilondo, Joseba. "The Hispanic Atlantic." *Arizona Journal of Hispanic Cultural Studies* 5, no. 89 (2001): 91–113.

Gadpaille, Michelle. "Eating Dirt, Being Dirt: Backgrounds to the Story of Slavery." *AAA: Arbeiten aus Anglistik und Amerikanistik* 39, no. 1 (2014): 3–20.

Gallo, Mario, dir. *Al compas de Cuba.* Havana: Instituto Cubano del Arte e Industria Cinematográficos, 1960. https://www.youtube.com/watch?v=QuI_aiDacRo.

García, Armando. "Freedom as Praxis: Migdalia Cruz's *Fur* and the Emancipation of Caliban's Woman." *Modern Drama* 59, no. 3 (Fall 2016): 343–62. https://doi.org/10.3138/md.0705R.

Garcia-Navarro, Lulu. "Brooklyn Is Magical in 'Shadowhouse Fall.' " *NPR*, September 17, 2017. https://www.npr.org/2017/09/17/551604574/brooklyn-is-magical-in-shadowhouse-fall.

García-Peña, Lorgia. *The Borders of Dominicanidad: Race, Nation, and Archives of Contradiction.* Durham, N.C.: Duke University Press, 2016.

———. "Translating 'Blackness': Dominicans Negotiating Race and Belonging across the Atlantic." Special issue, "Dominican Black Studies," *The Black Scholar* 45, no. 2 (Summer 2015): 10–20.https://doi.org/10.1080/00064246.2015.1012993.

Gilmore, Ruth Wilson. *Golden Gulag: Prisons, Surplus, Crisis, and Opposition in Globalizing California.* Berkeley: University of California Press, 2007.

Gilroy, Paul. *The Black Atlantic: Modernity and Double Consciousness.* Cambridge, Mass.: Harvard University Press, 1995.

Girmay, Aracelis. *The Black Maria.* Rochester, N.Y.: BOA Editions, 2016.

Glissant, Édouard. *Caribbean Discourse: Selected Essays.* Translated by J. Michael Dash. Charlottesville: University of Virginia Press, 1989.

———. *Poetics of Relation.* Translated by Betsy Wing. Ann Arbor: University of Michigan Press, 1997.

Godreau, Isar P. *Scripts of Blackness: Race, Cultural Nationalism, and US Colonialism in Puerto Rico.* Champaign: University of Illinois Press, 2015.

Gómez-Barris, Macarena.*The Extractive Zone: Social Ecologies and Decolonial Perspectives.* Durham, N.C.: Duke University Press, 2017.

Gonzalez, Juan. *Harvest of Empire: A History of Latinos in America.* New York: Penguin, 2000.

González-Wippler, Migene. *Santería: The Religion, Faith, Rites, Magic.* Woodbury, Minn.: Llewellyn Worldwide, 1994.

Graziano, Frank. *Undocumented Dominican Migration*. Austin: University of Texas Press, 2013.

Green, Tobias. "Fear and Atlantic History: Some Observations Derived from the Cape Verde Islands and the African Atlantic." *Atlantic Studies* 3, no. 1 (2006): 25–42. https://doi.org/10.1080/14788810500525424.

Grillo, Evelio. "Black Cuban, Black American." In *The Afro-Latin@ Reader: History and Culture in the United States*, edited by Miriam Jiménez Román and Juan Flores, 99–112. Durham, N.C.: Duke University Press, 2010.

Grosfoguel, Ramón. "Colonial Difference, Geopolitics of Knowledge, and Global Coloniality in the Modern/Colonial Capitalist World-System." *Review (Fernand Braudel Center)* 25, no. 3 (2002): 203–24.

———. *Colonial Subjects: Puerto Ricans in a Global Perspective*. Berkeley: University of California Press, 2003.

———. "Decolonizing Post-Colonial Studies and Paradigms of Political-Economy: Transmodernity, Decolonial Thinking, and Global Coloniality." *TRANSMODERNITY: Journal of Peripheral Cultural Production of the Luso-Hispanic World* 1, no. 1 (January 2011): 1–38. https://escholarship.org/uc/item/21k6t3fq.

Gumbs, Alexis Pauline. *Spill: Scenes of Black Feminist Fugitivity*.Durham, N.C.: Duke University Press, 2016.

Hanna, Monica. "'Reassembling the Fragments': Battling Historiographies, Caribbean Discourse, and Nerd Genres in Junot Díaz's *The Brief Wondrous Life of Oscar Wao*." *Callaloo* 33, no. 2 (March 2010): 498–520.

Hau'ofa, Epeli. "Our Sea of Islands." In *A New Oceania: Rediscovering Our Sea of Islands*, edited by Epeli Hau'ofa, Vijay Naidu, and Eric Waddell, 2–16. Suva, Fiji: University of the South Pacific, 1993.

Haynes, Tonya. "Mapping Caribbean Cyberfeminisms." *sx archipelagos* no. 1 (May 2016).

Hernández Hiraldo, Samiri. *Black Puerto Rican Identity and Religious Experience*. Gainesville: University Press of Florida, 2006.

Hey-Colón, Rebeca. "Transformative Currents: An Exploration of the Sea and Identity in the Works of Angie Cruz and Nelly Rosario." In *Negotiating Latinidades, Understanding Identities within Space*, edited by Kathryn Quinn-Sánchez, 9–30. Newcastle upon Tyne, Eng.: Cambridge Scholars, 2015.

Hom, Sabrina L. "Between Races and Generations: Materializing Race and Kinship in Moraga and Irigaray." *Hypatia* 28, no. 3 (Summer 2013): 419–35. https://doi.org/10.1111/j.1527-2001.2012.01271.x.

Horn, Maja. *Masculinity after Trujillo: The Politics of Gender in Dominican Literature*. Gainesville: University Press of Florida, 2017.

Hymes, Dell. "Ways of Speaking." In *Explorations in the Ethnography of Speaking*, edited by Richard Bauman and Joel Sherzer, 433–51. New York: Cambridge University Press, 1974.

Ibeyi. *Ibeyi*. London: XL Recordings, 2015.

Ilombe del Pozo Epita, Raquel. *Ceiba*. Madrid: Editorial Madrid, 1978.

———. *Ceiba II*, edited by Benita Sampedo Vizcaya and Baltasar Fra Molinero. Madrid: Editorial Verbum, 2014.

Irizarry, Ylce. "Because Place Still Matters: Mapping Puertorriquenidad in *Bodega Dreams*." *Centro Journal* 27, no. 1 (Spring 2015): 152–85.

James, C. L. R. *The Black Jacobins: Toussaint L'Ouverture and the San Domingo Revolution.* New York: Random House, 1963. First published in 1938 by Secker and Warburg (London).

Jaramillo, María Mercedes, and Lucía Ortiz. *Hijas del muntu: Biografías críticas de mujeres afrodescendientes de América Latina.* Bogota, Colombia: Panamericana Editorial, 2011.

Jean-Charles, Régine Michelle. *Conflict Bodies: The Politics of Rape Representation in the Francophone Imaginary.* Columbus: Ohio State University Press, 2014.

Jeffries, Stuart. "Angela Davis: 'There is an Unbroken Line of Police Violence in the US That Takes Us All the Way Back to the Days of Slavery.'" *Guardian*, December 14, 2014. https://www.theguardian.com/global/2014/dec/14/angela-davis-there-is-an-unbroken-line-of-police-violence-in-the-us-that-takes-us-all-the-way-back-to-the-days-of-slavery.

Jiménez Román, Miriam. "Boricuas vs. Nuyoricans—Indeed! A Look at Afro-Latinos." *ReVista: Harvard Review of Latin America* (Spring 2008): 8–11.

Jiménez Román, Miriam, and Juan Flores, eds. *The Afro-Latin@ Reader: History and Culture in the United States.* Durham, N.C.: Duke University Press, 2010.

Johnson, Jessica Marie. *Practicing Freedom: Black Women, Intimacy, and Kinship in New Orleans AtlanticWorld.* Philadelphia: University of Pennsylvania Press, 2020.

Jones Ndjoli, Edjanga. *Heredarás la tierra.* Barcelona: Ediciones Carena-Acidalia, 2015.

Jorge, Angela. "The Black Puerto Rican Woman in Contemporary Society." In *The Puerto Rican Woman: Perspectives on Culture, History, and Society*, edited by Edna Acosta-Belén, 180–87. New York: Praeger, 1986.

Kelley, Robin D. G. *Freedom Dreams: The Black Radical Imagination.* New York: Beacon, 2003.

Kiple, Kenneth F. *The Caribbean Slave: A Biological History.* New York: Cambridge University Press, 1984.

Kunsa, Ashley. "History, Hair, and Reimagining Racial Categories in Junot Díaz's *The Brief Wondrous Life of Oscar Wao.*" *Critique: Studies in Contemporary Fiction* 54, no. 2 (April 2013): 211–24. https://doi.org/10.1080/00111619.2011.574747.

Lam, C. Christina. "Trauma and Testimony: Embodied Memory in Loida Maritza Pérez's *Geographies of Home.*" *Rocky Mountain Review of Language and Literature* 69, no. 1 (Spring 2015): 37–48.

Lamming, George. *The Pleasures of Exile.* Ann Arbor: University of Michigan Press, 1992.

Laó-Montes, Agustín. "Afro-Latinidades and the Diasporic Imaginary." *Iberoamericana* 5, no. 17 (2005): 117–30.

Lázare, Sarah, and Virginia Fons. "Los procesos procreativos desde la antropología: El caso de las madres de Barcelona por un parto respetado." *Quaderns-e de l'Institut Català d'Antropologia* 21, no. 2 (2016): 21–37.

lê, thi diem thúy. *The Gangster We Are All Looking For.* New York: Knopf, 2003.

Lew, Janey. "In Place/Of Solidarity: Acknowledgement and Reciprocity with/in Indigenous and Asian Canadian Writing." Ph.D. dissertation, University of California, Berkeley, 2018.

Lewis, Marvin A. *Equatorial Guinean Literature in Its National and Transnational Contexts*. Columbia: University of Missouri Press, 2017.

———. *An Introduction to the Literature of Equatorial Guinea: Between Colonialism and Dictatorship*. Columbia: University of Missouri Press, 2007.

Lewis, Oscar. *La Vida: A Puerto Rican Family in the Culture of Poverty—San Juan and New York*. New York: Random House, 1966.

Liao, Alice. "Contra Queer: The Metaphoric Incommensurability between Queer Politics and Coming Out." *Journal of Information Ethics* 19, no. 2 (fall 2010): 17–32.

Lifshey, Adam. "'No podemos soñar': A Hispanophone African Literary Displacement of the Spanish-American War of 1898." *Hispanic Journal* 27, no. 1 (Spring 2006): 119–34.

Lipski, John. "The Spanish Language of Equatorial Guinea." *Arizona Journal of Hispanic Cultural Studies* 8, no. 1 (2004): 115–30.

López, Irene. "'But You Don't Look Puerto Rican': The Moderating Effect of Ethnic Identity on the Relation between Skin Color and Self-Esteem among Puerto Rican Women." *Cultural Diversity and Ethnic Minority Psychology* 14, no. 2 (2008): 102–8. http://dx.doi.org/10.1037/1099-9809.14.2.102.

López Oro, Paul Joseph. "Digitizing Ancestral Memory: Gariguna Settlement Day in the Americas and in Cyberspace." In *Indigenous Interfaces: Spaces, Technology, and Social Networks in Mexico and Central America*, edited by Jennifer Carolina Gómez Menjívar and Gloria Elizabeth Chacón, 165–79. Tucson: University of Arizona Press, 2019.

———. "'Ni de aquí, ni de allá': Garífuna Subjectivities and the Politics of Diasporic Belonging." In *Afro-Latin@s in Movement: Critical Approaches to Blackness and Transnationalism in the Americas*, edited by Petra R. Rivera-Rideau, Jennifer A. Jones, and Tianna Paschel, 61–83. New York: Palgrave Macmillan, 2016.

Lorde, Audre. "Age, Race, Class, and Sex: Women Redefining Difference." In *Sister Outsider: Essays and Speeches*, 114–23. Berkeley, Calif.: Crossing, 2012.

———. *Our Dead Behind Us: Poems*. New York: W. W. Norton, 1986.

———. "Scratching the Surface: Some Notes on Barriers to Women and Loving." *The Black Scholar* 9, no. 7 (April 1978): 31–35. https://doi.org/10.1080/00064246.1978.11414006.

———. *Sister Outsider: Essays and Speeches*. Berkeley, Calif.: Crossing, 2012.

Lowe, Lisa. *The Intimacies of Four Continents*. Durham, N.C.: Duke University Press, 2015.

Lugones, María. "Heterosexualism and the Colonial/Modern Gender System." Special issue, "Writing Against Heterosexism," *Hypatia* 22, no. 1 (Winter 2007): 186–209.

———. *Pilgrimages/Peregrinajes: Theorizing Coalition against Multiple Oppressions*. Lanham, Md.: Rowman and Littlefield, 2003.

———. "Toward a Decolonial Feminism." Special Issue, "Feminist Legacies/Feminist Futures: The 25th Anniversary Issue," *Hypatia* 25, no. 4 (Fall 2010): 742–59.

Lyons, Paul, and Ty P. Kawika, eds. Special issue, "Pacific Currents," *American Quarterly* 67, no. 3 (September 2015).

Mahler, Anne Garland. "The Writer as Superhero: Fighting the Colonial Curse in Junot Díaz's *The Brief Wondrous Life of Oscar Wao*." *Journal of*

Latin American Cultural Studies 19, no. 2 (August 2010): 119–40. https://doi.org/10.1080/13569325.2010.494928.

Makalani, Minkah. *In the Cause of Freedom: Radical Black Internationalism from Harlem to London, 1917–1939*. Chapel Hill: University of North Carolina Press, 2011.

Maldonado-Torres, Nelson. *Against War: Views from the Underside of Modernity*. Durham, N.C.: Duke University Press, 2008.

———. "The Decolonial Turn." Translated by Robert Cavooris. In *New Approaches to Latin American Studies: Culture and Power*, edited by Juan Poblete, 127–43. New York: Routledge, 2017.

———. "Decoloniality at Large: Towards a Trans-Americas and Global Transmodern Paradigm." Special issue, "Thinking through the Decolonial Turn," *TRANSMODERNITY: Journal of Peripheral Cultural Production of the Luso-Hispanic World* 1, no. 3 (2012): 1–10.

———. "Epistemology, Ethics, and the Time/Space of Decolonization: Perspectives from the Caribbean and the Latina/o Americas." In *Decolonizing Epistemologies: Latina/o Theology and Philosophy*, edited by Ada María Isasi-Díaz and Eduardo Mendieta, 193–206. New York: Fordham University Press, 2012.

———. *Fanonian Meditations and Ten Theses on Coloniality and Decoloniality*. Durham, N.C.: Duke University Press, forthcoming.

———. "On the Coloniality of Being: Contributions to the Development of a Concept." Special issue, "Globalization and the De-Colonial Options," *Cultural Studies* 21, no. 2–3 (March/May 2007): 240–70. https://doi.org/10.1080/09502380601162548.

———. "Reconciliation as a Contested Future: Decolonization as Project or Beyond the Paradigm of War." In *Reconciliation, Nations and Churches in Latin America*, edited by Iain S. Maclean, 225–45. Brookfield, Vt.: Ashgate, 2006.

Martínez-San Miguel, Yolanda. *Caribe Two Ways: Cultura de la migración en el caribe insular hispánico*. San Juan, P.R.: Ediciones Callejón, 2003.

———. "Coloniality of Diasporas: Racialization of Negropolitans and Nuyoricans in Paris and New York." In *Hispanic Caribbean Literature of Migration: Narratives of Displacement*, edited by Vanessa Pérez Rosario, 189–206. New York: Palgrave Macmillan, 2010.

———. *Coloniality of Diasporas: Rethinking Intra-Colonial Migrations in a Pan-Caribbean Context*. New York: Palgrave Macmillan, 2014.

Martin-Márquez, Susan. *Disorientations: Spanish Colonialism in Africa and the Performance of Identity*. New Haven, Conn.: Yale University Press, 2008.

Mbembe, Achille. *On the Postcolony*. Studies on the History of Society and Culture, vol. 41. Berkeley: University of California Press, 2001.

Mbomío Bacheng, Joaquín. *Matinga, sangre en la selva*. Barcelona: Editoriales Mey, 2013.

McCormack, Donna. *Queer Postcolonial Narratives and the Ethics of Witnessing*. New York: Bloomsbury Academic, 2014.

McKittrick, Katherine. *Demonic Grounds: Black Women and the Cartographies of Struggle*. Minneapolis: University of Minnesota Press, 2016.

———, ed. *Sylvia Wynter: On Being Human as Praxis*. Durham, N.C.: Duke University Press, 2014.

Mehta, Brinda J. *Diasporic (Dis)locations: Indo-Caribbean Women Writers Negotiate the Kala Pani.* Jamaica: University of the West Indies Press, 2004.

Méndez, Susan C. "Afro-Caribbean Spiritual Practices, Race, Gender, and Violence in Loida Maritza Pérez's *Geographies of Home.*" *Afro-Hispanic Review* 31, no. 1 (Spring 2012): 105–18.

Méndez, Xhercis. "Decolonial Feminist Methodologies." Paper presented at the annual meeting of the Caribbean Philosophical Association, Dakar, Senegal, June 2018.

———. "Notes Toward a Decolonial Feminist Methodology: Revisiting the Race/Gender Matrix." *Trans-Scripts* 5 (2015): 41–56.

———. "Transcending Dimorphism: Afro-Cuban Ritual Praxis and the Rematerialization of the Body." *Journal for Cultural and Religious Theory* 13, no. 1 (winter 2014): 101–21.

Méndez, Xhercis, and Yomaira Figueroa. "Not Your Papa's Wynter: Women of Color Contributions toward Decolonial Futures." In *Beyond the Doctrine of Man: Decolonial Visions of the Human*, edited by Joseph Drexler-Dreis and Kristien Justaert, 60–88. New York: Fordham University Press, 2020.

Merla-Watson, Cathryn Josefina. "The Altermundos of Latin@ Futurism." *Alluvium* 6, no. 1 (2017). https://doi.org/10.7766/alluvium.v6.1.03.

Merla-Watson, Cathryn Josefina, and B. V. Olguín. "Introduction: ¡Latin@futurism Ahora! Recovering, Remapping, and Recentering the Chican@ and Latin@ Speculative Arts." *Aztlán: A Journal of Chicano Studies* 40, no. 2 (Fall 2015): 135–46.

Mignolo, Walter D. "The Geopolitics of Knowledge and the Colonial Difference." *South Atlantic Quarterly* 101, no. 1 (Winter 2002): 57–96.

———. "Introduction: Coloniality of Power and De-Colonial Thinking." Special issue, "Globalization and the De-Colonial Options," *Cultural Studies* 21, no. 2–3 (March/May 2007): 155–67. https://doi.org/10.1080/09502380601162498.

———. *Local Histories/Global Designs: Coloniality, Subaltern Knowledges, and Border Thinking.* Princeton, N.J.: Princeton University Press, 2012.

Miñoso, Yuderkys Espinosa, Diana Gómez Correal, and Karina Ochoa Muñoz, eds. *Tejiendo de otro modo: Feminismo, epistemología y apuestas descoloniales en Abya Yala.* Popayán, Colombia: Editorial Universidad del Cauca, 2014.

Mintz, Sidney. "The Caribbean Region." *Daedalus* 102, no. 2 (1974): 45–71.

Miyagawa, Mitch. "A Sorry State." Walrus, December 12, 2009, updated May 1, 2017. https://thewalrus.ca/a-sorry-state/.

———. *A Sorry State.* Whitehorse, Can.: Up and Away Productions, 2012.

Mohanty, Chandra Talpade. *Feminism without Borders: Decolonizing Theory, Practicing Solidarity.* Durham, N.C.: Duke University Press, 2003.

Monahan, Michael J. "Recognition beyond Struggle: On a Liberatory Account of Hegelian Recognition." *Social Theory and Practice* 32, no. 3 (July 2006): 389–414.

Moraga, Cherríe, and Gloria Anzaldúa, eds. *This Bridge Called My Back: Writings by Radical Women of Color.* 4th edition. Albany: State University of New York Press, 2015.

Morales, Aurora Levins. *Medicine Stories: History, Culture, and the Politics of Integrity.* Boston: South End, 1998.

Morales, Iris, dir. *¡Pa'lante, Siempre Pa'lante! The Young Lords.* New York: Third World Newsreel, 1996.

Morejón, Nancy. "Toward a Poetics of the Caribbean." *World Literature Today* 76, no. 3/4 (Summer/Autumn 2002): 52–53.

Moreno, Marisel C. *Family Matters: Puerto Rican Women Authors on the Island and the Mainland.* Charlottesville: University of Virginia Press, 2012.

Morgan, Jennifer L. "*Partus sequitur ventrem*: Law, Race, and Reproduction in Colonial Slavery." *Small Axe: A Caribbean Journal of Criticism* 22, no. 1 (55) (March 2018): 1–17. https://doi.org/10.1215/07990537-4378888.

Moya, Paula M. L. "The Search for Decolonial Love: An Interview with Junot Díaz." *Boston Review*, June 26, 2012. http://bostonreview.net/books-ideas/paula-ml-moya-decolonial-love-interview-junot-d%C3%ADaz.

Muñoz, José Esteban. *Disidentifications: Queers of Color and the Performance of Politics.* Minneapolis: University of Minnesota Press, 1999.

Nakano Glenn, Evelyn. "Settler Colonialism as Structure: A Framework for Comparative Studies of U.S. Race and Gender Formation." *Sociology of Race and Ethnicity* 1, no. 1 (January 2015): 52–72. https://doi.org/10.1177/2332649214560440.

Ndlovu-Gatsheni, Sabelo J. *Coloniality of Power in Postcolonial Africa: Myths of Decolonization.* Codesria, Senegal: African Books Collective, 2013.

Ndongo-Bidyogo, Donato. *Las tinieblas de tu memoria negra.* Madrid: Editorial Bronce, 1987.

———. *Shadows of Your Black Memory.* Translated by Michael Ugarte. Chicago: Swan Isle, 2007.

Negrón-Muntaner, Frances. "Bridging Islands: Gloria Anzaldúa and the Caribbean." *PMLA* 121, no. 1 (January 2006): 272–78. https://doi.org/10.1632/003081206X129792.

Nelson, Alondra, ed. Special issue, "Afrofuturism," *Social Text* 20, no. 2, (71) (Summer 2002).

Nerín, Gustau. *Guinea Ecuatorial, historia en blanco y negro: Hombres blancos y mujeres negras en Guinea Ecuatorial (1843–1968).* Ediciones Península, 1998.

Ngũgĩ wa Thiong'o. *Decolonising the Mind: The Politics of Language in African Literature.* Portsmouth, N.H.: Heinemann, 2011.

———. *Something Torn and New: An African Renaissance.* New York: Basic Books, 2009.

Nixon, Angelique V. "'Relating across Difference': Caribbean Feminism, bell hooks, and Michelle Cliff's Radical Black Subjectivity." In *The Caribbean Woman Writer as Scholar: Creating, Imagining, Theorizing*, edited by Keshia N. Abraham, 331–73. Coral Springs, Fla.: Caribbean Studies, 2009.

Nkealah, Naomi. "(West) African Feminisms and Their Challenges." *Journal of Literary Studies* 32, no. 2 (2016): 61–74.

Nkrumah, Kwame. *Neo-Colonialism: The Last Stage of Imperialism.* New York: International, 1965.

Nsue Otong, Carlos. "Salud: A Nicholas Guillen." *El Patio: La Revista de la Cultural Hispano-Guineana*, no. 25 (June 1993): 6.

Nussbaum, Abigail. "*The Brief Wondrous Life of Oscar Wao* by Junot Díaz." *Asking the Wrong Questions* (blog), July 19, 2008. http://wrongquestions.blogspot.com/2008/07/brief-wondrous-life-of-oscar-wao-by.html.

Obejas, Achy. *Days of Awe.* New York: Ballantine, 2001.

Oboler, Suzanne, and Anani Dzidzienyo, eds. *Neither Enemies nor Friends: Latinos, Blacks, Afro-Latinos*. New York: Palgrave Macmillan, 2005.

Obono, Trifonia Melibea. *La bastarda*. Madrid: Flores Raras, 2016.

———. *La Bastarda*. Translated by Lawrence Schimel. New York: Feminist, 2018.

———. *Herencia de bindendee*. Madrid: Ediciones del Auge, 2016.

———. "Igualdad y propaganda: Lo que se canta en los Coros de Animación en Guinea Ecuatorial." Paper presented at III Seminario Internacional sobre Guinea Ecuatorial, Universidad Nacional de Educación a Distancia, Madrid, Spain, July 6, 2016.

Older, Daniel José. *Shadowhouse Fall (The Shadowshaper Cypher Series #2)*. New York: Scholastic, 2017.

———. *Shadowshaper (The Shadowshaper Cypher Series #1)*. New York: Scholastic, 2015.

Olivares, Christina. "Letter." *About Place Journal* 3, no. 4 (October 2015). https://aboutplacejournal.org/issues/future-imagined/section-5/christina-olivares.

Oliver, Kelly. *Witnessing Beyond Recognition*. Minneapolis: University of Minnesota Press, 2001.

Online Etymology Dictionary, s.v. "Reparation." http://www.etymonline.com/index.php?term=reparation.

Osamu, Nishitani. "Anthropos and Humanitas: Two Western Concepts of 'Human Being.'" In *Translation, Biopolitics, Colonial Difference*, edited by Naoki Sakai and Jon Solomon, 259–74. Aberdeen, Hong Kong: Hong Kong University Press, 2006.

Otero, Solimar. "Barrio, Bodega, and Botánica Aesthetics: The Layered Traditions of the Latino Imaginary." *Atlantic Studies* 4, no. 2 (2007): 173–94.

Oxford English Dictionary, s.v. "Reparation." http://www.oed.com/view/Entry/162653?redirectedFrom=reparation#eid.

Palacios, Agustín. "Multicultural Vasconcelos: The Optimistic, and at Times Willful, Misreading of *La Raza Cósmica*." *Latino Studies* 15, no. 4 (2017): 416–38.

Parks, Gordon, dir. *The World of Piri Thomas*. New York: National Educational Television and Radio Center, 1968.

Paschel, Tianna S. *Becoming Black Political Subjects: Movements and Ethno-Racial Rights in Colombia and Brazil*. Princeton, N.J.: Princeton University Press, 2016.

Pérez, Laura E. "Enrique Dussel's *Etica de la liberación*, U.S. Women of Color Decolonizing Practices, and Coalitionary Politics amidst Difference." *Qui Parle: Critical Humanities and Social Sciences* 18, no. 2 (Spring/Summer 2010): 121–46. https://doi.org/10.5250/quiparle.18.2.121.

Pérez, Loida Maritza. *Geographies of Home*. New York: Penguin, 1999.

Pérez-Rosario, Vanessa. "On the Hispanophone Caribbean Question." *Small Axe: A Caribbean Journal of Criticism* 20, no. 3 (51) (November 2016): 21–31.

Pérez-Torres, Rafael. *Movements in Chicano Poetry: Against Myths, Against Margins*. New York: Cambridge University Press, 1995.

Phaf-Rheinberger, Ineke. "Migration versus Stagnation in Equatorial Guinea: The Sea as the Promise of Modernity." *Research in African Literatures* 48, no. 3 (Fall 2017): 55–71.

Philip, M. NourbeSe, and Setaey Adamu Boateng. *Zong!* Middletown, Conn.: Wesleyan University Press, 2008.

Pinnix, Aaron. "Sargassum in the Black Atlantic: Entanglement and the Abyss in Bearden, Walcott, and Philip." *Atlantic Studies* (2018): 1–29. https://doi.org/10.1080/14788810.2018.1510700.

Pinto, Samantha. *Difficult Diasporas: The Transnational Feminist Aesthetic of the Black Atlantic.* New York: NYU Press, 2013.

Portes, Alejandro, and Ruben Rumbaut. *Immigrant America: A Portrait.* Berkeley: University of California Press, 1990.

Pozzi, Carlos. "Race, Ethnicity, and Color among Latinos in the United States." In *This Side of Heaven: Race, Ethnicity, and Christian Faith*, edited by Robert J. Priest and Alvaro L. Nieves, 47–62. New York: Oxford University Press, 2007.

Price, Sally, and Richard Price. *Romare Bearden: The Caribbean Dimension.* Philadelphia: University of Pennsylvania Press, 2006.

Priest, Robert J., and Alvaro L. Nieves, eds. *This Side of Heaven: Race, Ethnicity, and Christian Faith.* New York: Oxford University Press, 2007.

Quijano, Aníbal. "Coloniality of Power and Eurocentrism in Latin America." *International Sociology* 15, no. 2 (June 2000): 215–32. https://doi.org/10.1177/0268580900015002005.

Quiñonez, Ernesto. *Bodega Dreams.* New York: Vintage, 2000.

Ramírez, Catherine S. "Afrofuturism/Chicanafuturism: Fictive Kin." *Aztlán: A Journal of Chicano Studies* 33, no. 1 (Spring 2008): 185–94.

Ramírez, Dixa. *Colonial Phantoms: Belonging and Refusal in the Dominican Americas, from the 19th Century to the Present.* New York: NYU Press, 2018.

Repinecz, Martin. "Raza or Race? Slavery and Transatlantic Family Ties in Equatorial Guinean Literature." *Hispanic Studies Review* 4, no. 1 (2019): 121–35.

Richardson, Jill Toliver. "Gendered Migrations: The Migratory Experience in Loida Maritza Pérez's *Geographies of Home*." *Label Me Latina/o* 1 (2011): 1–24.

Rivera, Lilliam. *The Education of Margot Sanchez.* New York: Simon and Schuster, 2017.

Rivera, Lysa. "Future Histories and Cyborg Labor: Reading Borderlands Science Fiction after NAFTA." *Science Fiction Studies* 39, no. 3 (November 2012): 415–36.

Rivera, Raquel. *New York Ricans from the Hip Hop Zone.* New York: Palgrave Macmillan, 2003.

Rivera-Rideau, Petra R. "'If I Were You': Tego Calderón's Diasporic Interventions." *Small Axe: A Caribbean Journal of Criticism* 22, no. 1 (55) (March 2018): 55–69. https://doi.org/10.1215/07990537-4378924.

———. *Remixing Reggaetón: The Cultural Politics of Race in Puerto Rico.* Durham, N.C.: Duke University Press, 2015.

Rizo, Elisa. "Equatorial Guinean Literature in a Context of State-Promoted Amnesia." *World Literature Today* 86, no. 5 (September/October 2012): 32–36.

Roberts, Brian Russell, and Michelle Ann Stephens, eds. *Archipelagic American Studies.* Durham, N.C.: Duke University Press, 2017.

Roberts, Neil. *Freedom as Marronage.* Chicago: University of Chicago Press, 2015.

Rodríguez, María Cristina. *What Women Lose: Exile and the Construction of Imaginary Homelands in Novels by Caribbean Writers.* New York: Peter Lang, 2005.

Rohrleitner, Marion, and Sarah E. Ryan, eds. *Dialogues across Diasporas: Women Writers, Scholars, and Activists of Africana and Latina Descent in Conversation*. Lanham, Md.: Rowman and Littlefield, 2013.

Rosario, Nelly. *Song of the Water Saints*. New York: Vintage Contemporaries, 2002.

Rose, Wendy. *Going to War with All My Relations: New and Selected Poems*. Flagstaff, Ariz.: Northland, 1993.

Rutgers Center for Cultural Analysis. "Archipelagos." Rutgers University, New Brunswick, N.J., 2015–16. http://cca.rutgers.edu/annual-seminar/past-seminars/308-archipelagoes.

Sáez, Elena Machado. "Dictating Desire, Dictating Diaspora: Junot Díaz's *The Brief Wondrous Life of Oscar Wao* as Foundational Romance." *Contemporary Literature* 52, no. 3 (Fall 2011): 522–55.

———. *Market Aesthetics: The Purchase of the Past in Caribbean Diasporic Fiction*. Charlottesville: University of Virginia Press, 2015.

Said, Edward W. *Reflections on Exile and Other Literary and Cultural Essays*. London: Granta, 2001.

Sampedro Vizcaya, Benita. "African Poetry in Spanish Exile: Seeking Refuge in the Metropolis." *Bulletin of Hispanic Studies* 81, no. 2 (2004): 201–14.

———. "Engaging the Atlantic: New Routes, New Responsibilities." *Bulletin of Hispanic Studies* 89, no. 8 (2012): 905–22.

———. "Inscribing Islands: From Cuba to Fernando Poo and Back." In *Transatlantic Studies: Latin America, Iberia, and Africa*, edited by Cecilia Enjuto-Rangel, Sebastiaan Faber, Pedro García-Caro, and Robert P. Newcomb. Liverpool, Eng.: Liverpool University Press, 2019.

———. "Rethinking the Archive and the Colonial Library: Equatorial Guinea." *Journal of Spanish Cultural Studies* 9, no. 3 (November 2008): 341–63. https://doi.org/10.1080/14636200802563600.

———. "Routes to Ruin." *Lengua y Literatura* 7, no. 2 (November 2012). https://lljournal.commons.gc.cuny.edu/2012–2-sampedro-texto/.

Sánchez, Erika. *I Am Not Your Perfect Mexican Daughter*. New York: Alfred A. Knopf, 2017.

Sánchez, Marta E. "La Malinche at the Intersection: Race and Gender in *Down These Mean Streets*." *PMLA* 113, no. 1 (January 1998): 117–28.

———. *"Shakin' Up" Race and Gender: Intercultural Connections in Puerto Rican, African American, and Chicano Narratives and Culture (1965–1995)*. Austin: University of Texas Press, 2005.

Sánchez González, Lisa. *Boricua Literature: A Literary History of the Puerto Rican Diaspora*. New York: NYU Press, 2001.

Sánchez-Pardo, Esther. "Adrift on the Black Mediterranean Diaspora: African Migrant Writing in Spain." *Social Identities* 17, no. 1 (January 2011): 105–20.

Sandín, Lyn Di Iorio. *Killing Spanish: Literary Essays on Ambivalent US Latino/a Identity*. New York: Palgrave Macmillan, 2004.

Sandoval, Chela. *Methodology of the Oppressed*. Minneapolis: University of Minnesota Press, 2000.

Santiago-Valles, Kelvin. "Policing the Crisis in the Whitest of All the Antilles." *CENTRO: Journal of the Center for Puerto Rican Studies* 8, no. 1–2 (1996): 43–55.

———. "Puerto Rico." In *No Longer Invisible: Afro-Latin Americans Today*, edited by Minority Rights Group, 139–61. London: Minority Rights Publications, 1995.

———. "'Race,' Labor, 'Women's Proper Place,' and the Birth of Nations: Notes on Historicizing the Coloniality of Power." *CR: The New Centennial Review* 3, no. 3 (Fall 2003): 47–69.

Santos-Febres, Mayra. *Sobre piel y papel*. 2nd edition. San Juan, P.R.: Ediciones Callejon, 2005.

Santos Pérez, Craig. "Transterritorial Currents and the Imperial Terripelago." Special issue, "Pacific Currents," edited by Paul Lyons and Ty P. Kawika, *American Quarterly* 67, no. 3 (September 2015): 619–24.

Schmidt, William E. "Southern Practice of Eating Dirt Shows Signs of Waning." *New York Times*, February 13, 1984. https://www.nytimes.com/1984/02/13/us/southern-practice-of-eating-dirt-shows-signs-of-waning.html.

Scott, Rebecca J. "Gradual Abolition and the Dynamics of Slave Emancipation in Cuba, 1868–1886." *Hispanic American Historical Review* 63, no. 3 (August 1983): 449–77.

Seyhan, Azade. *Writing Outside the Nation*. Princeton, N.J.: Princeton University Press, 2000.

Sharpe, Christina. *In the Wake: On Blackness and Being*. Durham, N.C.: Duke University Press, 2016.

———. *Monstrous Intimacies: Making Post-Slavery Subjects*. Durham, N.C.: Duke University Press, 2009.

Sheller, Mimi. *Citizenship from Below: Erotic Agency and Caribbean Freedom*. Durham, N.C.: Duke University Press, 2012.

Simpson, Leanne Betasamosake. "Land as Pedagogy: Nishnaabeg Intelligence and Rebellious Transformation." *Decolonization: Indigeneity, Education & Society* 3, no. 3 (2014): 1–25.

Singel, Wenona T., and Matthew L. Fletcher. "Power, Authority, and Tribal Property." *Tulsa Law Review* 41, no. 1 (2005): 21.

Sipi Mayo, Remei. "Crónica de un viaje a Guinea Ecuatorial: Entrando y saliendo de la modernidad (entre corrupción, turismo y tradición)." *Afro-Hispanic Review* 28, no. 2 (2009): 163–71.

———. *Inmigración y género: El caso de Guinea Ecuatorial*. Donostia-San Sebastián, Spain: Gakoa Liburuak, 2002.

Smith, Barbara, and CenCen. "The Blood—Yes, the Blood: A Conversation." In *Home Girls: A Black Feminist Anthology*, edited by Barbara Smith, 31. New Brunswick, N.J.: Rutgers University Press, 2000.

Smith, Linda Tuhiwai. *Decolonizing Methodologies: Research and Indigenous Peoples*. 2nd edition. London: Zed Books, 2012.

Smythe, SA. "Smythe, The Black Mediterranean, and the Politics of Imagination." *Middle East Report: Suffering and the Limits of Relief*, no. 286 (Spring 2018): 3–9. https://essaysmythe.files.wordpress.com/2018/06/smythe-the-black-mediterranean-and-the-politics-of-imagination.pdf.

Solnit, Rebecca, and Joshua Jelly-Schapiro. *Nonstop Metropolis: A New York City Atlas*. Berkeley: University of California Press, 2016.

Spencer, Robert. "Ngũgĩ wa Thiong'o and the African Dictator Novel." *Journal of Commonwealth Literature* 47, no. 2 (June 2012): 145–58. https://doi.org/10.1177/0021989412447490.

Spillers, Hortense J. "Mama's Baby, Papa's Maybe: An American Grammar Book." *Diacritics* 17, no. 2 (1987): 65–81.

Staggs, Matt. "Author Daniel José Older Talks Santeria, Cockroach Men, and Changing Minds through Fiction." Unbound Worlds, November 2, 2016. https://www.unboundworlds.com/2015/10/author-daniel-jose-older-talks-santeria-cockroach-men-and-changing-minds-through-fiction/.

Steady, Filomena. "African Feminism: A Worldwide Perspective." In *Women in Africa and the African Diaspora*, edited by R. Terborg-Penn, S. Harley, and R. Benton Rushing. Washington, D.C.: Howard University Press, 1987.

Stern, Daniel. "One Who Got Away." *New York Times*, May 21, 1967.

Stoler, Ann Laura. *Duress: Imperial Durabilities in Our Times*. Durham, N.C.: Duke University Press, 2016.

———. "Intimidations of Empire: Predicaments of the Tactile and Unseen." In *Haunted by Empire: Geographies of Intimacy in North American History*, edited by Laura Ann Stoler, 1–22. Durham, N.C.: Duke University Press, 2006.

———. "Tense and Tender Ties: The Politics of Comparison in North American History and (Post) Colonial Studies." *Journal of American History* 88, no. 3 (December 2001): 829–65. https://doi.org/10.2307/2700385.

Sundiata, Ibrahim K. "The Diaspora and a Very Small Place in Africa." *Transition*, no. 119 (2016): 140–52.

Taylor, Taryne Jade. "A Singular Dislocation: An Interview with Junot Díaz." *Paradoxa* 26 (2014): 97–110.

Taylor-García, Daphne V. *The Existence of the Mixed Race Damnés: Decolonialism, Class, Gender, Race*. Lanham, Md.: Rowman and Littlefield, 2018.

Thomas, Piri. *Down These Mean Streets*. Los Angeles: Graymalkin Media, 2016. First published in 1967 by Alfred A. Knopf (New York).

Thompson, Audrey. "Listening at an Angle." *Philosophy of Education* (2010): 1–10. https://ojs.education.illinois.edu/index.php/pes/article/view/2990/1071.

Thompson, Robert Farris. *Flash of the Spirit: African and Afro-American Art and Philosophy*. New York: Vintage Books, 1983.

Tinsley, Omise'eke Natasha. "Black Atlantic, Queer Atlantic: Queer Imaginings of the Middle Passage." *GLQ: A Journal of Lesbian and Gay Studies* 14, no. 2–3 (June 2008): 191–215. https://doi.org/10.1215/10642684-2007-030.

Torres-Padilla, José L., and Carmen Haydee Rivera, eds. *Writing Off the Hyphen: New Perspectives on the Literature of the Puerto Rican Diaspora*. Seattle: University of Washington Press, 2008.

Torres-Saillant, Silvio. *Caribbean Poetics: Toward an Aesthetic of West Indian Literature*. 2nd edition. Leeds, Eng.: Peepal Tree, 2013.

———. "The Tribulations of Blackness: Stages in Dominican Racial Identity." *Latin American Perspectives* 25, no. 3 (May 1998): 126–46.

Torres-Saillant, Silvio, and Ramona Hernández. *The Dominican Americans (The New Americans)*. Westport, Conn.: Greenwood, 1998.

Tracy, Liz. "Ibeyi Mixes Music and Santería to Make Something Truly Original." *Miami New Times*, February 21, 2017.

Tuck, Eve, and K. Wayne Yang. "Decolonization Is Not a Metaphor." *Decolonization: Indigeneity, Education, and Society* 1, no. 1 (2012): 1–40.

Ugarte, Michael. *Africans in Europe: The Culture of Exile and Emigration from Equatorial Guinea to Spain*. Champaign: University of Illinois Press, 2010.

———. "Spain's Heart of Darkness: Equatorial Guinea in the Narrative of Donato Ndongo." *Journal of Spanish Cultural Studies* 7, no. 3 (November 2006): 271–87. https://doi.org/10.1080/14636200601084071.

———. "Where Do We Fit? The Place of Afro-Hispanic and Afro-Iberian Studies in US University Curricula." In *In and Out of Africa: Exploring Afro-Hispanic, Luso-Brazilian, and Latin-American Connections*, edited by Joanna Boampong, 10–17. Newcastle upon Tyne, Eng.: Cambridge Scholars, 2012.

Umansky, Lauri. "The Sister Reply: Black Nationalist Pronatalism, Black Feminism, and the Quest for a Multiracial Women's Movement, 1965–1974." *Critical Matrix* 8 (December 1994): 19–50.

"U.S. Department of State Country Report on Human Rights Practices 1993–Equatorial Guinea." United Nations High Commissioner for Refugees, January 30, 1994. https://www.refworld.org/docid/3ae6aa4c14.html.

Valdés, Vanessa K. *Oshun's Daughters: The Search for Womanhood in the Americas*. Albany: State University of New York Press, 2014.

Vargas, Jennifer Harford. "Dictating a Zafa: The Power of Narrative Form in Junot Díaz's *The Brief Wondrous Life of Oscar Wao*." *MELUS* 39, no. 3 (July 2014): 8–30.

Vermeer, Donald E., and Dennis A. Frate. "Geophagy in a Mississippi County." *Annals of the Association of American Geographers* 65, no. 3 (September 1975): 414–24.

Walcott, Derek. "The Sea Is History." In *Collected Poems: 1948–1984*. New York: Farrar, Straus and Giroux, 1986.

Wehbe-Herrera, Aishih. "Transnational Legacies and Masculinity Politics in *The Brief Wondrous Life of Oscar Wao*." In *Masculinities and Literary Studies: Intersections and New Directions*, edited by Joseph M. Armengol, Marta Bosch-Vilarrubias, Àngels Carabí, and Teresa Requena-Pelegrí, 56–65. New York: Routledge, 2017.

Weheliye, Alexander. *Habeas Viscus: Racializing Assemblages, Biopolitics, and Black Feminist Theories of the Human*. Durham, N.C.: Duke University Press.

Whalen, Carmen Theresa. "Bridging Homeland and Barrio Politics: The Young Lords in Philadelphia." In *The Puerto Rican Movement: Voices from the Diaspora*, edited by Andrés Torres and José Velázquez, 107–23. Philadelphia: Temple University Press, 1998.

Whyte, Kyle P. "Indigenous Science (Fiction) for the Anthropocene: Ancestral Dystopias and Fantasies of Climate Change Crises." *Environment and Planning E: Nature and Space* 1, no. 1–2 (May 2018): 224–42. https://doi.org/10.1177/2514848618777621.

———. "Living in Our Ancestors' Dystopia: Indigenous Research Confronts Climate Change." NPM Media Centre, November 18, 2016. http://mediacentre.maramatanga.ac.nz/content/professor-kyle-powys-whyte-potawatomi.

Williams, Eric. *Capitalism and Slavery*. Chapel Hill: University of North Carolina Press, 1994. Originally published in 1944.

Wilson, Ciann, Tiffany King, Maile Arvin, Andrea Smith, Zainab Amadahy, Jay Khan, and Alexandria Williams. "Relationships as Resistance: Dismantling Anti-Black Racism and Settler Colonialism." Closing plenary discussion at the annual Critical Ethnic Studies Conference, Toronto, Canada, May 3, 2015.

Wolfe, Patrick. *Settler Colonialism and the Transformation of Anthropology: The Politics and Poetics of an Ethnographic Event*. London: Cassell, 1999.

Wood, Geoffrey. “Business and Politics in a Criminal State: The Case of Equatorial Guinea.” *African Affairs* 103, no. 413 (2004): 547–67.

Wynter, Sylvia. “Afterword: Beyond Miranda’s Meanings: Un/silencing the ‘Demonic Ground’ of Caliban’s ‘Woman.’ ” In *Out of the Kumbla: Caribbean Women and Literature*, edited by Carol Boyce Davies and Elaine Savory Fido, 355–72. Trenton, N.J.: Africa World, 1990.

———. “The Ceremony Must Be Found: After Humanism.” *Boundary* 2, no. 12/13 (1984): 19–70.

———. “1492: A New World View.” In *Race, Discourse, and the Origin of the Americas: A New World View*, edited by Vera Lawrence Hyatt and Rex Nettleford, 5–57. Washington, D.C.: Smithsonian Institution, 1996.

———. “Unsettling the Coloniality of Being/Power/Truth/Freedom: Towards the Human, After Man, Its Overrepresentation—An Argument.” *CR: The New Centennial Review* 3, no. 3 (fall 2003): 257–337. https://doi.org/10/1353/ncr.2004.0015.

Young, Sera L. *Craving Earth: Understanding Pica: The Urge to Eat Clay, Starch, Ice, and Chalk*. New York: Columbia University Press, 2011.

Zamora, Omaris Z. “Refashioning Blackness, Refashioning Our Histories.” *Portal*, no. 8 (2013): 24–25.

———. “(Trance)forming AfroLatina Embodied Knowledges in Nelly Rosario’s *Song of the Water Saints*.” Special issue, “Black and Latin@: Conceptualizing Afro-Latinidad in Afro-Latina/o Literature and Performance,” edited by Michele Shaul and Kathryn Quinn-Sánchez, *Label Me Latina/o* 7 (Summer 2017).

Zamora Loboch, Francisco. *Desde el viyil y otras crónicas*. Madrid: Sial Casa de África, 2008.

———. *La república fantástica de Annobón*. Madrid: Sial Casa de África, 2018.

Zeleza, Paul Tiyambe. “The Politics and Poetics of Exile: Edward Said in Africa.” Special issue, “Edward Said, Africa, and Cultural Criticism,” *Research in African Literatures* 36, no. 3 (Autumn 2005): 1–22.

Zentella, Ana Celia. *Growing Up Bilingual: Puerto Rican Children in New York*. Malden, Mass.: Blackwell, 1997.

INDEX

www.ingramcontent.com/pod-product-compliance
Ingram Content Group UK Ltd.
Pitfield, Milton Keynes, MK11 3LW, UK
UKHW040336060326
468712UK00004B/479

9 780810 142428